COUNTERREVOLUTION
IN CHINA

For those who made 1986 in Hong Kong
the spectacular it was:

Monte Bullard
Sterling Seagrave
Denny Lane
Ed O'Dowd
Tony Paul

COUNTERREVOLUTION
IN CHINA
Wang Sheng and the Kuomintang

THOMAS A. MARKS

Academy of the Pacific
Honolulu, Hawaii

FRANK CASS
LONDON • PORTLAND, Or.

First published 1998 in Great Britain by
FRANK CASS PUBLISHERS
Newbury House, 900 Eastern Avenue, Newbury Park,
London IG2 7HH, England

and in the United States of America by
FRANK CASS PUBLISHERS
c/o ISBS
5804 N. E. Hassalo Street
Portland, Oregon 97213-3644

Website: http://www.frankcass.com

British Library Cataloguing in Publication Data

Marks, Thomas A.
    Counterrevolution in China : Wang Sheng and the Kuomintang
    1. Wang, Sheng 2. Generals – China – Biography 3. Statesmen –
    China – Biography 4. China – History – Republic, 1912–1949
    5. China – Politics and government – 1912–1949
    I. Title
    951'.042'092

ISBN 0–7146–4700–4 (cloth)
ISBN 0–7146–4238–X (paper)

Library of Congress Cataloging-in-Publication Data

Marks, Thomas A.
    Counterrevolution in China : Wang Sheng and the
    Kuomintang / by
    Thomas A. Marks.
        p. cm.
    Includes bibliographical references and index.
    ISBN 0-7146-4700-4 (cloth). – ISBN 0-7146-4238-X (pbk.)
    1. Wang, Sheng, d1917- . 2. Generals–Taiwan–Biography
    3. Taiwan–Politics and government–1949- I. Title
    DS799.82.W346M37   1996
    951.24'905'092–dc20
    [B]   96-13891
                                                                  CIP

Printed in Great Britain by
Bookcraft (Bath) Ltd., Midsomer Norton, Avon

Contents

Illustrations

Maps

Figures

Preface

Few episodes have been as ill-served by historians as the effort by the Nationalist Party, the Kuomintang (KMT), to carry out a revolution in China. Long overshadowed by its victorious rival, the Chinese Communist Party (CCP), it is only in recent years that the KMT interlude has begun to attract more sustained examination. Few studies, though, carry their scholarship through to its logical end, Taiwan, where the KMT has succeeded in building the society and state it in many respects sought to create on the mainland. Indeed, small wonder – in a field where not a single adequate biography of such central figures as Chiang Kai-shek or Chiang Ching-kuo exists – that we find little of scholarly note on the revolution of the Chinese Republic.

It was this relatively unexplored state of affairs which I found so exciting when, in the summer of 1993, the opportunity arose to conduct a year's research under the auspices of the Asian Militaries Research Society in Carmel, California. Previous service in Taiwan during the Vietnam War combined with a fortuitous intersection of personal contacts to provide the opening for this biography of Wang Sheng. His association with key personalities and institutions of the KMT provides a unique vantage point from which to explore the KMT and its vision of revolution, particularly as embodied in Sun Yat-sen's *San Min Chu-i*.

This vantage point could never have been explored, however, without the cooperation afforded by the scores of individuals, not least of whom was Wang Sheng himself, who consented to the interviews which serve as my most important source of information. These discussions, in turn, would not have been possible without the translation and interpersonal skills of Shan Bullard; Wendy Tsai; Major Jerry Pang, PhD; and Major General Lee Tung-ming ('Tom'), PhD. The latter two individuals are active duty Political Warfare officers who gave unstintingly of their time in an effort to ensure the accuracy of the text, particularly the manner in which important translations were rendered. This, too, was a role assumed by Colonel (Retired) Monte R. Bullard, PhD, a former professor, without whose intercession and patient guidance this study would never have reached completion.

1 The End of an Era

Inseparable duo: Chiang Ching-kuo (center front) and Wang Sheng (left) during 1967 inspection of the offshore islands.

ON 10 MAY 1983, a day apparently of no special note in the
Republic of China, the country's president, Chiang Ching-
kuo, asked Wang Sheng to come to his office in Taipei. The brief
telephone call to Wang, the general who headed the military's
General Political Warfare Department, or 'GPWD' as it was often
termed, was a normal thing.[1] The two men had known each other
for half a century. To many, in fact, they were the numbers one and
two – respectively – in the political hierarchy of the Kuomintang,
the Nationalist Party, 'the KMT', which, in exile from China, had
constructed and ruled the *de facto* island-state of Taiwan.

As he entered the room, Wang, then 67, saluted and said, 'Mr
President, how are you?', to which Chiang replied, 'Director
Wang'. It was a ritual which had been repeated innumerable times.
Only five years apart in age, they were nonetheless separated by an
immense gulf. For all the talk of relative positions in the KMT
hierarchy, it had always been like this, one the teacher, one the
dutiful pupil, the very relationship of their meeting those long
years ago in China's Jiangxi province, cradle of the communist
revolution of which they were both firm foes.

So much had happened in the intervening years, yet so much
had stayed the same: two figures whose personal relationship
remained defined by their relationship to their country. For the
previous eight years, those during which Wang Sheng had been the
official head of GPWD, he had in public been 'Director Wang'.
Chiang Ching-kuo had been 'President Chiang'. When they were
alone, Chiang often became 'Education Director', the position he
had held those many years previously in Jiangxi. Wang Sheng
became 'Hua-hsing'.

That, of course, was not the name his parents had given him,
which was Wang Shiu-chieh. But that name had disappeared along
the way. Wang Sheng was the student name which had stuck.
Another teacher, though, had taken to calling him Wang Hua-
hsing, so sometimes Chiang Ching-kuo called him that. Or he
would use the two titles that Wang Sheng had held while Chiang's
direct subordinate in the Political Warfare hierarchy, 'Chief of
Education Wang' or 'Assistant Commandant Wang'.

Yet this time it was 'Director Wang'. And 'President Chiang'
motioned to the sofa. Wang Sheng sat on the left, Chiang on the
right. Not well – driven by diabetes, his health had been in serious
decline for several years – Chiang Ching-kuo was very serious.

It had been but several weeks since Wang Sheng had returned from a short trip to the United States at the request of the unofficial US Embassy, the American Institute in Taiwan (AIT). Aside from the usual gossip occasioned by the timing, the whole business had seemed uneventful enough.

Certainly the inevitable carping and criticism, though, had proved irritating. The name Wang could also mean 'king', and Sheng could mean 'raise' or 'to rise up'. Hence, as Chiang Ching-kuo deteriorated, went the gossip, Wang Sheng, or 'Rising King', was moving to solidify his position with the Americans so that there would be no disruption, come the transfer of power, in the Republic's relations with its chief international backer.

Ironically, the trip had been cleared by Chiang Ching-kuo himself. The timing had been right. After three difficult years of 'extra duty', heading a special body set up by President Chiang to coordinate Taiwan's response to China's united front assault, Wang Sheng had found himself back in his familiar GPWD routine when Chiang abruptly terminated the '*Liu Shao Kang* Office'. The American invitation, apparently stemming from Washington's own perception of Wang's position in the ruling KMT hierarchy, had been pressed since 'derecognition' of Taiwan in favor of the mainland in 1979. Sensing the need for a break, all concerned had agreed that the time had come to accept.

As far as such episodes went, the Wang Sheng tour was decidedly low key. Accompanied by only a single interpreter and his wife, Wang Sheng had met with American officials and academics concerned with Taiwan and China. At one point the issue of the presidential succession came up, in response to a question asked by the scholar A. Doak Barnett. Wang replied that Chiang Ching-kuo's health was good, his mind clear; and, in any eventuality, the ROC constitution, which stipulated that the vice-president would step into the shoes of the president should such become necessary, would dictate events.

That the issue of the transition was openly broached by the Americans to Wang had created some stir in Taiwan, but both the question and the response had been straightforward. It was reported in a regular communication sent back to Taiwan.

When he returned, Wang Sheng discussed his trip directly but briefly with Chiang Ching-kuo. The president seemed different in a vague sort of way, a bit cold, but that could be attributed to his continuing illness. Wang Sheng thought nothing more of it and

Fateful visit: Wang Sheng is greeted by William Casey, Director of the Central Intelligence Agency (CIA), during his brief 1983 trip to the US.

went back to his work. There were no meetings between the two.

Now, in May, they made small talk. Then Chiang Ching-kuo came to the point. 'You've been doing the same job for too long', he said, 'so we're going to transfer you to a position in armed forces joint-training'. A few more words, and the meeting was over. It had lasted just five minutes.

Thus ended one of the most powerful, though certainly one of the most ambiguous, careers in the long history of the KMT and the system it sought to build and protect. 'Rising King' had fallen, summarily and completely, ushering in a new phase of the Republican revolution.

In retrospect, one has images of storm clouds gathering and ominous portents, followed by the climactic struggle. Reality was far more prosaic.

Even the sacking was lacking in drama. For Chiang Ching-kuo had said nothing of demotion or disgrace. He had spoken only of a general being transferred. Certainly Wang Sheng was no ordinary general, as we shall see, but he was, in the final analysis, just a general filling a billet. Moving to another position would have been unusual, given Wang's singular involvement with Political Warfare, but not extraordinary.

There was even a certain logic to the meeting. Three years earlier, just before *Liu Shao Kang* had been established, Chiang Ching-kuo had asked Wang Sheng to his house for a friendly chat. At the time, Wang was thinking about how he could get a new job. 'I was running Political Warfare', he was to observe later. 'This was very wearing. You're the guardian for the whole military. Any night the phone would ring, I'd jump up, frightened, knowing there might be some disaster'.[2]

Wang Sheng, a product of a military sense of duty and a Chinese sense of obligation, could not directly tell Chiang Ching-kuo, his superior and lifelong teacher, that he did not want his job anymore, so he tried to find another way. Referring to the time when Chiang had been GPWD head, and Wang the deputy, he said, 'When you took this job the first time, it was for a two year term. When you stayed on, it was for only another term. You left in order to keep things legal. Next year I'll have been here three terms. If I continue to stay on, I'll violate the system'.[3]

Chiang Ching-kuo, though, did not see the connection Wang Sheng was trying to make and said only, 'It is a difficult question but another problem'.[4]

Then, after a few days, he called Wang Sheng and said that he had checked the matter out: 'There is no statutory limit on the head of the Political Warfare Department. Term limits were just something we had assumed existed'.[5]

That was the end of the issue. Wang Sheng was unable to get himself to ask formally that he be given a new assignment. Nevertheless, he did not let the matter drop. In particular, when Chiang Ching-kuo directed him to set up *Liu Shao Kang*, Wang tried his mentor's patience by seeking to decline. In the end, the fateful chain of events was set in motion.

When Chiang Ching-kuo finally called Wang Sheng in, however, that eighth year as Director of GPWD, and told him that he had been there too long and was being given a new job, it did not seem ominous. Indeed, Wang was relieved. He needed a change. 'Fine' was all the response he mustered.

'For sixteen years I had been the deputy director and executive deputy general beneath Chiang Ching-kuo', he recounts, 'then eight years as the director, a total of 24 years of very difficult work. So I felt as though ten thousand pounds had been lifted from my shoulders'.[6]

Wang Sheng returned to his office. Immediately thereafter, the transfer order was announced. He was to become the Director of Joint Operations and Training. Finally, Wang was stunned: 'If I had been transferred to a very important position, such an action would have been comprehensible, but I had been transferred to a very insignificant position'.[7]

There now was no doubt that the action was considered extraordinary. No time was allowed for a normal rotation. The GPWD Executive Officer, a lieutenant general, was not even in Taipei but in the southern part of the island participating in a field exercise. The Chief of the General Staff, Hau Po-tsun, was also there to watch the exercise.

A reaction to the announcement started immediately. The Chief of Staff heard the news and called back to Wang Sheng's office. He said that the change had caused uneasiness among the troops and suggested that Wang meet him immediately to calm matters and to plan an orderly transition. Wang briefly demurred, observing that it did not seem to be necessary to do such a thing. But General Hau insisted that he do so 'for the country's sake'. Wang agreed to go if Hau would issue an order, which he did. 'I was a fool for conceding', Wang was to observe much later, 'For the country's sake, I went. But certainly this caused a great deal of trouble for all of us!'[8]

He went down south, where he made a round of farewell calls. Again, in retrospect, it was naive. In the military way of looking at things, the sudden removal of a key officer, the GPWD boss, made necessary efforts to emphasize continuity. This undoubtedly was General Hau's logic. Furthermore, GPWD's central role in looking after the welfare of officers and men alike demanded that the reservoir of goodwill Wang had accumulated be respected by an adequate and heartfelt sendoff. Just as predictably, given the circumstances of Wang's transfer, this was not how the political world would see matters.

Chiang Ching-kuo and others saw Wang's moves as disruptive. On the surface, though, the farewell tour, which eventually expanded to units countrywide, was calm enough and well within the bounds of normal military protocol. In one instance, at a Marine assembly hall in the south, he spoke to over a thousand officers of field grade (major) and above, all from the area. The Chief of Staff's orders were that all would attend. Marine General To Yo-shing was the base commander. Wang discussed the need to move on, emphasizing that their duty was to protect the country. He cautioned them not to use his sudden transfer as 'cause for sadness'.[9]

It was all very moving. After the talk at the assembly hall there was a meal. As it began, General To Yo-shing brought his cup to Wang, toasted him, saying, 'Mr Director, we all feel sad about your new appointment', and became teary-eyed. It was indicative of a general feeling.

Former colleagues were to remember 'General Wang Sheng', as he invariably was termed by them, thus: 'Taiwan's principal expert at fighting communism';[10] 'one of the most diligent and incorruptible men in the military';[11] 'a man totally loyal to his country and dedicated to the people';[12] 'a man completely loyal to President Chiang Ching kuo and the Kuomintang and prepared to sacrifice himself';[13] 'a totally selfless person, without personal ambition, who was dedicated to helping others';[14] 'a pragmatic administrator who eschewed patronage systems and factions';[15] 'a military officer who was dedicated to education for himself and to help young military officers obtain a liberal education, especially in foreign universities';[16] 'one of the few important military officers who interacted regularly with scholars in the academic community';[17] 'a very capable person with strong political wisdom';[18] 'a great communicator who was very persuasive but very soft-hearted in dealing with subordinates';[19] 'a loyal subordinate who never sought political power';[20] 'a good man who did a lot for his country against communism and corruption';[21] and 'the right man, in the right job, at the right time in Taiwan'.[22]

Altogether, Wang Sheng made three major speeches. In addition to the one in the south, he gave one to the Defense Department; another to *Fu Hsing Kang* College, the training ground for Political Warfare officers and, in many respects, a Wang Sheng creation. There, many students and instructors wept.

There was also a good bit of reaction in the civilian community. Approached by one young man at a wedding, Wang was told tearfully, 'The day you left, I lost my mother'.

Yet there was another side to the reaction. While many wept at Wang's departure, others rejoiced. For they believed he was Chiang Ching-kuo's powerful henchman, a man who controlled thousands upon thousands of secret police – and who was responsible for the brutal suppression of 'popular movements' in Taiwan.[23] A purported exposé of Kuomintang oppression, written later, was to label him as the 'widely feared...successor to CCK [Chiang Ching-kuo]', as well as 'perhaps the most feared man on the island'. He was a 'hard-line political czar', 'having direct command of a security network that permeated Taiwanese society', 'the man who manipulated student demonstrations against the United States'. He was the 'notorious boss of the military's Political Warfare Department', who was 'widely considered among the three most powerful men in Taiwan'. He was 'responsible for the continuation of martial law'. 'Perhaps the most feared man on the island', he was one 'in control of thousands of political agents and informants' and 'author of truly vitriolic tracts' attacking communism. He was, to be blunt, the man who helped Chiang Ching-kuo 'terrorize life in Taiwan'.[24] Finally, if he had not participated directly, he had surely helped to create the atmosphere which resulted in the murder of an American citizen, Henry Liu (pen name, Chiang Nan), whose writing had been harshly critical of the Kuomintang.[25]

In short, Wang Sheng was not an old soldier who could just fade away. Even his efforts to settle into a new low profile routine did not end the adulation and critique of his past role. The joint training job, he found unchallenging and repetitive. Yet it seemed to offer a chance to catch up on his reading and family affairs, a chance to work something vaguely resembling a nine-to-five job. But every day there were visitors non-stop seeking his counsel. This combined with reports, in particular, of Wang's speech in the south, to worry Chiang Ching-kuo.

'I thought I had performed a great service in calming the military', Wang analyzes.

> But the president had been told that some soldiers perceived my talk to be arrogant. It was reported that I had said – who is the most ardent anti-communist? I'm the only one who can do this work. Ironically, I even sent a tape of the speech to Chiang Ching-kuo so that he could see there was but one line which was being misinterpreted.[26]

It was to no avail. To those around him, Chiang Ching-kuo asked, 'How did General Wang become so wild, so conceited, so arrogant?'[27] Such questioning could not escape Wang Sheng's notice:

> Hearing such words, I knew Chiang Ching-kuo's judgement had weakened. After fifty years of friendship, he should have known my mind. He was acting on rumors rather than checking them out. That was not like him. That's when I knew his mind was going. In my new job, I was being overwhelmed with visitors. Most were high, influential people. I was spending all my energy on this! All they wanted to do was to comfort me. Chiang Ching-kuo should have been pleased at such solicitude in the upper echelons. But people told him that this was evidence of how powerful I had become. This created a cloud. Paranoia set in. That was why he decided to put me far away from the country.[28]

This analysis seems accurate. From his earliest days in the KMT cause, Chiang Ching-kuo had worked assiduously to avoid that which KMT stalwarts viewed as the single greatest cause for their loss of the mainland, factionalism. Whether there was more to it than that is best left for later discussion. For the moment, we can judge that Chiang Ching-kuo's immediate concern was that Wang Sheng at home continued to be a source, through his faithful following, of division. So he decided 'to send him far away'.

Just how far he could not bring himself to tell directly to his loyal subordinate, his friend and comrade. Instead, he detailed the task to Premier Sun Yun-husan (also rendered as Yun-suan), or Y. S. Sun, as he was normally called by the Americans. A member of the KMT inner circle as well, a friend of Wang's, Sun explained to Wang that he had been chosen for an ambassadorship. He did so in a gentlemanly way, explaining that Wang's expertise, his skill, and his experience were needed for a task that would serve the nation. He had also been requested by the president of Paraguay, whom he had known for some time.[29]

Wang tried to decline. He protested that it did not make a whole lot of sense. Sending him to be an ambassador was not quite proper and might cause the country to pay a high price if he proved inadequate to the task. He thought, 'I'm a military man; I have no experience for such a thing'. But he said out loud, 'At this moment, I am still a military man. I obey orders. If you tell me to go, if those are the President's orders, I will obey'.[30]

'I heard later that Chiang Ching-kuo was very pleased to hear that I would go if ordered since I was a soldier', Wang notes.[31]

> Chiang Ching-kuo summoned me. Whereas previously he had been stiff, now he had a lighter attitude. He addressed me as 'ambassador'. I said being an ambassador was not my cup of tea and that I was not suitable, but that if he ordered me to go, I would. He said an ambassador was a very important position and something I should experience. He said, 'I know you will do a good job. Within this country, you may become the focus of a faction'. I answered, 'You ought to know me. I'm almost seventy. You ought to know me. Don't use your own fist to hit your head'. Chiang Ching-kuo replied, 'My thinking is still very clear'. I was unable to continue. I bowed and left.[32]

And so Wang Sheng was sent as ambassador to Paraguay, a country a ten and a half hour flight from Miami, Florida. Before he left, he met one last time with Chiang Ching-kuo. The president was at ease and solicitous in his mannerisms. There was no doubt in his mind that he was sending Wang Sheng into exile and that Wang Sheng, out of loyalty to the KMT and Taiwan, was going. They sat beside each other again on the sofa, and Chiang Ching-kuo wished Wang Sheng well. They were never to see each other again.

After Wang Sheng arrived in Paraguay, he was dropped from the KMT Standing Committee, the inner circle of 27 who determined the parameters of national policy. He remained a member of the Central Committee. He did not return to Taiwan until 1990, two years after the death of his mentor, Chiang Ching-kuo. An era had ended.

NOTES

1. The military rank structures of the US and Taiwan (ROC) are basically the same, having equivalent grades at each level. Unlike the US military, however, which uses four stars to designate a full 'general', Taiwan's armed forces use three stars for the counterpart. Further, though all 'generals' in the ROC system physically wear 'three-stars', there is a further division, for pay purposes, between 'upper level' and 'lower level' generals. Wang Sheng was a 'lower level general', which would rank as a US four-star equivalent, or 'general'.
2. Interview with Wang Sheng, 16 July 1993 in Taipei.
3. Ibid.
4. Ibid.
5. Ibid.
6. Ibid.
7. Ibid.
8. Ibid.
9. Ibid.
10. Interview with Yu Kuang, chief of ROC Advisory Mission to Cambodia during the Vietnam War, 19 July 1993 in Taipei. Though this and the quotes which follow come from specific individuals, there was considerable overlap in their analyses of Wang Sheng's personal and professional qualities, extending in particular to their choice of adjectives. Hence virtually any source could be used to support particular quotations.
11. Interview with Tracy T.S. Cheng, former professor at National Taiwan University (began work with Wang Sheng during the civil war period), 14 July 1993 in Taipei.
12. Interview with Kiang [Jiang] Yen-shih, Secretary-General of the ROC Office of the President and former KMT Secretary-General, 20 July 1993 in Taipei.
13. Interview with Chang Shih-jieh, Chinese Unified Union Advisor (Wang Sheng colleague since civil war period), 26 July 1993 in Taipei.
14. Interview with Central Military Academy (CMA) Class 16 members, 16 July 1993 in Taipei.
15. Interview with Kung Chiu-chuan, professor at Tamkang University (Wang Sheng colleague since World War II period), 12 July 1993 in Taipei.
16. Ibid.
17. Interview with Thomas B. Lee, Director of Graduate Institute of American Studies at Tamkang University, 29 July 1993 in Taipei.
18. Interview with Li Huan, former premier of ROC, 23 July 1993 in Taipei.
19. Interview with Tseng Cheng-te, former Commercial Attaché in ROC Embassy to Paraguay, 19 July 1993 in Taipei.
20. Interview with Soong Chang-chih, former defense minister of ROC, 13 July 1993 in Taipei.
21. Interview with Sun Yun-husan, former premier of ROC, 29 July 1993 in Taipei.
22. A phrase used repeatedly by interviewees, July 1993 in Taipei.
23. Chiang Na [Henry Liu], 'Wang Sheng's Mysterious Misstep' [translated], *Ch'i-shih Nien-tai Yueh Kan (The Seventies Monthly)* (June 1983), pp.55–7. Such accusations also

came out in interviews with Hsieh Tsung-ming (Roger), member of Legislative Yuan, 22 and 26 July 1993 in Taipei.
24. David E. Kaplan, *Fires of the Dragon* (New York: Atheneum Press, 1992). See pp.175–6, 196, 259, 268, 328, 334.
25. Ibid.
26. Interview with Wang Sheng, 16 July 1993 in Taipei.
27. Ibid.
28. Ibid.
29. Interview with Sun Yun-husan, former premier of ROC, 29 July 1993 in Taipei.
30. Interview with Wang Sheng, 16 July 1993 in Taipei.
31. Ibid.
32. Ibid.

2 Jiangxi: The Making of a Counterrevolutionary

A youthful Wang Sheng as rendered by a colleague.

TO SPEAK of the passing of an era is to hint at profound change; to imply a succession in world views, a generational shift. Certainly this occurred in Taiwan in the years which followed Wang Sheng's exile. As he flew to Paraguay, he left behind him a 'Free China' that was but an island and its outliers, a domain the size of Massachusetts and Connecticut combined, which was all that remained of the Republic of China that had once ruled the huge mainland. The Republic was beginning to prosper, true, yet remained only a promise, economically and politically, its democracy imperfect and authoritarian. Less than a decade later, when he returned, it was to a nation which ranked among the strongest economically in the world, a fledgling democratic power with a rich cultural life. More significantly, the generations who had built this 'Taiwan miracle', as it was so often called,[1] had handed leadership over to new blood. Those such as Wang Sheng had passed the torch.

It was a torch which had been lighted decades before in China itself, when the 1911 collapse of the Qing (Ch'ing, Manchu) dynasty brought an end to imperial rule. There followed the chaotic years of the warlords, a time of bloodshed and suffering tempered, at least partially, only in 1927 with the consolidation of the Republic. It was a republic, though, which did not even dominate its core area of provinces centered on the great treaty ports such as Canton and Shanghai. It was these that had been seized in the so-called Northern Expedition, headed by the emerging star of the Kuomintang (KMT), Chiang Kai-shek, father of Chiang Ching-kuo and leading KMT figure following the death in 1925 of the 'father of the republic', Sun Yat-sen.[2] From the moment of Sun's passing, it had been Chiang who increasingly dominated the KMT and the future of China.

In 1927 this future was anything but clear, for the revolutionary endeavor, the drive to replace the old-regime with something new, had early on splintered into two contending forces, both Russian-advised, the Kuomintang and the Chinese Communist Party (CCP). The CCP was not yet, in those early years, led by Mao Tse-tung, and so was not 'Maoist'. What it sought was a Marxist-Leninist solution to China's problems, the most salient of which were a loss of national independence and internal socio-economic-political structures which insured that life, to use the old phrase, was nasty, short, and brutish. In the chaotic post-imperial world, it was the local elite, or gentry, which increasingly determined the rhythms of existence. Though ultimately beholden to regional warlord power, the gentry were thrust to the fore by the very vastness of China and the size of its population. Of necessity, warlord power was concentrated in towns or cities. Thus it was the gentry who were masters of their localities and the directors of the forces of local order. Predictably, too, it was they who were the targets of the CCP.

Neither could the gentry gain protection from the KMT, at least not initially. Far from being their ally, the KMT also saw them as a counterrevolutionary force, a link with the past impeding those new structures necessary to restore China to its previous glory and its rightful place in the family of nations. Thus it was logical that initially the CPP and the KMT worked together in a united front against the warlords and, by implication, their local representatives (i.e. structurally if not actually), the gentry. This marriage of convenience ended, however, even as the Northern Expedition drew to a conclusion. In 1927 and 1928, estranged by the CCP's efforts to emphasize class struggle and to mobilize into its ranks forces Chiang saw as a threat, the KMT leader turned on his erstwhile allies and purged them. In disarray, the CCP fled from the areas in which it had, following its Marxist-Leninist doctrine, concentrated its efforts, the cities, to the only place where it could find safety, the countryside. There Mao, who had early on attempted to reorient the party towards the teeming millions who dwarfed in numbers any purported, doctrinal 'proletariat', was ultimately to emerge as CCP helmsman. And there the KMT, needing to mobilize forces to do battle with the communists, turned to the gentry in an alliance which was to last throughout an increasingly more widespread and bitter civil war. Chiang Kai-shek, in other words, sought to build upon the structures which were embedded in Chinese society; Mao Tse-tung worked to mobilize new forces for the creation of new structures.

Wang Sheng, of course, was to have his identity formed by the playing out of this drama, but this is to get ahead of the story. For the moment, suffice to note the point and move ahead. The end to the tale is already well known. Yet therein lies the confusion which we see in those attempting to describe Wang Sheng himself. He became an historical figure precisely because he picked the 'losing side' in the struggle, the Kuomintang. For as is now clear, in reality those who lost the war, the Nationalists, won the peace. It was their state which realized the dreams of the early revolutionaries for a China which was independent, prosperous, and free. And Wang Sheng played a crucial role.

Maoist Insurgency

At this point, there is no need to review in more detail than above the early framework of the Chinese revolution and its growing civil war. Nonetheless, there are several points which must be made. Certainly Mao Tse-tung and the Chinese Communist Party (CCP) emerged the short-term victors when, in 1949, after a struggle of more than two decades, they drove the Kuomintang from the field. From this fact, though, it does not follow that the outcome was preordained, an inevitable consequence of the flawed structure or incorrect leadership of 'pre-liberation' China. This, of course, has been a dominant theme of American scholarship on China.[3] Actually, the evidence would seem to come closer to supporting an earlier view, that which saw activists exploiting grievances, than to the alternative, that which saw the revolutionary élite as springing from the masses. Indeed, as we now know from a wide body of material, the initial recruits of the Maoist revolutionary endeavor in China were not drawn from the masses *per se* but from fringe elements of the populace, especially secret societies, bandits, and linguistic minorities located in locales of minimal official presence, such as border areas. Only when the revolutionary movement became a going concern was it able to exploit the mechanisms and contradictions in the old-regime, as it did in the key province of Jiangxi, where the communists had their most important pre-World War II 'liberated area', or soviet. Thus the structural conditions of the old-regime in China cannot be seen to have *caused* the communist insurgency.[4] The role of leadership – of the choices made by both sides – was crucial.

When all is said and done, communist revolutionary warfare in China was a technique for purposive action.[5] It was a means to an end, political power – political power to be seized for the purpose of overthrowing the existing order. It was not, as so many of its misguided adherents have claimed, an alternative form of democratic governance.[6] To the contrary, as will become clear in this work, democracy has been the most viable counter to the Maoist approach. The CCP insurgency, in other words, was about politics, about reshaping the process of 'who got what'. It was the conscious effort to supplant one political structure with another. Taken to its logical end, it became that which Mao claimed to be waging, *revolutionary warfare*, the conscious effort by insurgents 'to make a revolution' by seizing state power using politico-military means. Those who resisted it, such as the KMT and Wang Sheng, therefore, engaged by definition in *counterrevolutionary warfare*. They were counterinsurgents.

This becomes entirely logical when it is recalled that, following the Northern Expedition, it was the KMT which became the state power in China. Whereas previously the Nationalists had been the revolutionaries, they now found themselves *countering* would-be revolutionaries. Hence, if for temporal reasons alone, they had become revolutionaries waging counterrevolution. When the roles were ultimately reversed again in 1949, with the communist victory on the mainland, the KMT on Taiwan was again in the revolutionary position *vis-à-vis* the established power.

A crucial point, of course, is that in all these endeavors it is men who comprise revolution and counterrevolution. Structural circumstances, as either Mao or Wang Sheng would say, mean nothing save they are made real through human action. External manifestations of *insurgency* or *counterinsurgency,* such as terror or guerrilla war or mobile war, are all but tools to accomplish the political end, the remaking or defense of the political system. The precise level of force required by either side to achieve its goals depends upon the strength of the system under attack. Guerrilla warfare may suffice in one case; full-fledged conventional action may ultimately prove necessary in another. Likewise, the correct strategy to be followed will depend upon the particulars of the case at hand. Regardless, that which links strategy to the tactical use of force is the operational utilization of political infrastructure, covert in the case of the insurgents, open and legally established in the case of those who support the existing system.

Thus it is that the *raison d'être* of military power in such a context, in whatever form and for either side, is the projection and protection of the political infrastructure, leading ultimately to victory. Mao is only the most famous of the various revolutionaries who have related this reality. He set forth a three-step process (strategic defensive, stalemate, and offensive) and found it necessary, in the end, to transform his guerrilla armies into massive conventional forces to remove the last vestiges of KMT power. (Castro, we may note by way of contrast, found a Cuba so decayed that minimal guerrilla action was needed to bring the edifice crashing down.) Likewise, prominent counter-revolutionaries have achieved a certain notoriety; but since, in China, they were the losing party in the battle, KMT theorists of counterrevolution have not been much in evidence. Only Wang Sheng was to be a consistent exception, at least in the Chinese-speaking world.

Turning to the insurgent side of the equation, regardless of the military strength required to achieve the political aim, the critical fact is that it is dictated by the demands for protection of the alternate political system being constructed to carry out the revolution, not by military means *per se*. This, to be sure, is the ideal. Numerous other mundane factors, such as logistics or demographic realities, will affect insurgent courses of action. Yet it is the inspiration that is important. Step by step, the revolutionaries in China created an alternative political movement, then used it to seize power. Having done this, they implemented far-reaching changes – revolutionary changes.

Mao's strategy itself did not spring full-grown from his mind. It matured only by fits and starts. As such, it really had several parts, and the relationship between them is not always appreciated. Specifically, during the Jiangxi Soviet period, 1927–34, techniques of correct tactical employment of force, as well as for dealing with the masses, were developed. Yet these proved insufficient to prevent the Jiangxi Soviet from being crushed by Chiang Kai-shek's five encirclement campaigns.[7] Subsequently, during the Yenan period, that which followed the 'Long March' but prior to full-scale war with Japan in 1937, further 'mass line' techniques were developed (i.e., those for mobilizing the populace). Only with the Japanese occupation, however, and the adoption of the 'united front' as a strategic template (as opposed to its use merely as a tactical gambit), could a synthesis emerge which we would recognize today as Maoist revolutionary warfare.

There continues to be controversy over the role 'aroused Chinese peasant nationalism' played in mobilizing manpower for the CCP, but Chalmers Johnson is obviously correct in judging that without the Japanese occupation there would not have been Maoist insurgency.[8] One need not even enter into the debate as to whether it was nationalism or social action which activated the peasantry. Both were important and played varying roles depending upon the specific region in question; the real key was the destruction of the Kuomintang resource and manpower base by the Japanese, a reality which meant the state – incomplete and inefficient though it was, even after the Northern Expedition – was no longer able to muster the power which had previously proved sufficient to crush the communists. Indeed, it is not an overstatement to state that without the Japanese invasion, there might well have been no Mao. The collapse of the KMT in the 1945–49 civil war was an anticlimax. The Nationalist cause was mortally wounded before the battle was joined.[9]

Such an analysis surely flies in the face of much accepted wisdom but is more accurate. Jiangxi was the communist movement prior to war with Japan; and in Jiangxi the CCP was beaten. Following the Fifth Encirclement Campaign, the KMT began several significant approaches and programs designed to further its vision of China's future. These plans met with varying degrees of success before they, too, fell victim to the flames of war. In them, though, may be found the genesis of modern Taiwan.

A Youth in Longnan

It was not, we have noted above, in the rural hinterlands of provinces such as Jiangxi that the communists first attempted to make their movement a going concern. Instead , it was in the cities of southern China, particularly Canton and Shanghai, where they could find a proletariat which needed only the leadership of a Leninist revolutionary party to throw off its chains. Only with their hammering in the urban centers did it become necessary for the would-be revolutionaries to go to the masses. There were those such as Mao, and a host of lesser known local would-be revolutionaries, already there. Most of these individuals, including Mao himself, were sprung from the gentry. More often than not, they were students and teachers who used the existing institutions and structures of Chinese society to build their movements. Once they gained a certain following, they went to work amongst those they judged to be the exploited, particularly the landless poor.[10] Since their proffered solution was one which saw the overthrow of existing institutions, they rapidly came into confrontation with the gentry.

As the conflict grew in scope and violence, the gentry's need for enhanced resources, particularly trained manpower, resulted in appeals to higher rungs of government for assistance. These responded, with the result that the contest which emerged was one characterized by alternative modes of mobilization. What is of most significance in this process is that, because it was a political battle between rival infrastructures, with each side marshalling armed power to protect its organizing efforts, the outcome in any particular area was never a foregone conclusion. Grievances thrown up by structural injustice, to include widespread gentry abuse of the populace,[11] could be used by the insurgent leadership to mobilize manpower; but the process could work for the counterinsurgents in support of the status quo as well, particularly if the gentry could be made to ameliorate its excesses.[12] Where the two sides differed fundamentally was in the use they were willing to make of existing societal structures.[13]

Amidst such a dynamic Wang Sheng was born on 28 October 1915[14] in Longnan, one of Jiangxi Province's 81 counties or *hsien* (see Map 1 for location of Jiangxi, Map 2 for Longnan). There were 28 provinces, excluding Tibet and Outer Mongolia, and approximately 1,964 *hsien* nationwide.[15] Jiangxi itself was by the time of Wang's youth to have 13,794,159 inhabitants in 173,089 square kilometers.[16] His own world, though, was ever so much smaller. Even Longnan, now grown to some 300,000 people, was then but 80,000. It was administratively divided into five districts embracing 22 villages or small towns. It was in one of these, now called Jingou (Chinkou), 'Golden Fishhook', near Longnan town, that young Wang Shiu-chieh, as his parents named him, lived – though then their village was Mut'itsun (Muticun), 'Wooden Flute Village'. It was so-named because of the whistling noise the wind made as it swept through the trees. The Wang household lay in a cluster of 20 homes half an hour's walk, about a kilometer, from the Longnan center (see Map 3). Most of the homes, including the Wang family's, were sun-baked mud brick structures; tiled roofs and wooden frames. Subsistence activities were the norm. Rice-growing provided the livelihood for most, augmented by vegetables and fruit. As cash crops, the inhabitants processed commodities such as cotton, tobacco, sugar cane, peanuts, and beans.[17]

This was an isolated world, yet it was integrated into the larger system of the Gan River, a tributary of the Yangtze. The transportation network was poor, and only a few roads led to the outside; Guangdong Province was eight hours to the south by foot. Thus it was on the river that the most important commercial

MAP 1
JIANGXI PROVINCE IN CHINA

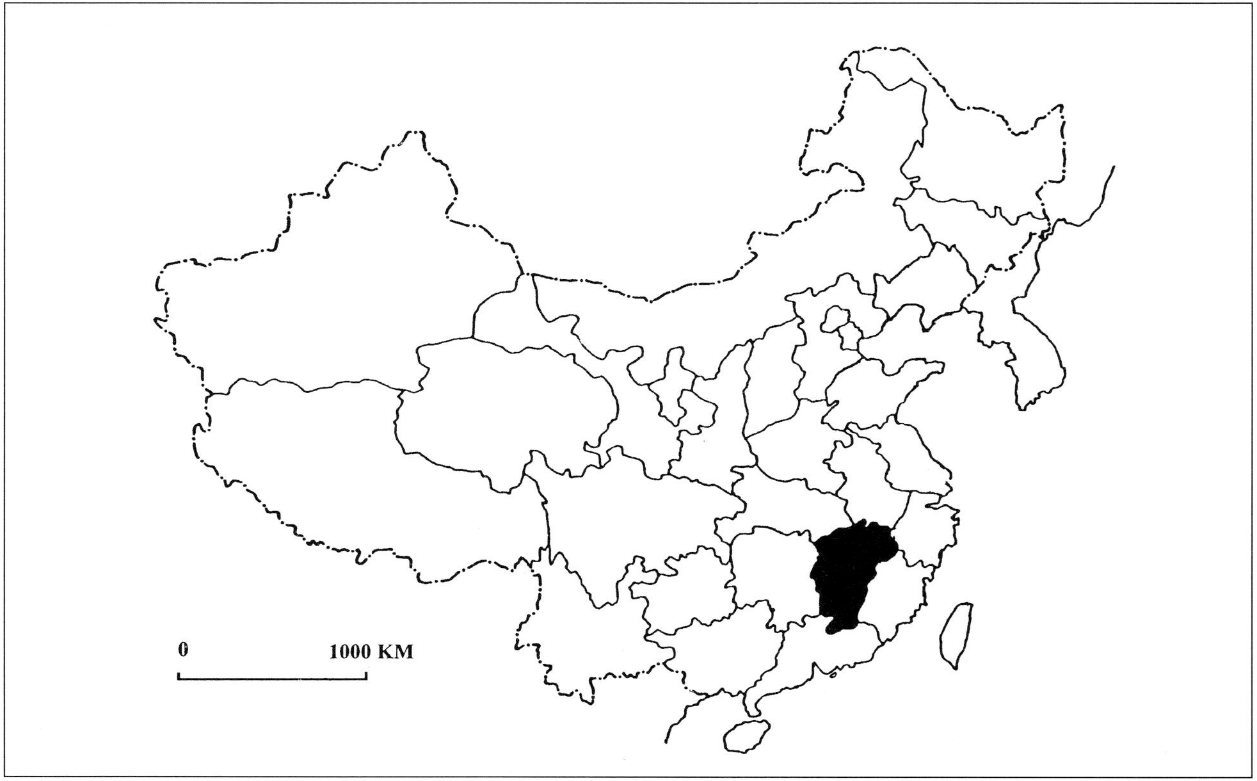

1000 KM

0

MAP 2
JIANGXI PROVINCE COUNTIES

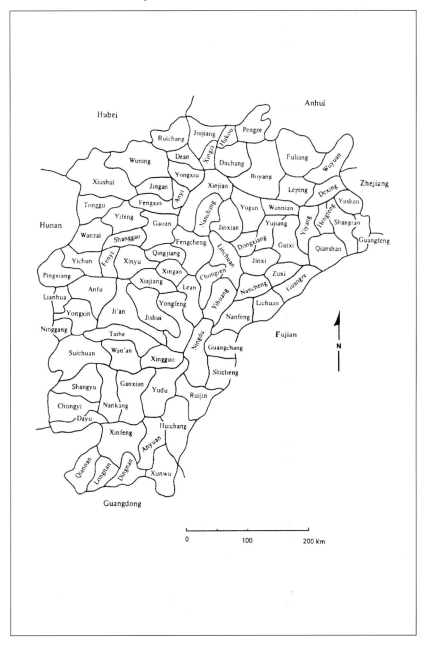

activity moved, in particular the exchange of salt, which Jiangxi lacked, for rice, needed by far-off Guandong. Cantonese, consequently, comprised a majority of the outsiders. Wood was another export, floated, like the two-way trade in salt and rice, to the provincial capital, Nanchang, thence to Nanjing (Nanking), the capital of the Republic, or, using various branches of the great rivers, to the bustling commercial center of Canton itself. In the Longnan area, the Jiangshu River, a branch of the Gan, could be used both ways for movement of such bulky items. Inland, on the roads, there were a few carts for shipping of goods, but most hauling was done by porters. Travellers got around almost exclusively on foot.

It was thus that the Wang family, ethnically Hakka, had originally come to Longnan. They had been in their area long enough to assimilate but had retained a commercial orientation.[18] Wang Sheng's father, Wang Pei-kuei (also known as Wang Kuei-san), ran a small business processing cotton and tobacco. As the chief of the clan, the small group of families with the same surname who lived together on the outskirts of Jin-gou, he presided over religious ceremonies and was the mediator in disputes. He was, in other words, a member of the gentry but certainly not in the sense that 'élite' is frequently interpreted. He could read and write but was not educated. His cotton mill was really only rented space in a public building, and all work was done by hand. When business was good, help could be hired. Elsewise, it was a family endeavor, joined in by Wang Sheng and his mother, Liu Huei-ying; an elder brother, Wang Chien-kang, and sister, Wang Hsiang-feng; and a younger brother, Wang Chien-hu.

The dislocation of the warlord years and the economic difficulties which culminated in the worldwide Great Depression made such family arrangements the norm. Hardship was great. The Wang business had not a single cart to carry its products; everything was moved on the family's backs. Wang Sheng's mother, a 'kind and hardworking woman', as one villager remembers, drove herself relentlessly despite a worsening illness. Recalls Wang Sheng, 'She overworked herself during those years. She would stay up until midnight, coughing with tuberculosis. Always I have that image of her – she worked and suffered. I would wake up in the dark and hear those two sounds, of her working the cotton and coughing'.[19]

At first young Wang Sheng must have been unaware of the

MAP 3
LONGNAN COUNTY

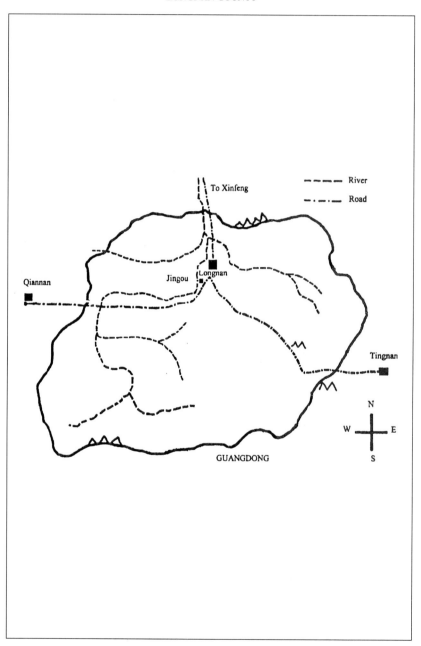

straits in which his family found themselves. Gradually, however, they impinged directly upon his life. From 1924–29, until he was 13 years of age, he was able to continue with his primary education at the county's Chih-liang Elementary School, working for the family on the side. He was a quick learner and applied himself, but to continue on with middle school would have required going to the regional center of Ganzhou, a four-day trek away, at a time when family finances were straitened and political instability mounting. Already the presence of local 'Communist Bandits' was interrupting the rhythms of daily life. In any case, by 1929 the family's money situation had become such as to preclude this option. Instead, Wang Sheng worked in Jingou and its vicinity to contribute his share. His brother owned in succession two stores, a small shop in Mut'itsun, then one for Chinese medicine in Qiannan, which he maintained with a partner. Wang Sheng worked as a clerk in the medicine store and also ran a print shop with a friend. He studied on his own at the insistence of his father and brother. From 1932 to 1935, he was able to return to a formal setting, Nanfang Institute of Chinese Literature, a clan creation which was a normal method for boys of the time to be educated. Though only attending half a year annually, the other half devoted to work, he was an apt pupil of his teacher, Liao Cheng-pu, who tutored him, as well as the other students, in the classical manner of 'the academy' (for which Socrates and the Greek philosophers were so well known).

Principally it was Chinese literature, philosophy, and social sciences which attracted Wang Sheng. As with countless others of his generation, he was drawn to tales of Chinese heroes – he especially liked Wen Tien-hsiang of the Southern Sung Dynasty – and to the three immemorial classic tales, *The Romance of the Three Kingdoms*, *Tales of the Monkey King*, and *Dream of the Red Chamber*. As perhaps indicative of the times, when China itself sought to build a republic, he also studied on his own a smattering of American history and was impressed by the quintessential American legends, Benjamin Franklin, Abraham Lincoln, and George Washington. He also was deeply interested in the moral framework posited by the Chinese philosophers Confucius and Mencius. His classmate, Chung Li-jieh, three years older, was to recall those years:

All Wang Sheng did was read all the time, study really hard, work hard. He got along with people well. All the time he stayed occupied. He was very, very goal-oriented, yet very introverted. We would talk. The topic was always about the country, society, our county – not like youngsters nowadays, who show less concern. We all lived in school together. At this part-time school, we didn't have extracurricular activities. All we did was study. This is why Wang Sheng has very good Chinese, because of his studying at that school.[20]

It was an education which was to serve him well. Throughout his life Wang Sheng was to be known for his ability to bring ideas together into a coherent whole, then to articulate his vision. His view of the moral order was profoundly affected by the classics; and he took away from his learning a world view which saw behavior, structures, and values as being of equal importance in forming a just order. The solution to the ills of society lay, first, in individual perfection; leading, second, to correct behavior; and, finally, brought together with other like-minded individuals in institutions dedicated to service as well as leadership. In pondering the intricacies of any situation, he was given to writing down his ideas – he had a strong memory – pulling the diverse threads into a coherent whole, all stroked with a sure hand in simple but elegant calligraphy.[21]

Evident, too, even at this early date, was Wang Sheng's astonishing capacity for work, linked to a growing patriotism which had first surfaced in the 'citizenship' lessons of elementary school. Clearly, he was profoundly affected by his family's own impoverishment, its downward social mobility, if one may use the term. 'I believe that life's tears can stain you', he has observed, 'but they can also push you forward'.[22] Likewise, he was much affected by the plight of that entity called only 'China'. Educational attainment provided a natural outlet for the synthesis he formed:

> I had a belief: scholarly knowledge is not anyone's monopoly. If you work hard, it can belong to you, not just to those with special degrees. My brother encouraged me to study. My father also encouraged me. No one told me, but it was obvious that to live in this world, you must have knowledge. Our country was so poor; we needed knowledge to improve. My thought was this: If the country is to advance, we must become educated.[23]

How Wang Sheng – a product of an isolated, remote,

impoverished environment, an environment where there was not even a newspaper, much less a telephone – came to link his own destiny with that of the Chinese nation is an enigma. For, as he was to comment years later, though he was aware of the existence of the Kuomintang, he did not actually hear of even so prominent a national figure as Chiang Kai-shek until he left home.[24] The genesis of his nationalism appears to lie in the particular confluence of threads in his corner of Longnan: the poverty of his gentry family; social unrest; vague but growing rumblings of revolutionary feeling, KMT and CCP; and the traditions of a classical education. Driven by a desire to lift himself and his family from the depths to which they had fallen, he saw his situation as part and parcel of similar national circumstances. Strong personal qualities, fostered by familial intercession, took flight and soared when placed within the world of traditional Chinese heroes and philosophers. A just world did not happen; it was *made*. It was made by those who acted, but acted in a very particular way, a 'Chinese' way.[25] Taught to think in terms of continuities and linkages, he was able to place himself in context, to link his personal circumstances to the declining fortunes of his society, as evidenced by economic hard times in general and the growth of 'bandit' forces, especially the communists. 'Bandit' forces offered nothing; they were external threats. *Restoration*, in the most profound sense of the word, *rebirth*, had to come from within, through the action of righteous men.

Wang Sheng put philosophy to work almost immediately. He found himself a soldier.

Counterinsurgency and the Mobilization of the Populace

His years of maturation had been marked by increasingly bitter fighting between the government and the communists. Though Longnan was not in the main area of confrontation, the counties around it were, and the CCP was active there (see Map 4), moving occasionally into Longnan itself. To the west was the CCP's Hunan-Quangxi base area, to the east the key Central Soviet base area. This main 'Jiangxi Soviet', as it was called, with its capital in Ruijin, controlled most of 16 counties and 3 million people at the beginning of 1934.[26] Initially, the KMT had attempted to deal with the advance of the CCP infrastructure by imposing a Western-style

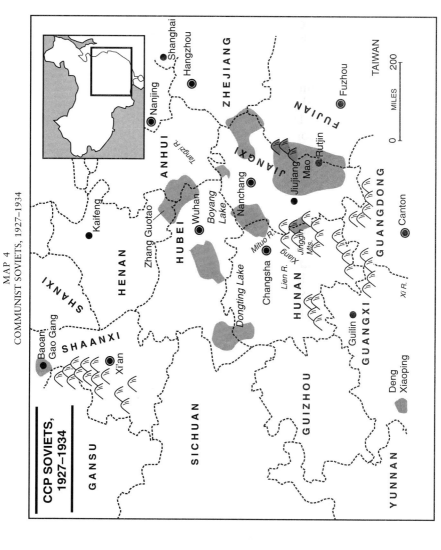

MAP 4
COMMUNIST SOVIETS, 1927–1934

CCP SOVIETS,
1927–1934

GANSU

SHAANXI

Baoan
Gao Gang

Xi'an

SHANXI

SICHUAN

HENAN

Kaifeng

Zhang Guotao

HUBEI

Wuhan

Boyang
Lake

Nanchang

Dongting Lake

Changsha

Mituo R.

Lien R.

Jinggang
Mts.

Xiang

HUNAN

GUIZHOU

Guilin

GUANGXI

Deng
Xiaoping

Xi R.

YUNNAN

ANHUI

Yangzi R.

Nanjing

Shanghai

Hangzhou

ZHEJIANG

JIANGXI

Jiujiang

Mao

Ruijin

FUJIAN

Fuzhou

TAIWAN

GUANGDONG

Canton

MILES

0   200

(Source: Spence, p.378)

police structure, established in September 1928, upon the province in the form of a Public Security Bureau (PSB) in each county. Nominally under its control was a paramilitary body, the county Police Force (PF), recruited explicitly to deal with law and order problems such as the communists. Since the impetus for this capability came from above, however, it proved quite ineffective, causing Nanjing to turn to the traditional source of local order, the gentry-recruited militia. These numerous bodies were gathered under one system, the *baowei tuan*,[27] ordered to be in place by the end of August 1930. Answering to the county magistrate, this organization 'conscripted all able-bodied men between the ages of 20 and 40 into tactical militia units organizationally corresponding to the neighborhood, village, district, and county self-governing institutions set up by the government'.[28]

Though more rooted in society, the *baowei tuan* also did not work out well. This and the government's defeat in the First Encirclement and Suppression Campaign (19 December 1930– 3 January 1931),[29] led Nanjing to revive yet another traditional approach, the *baojia* system, based upon organizing the entire populace in decimal hierarchies of mutual guarantee and collective responsibility. The PSB's were given the task of implementing the system; the *baowei tuan* was used to organize a truly universal militia. By 1934 the government had an available manpower pool of 2,137,036.[30] Meantime, of course, three more unsuccessful encirclement campaigns had taken place, the fourth ending in April 1933. While unsuccessful, the causes of these defeats had little to do with either insurgent popular mobilization or skillful guerrilla tactics, as is so frequently lauded. Instead, the main source of KMT disaster stemmed from the mixing of units, combining diverse warlord and KMT divisions which failed to support each other and consequently suffered defeat in detail when faced with superior CCP operational and tactical defensive moves. Entire 'government' divisions were lost in operations which had less to do with 'guerrilla tactics' so much as ignoring sound military fundamentals.[31]

The point is important, because it was not mass mobilization stemming from structural inequity which was allowing the CCP to win on the field of battle; it was military skill resulting in good tactics and sound operational designs (neither was there anything uniquely 'guerrilla' about these). Where mobilization came into play was in the production of manpower for the communist armies. Yet even in this area, control of the 'Jiangxi Soviet' and other base areas was not a matter of communist covert infrastructure gradually subverting and finally capturing an area. Instead, areas in contention were normally captured by CCP columns issuing from secure areas, *then* organized as part of the infrastructure. What this meant was that the communists, being unable as yet to form a liberated area, or alternate state, which could match the Republic in resources, were vulnerable to a competently prosecuted counterrevolutionary campaign. This was not long in coming.

The Second Encirclement and Suppression Campaign (1 April– 30 May 1931) had been essentially a rerun of the First Campaign, but beginning with the Third Campaign (1 July–20 September 1931), external factors mattered as much as communist defensive action in the actual defeat of the government forces. These were the Canton Secessionist Movement (May 1931) and the Mukden Incident (18 September 1931). The former threatened Nanjing's already tenuous hold on power; the latter resulted in the alienation of Manchuria to Japan. Likewise, the Fourth Campaign (1 January –29 May 1933) was halted due to renewed Japanese aggression.[32] Already, following the Third Campaign, Chiang Kai-shek had used the occasion of the Five Province Bandit Suppression Conference at Lushan, Jiangxi, to announce a 'Three Parts Military and Seven Parts Politics Policy' which focused upon popular mobilization through the strengthening of administrative structure and efficiency.[33] Under the guidance of Chiang Kai-shek intimate Hsiung Shih-hui (Xiong Shi-hui), who was Jiangxi governor from 15 December 1931 to 1941, counties were grouped under 13 intermediate bodies in an Administrative Inspectorate System (AIS). The inspectorates, in turn, reported to Nanchang, where Chiang Kai-shek had his military headquarters for most of 1927–35. Wholesale personnel changes followed, as did training for government personnel at all levels. Socio-economic initiatives, such as fostering cooperative societies and promoting the 'New Life Movement',[34] played a secondary role but logically grew from Chiang Kai-shek's emphasis upon the primacy of values and behavior in producing viable structures for a new, revolutionary order. The results were mixed, but when the Fourth Campaign was accompanied by a communist offensive outside the 'Jiangxi Soviet' area, as well as the inauguration of an aggressive CCP policy for land redistribution, the pieces of a viable government approach fell into place. Aroused at last by the communist menace to their position, the gentry and their ability to mobilize local resources moved decisively to the government side. The *sanbao* ('three *bao*'s') strategy, adopted in April 1933, 'called for the integration of security forces into the Communist-suppression effort through an expansion of the *baojia*, revitalization of the *baowei tuan*, and the construction of *baolei* (blockhouses) to blockade the soviet base area'.[35]

In conception the KMT's approach to popular mobilization was the opposite of that adopted by the CCP in that it sought to use existing structures, improved in honesty and administrative efficiency, to tap the manpower pool. The communists, in contrast, built new structures by bringing into political play popular forces marginalized by the existing system. Where both approaches were alike, however, was that they were strategic initiatives adopted by the contending élites, revolutionary and counterrevolutionary. Both, we may note further, involved co-option of local movements: the gentry-led social structure and militia, by Nanjing; regional insurgent groups rooted in parochial disaffection, by the CCP hierarchy. In the Fifth Encirclement Campaign (16 October 1933–14 October 1934) the KMT demonstrated its ability to derive greater power in this contest of mobilization. It used the militia to build and man a blockade of the 'Jiangxi Soviet', enforcing population and resources control as regular military units were used to move the network of blockhouses and barriers inexorably forward. The results for the CCP 'liberated area', always a questionable economic entity even in the best of times, were catastrophic. In autumn of 1934 the communists abandoned their would-be state and launched upon the epic 'Long March' which led them, a year later, to the wilds of Yenan.[36]

Stay-behind units remained, though (see Map 5), so a continuing task for the KMT was the complete pacification of Jiangxi. This counterinsurgency goal required insuring that the government infrastructure was impervious to assault from within or without. Initially, Military Pacification Regions were established, but these proved unwieldy, and their functions were transferred to the AIS, which itself was reorganized from 13 to 8 inspectorates. Within them, the *baojia* was extended and used both for control and reconstruction. From its rolls, all able-bodied men, 18–45 years, were conscripted into militia units called everything from the peace preservation corps to Righteous

MAP 5
AREAS OF COMMUNIST ACTIVITY, 1934–1937

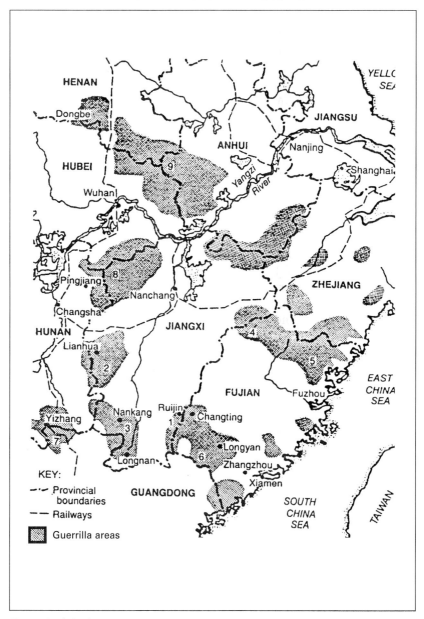

(Source: *Single Sparks*, p.67)

Warriors Communist Suppression Squads. 'While in the militia, they received a modest education and a heavy dose of political indoctrination. On the eve of the War of Resistance against Japan, there were over 118,000 men in these paramilitary units'. [37] One of them was Wang Sheng.

First Steps into the KMT Infrastructure

Initially, it had not appeared that Wang Sheng's life was to be marked by anything other than a collapse into obscurity. His mother had died, finally, of the tuberculosis. After leaving Nanfang Institute, he again worked where he could. By 1936 he was a tailor, the print shop having failed. A friend was in the local militia, the peace preservation corps structure, and encouraged him to join that. This Wang Sheng did in 1936, being recruited, due to his ability to read and write, as the unit clerk of the 12th Jiangxi Security Protection Regiment in Longnan. At the time the southern portion of Jiangxi, or Gannan,[38] was divided into two administrative districts, the eighth, which embraced the southeastern portion, to include many of the former CCP areas, and the fourth, under which fell 11 counties more to the southwest. Boundaries were to change, but at the time the regiment fell within the command authority of what was then the eighth pacification district of Gannan.[39] Wang Sheng was only 20 and was given the rank of second-lieutenant, the established grade for the unit clerk.

It was during this initial tour of duty that he recalls first actually hearing of Chiang Kai-shek. Acknowledged officially, at least internationally, as the leader of China, the general in reality exercised control principally over the provinces near the sea, those most affected by foreign influence and commercial penetration – and thus the source of KMT membership and power. By 1936, when Wang Sheng put on a uniform, Chiang was fighting for his life. Japanese incursions had grown ever more blatant, and pressure upon him to act in the national defense more intense. The problem he faced, however, was deceptively simple. He could not actually command 'his' armies. Rather, in a complex internal calculus, he was a first among equals, with a majority of 'government' armies actually those of real and potential rivals. Casualties to KMT forces, those which had grown out of the

Whampoa-officered troops that had carried out the Northern Expedition, had already been substantial, further undercutting Chiang's already tenuous position. Hence, while an all-out resistance struggle against the Japanese was the seemingly logical course, certainly the most popular, it was neither politically prudent nor even militarily possible.

Be this as it was, demands to concentrate against the foreign aggressor, rather than the fellow Chinese of the CCP, reached a head in December 1936 in the so-called Sian Incident. Chiang was held hostage by a group of regional officers demanding that the impending Sixth Campaign against the communists be called off in favor of a war of national resistance. The campaign was, in fact, cancelled, even as the Japanese made it irrelevant by using the Marco Polo Bridge Incident of 7 July 1937 as an excuse to invade the Chinese interior and to seize important coastal areas, such as Shanghai. Intense fighting mauled key KMT units, dealing Chiang Kai-shek a blow from which he never actually recovered. 'Within a year', Jonathan D. Spence has written, 'the Japanese overran east China, depriving the Guomindang [*sic*] of all the major Chinese industrial centers and the most fertile farmland, and virtually severing China's ties to the outside world. Chiang's new wartime base, Chongqing (Chungking), became a symbolic center for national resistance to the Japanese, but it was a poor place from which to launch any kind of counterattack'.[40] Chiang, in other words, though he remained the 'ruler' of China, was anything but, maintaining his position through inertia and the disarray of his domestic opponents. The very vastness of China's human and physical geography prevented the Japanese from delivering a knockout punch.[41]

This emasculation of Chiang Kai-shek's position, of course, was still ahead but it was increasingly to affect Wang Sheng's progress. For the moment, there were appeals that all patriotic young people mobilize against the Japanese. In 1937, after approximately a year with the 12th Jiangxi Security Protection Regiment, Wang Sheng transferred to a unit at a training depot in the adjoining county of Hsingfeng (Xinfeng). It needed a clerk. Seemingly an innocuous career move, the shift to the Strong Youth Training Battalion of the 6th Strong Youth Training Regiment[42] was to have, for him and the Republic, momentous consequences. For it was to lead him to Chiang Kai-shek's eldest son, Chiang Ching-kuo.

Chiang Ching-kuo's life in many ways parallelled that of Wang

Sheng. Born on 18 March 1910 of his father's first wife by an arranged marriage, he was inevitably thrust into the politics of China. His contact with the revolutionary ferment of the country's cities, though, drew him towards the left wing of the Kuomintang and the CCP, then still linked to the KMT through the first united front, even as his father moved towards the right. Bitter discussions resulted in the 15-year-old Ching-kuo being allowed to go with the initial group of 600 Chinese students selected for training at the Soviet Union's Sun Yat-sen University. Only just established, it was until its closing in 1930 to be a major training ground for Chinese communist leaders. Initially, too, since Moscow was working officially with the KMT rather than the CCP, it had in its student body many KMT youths. Relations between the two groups were always strained, at times bursting into open conflict, and collapsed altogether following Chiang Kai-shek's assault on the communists at Shanghai in April 1927. Most KMT students returned home.[43]

Among those who did not was Chiang Ching-kuo. Furthermore, he denounced his father[44] and threw himself more deeply into Communist Party work. Ultimately, in December 1929, he was to become an alternate member of the Russian Communist Party, and in May 1930 a graduate of the Central Tolmatchev Military and Political Institute of the Red Army in Leningrad. Steeped in the intricacies of communist theory and organization, as well as military practice, Ching-kuo would have seemed completely alienated not only from his father but also from his homeland. From June to October 1930 he even served as assistant director of the Chinese students at Sun Yat-sen University. Yet behind the scenes, in that chaotic world of university politics, he had become involved in the Trotsky versus Stalin debate. In 1927, before moving on to the Tolmatchev Institute, he joined a secret Trotskyite organization. He apparently actually withdrew from the group in 1928, but the die was cast. In June, fresh from Tolmatchev, he joined the staff of an institution so wracked with factionalism – it had already suffered major purges which involved the secret police – that it was shut down. Chiang Ching-kuo's fate was similar. After several assignments, as an electrical plant apprentice and a cadre on a cooperative farm, he was purged and exiled in January 1933 to Siberia to work in a gold mine. Rehabilitated to an extent, but still forced to engage in labor at a heavy machinery plant in the Urals, he married a Russian woman,

Faina Epatcheva Vahaleva, in March 1935 and promptly had a son. Purged yet again, but apparently rescued by the growth of renewed contacts between the KMT and CCP following the Sian Incident, in March 1937 he was allowed to return home.[45]

Only 27 but grown beyond his years, Chiang Ching-kuo was a different man than the impetuous, ideologically driven youth who had left China at 15. The years in the Soviet Union, which had begun so optimistically, in the flush of revolutionary fervor, had ended in the bitter cold and loneliness of Siberian exile. Even his marriage, though it was to last a lifetime, could be seen as a product of isolation; Faina was also alone when they met. Yet the harsh realities of Stalinism were to temper him in the same manner that 'life's tears' toughened Wang Sheng. Ironically, where it was revolutionary ardor that had led to Chiang Ching-kuo's estrangement from his father and China, so it was this same quality which was to make for his fall in the USSR and his eventual rise once he returned home. Trotskyism, which Ching-kuo found attractive, despite its clarion calls for continuing the world revolution, was nonetheless a more democratic and mass-based version of Marxist-Leninism than Stalinism, particularly as filtered through a young man's prism. Stalinism, he had experienced at first hand and knew to be a monster. What he took away, then, was a wealth of organizational and theoretical revolutionary experience, a thorough knowledge of communism and its shortfalls, and a renewed commitment to the continuing quest for a just society. The quest was no doubt something Chiang Kai-shek could understand immediately; in time he would come to appreciate his son's finesse in the other two areas.

Chiang Ching-kuo's reconciliation with his father has not been recorded but must have been heartfelt, because from then on Ching-kuo was to assume an evermore important role in KMT affairs. Initially, though, he was sent by Chiang Kai-shek to study the Chinese classics and to familiarize himself with the lay of the land, in every respect, particularly socially and politically. This he did quickly. By 1938 he was ready to begin a period of praxis. He was appointed assistant chief of the Office of Public Security, headquartered in Nanchang, by the Jiangxi governor and Chiang Kai-shek intimate, Hsiung Shih-hui. Simultaneously, he was designated head of the Military Training Department of the Jiangxi Political School, a KMT organization. Under his purview fell the various units of local defense. In May, Hsiung, who was also

serving as the President of the Jiangxi Political School, named
Chiang Ching-kuo a major-general to head a newly established
Supervisory Office for Training of Recruits.[46] He made his
headquarters in Ganzhou, in southern Jiangxi.

In fact, he arrived to assume his duties even as Wang Sheng,
propelled upward by unit expansion brought on by war with
Japan, was sent to Ganzhou to serve at regimental headquarters.
His unit fell under the authority of Chiang Ching-kuo's
Supervisory Office. Assigned as *aide de camp* to Colonel Liu, the
regimental commander, Wang Sheng found himself one day,
together with 500–600 other people, in the center of Ganzhou
struggling to hear Chiang Ching-kuo give a speech. Though he
worked directly under Ching-kuo, in a sense, Wang Sheng had
never met the man, who spoke without a microphone, slowly and
in Mandarin which had still not recovered from his long spell of
using principally Russian. Yet the short figure was full of energy
and articulated a message of service to the country and resistance
against the Japanese. It was a message which went over well with
Wang Sheng: 'I thought, this guy has the strength to carry on the
work. He is very patriotic'.[47]

Their paths still did not cross directly, but Wang Sheng had
formed his first – and favorable – impression of Chiang Ching-kuo.
Wang Sheng's own high qualities were likewise noted by Colonel
Liu, who used him for tasks of increasing importance, despite his
relative inexperience. When it came time for the newly trained
personnel of the regiment to move to the front, in northern
Jiangxi, it was Wang Sheng who was given the task of leading them
there. Similarly, in the months that followed, he delivered batches
of replacements. Throughout, regardless of where he found
himself, he took materials to study, as he had since leaving Nanfeng
Institute. This trait was rewarded when, in late 1938, he passed the
competitive examination for admission to the Central Military
Academy (CMA). He entered in February 1939.

Joining the Elite

The Central Military Academy had a distinguished lineage.
Previously Whampoa Military Academy, the famed institution
which gave birth to KMT military power (and hence that of the
Republic), it had become CMA upon its move from Canton to

Nanjing. Subsequently, with the relocation of the capital itself to Chongqing (Chungking), the school functioned as a central institution and nine branch schools. Annual intakes were still numbered – Wang Sheng was in Class 16, which had more than 3,000 members, 300 of them women – but classmates would frequently not have been trained together. Likewise, the extraordinarily close personal link between Chiang Kai-shek and, initially, Whampoa, then CMA, was broken. Though the students were still the products of a competitive selection process, the focus of the training was no longer tutelage for great things, as had previously been the case, but rather upon the production of tactical leaders for an army whose junior ranks were already decimated.[48]

Daily life at the Jiangxi Branch School (or Number Three Branch School of the Central Military Academy, as it was also called) was a 0600–2100 regimen, an equal mix of political and military training. The number of instructors reflected this, with about 20 performing military functions, an equal number the political tasks. The students observed that the military instructors were invariably at a higher level than their political counterparts, some of whom had no experience with a military organization at all. Shortly after classes began the school had to move due to continued Japanese pressure in northern Jiangxi, which eventually resulted in the fall of Nanchang, the Jiangxi capital (27 March 1939). Spirits, though, remained high. Observes CMA Class 16 member Lin Jung-chu:

> The members of our class came from all directions, because in the war against the Japanese, we had seen their brutality. They killed Chinese and engaged in savage, barbarian behavior. They frightened the Chinese. At that time in China, we had a saying – 'you don't use good steel to make nails or good men to make soldiers' – but during the war everyone went in the military. My hometown is in Nanjing. We witnessed the Japanese slaughter. We hated the Japanese from the bottoms of our hearts, so many youths vowed to fight them.[49]

This sense of shared purpose, of working to save the Chinese nation, is echoed in the experiences of Sha Chi-liang, another CMA Class 16 member:

> My family was middle class and lived in the Japanese Concession in Shanghai. I was a University of Shanghai

graduate. War broke out between China and Japan on 7 July 1937; on 13 August we bolted from the Japanese to the British Concession. As we were fleeing, the Japanese soldiers pulled me from the car, made me bow to them, and kept kicking me, calling me things like 'son of a bitch'. This made me very angry. I thought, 'How can I live like this? The Chinese world is finished'. The newspaper reports said Japan would conquer China in just three months. I stayed at the YMCA. Then came the rape of Nanjing, when the Japanese killed so many thousands of people. I was supposed to go to the States for further schooling, to graduate school. But I joined the army, where I was put in the political section. They sent me to the Strong Youth Training Corps in the mountains. My involvement with the military was purely involuntary! My schooling had been for commerce, so the military life at Central Military Academy was very difficult for me. I could not pass my courses, so Wang Sheng helped me. We were about the same size, so we became very close. It was because of him that I graduated.[50]

Indeed, if there is anything the members of the Third Branch (the Jiangxi component) of CMA Class 16 shared, it was memories of Japanese aggression and the central role Wang Sheng came to play in their lives. As with the case of Sha Chi-liang, Tai Ch'i-hung's tale combines the two:

I was seventeen, so according to government regulations, which said you had to be eighteen, I was not supposed to be in service; but I hid my age and enlisted. Before I could leave my town, it was bombed. The walls of the house I was in collapsed, and I was buried in the rubble. When I woke up, my friend was dead beside me. After I left, I carried what I could with me and was put into the Service Corps. I passed an exam in Gian and became a cadet at the Central Military Academy. Wang Sheng and I belonged to the same company. We had no dorms; we had to shovel manure out of stables to make space for ourselves. When we had to move from Gian to Yutu, there was no transportation. So we walked for five days. It was hardest when it rained, because this caused the rivers to rise. We constantly had to cross rivers, carrying all of our weapons and equipment, 40 kilos in all, a very heavy load

which soon began to feel like 70! Our equipment included a
little stool and a wooden writing slate, because we still had to
have classes during our march. Wang Sheng was very
considerate. He took care of the little ones. When Liu Ch'i-
hsiung fell into the river, no one dared to go in after him. He
was drowning, so Wang Sheng jumped in after him and saved
him. It was a terrible time. Our sole motivation for being
there was to fight the Japanese.[51]

It was a sentiment repeated many times. Says Liu Ch'i-hsiung
himself:

When I left for the military academy, my parents were very
sad, but we had to fight the Japanese. That was our sacred
duty. No matter what age or sex, male or female, adult or
child, regardless of region, every Chinese stood up to fight
them. It was even a slogan. I was only seventeen, but we had
to fight to save our country. I studied with Wang Sheng that
one year. We had a close relationship. He was the natural
leader amongst the group, not because he had a formal
position. He was so helpful, so enthusiastic, and so patriotic
that there were those who were envious of him. He was also
a very honest man.[52]

Remarkably, if there is a salient theme to these observations,
beyond their fulsome praise of Wang Sheng, it is consistently how
his classmates recognized his willingness to help those who found
themselves in difficult straits. At one end of the behavioral
spectrum, he was physically courageous, a trait mentioned
repeatedly in interviews: 'He really had guts. He was a brave,
courageous man'.[53] Not only did he place himself directly in harm's
way, rescuing a drowning classmate or – 'At that time, there were
spies around our camp, so we had to stand guard. Wang Sheng
would accompany those who were frightened on guard'.[54] He
sought to get into the larger fight – 'He was not interested in
political warfare. He wanted to be a combat commander, to plunge
into war, to go to the war zone'.[55] At the other end of the spectrum,
he was solicitous of those around him, especially the young, the
weak, and the troubled. Many of his classmates were younger, with
less experience than he possessed, and he seemed to thrive on the
chance to lighten their loads: 'I was a little bit slow', remembers
Ch'en Shen, 'But Wang Sheng encouraged me to ask questions, to

ask for clarification of anything I did not understand. He told me I had to be willing to ask questions'.[56] Likewise, adds Tsai Ping-jung, 'Because I was small, physical training was very, very tough. Wang Sheng showed me how to pass the physical training test. So I appreciated him very much. He also showed me how to take notes in class. He was a good writer and could summarize points well'.[57] Interestingly, such compassion for others existed side-by-side with his own passion for strict discipline. 'He liked the instructors who were tough', observes Sun Hwa-chieh.[58] Yet he never seems to have become a martinet. Instead, as Lin Jung-chu summarizes, 'He was our spiritual leader'.[59] Not surprisingly, Wang Sheng graduated first in the Jiangxi branch class.

His prowess had not gone unnoticed. While Wang Sheng was in the Central Military Academy, Chiang Ching-kuo was attending the Party and Government Administration Training Course in Chongqing (Chungking) from 17 April to 15 May 1939. At the same time, he became Secretary of the planned Jiangxi branch of the government's *San Min Chu-i* Youth Corps. Established on 7 July 1938 as an independent KMT body, the Youth Corps had 'a special duty to organize and train the nation's youth [defined as those 16–25 years of age] so that it may be able to shoulder the responsibilities and work concerning social welfare and spiritual salvation'.[60] In other words, by using Sun Yat-sen's Three Principles, the *San Min Chu-i* – nationalism, democracy, and people's livelihood – the eager young were to work to further the reshaping of China. This was a revolutionary task, as the KMT saw it. Since it was in support of the established state power, however, it could objectively be judged counterrevolutionary, because an explicit purpose was to appeal to a favorite target of the CCP revolutionaries – youth.

Such theory was not the immediate concern of Chiang Ching-kuo. What he needed were good individuals to staff his organization. A *San Min Chu-i* Youth Corps (Jiangxi Branch) Cadre Training Course was set up at Ch'ihchuling for this purpose. Ching-kuo asked Hu Kuei, director of the Political Department at the Central Military Academy, to recommend students.[61] The top 72 students from the CMA Class 16 in Jiangxi, to include Wang Sheng, as well as 72 selected college graduates, were sent – altogether 144 men and women, thus a 50-50 mix of military and civilians.[62] Chiang Ching-kuo himself was the course director.

Training followed a familiar pattern. The uniformed cadre

awoke to a bugle for physical training, then spent the days, on into the nights, in political and military training. The emphasis was on developing revolutionary spirit and techniques for mobilizing such enthusiasm. Chiang Ching-kuo himself would join in the routine, to include the physical training, at least several times each week. He could not always be there, as he had other duties in Gannan, but his presence was regular enough that he soon came to know all participants. To facilitate remembering their names, he would personally call the roll on the days when he was in camp. Then he would conduct classes himself. Again, it was Wang Sheng who emerged at the head of the group when it was time to graduate at the end of the three months allotted. This time Chiang Ching-kuo knew the man. What he liked about Wang Sheng was his quickness of mind; his energy, sincerity, and patriotism. For his part, Wang Sheng recalls:

> I was still young [23], so sometimes I'd get up and ask questions of him – but very few. There were times when we talked one on one. He was very, very busy; very sincere; very patriotic. When I had heard him in the park, I had been impressed but not overwhelmed. He was so young [29], but now that I got to know him, I realized that he had substance.[63]

The feeling was mutual. From the graduating class Chiang Ching-kuo selected four individuals, two military and two college, for special assignment with him. Wang Sheng was the first he named.[64] It was the beginning of a team which was to last for nearly 50 years.

In such a development – in the Cadre Training Course – we see the contradictions and potentialities which were both the weaknesses and strengths of the KMT tenure on the mainland. Ironically, the angle which seems to preoccupy modern Chinese commentators is that of faction, the notion that by training 'his own cadres', as Lo Hsuan termed them, Chiang Ching-kuo became but another player in the warlord maneuvering which passed for politics in China.[65] In one sense this was true; he was training his own people. In another sense, the argument is flawed, because Ching-kuo was occupying a relatively low-level KMT position to which he was appointed by another KMT appointee (admittedly a family confidant), and could just as easily be removed (he was not yet established as his father's heir). Training young college graduates or military men could hardly provide a power base in the most concrete sense of the word. Neither does such seem to have been Chiang Ching-kuo's intent. Instead, he was doing exactly what institutions such as the Central Military Academy were doing in training individuals such as Wang Sheng, providing competent individuals to staff the revolution, the effort to rebuild China. The acid test was neither the training of personnel nor the acceptance of responsible positions; it was any one individual's willingness to function within the system for a common good beyond personal gain. Chiang Ching-kuo, as he was to demonstrate throughout his career, met this test.

Therein lay precisely the weakness of the Republic. The very manner in which the Northern Expedition of 1926–27 had consolidated KMT power, coopting warlords rather than ousting them and mobilizing new social forces, as advocated by the CCP and the KMT's own left wing, resulted in a paucity of individuals committed to *the revolution*. The only remedy was to educate the young. This certainly was the communist solution. The difference was that the CCP chose to create new institutions altogether, to carry out the national revolution by tapping the forces of the welling social revolution. The KMT sought only a national revolution, to staff its modifications of the old structure with new blood schooled in traditional values and virtuous in thought and behavior.[66] This was what lay behind Chiang Kai-shek's support for the Youth Corps itself[67] and even such shadowy and much-misunderstood bodies as the *Lixingshe*, or Blue Shirts.[68] Constantly disappointed that the 'old blood' with which he was surrounded, particularly in the revolutionary party, the KMT, was unable to remake itself in the mold necessary for internal restoration and national liberation – the failure of the so-called 'New Life Movement' must be seen in this context – he sought to invest in the future by molding young minds to a calling in every sense analogous to that of the Christian priesthood.

If the very structure Chiang Kai-shek sought to modify may be deemed tragically flawed, as it has been by so many, his efforts were doomed to failure. Yet this would hardly seem to be a foregone conclusion. What was probably at issue was not the structures but rather the temporal element: Could the Republic survive a contest of resource mobilization with other contenders while it struggled to acculturate and train new personnel, who, if nothing else, would move into the structure as the old officeholders died off or were put out to pasture? While the KMT still had access to resources in the pre-War of Resistance years, it did successfully withstand challenges to its position and extend its domain. Once, however – as we have noted earlier – it was cut off from these resources by the Japanese, it was vulnerable. In the event, it was CCP mobilization which provided the knockout blow because the communist method of organizing proved the more appropriate to the radically altered environment of Japanese occupation (1937–45).

Yet the KMT, as seen in the composition of the Cadre Training Course, was not monolithically so rooted in existing structures that it was self-destructive. KMT schools and organizations consistently mobilized new groups, such as women, and endeavored to harness them. That it may have done so inefficiently is quite a different matter from holding that ossification was the norm. Under Chiang Ching-kuo, as we shall see, this was anything but the case. His proving ground was to be Gannan.

Gannan: Revolution in the Counterrevolution

That Chiang Ching-kuo was only able to *supervise* the Cadre Training Course was due to the multiplicity of offices he held. Most importantly, he was Commissioner of the Fourth District in the administrative inspectorate system, as well as Commanding Officer of the Security Preservation Corps. Obviously, the relationship between his father, Chiang Kai-shek, and the Jiangxi governor, Hsiung Shih-hui, played a significant role in his being elevated to such responsibility at so young an age – he was still only 30 in mid-1940 when the Cadre Training Course took place. Yet, as events were to demonstrate, he kept the positions because he proved not only a competent but also an inspirational leader. Like Wang Sheng, he motivated those whom he met. And so it was with considerable pride and anticipation that Wang Sheng assumed his new position as an Inspector in the Fourth District Commissioner's office, directly responsible for overseeing three counties near that of his birth: Xinfeng, Anyuan, and Xunwu (refer to Map 2). Concurrently, he was made the Political Director for the self-defense battalion of the district.

For a 24-year-old, this was an impressive task; though no more so than that which Chiang Ching-kuo had set for himself. His Fourth District had 11 counties embracing 23,000 square kilometers and a population of 1.6 million.[69] Included therein were some of the most marginal areas in the province – recall that it was Xunwu, for instance, which Mao Tse-tung chose for his first major effort at social investigation.[70]

Ching-kuo set forth a Three-Year Development Plan designed to make Gannan a model area for the entire country. Everyone was to have a job, have food, be clothed, be housed, and be educated.[71] The first year was to be taken up by pacification, the next two by development itself, followed with a longer effort of another three or even five years. Besides directing the effort as a whole, Chiang Ching-kuo was magistrate for one of his eleven counties, Ganxian, wherein lay the important center of Ganzhou itself. Concurrently, as had become the norm, he headed both the Jiangxi Administrative Office for Wounded Soldiers (Ganzhou Branch), subordinate to the Ministry of War, and the Salt Tax Bureau responsible for the four provinces of Zhejiang (Chekiang), Anhui (Anhwei), Fujian (Fukien), and Jiangxi (Kiangsi).[72]

Despite the extent of his responsibilities, Chiang Ching-kuo performed well. During the first year, the *baojia* system was set firmly in place, and the militia was expanded after being brought under centralized control – a move reportedly opposed by most of the country magistrates but carried out nonetheless. Mobile operations sought out 'bandits'. Crime and corruption were suppressed vigorously. Law and order improved so much that the people began to refer to him as 'Chiang the Blue Sky', 'a nickname traditionally given to the incorrupt officials who brought 'bright days' to the people'.[73] He earned further trust by mingling with the people and refusing to put on the usual airs of officialdom. Always his theme was service to the people.

There was resistance, particularly from those whose vested interests were affected by the sweeping and effective housecleaning Chiang Ching-kuo instituted. A steady stream of missives and supplicants went to Chongqing (Chungking) to protest directly to Chiang Kai-shek. These increased as the prohibition on the 'Three Balls of Fire' – gambling, opium, and prostitution – were more sternly enforced, and corrupt and abusive officials and gentry were attacked. Recounts one source:

At the time, there were between ten and twenty members of the gentry in the government of southern Jiangxi who, seemingly unaware of the importance of the war effort, still smoked opium and continued in their dissolute ways. They lodged a complaint with the provincial governor, Hsiung Shih-hui, saying that Chiang's way of doing things was 'red' and that he used communist slogans. They feigned compliance with Chiang's orders but secretly opposed him. Chiang became aware of this and gave his subordinates in the Commissioner's office and county government stern reproaches. He emphasized that he would be very tough on lawbreakers. Following this, Chiang had two prominent gamblers arrested, the wives of two Jiangxi officials. He punished them as he did all other gamblers: they were forced to kneel in front of the 'Memorial to Soldiers Killed in Battle in the Sino-Japanese War' in central Ganzhou for three days, six hours per day. He had the son of Nanchang Midland Bank official Fu Tzu-t'ing and five other people executed for smoking opium. These stern measures shook southern Jiangxi, causing some people to call Chiang, 'Chiang Blue Sky'.[74]

The claim that Chiang Ching-kuo was at best a CCP fellow-traveller, at worst an agent of the Soviet Union and international communism, was the one levelled most often.[75] Nothing could have been further from reality. To the contrary, he had the security forces push ahead relentlessly with pacification. There was nothing Chiang Ching-kuo did that Chiang Kai-shek did not know about and approve, either directly or tacitly. Obviously, the effort to create a 'model district' was not going to be derailed by resistance or gossip. What Chiang Ching-kuo was doing in Gannan was what Chiang Kai-shek hoped to see happen in the country at large. A start had to be made somewhere, and the elder Chiang was turning to people upon whom he felt he could rely, most notably his son. That his decision bore fruit was a result of what turned out to be Chiang Ching-kuo's formidable abilities. The younger Chiang's greatest weapon was his ability to inspire and his willingness to seek out good people wherever he could find them. His recognition of Wang Sheng and appointment of him to an important position, despite his youth and relative inexperience – particularly when considered in traditional Chinese terms – were

illustrative. The case of Liu Jing-shing (Jingxing), who became
Gannan Finance Section Chief and thus ended up working closely
with Wang Sheng, is telling for what it reveals of Chiang Ching-
kuo's methods for bringing competent, trustworthy individuals
into his team:

> I was from a typical farmer's family. For generations there was
> no one in my family who had worked for the government,
> and we were even afraid of becoming officials. Both my
> grandpa and my father warned me that we should stay away
> from any official position...When I returned to my hometown
> in 1940 for a summer vacation [from university, where he was
> working on a degree in economics], I wrote a letter to Chiang
> Ching-kuo, stating my admiration and support for his plan for
> developing Gannan. I soon received his reply. In his letter he
> expressed his gratitude to me and invited me to his office to
> have a talk. I went there at the appointed time. He gave me a
> sincere and detailed explanation of his ideals, goals, and
> practical plan. He emphasized that the anti-Japanese War was
> a long and arduous one, closely tied to the fate of the Chinese
> nation. We had no choice but to succeed. Elsewise, the entire
> nation would perish. Thus we had to fight against Japan and,
> in the meantime, develop the country. The development
> would allow us to overcome the losses suffered during the
> war. Only in this way could we persevere until ultimate
> victory. Chiang Ching-kuo also expressed his hope that all the
> educated youth in Gannan would wholeheartedly throw
> themselves into the development of their hometown and their
> country and would, in turn, call upon the people to support
> the government. This was the first time I had met Chiang
> Ching-kuo and the first time I had heard his friendly, frank,
> just talk. He gave all of himself to the cause, even sacrificing
> his personal enjoyment. Regardless of hardships and
> difficulties, he came to help us build our hometown. Greatly
> moved by his sincerity and modesty, as well as his zeal to turn
> his plan into reality, I immediately promised to return to join
> him as soon as I graduated. I would do whatever he asked me
> to do. Just like that, I threw away that which I had believed –
> 'Never be an official' – and from that day on, I knew that my
> mission was to dedicate my life to my country.[76]

Many others reacted like Liu, answering Chiang Ching-kuo's clarion call. What separated the methodology from 'faction building' or simple favoritism was the overriding position given to the quest for *results*. The emphasis was on *service* – and woe to those who forgot this simple fact. Often repeated is the story of a visit Chiang Ching-kuo made to a reception center for refugees. As he inspected the food, he was approached by a young man who said that the good meal they were enjoying was the only one they had been served. Not only did Chiang Ching-kuo reprimand the center head on the spot, warning him not to get caught embezzling money, but he arranged for the young man, Wei An-jen, to receive a position as a clerk. Later, he appointed him as the county magistrate for Dingnan (refer to Map 2). When Wei An-jen's performance was found wanting, however, he was immediately removed from the position.[77]

That he considered these matters carefully is demonstrated by Chiang Ching-kuo's setting them down in his essay 'Revolution and Revolutionary Cadres'.[78] Therein, he emphasized the importance of using good, capable individuals appropriately, and of tapping new talent. Just how far he was willing to go was highlighted when Chiang Ching-kuo found to be true the stories of two prisoners in the Ganzhou jail that they had been unjustly imprisoned. Not only were they released, but Ching-kuo took them on as his personal bodyguards.[79]

Thus Chiang Ching-kuo proceeded. In this early stage of the Gannan Development Plan, the two overriding concerns were finding the proper personnel and insuring security for the populace. Wang Sheng turned out to be just the man in the difficult area Chiang Ching-kuo had given him. 'These were counties', Wang Sheng has noted, 'which were backwaters. They had the least transportation, extremely poor conditions, the highest number of bandits, and corrupt high-ranking officers. I was sent over to clear up this area'.[80]

What made the southern Jiangxi counties special, especially Xunwu, was their position along the border with Guandong. Consequently, they were frequently claimed by both Jiangxi and Guandong – and just as frequently effectively administered by neither. The result was a typical frontier atmosphere and ethos, which the communists had earlier been able to use to their advantage when they were maneuvering for control. Driven out, their mechanisms of social control had gone with them. Daily life became precarious, and many of the populace entered into those activities which seemed to threaten social order still further. 'This place', Wang Sheng adds in a memoir, 'was characterized by opium smoking, gambling, bandits and prostitutes; in other words, a place of crime and corruption'.[81]

In designing an approach to deal with the situation, Wang Sheng realized that he faced the opposite of what had prevailed during the Encirclement Campaigns. Then, the government forces had been attempting to force their way into insurgent-held areas which used a popular base to support a mobile defense. Now, with any possible enemy main force units gone, pacification was the business at hand, and disorder was the foe. What the populace needed, above all, was the security which would allow them to get on with their lives.[82] Thus the target was truly the 'bandits' of whatever stripe – roaming bands which had little insurgent infrastructure to support them. What covert apparatus remained could be rooted out through the inexorable expansion of the *baojia* system and formation of militia under the control of the returning gentry. The key, of course, was the quality of the gentry placed in these leadership positions.

That, Chiang Ching-kuo might have noted, was the point; hence Wang Sheng's presence. Making his headquarters in Xinfeng county, Wang Sheng used the three companies (120 men each) of the self-defense battalion to set up a series of strongpoints wherever there was 'bandit' presence. He himself served as their weapons instructor,[83] then deployed them. The most difficult areas, predictably, were in the voids of official control which had flourished along county boundaries. To pacify these, the companies constructed blockhouses, much like those used in the Encirclement Campaigns, in the heart of a target area and maintained a strong presence by patrolling the area and assisting the population. Simultaneously, 90 of the best men, 30 from each company, were placed in a special unit. Armed with German-made machine-pistols, they hunted out their adversaries. The original intent had been to arm a hundred, but there were not enough machine-pistols.[84] Regardless, they patrolled. Wang Sheng frequently accompanied them. 'They were the bravest and strongest', he observes. 'They wore civilian clothes and kept their food with them. They would gather information on where criminal activity was going on; then they would march at night and wipe them out before they knew what was going on. We would inform the local commander, and he would reinforce us if we needed help'.[85]

So successful was the approach, that the main 'bandit' areas were pacified within three months. To prove the point, Wang Sheng would take four soldiers and walk about the area: 'Once I did this, the residents were no longer afraid'. Chiang Ching-kuo himself came to assess the reasons for such results. He, too, would go where he chose. 'He was not afraid of hardships', Wang Sheng observes. Thus it was no surprise that Ching-kuo insisted upon going with units in the field. He and Wang Sheng worked well together. Wanting to extend his operations, Wang Sheng asked Chiang Chang-kuo for 40 additional machine-pistols – 'at that time, machine-pistols were the best weapons for close fighting'[86] – but heard nothing for several weeks. Pressing the issue, he was told, 'You can't just use bullets but also economics and culture'.[87] Few statements could have expressed his philosophy more succinctly. It was a particular mix of the Western 'get the job done' with the Chinese 'attend to the people's welfare, and all shall be well'. Virtually a cliché when viewed from afar, it was the manner in which Chiang Ching-kuo wanted his campaign run. When he personally led the attack on a powerful secret society leader's compound, where hundreds of rifles were captured, he had the captured 'bandit' tied to a stretcher and carried all the way to Ganzhou, so that the people would see his fate. The intelligence leading to his capture had come from a populace squeezed by his protection rackets, and the people lined the road and cheered.

Small victories such as this, while building reputations and attesting to the personal courage of the key players on the scene, were but the foundation upon which a more permanent structure could be constructed. In mid-1941 Chiang Ching-kuo had Wang Sheng move to his headquarters in Ganzhou and become Military Section (or Division) head. About the same time, Liu Jing-shing made good on his earlier promise to Chiang Ching-kuo and returned to work in the Gannan Finance Section. Wang Sheng took to calling him 'elder brother', despite the latter's being five years his junior, because by October of the same year, the university-educated Jing-shing had become Finance chief. As such, he and Wang Sheng worked hand in glove. For among Wang Sheng's main tasks was supervision of the *baojia* system.[88] Just as it was used for militia enrollment, so did it serve as the organizational basis for development activities – activities for which Liu was pressed to

find funding. This he did by revamping Gannan's taxation system.
A key aim of this revamping was to create an independent
resource base for county and city governments. This would
facilitate local autonomy, hence democratic growth. In the fluid
situation after the successful Fifth Encirclement Campaign, to be
sure, the pacification approach worked out by Hsiung Shih-hui
and his staff did not stress 'democracy' in any sense of the word.
It remained a KMT goal, as expressed in the *San Min Chu-i*, but
the immediate emphasis was upon the more pressing concerns of
'people's livelihood'. This was essential. Internal war had left the
economy in shambles. William Wei points out, further, that
between 1931 and 1935 the province lost more than 2,000,000
inhabitants. Yiyang county, in the northeast corner (see Map 2),
lost approximately 67 per cent of its entire population![89] The
subsequent war with Japan had only aggravated these conditions.
Beginning as early as 1934, the government fostered rural welfare
schemes such as a Rural Welfare Centers project and a program for
community schools (*baoxue*). The former effort envisaged ten
centers that would bring together expertise from appropriate
government agencies in order to disseminate technical information
and train villagers in skills for life improvement. The latter effort
moved aggressively to establish a community school for each *bao*
organization of the *baojia* system (i.e. a school for each hundred
families).

These and other programs were carried out for the ultimate
goal, it bears repeating, of building a just society. Physical well
being, as crucial as it was to the people, would result from correct
values and conduct. Analyzes Liu Jing-shing:

> To reach the [five] goals [of the Gannan Development Plan],
> there was a need to set up schools and libraries, construct
> factories, build roads and airports, and so forth. More
> importantly, the *San Min Chu-i* (Nationalism, Democracy, and
> People's Livelihood) should take root in people's minds
> through education, propaganda, and so forth. This
> encouraged people to work hard for themselves and for their
> country as well. Therefore, in the course of carrying out the
> plan, there was an emphasis on these tasks: cultivating a new
> outlook of life and training modern citizens (everyone should
> get rid of their feudal ideas, accept the Three Principles [*San
> Min Chu-i*], be hardworking, and be healthy emotionally and

physically). When this happens the people of Gannan will be
able to glow with happiness and good health. They should
work, read, and love each other and love their country. There
should be no illiteracy, no repression or deceit, no
exploitation or blackmail, no disturbances or fights.[90]

What characterized the effort was its intensity and the
imagination applied to solving problems. At all levels, members of
the *San Min Chu-i* Youth Corps were brought in to staff
government and given the authority to go with whatever would
work. Resources were to be locally generated, with the higher
echelons providing support. Cooperatives, for instance, were set up
for agricultural and construction materials, with officials providing
the expertise and the regional government the start-up capital. A
rural credit bank was likewise instituted to finance the purchase of
fertilizer by peasants. Everything was done on a level
commensurate with the setting. Payment for materials and services,
to cite one of the more colorful illustrations, could be made in eggs.

In strategy sessions, Chiang Ching-kuo hammered home his
point: service to the people. Those who could not measure up, or
keep the pace, were sent packing. It was an extraordinary time for
the young people who were thus mobilized. To further
demonstrate what he had in mind, Chiang Ching-kuo planned to
develop a model county within the larger Gannan Development
Plan area. That which he had in mind was Ganxian; for in addition
to being the overall Commissioner for the region, Chiang Ching-
kuo had been appointed as magistrate of Ganxian, wherein lay
Ganzhou. Even his formidable energies, though, did not allow
him to take on yet another project. So he turned to Wang Sheng,
who was given a district to make 'the model'. Still only aged 25,
Wang Sheng found himself running 'seven little units of 500
families each in this effort to build a model area'. Four *chen* (urban
wards) were in Ganzhou itself; three *hsiang* (rural wards) were in
the outskirts. For seven months, spending a day each week in one
of his units, Wang Sheng strove to improve the lives of 'his' people.
Never in uniform, he wore simple clothes, with a straw cape in
case of rain, and walked everywhere. 'We had five goals', he has
reiterated:

> Everyone is to have food, clothes, a house, a job, and a school
> to attend. The communists were going through the struggle

period of the 'land to the tiller', so they were tearing down while we were building up. We knew what they were doing, because we got information through intelligence agents. Our approach was to build up the area, wipe out illiteracy, give a school to every hundred families [*bao*]. In the countryside, we fixed the roads, fixed the bridges. Every *bao* was to have a reservoir for irrigation and fishing. We showed them how to select the right kind of seed, how to avoid sickness from certain plants. We taught agricultural specialties, how to increase the harvest, and how to earn side income.[91]

In all this, Wang Sheng's aim was to work himself out of the job. Though he was assisted by *San Min Chu-i* Youth Corps cadre, eventually their roles, together with that of Wang Sheng, were assumed by individuals in each ward. This was necessary, in any case, for Wang Sheng; because in addition to his Military Section and his district, he was the Special Assistant for Security to the Mayor of Ganzhou. As the war with Japan see-sawed, military matters took up growing amounts of time. Most vexing were the demands for the filling of recruiting quotas for the army. The soldiers' lot at that time was not a happy one. So bad was their treatment that many recruits, press-ganged into service and fed miserable rations while chained, perished before they even reached the induction centers.[92] Small wonder that potential draftees would go to extraordinary lengths to avoid reporting for duty. What Wang Sheng knew, though, was that there was an alternative. The standard approach to recruiting contrasted only too sharply with that utilized by the numerous patriotic organizations active in the war effort, such as the Youth Corps, which went to considerable lengths not only to bring in volunteers but also to provide them with training in both military and life skills. Hence he sought to institute similar procedures, whereby joining the military became truly a patriotic exercise of citizenship as apposed to merely another onerous requirement from above. In this he was aided immeasurably by the fact that, at least in their initial service, recruits were placed in units located within their home provinces. Ergo, the 'chain of custody' for a recruit could be influenced through the intercession of upright officials.

This Wang Sheng did. The acid test came when a demand for another 3,000 men came down.[93] The key to such mobilization, obviously, was in impressing all that it was indeed universal service, hence fair. To establish this impression, Wang Sheng first insured that the sons of the seven 'very rich, very influential' clans in his area, all of whom had hitherto avoided service, were inducted. He was unyielding in his dictate that all must come forward for the good of the country. Bribes were offered, threats made, all to no avail. In one instance, the son of a rich family related to the deputy director of the Ganzhou orphanage, run under the patronage of Chiang Ching-kuo's wife, attempted to have him exempted from service. 'Chiang Ching-kuo called me in', he recounts, 'and asked for an explanation. I said, if he is exempt under the regulations, I'll serve in his place. If you want him released, give him a written excuse. He didn't'.[94] Certainly there was resistance, but once it became established that the draft was not a cross only the poor had to bear, resistance declined substantially. This trend was accentuated by insuring that those induction centers under Wang Sheng's authority were models of good treatment. Indeed, special red ribbons were presented to those who joined, to be worn on the chest, and parades held to laud their patriotism. 'Soon everyone thought it was a glorious thing'.[95]

Brave New World

Wang Sheng had indeed done a fine job. As the development effort became more routinized, administrative personnel could take over what he had created. Finally, it was felt he could move on. In preparation for the First National Congress of the *San Min Chu-i* Youth Corps, which was held in March 1943, Wang Sheng was sent to Chongqing (Chungking), where he took part in the third three-month Cadre Training Class of the Central Training Regiment. He graduated as the second man in this school. Then Wang Sheng was involved in the Congress itself; it had for him several significant outcomes. First, Chiang Ching-kuo was elected Secretary for the national body, a key position from which to influence its operations, since the nominal Corps Leader was Chiang Kai-shek himself; the Secretary-General, Chang Chih-chung, the head of the Political Department of the Military Commission. Both had so many concurrent duties that they could not directly supervise the Youth Corps.[96] Second, a Central Cadre Academy (also called the Central Government Cadre School) was approved.[97] It was to have two branches, a Research Division for university graduates and a

Special Training Division for high school graduates. Chiang Ching-kuo himself was to be the school's academic Director; again, the effective head since his father was the nominal head. By now the logical consequence should be plain: he wanted Wang Sheng, among others, to attend.

What should also be plain, as well, is that this was a continuing effort by Chiang Kai-shek to develop a new generation of revolutionary leaders. The Youth Corps had already lost its battles with the Kuomintang over which organization was officially to be recognized as caretaker of *the* revolution. That, tired and disappointing though it might be, was to be the KMT, with the Youth Corps subordinate. Nevertheless, acting through his son, Chiang Kai-shek obviously had not given up his hopes of producing the righteous leadership necessary to the internal and external liberation of China. As the Youth Corps continued to grow – by 1942 it officially numbered 423,144 – its members were encouraged to enter leadership positions in diverse fields at various levels. A national organization, similar in most respects to that of the Kuomintang, and competing fiercely with it for members, existed in all provinces and reported to a national headquarters. An ongoing effort sought to train *all* Youth Corps members so that they might form the cadre and officials of the future. The Central Cadre Academy was nothing less than an attempt to create a capstone organization, a university with upper and lower divisions, to educate those selected as likely to move into the top echelons of this new political leadership. It would go beyond the mere organizational 'training' in the three-month sense, as embodied in the Cadre Training Class format, and move into the realm of higher order theoretical and practical political studies, granting master's and bachelor's degrees.[98]

The prospects were exciting. While the project was getting off the ground, Wang Sheng was posted in mid-1943 back to Jiangxi in the Organization and Training Division of the provincial branch of the *San Min Chu-i* Youth Corps. He spent several months overseeing training programs for Youth Corps members, then was moved 'upstairs' to become Secretary to the Director of the division, the third-ranking individual in the provincial hierarchy of the Youth Corps. He was not happy with the position, and his continued selection for plum assignments caused some resentment among his peers. Hence, he asked to be relieved of the position and was sent instead to a civil servant's school for six months to

prepare for the tough competitive examination which would
determine those selected for the first class of the Research Division
of the soon-to-open Central Cadre Academy. In the event, some
7,000 applicants vied for the appointments; Wang Sheng was one
of the 300[99] who made the cut, though barely so; another 400
students were selected for the Special Training Division. Classes
began in January 1944. A student in the Research Division was
supposed to work for two years and graduate with an MA. In
addition to Wang Sheng, its membership included others who were
to assume prominent positions in Taiwan, most notably Li Huan,
who eventually became premier. As events transpired, the class was
forced to graduate early, after just a year and without their degrees.
It was undone by a combination of circumstances which drained
off so much manpower that the school ceased to be viable.

Specifically, as 1944 progressed, China's situation became
increasingly more desperate. Every possible soldier was needed,
for in April 1944 the Japanese launched an ambitious offensive,
Operation *Ichigo*, which continued in its main operations for eight
months, then sputtered on in smaller thrusts. Aimed at forging a
land route by which natural resources, especially oil, could be
transferred safely from Southeast Asia virtually to Japan's
doorstep, *Ichigo* dealt China a blow from which it never recovered.
As the Japanese seized vast areas hitherto untouched, they
specifically targeted central government, as opposed to provincial,
units and thus fractured the KMT military structure to such an
extent that 'by the end of 1944, the government no longer
possessed an effective fighting machine for the defense of China
proper, and the Japanese were probably correct in predicting that
none could be revived in the next two years'.[100] So intense was the
fighting – it has been seriously underestimated by historians,
particularly those who claim the KMT expended little if any effort
against the Japanese during the war – that student exemption from
conscription was finally cancelled and a general call for volunteers
issued. Many who answered outright were at the Central Cadre
Academy.

Virtually simultaneously, in October 1944, even as it appealed
to the youth of the nation to come to its defense, the government
instituted a Youth Army (also translated as Youth Volunteer Militia
or Youth Expeditionary Force), to be made up of educated troops
who could absorb the training necessary to turn them into
mechanized divisions. These were to be formed and trained by the

Americans – initially in India for use in, immediately, Burma and, possibly later, Southeast Asia – as part of their effort to create 39 retrained and re-equipped divisions constituted along American lines. Consequently, further Central Cadre Academy students, as well as Youth Corps members in general, simply quit to join the Youth Army.[101]

The patriotic reservoir tapped by the appeal was indeed astonishing. The immediate consequence was that by early 1945 some 120,000 educated youths were in uniform, and the government had established a Youth Army Training Headquarters to manage the endeavor. Chiang Ching-kuo, now a lieutenant general at age 35, was made director of its Political Department. The longer term consequences were not so heartening. In addition to the youths in training, there were innumerable others from the Youth Corps or other sectors who went directly into the line, spurred on in their country's time of peril by Chiang Kai-shek's appeal, 'An inch of blood for every inch of land, ten thousand youths for ten thousand soldiers'.[102] All had some education, so losses were felt doubly by China as its future hemorrhaged out through the gaping wounds which were the battlefields of a World War II sputtering to a conclusion on the Asian mainland even as fierce battles raged in the Pacific.

One of the casualties, it must be added, was Gannan, which in late 1944 and early 1945, fell to the Japanese. They could occupy only major centers, but their assault destroyed the work which had been so painstakingly completed. Even Wang Sheng's home county of Longnan fell. Working there at the time was none other than Wang Sheng's former counterpart in the Gannan administration, Liu Jing-shing. In true fashion, he was performing in much the same fashion as Wang Sheng had done in Ganzhou; he had, in fact, come to Longnan in 1943 at about the same time as Wang Sheng departed for Chongqing (Chungking). Liu had been appointed General Secretary of the Longnan branch of the *San Min Chu-i* Youth Corps (which actually had four counties under its jurisdiction). His arrival was timely, for communist remnants were again active in the rough border area with Guangzhou, and disturbances had occurred. Liu coordinated with Chiang Ching-kuo, who flew to the area and dealt with the situation directly. Removing derelict officials and replacing them with Youth Corps members, as well as directing stability operations, he restored the situation quickly. When he left, Liu, though not nominally in charge, performed in the manner Chiang Ching-kuo had inspired and expected throughout Gannan. He visited every village in Longnan to ascertain their needs, then created Youth Corps organizations in each to work towards the accomplishment of the agreed-upon goals. He had made considerable headway and had an entire infrastructure in place when the process was interrupted by the arrival of the Japanese. Liu and his Youth Corps cadre retreated to the hills, where they waged guerrilla war until the Japanese surrender in August 1945.

Surrender was still eight months off, however, when the Central Cadre Academy, depleted of its manpower, released its students. Wang Sheng was assigned as the Political Officer of the Youth Army's Southeast Branch Training Base. As such he was in charge of fostering loyalty and looking to the morale and welfare of the troops. He was given the rank of lieutenant-colonel, and his ultimate boss, again, was Chiang Ching-kuo. Though the latter had only just been formally named Youth Army Political Department head, he had participated in planning the organization from the start. He assigned the political officers to the several Youth Army training bases including that to which Wang Sheng now found himself posted. There, he had a staff of 120 people responsible for working with two divisions, the 208th and 209th. One of the regimental commanders in the 208th, Wang Yung-shu, would later rise to the highest levels in Taiwan. For the moment his signal achievement was to detain a communist spy in his unit named Jiang Tse-min. The normal procedure would have been to execute him, but Wang Yung-shu liked Jiang Tse-min, so he gave him a lecture and turned him loose. Jiang is now President of the People's Republic of China![103]

Normally duty was more routine; Wang Sheng remained in the position through the end of the war and on into November 1945. Meantime, however, he had married. The event illustrated well the extent to which pockets of China were entering a brave new world.

Her name was Hu Hsiang-li, and she was a product of the new forces unleashed by war and revolution. A bundle of energy, articulate and sure of herself, she had graduated initially from the Jiangxi Physical Education Specialty School, then gone on to the Central Military Academy itself after Wang Sheng had left. Posted to Ganzhou, her hometown, she met the intense man from Longnan while he was working there as Secretary to the Director of the Organization and Training Division. When Wang Sheng set up training camps for *San Min Chu-i* Youth Corps members, she was invariably a supervisor for the women. Though pursued by any number of suitors, she was struck by Wang Sheng's demeanor. He was as quiet as she was outspoken. What they shared was an intense devotion to duty and an ability to triumph over the vicissitudes of life. 'Neither showed a relaxed side', recalls Liao Kuang-hsuan, who worked with the two in Gannan. 'She had three positions, administrative jobs in three schools simultaneously. She wore a military uniform all the time, never used makeup; very frugal – very serious'.[104]

Hu Hsiang-li.

That Hu Hsiang-li was the perfect match seemed obvious – at least to her. Yet Wang Sheng hesitated. 'Love is a very strange thing', he recounts. 'She didn't care about my status, but I did care. I already had a wife. I went home and settled the matter'.[105] It was the ultimate collision of worlds, the new and the old. As a boy of seven or eight, Wang Sheng, as was the custom in Chinese rural society, had been married to another youngster, Liao Kung-wei. The original agreement had been struck between the families while the girl's mother was pregnant with her. Following the actual ceremony, Liao Kung-wei had returned to her family, coming to reside with her husband only when both were grown and shortly before Wang Sheng entered the militia in 1936. They were to have a boy, who died in infancy, and a daughter, Wang Hua. It soon became clear, though, that they were of different worlds. She had no education, was unlikely to obtain any, and was a child of the soil. He was steeped in the classics and on the verge of a great journey. Had Wang Sheng remained in the closed world of the village, the differences might have been papered over; but his entry into the Youth Corps, with its revolutionary mores and commitment to creation of a new world, brought the contradiction to a head. 'There was nothing wrong with her', Wang Sheng observes. 'She was a good lady. She was very young [I reasoned], so if she returned to a farm, she could live in one place, and her lack of education would not be a handicap. We just settled it between families when I went away'.[106] To insure that it was formally settled, however, he returned to Longnan; then he and Hu Hsiang-li were married. In the years ahead, she was to give him three sons and two daughters.[107]

In his romance with Hu Hsiang-li, Wang Sheng revealed a side of him long repressed. His background had hardened him, especially the fate of his mother. His father, too, died but some years after his mother, during Wang Sheng's early years in the Youth Corps (1939–43). The impact was strong: 'When my parents passed away, they were so poor we had a hard time buying a coffin. They both passed away within five or six years of each other. I swore to myself that although I couldn't give them a good funeral, one day I would help those who were in the same position I was in then'.[108] To fulfil this vow, of course, required that he become a *somebody*. Hence, on a personal level, he was determined to rise and threw himself into his work to an extent which left those around him in awe at his dynamism and endurance. On a higher plane, he saw the need to remake China and saw the role he could play. In Hu Hsiang-li he had found a fellow seeker. Significantly, she was an equal, a woman who was a consequence of egalitarian trends which had been building in Chinese society for decades and were a powerful source of attraction to the Kuomintang and its organs for young women seeking to throw off the shackles of millennia.[109] Just as significantly, though, Hu Hsiang-li was not only someone with whom Wang Sheng could share his journey but someone he could love. Their intimacy brought back the soft edges which had been subsumed by the drive to excel and rescue a nation. Her intuition had been correct: She was the perfect match for Wang Sheng. He was to be as devoted to her as he had become to Chiang Ching-kuo.

Ironically, a decade later, Allen Whiting, writing for the *Saturday Evening Post*, was to say of Chiang Ching-kuo, 'He never trusts anyone, nor does anyone trust him'.[110] A remark more wide of the target would be hard to find. In Gannan, as throughout his life, Chiang Ching-kuo seems to have placed complete trust in individuals until their missteps forced him to do otherwise. In dealing with the reminiscences of those present at the time, we find neither fear nor unease but instead youthful exuberance for building their brave new world. Even the phraseology still used by participants, fifty years after the events in question, is revolutionary. They clearly saw themselves as engaging in a momentous undertaking.

'We must establish a brotherly unity' was a Chiang Ching-kuo slogan popularized at the Cadre Training Course. And in a sense they were. When Chiang Ching-kuo's mother was killed in Japanese bombing in 1939, recalls Kung Chiu-Chuan, a staff member in Ganzhou, a pall had descended upon the group. When Wang Sheng was sent to Chongqing (Chungking) for training at the end of 1942:

> Another trainee, one of Wang Sheng's good friends, a young and honest man, was sent with him for training. His friend was killed on the way. So Wang Sheng buried his body, prayed, and promised in his heart, 'After graduation, I will take your body back to the place where we became so close'. The next year, when the sun was very intense, Wang Sheng went there, as he had promised, and dug up the grave. The body had already deteriorated. It was awful; enough to make you sick. But he cleaned the bones – I can't recall whether it was with water or petrol – put them in a jar, and carried them on his back. He came all the way back – he was gone for ten days in the middle of wartime – even as the Japanese bombed and attacked. He brought the bones back to our camp. We got together and made a small graveyard with a stone marker. Chiang Ching-kuo was very moved. He later wrote an essay about what it is to be a good man. So you can see how we were. We were so close. We did not use ranks or formality. We knew each other for what we were.[111]

Yet they were not a 'band of brothers'. Though friendships formed, particularly amongst those engaged in the same offices or common tasks, there was never any doubt but that Chiang Ching-kuo was their leader. He appears to have been on intimate terms with only one person, to be discussed shortly. Indeed, for an individual such as Wang Sheng, irrespective of his continuing association with Chiang Ching-kuo and their slight difference in age (only five and a half years), there remained a moat of *standing* which was never crossed, then or later. It had nothing to do with birth or class but everything to do with position in Chinese culture. For in Chiang Ching-kuo, Wang Sheng had found a teacher whom he would revere as such the rest of his days, the master of the Chinese classics. They were never to assume a first-name basis; and if there was any weakness in Wang Sheng's performance, then and later, it was that he seemed incapable of reaching beyond his devotion to his leader and his duty to touch the human side of Chiang Ching-kuo, a leap he made only with Hu Hsiang-li.

This human side was there and had appeared early in Chiang Ching-kuo's tenure as Gannan commissioner. Precisely how he met Chang Ya-juo seems unclear, but the young lady apparently was working as a clerk at the Ganxian Mobilization Commission.[112] To escape the unwanted attentions of a superior, she applied for the Cadre Training Course. Rebuffed, she succeeded after an articulate personal appeal to Chiang Ching-kuo.[113] At the course, she blossomed. In response to the exhortations for 'brotherly unity', she teasingly insisted that her classmates refer to her as 'big brother'. Though several sources believe a sexual relationship developed at this time between the young cadre-in-training and her commissioner superior, this is doubtful. Still more doubtful is the claim that Wang Sheng acted as the go-between.[114] What does seem to have happened is that she and Chiang Ching-kuo were attracted to each other, because when the course ended, she was posted to the secretariat of the commissioner's office. There a love affair did occur. Chang Ya-juo played a low-key but important role in the day-to-day workings of the secretariat and, as such, often travelled with Chiang Ching-kuo as part of his staff. She was to give birth to twins but died shortly thereafter.[115]

The episode is important not for its titillating details but rather for what it tells us about Chiang Ching-kuo. In 1940 he would have been just 30, full of life, hopes and dreams. From all accounts,

Chang Ya-juo, 27 years in the spring but already the widowed mother of two sons,[116] was the same – and lovely besides. It was a match made in heaven. That Ching-kuo already had a wife is awkward but actually goes a good way towards explaining the Jiangxi match: Chang Ya-juo was the first *Chinese* woman Chiang Ching-kuo had ever known (and would remain such). He had left home at 15; had existed in the Soviet Union under exceptionally difficult circumstances; and, at the depths of his loneliness and despair, had met a Russian woman, Faina, equally marooned in the world, with whom he could share his miserable existence. The fates, however, smiled, and eventually they not only saw Ching-kuo back to China but to Jiangxi where he could throw himself with a passion into his lifelong dream, the building of a new China. Amidst this passion appeared one equally possessed, Chang Ya-juo. Plainly, they were in love. That there had to be a tomorrow seems not to have entered into their calculations. Ya-juo knew of Ching-kuo's wife but made the decision to ignore the fact. How Ching-kuo himself would have ultimately handled the situation can only remain speculation. Undoubtedly, it would have posed problems, because he was never ungrateful to Faina and recognized the terrible straits he would leave her in should he set her adrift. With Ya-juo's death, the point became moot. A piece of Chiang Ching-kuo died, too, and in his emotional life, he retreated into himself. He is never known to have had another love.

In retrospect, it is remarkable – and in a sense predictable – that for both Chiang Ching-kuo and Wang Sheng their efforts to make a revolution within the counterrevolution should lead to matches with women who were products of the liberation. What is significant, in addition to the degree to which the ladies concerned appear to have been partners in every sense of the word, is that similar episodes were being played out in the communist camp as well. One does not have to wax lyrical or overplay the card to see that profound changes were at hand. The barest biographical facts on both sides make this clear, particularly the co-equal attendance at élite institutions such as the Central Military Academy. This break with the shackles of traditional society was illustrative of the goals laid out by Chiang Ching-kuo and then implemented, with his active participation, by Wang Sheng, Hu Hsiang-li, Chang Ya-juo, and the numerous others we have encountered in this chapter. So, too, was their emphasis upon retaining that which was good in Chinese society, particularly the notion that only through reform of values and behavior could just structures be created. Former cadre Kung Chiu-chuan summarizes this well:

Crucial to any understanding of Chiang Ching-kuo, Wang Sheng, and the Kuomintang is the Jiangxi wartime period. We all were young, full of warm ideas, models of self-sacrifice. We took an oath to sacrifice everything for the country. It was really a great period. We were so filled with idealism, with no sense yet of fear, frustration, or disappointment. We had only a feeling of strength. If the country was suffering, we knew it was our duty to help. We had one ambition and that was to serve – everyone was filled with *purpose*.[117]

NOTES

1. For use of the term and discussion of its content see, among several possibilities, Thomas B. Gold, *State and Society in the Taiwan Miracle* (Armonk, NY: M.E. Sharpe, 1986); e.g. p. vii: 'I have not put quotation marks around the word "miracle" in the title of this book for the simple reason that I think the people of that island non-nation have made miraculous progress at rapid growth, structural change, improved livelihood, and political democratization. I do not mean miraculous in the sense of a unique, non-recurring God-given event, but rather as a wondrous recovery by dint of every human effort from a morass of destruction and despair. See also Shaw Yu-ming, *Beyond the Economic Miracle: Reflections: Reflections on the Republic of China on Taiwan, Mainland China, and Sino-American Relations*, 2nd ed. (Taipei: personal imprint; Kwang Hwa Publishing Co., 1990); e.g. p. 11: 'The economic performance of the Republic of China over the past 40 years has been internationally regarded as something of a miracle'.
2. On Sun Yat-sen see C. Martin Wilbur, *Sun Yat-sen: Frustrated Patriot* (New York: Columbia UP, 1976). There is no good biography of Chiang Kai-shek. Among the works available are: Pichon P.Y. Loh, *The Early Chiang Kai-shek: A Study of his Personality and Politics, 1887–1924* (New York: Columbia UP, 1971); Robert Payne, *Chiang Kai-shek* (New York: Weybright and Talley, 1969); Hollington K. Tong, *Chiang Kai-shek* (Taipei: China Publishing Company, 1953); and, certainly the most widely cited, if for its title alone, Brian Crozier, *The Man Who Lost China: The First Full Biography of Chiang Kai-shek* (New York: Scribner's, 1976). Actual scholarship on Chiang Ching-kuo has yet to be undertaken, though some popular treatments have begun to appear in Chinese. See e.g. Yang Tsun, *Chiang Ching-kuo Wai Chuan: Tsung Chiko dau Gannan* [*Chiang Ching-kuo's Untold Story: From Chiko to Gannan*] (Taipei: New Tide Cultural Enterprises, 1993).
3. Though he writes with considerable skill and nuance, this would seem to be essentially the approach taken by John King Fairbank, *The United States and China*, 4th ed. (Cambridge, MA: Harvard UP, 1983). As I read him, he holds, as do many scholars, that there were certain welling forces ('contradictions' would be the Marxist term which has entered more general usage) which had to be addressed by any post-dynastic political movement. Since the CCP did so, Fairbank appears to say, it emerged victorious. This sidesteps an important issue; namely, that the KMT may also have tried to deal with these forces but done so in an inadequate fashion, either due

to its own shortcomings or under the influence of external forces (or a combination of both). Increasingly, scholarship would seem to support such a case. The shift, though seemingly subtle, is important: It lifts modern Chinese history out of tautology – there was a revolution, so there must have been contradictions – and returns it to analysis where the role of deliberate action (also: voluntarist, purposive action) and contingency interact with structure to produce the result. In a phrase: History does make men; but just as surely, men make history. Still, one should not suppose the issue is going to be resolved anytime soon. In a wonderfully trenchant analysis, with which Fairbank would undoubtedly agree, Col. David D. Barrett, who played an important role in the US China presence during World War II, observed in 1968 to Lyman Van Slyke (Stanford University): 'In all sincerity, at the risk of oversimplification, it is doubtful if anything could have prevented us from "losing" China as we did as long as we remain essentially an anti-Communist country, for China was doomed to go Communist as [surely as] the sparks fly upward, as long as it was governed by the Kuomintang. The blind stupidity and arrogant stubbornness of Chiang Kai-shek did much to accelerate the loss of China to the Reds, and our well-meant but fumbling and poorly directed efforts to help were of little avail, and with the economy of the country in complete chaos, collapse of the government, which of course meant a take-over by the well organized opposition, was inevitable'. See John N. Hart, *The Making of an Army 'Old China Hand': A Memoir of Colonel David D. Barrett*, Chinese Research Monograph No. 27 (Berkeley, CA: Center for Chinese Studies, 1985), p. 73.

4. This is a conclusion also reached by Roy Hofheinz, Jr. in his 'The Ecology of Chinese Communist Success: Rural Influence Patterns, 1923–45', in A. Doak Barnett, ed., *Chinese Communist Politics in Action* (Seattle, WA: U. of Washington Press, 1969), pp. 3–77. He finds the most significant factor in explaining whether an area became involved in the insurgency to be the presence of CCP cadres themselves. William Wei agrees with this in his 'Insurgency by the Numbers I: A Reconsideration of the Ecology of Communist Success in Jiangxi Province, China', *Small Wars and Insurgencies* [London, hereafter *SWI*], 5/2 (Autumn 1994), pp. 201–17, but emphasizes, too, the importance of structural factors. He points out that the role of these factors becomes evident when statistical measures are used to analyze available data, as he has done, rather than relying solely upon map comparison, as in Hofheinz. I have pursued the viability of ecological explanation in my 'Insurgency by the Numbers II: The Search for a Quantitative Relationship Between Agrarian Revolution and Land Tenure in South and Southeast Asia', *SWI* [London], 5/2 (Autumn 1994), pp. 218–91.

5. Portions of this discussion have been used in several of my previous works: 'Making Revolution: *Sendero Luminoso* in Peru', *SWI* [London], 3/1 (Spring 1992), pp. 22–46; *Making Revolution: The Insurgency of the Communist Party of Thailand in Structural Perspective* (Bangkok: White Lotus Press, 1995); and *Maoist Insurgency since Vietnam* (London: Frank Cass, 1996).

6. See e.g. Mark Selden, 'People's War and the Transformation of Peasant Society: China and Vietnam', in Mark Selden and Edward Freedman (eds.), in *America's Asia*, offprint (nfd). In one telling passage, he observes: 'The thesis of this essay is as follows: Out of the ashes of military strife which enveloped China and Vietnam in protracted wars of liberation emerged a radically new vision of man and society and a concrete approach to development. Built on foundations of participation and community action which challenge élite domination, this approach offers hope of more *humane* forms of development and of effectively overcoming the formidable barriers to the transformation of peasant societies' [emphasis in original].

7. Numerous works are available on this early period. Among the most useful, in discussing soviet formation, are Linda Grove, 'Creating a Northern Soviet', *Modern China*, 1/3 (July 1975), pp. 243–70; and Shinkichi Eto, 'Hai-lu-feng – The First Chinese Soviet Government', Parts I & II, *China Qtly*, 8 (Oct.–Dec. 1961), I: pp.

161–83; 9 (Jan.–March 1962), II: pp. 149–81. For the Jiangxi period in general, cf. Philip C.C. Huang, Lynda Schaefer Bell, and Kathy Lemons Walker, *Chinese Communists and Rural Society, 1927–1934*, Chinese Research Monograph No. 13 (Berkeley: Center for Chinese Studies, 1978). Particularly good for Jiangxi specifics are two works by Stephen C. Averill: 'Party, Society, and Local Elite in the Jiangxi Communist Movement', *Jnl of Asian Studies*, 46/2 (May 1987), pp. 279–303, and 'Local Elites and Communist Revolution in the Jiangxi Hill Country', Ch. 11 in Joseph W. Esherick and Mary Backus Rankin (eds.), *Chinese Local Elites and Patterns of Dominance* (Berkeley, CA: U. of California Press, 1990), pp. 282–304; likewise, James M. Polachek, 'The Moral Economy of the Kiangsi Soviet (1928–1934)', *Jnl of Asian Studies*, XLII/4 (Aug. 1983), pp. 805–29. One may also profitably consult Mao Tse-tung's own *Report From Xunwu*, released in a new edition, Roger Thompson (ed. and trans.), (Stanford UP, 1990); his introduction is useful.

In dealing with the KMT counterinsurgency, no research approaches that of William Wei, *Counterrevolution in China: The Nationalists in Jiangxi During the Soviet Period* (Ann Arbor, MI: U. of Michigan Press, 1985). Though he incorporates his previous work into his text, his articles are worth reviewing on their merits, particularly for the insight they give into the state's response to Maoist insurgency: 'The Role of the German Advisors in the Suppression of the Central Soviet: Myth and Reality', in Bernd Martin (ed.), *The German Advisory Group in China: Military, Economic, and Political Issues in Sino-German Relations, 1927–1938* [or *Die deutsche Beraterschaft in China 1927–1938* (Düsseldorf: Droste, 1981); 'The Guomindang's Three Parts Military and Seven Parts Politics Policy', *Asian Profile* [Hong Kong], 10/2 (April 1982) pp. 111–27; 'Warlordism and Factionalism in the Guomindang's Encirclement Campaigns in Jiangxi', in *Illinois Papers in Asian Studies 1983, Pt. II: Kuomintang Development Efforts during the Nanking Decade* (Urbana, IL: Center for Asian Studies, U. of Illinois, 1983), pp. 87–120; 'Law and Order: The Role of Guomindang Security Forces in the Suppression of the Communist Bases During the Soviet Period', Ch. 2 in Hartford and Goldstein, *op.cit.*, 34–61 (notes on 182–8); 'Five Encirclement and Suppression Campaigns (1930–1934)', in Edwin Pak-wah Leung (ed.), *Historical Dictionary of Revolutionary China, 1839–1976* (New York: Greenwood Press, 1992), pp. 121–3; and 'Insurgency by the Numbers I (note 4).

8.   The debate was started by the publication of Chalmers Johnson, *Peasant Nationalism and Communist Power in China* (Berkeley, CA: U. of California Press, 1962). For a critique of his approach see Donald G. Gillin, 'Review Article: 'Peasant Nationalism' in the History of Chinese Communism', *Jnl of Asian Studies*, XXIII/2 (Feb. 1964), pp. 269–87. Johnson himself considers the controversy and discusses his point further in 'Peasant Nationalism Revisited: The Biography of a Book', *China Qtly*, 72 (Dec. 1977), pp. 766–85. For explication of the Yenan approach, cf. another Johnson critic, Mark Selden, *The Yenan Way in Revolutionary China* (Cambridge, MA: Harvard UP, 1971). Also useful is his earlier 'The Guerrilla Movement in Northwest China: The Origins of the Shensi-Kansu-Ninghsia Border Region', Parts I & II, *China Qtly*, 28 (Oct.–Dec. 1966), I: pp. 63-81; 29 (Jan.–March 1967), II: pp. 61–81. Carl E. Dorris suggests modification of the 'Yenan thesis' in his interesting 'Peasant Mobilization in North China and the Origins of Yenan Communism', *China Qtly*, 68 (Dec. 1976), pp. 697–719. For a benchmark work on the CCP during World War II, see the important *The Chinese Communist Movement: A Report of the United States War Department, July, 1945*, Lyman P. Van Slyke, ed. (Stanford UP, 1968).

9.   An excellent work on the damage inflicted upon the KMT by the Japanese invasion is Ch'i Hsi-sheng, *Nationalist China at War* (Ann Arbor: U. of Michigan Press, 1982). For the civil war period, cf. Suzanne Pepper, *Civil War in China* (Berkeley, CA: U. of California Press, 1978). Fine consideration of the KMT regime, its strengths and weaknesses, are two works by Lloyd E. Eastman: *The Abortive Revolution: China Under Nationalist Rule, 1927–1937* (Cambridge, MA: Harvard UP, 1974); and *Seeds of*

Destruction: Nationalist China in War and Revolution, 1937–1949 (Stanford UP, 1984).
10. See esp. Averill, 'Party, Society, and Local Elite in the Jiangxi Communist Movement', as well as his 'Local Elites and Communist Revolution in the Jiangxi Hill Country' (both note 7).
11. Cf. Phil Billingsley, 'Bandits, Bosses, and Bare Sticks: Beneath the Surface of Local Control in Early Republican China', *Modern China*, 7/3 (July 1981), pp. 235–88.
12. For a theoretical discussion on resource mobilization and the role it plays in internal conflict, cf. Charles Tilly, *From Mobilization to Revolution* (Reading, MA: Addison-Wesley, 1978); for structural consideration cf. Theda Skocpol, *States and Social Revolutions* (NY: CUP, 1979). Consideration of revolution in general may be found in several other benchmark works. See e.g. Jack A. Goldstone, 'Theories of Revolution: The Third Generation', *World Politics*, XXXII/3 (April 1980), pp. 425–53. The basic themes discussed in his article appear in expanded form, with readings, in Goldstone (ed.), *Revolutions: Theoretical, Comparative, and Historical Studies* (Chicago: Harcourt Brace Jovanovich, 1985). See also Walter L. Goldfrank, 'Theories of Revolution and Revolution Without Theory: The Case of Mexico', *Theory & Society*, 7 (1979), pp. 135–65.
13. Wei, *Counterrevolution in China* (note 7), pp. 3–4 describes this process thus: 'The actions of the Guomindang [*sic*] indicate that, while it recognized the need for a mass movement, it was averse to Communist [*sic*] approaches that sought to generate popular support by restructuring society and making it more equitable. Rejecting radical agrarian measures that might have pre-empted the CCP's popular base, the Guomindang chose instead to extend and intensify its local administrative authority and to rely on its military-civil bureaucracy and upon the manipulation of traditional types of authority, specifically the élite sector of society, to gain compliance of the people. The Nanjing government was convinced that 'the strength of the rural communities rested upon the old gentry and that at all costs the power of the gentry should be restored'. Nationalist leaders appreciated the fact that since the collapse of the Qing dynasty, power had steadily devolved into the hands of the local élite. They would seek to take advantage of the élite's normative and coercive influence in rural society to mobilize the masses to carry out its blockade-blockhouse strategy. The principal agencies used to accomplish this end were élite-controlled security forces'. Internal quotation used by Wei is from James C. Thomson, Jr., *While China Faced West: American Reformers in Nationalist China, 1928–1937* (Cambridge, MA: Harvard UP, 1969), p. 31.
14. Interview with Wang Sheng, 13 July 1993 in Taipei. Official records in Taipei list Wang's day of birth correctly, 28 October, but have the year as 1917, which is incorrect. Other sources have at times used 1914.
15. Cf. Hung-mao Tien, *Government and Politics in Kuomintang China 1927-1937* (Stanford UP, 1972), esp. Ch. 5: 'Provincial and County Government: An Overview', pp. 89–95. Commenting generally on the administrative setup of the Republic, Tien (pp. 89–90) notes: 'China's provinces differ greatly in size and population. In the 1930s the areas of the 28 provinces varied from about 39,000 sq. miles to over 633,000 sq. miles; and their populations ranged from about 400,000 to over 50,700,000. There were also significant differences in the number of counties each province had. The total number of counties in the 28 provinces in 1935 was *estimated* [emphasis added] to be 1,964. Szechwan had the most, 148 counties, and Ningsia the least, 11. At the county level, too, variations in size and population were considerable. Counties ranged from 28 sq. miles to over 225,300 sq. miles and from 234 to 1,568,492 residents. The size and population of some counties actually exceeded those of some provinces. Thus, when speaking of a province or a country [*sic*], we must be constantly aware of the great range of individual differences'.
16. Figures are those given for 1940 in Hollington K. Tong (ed.), *China Handbook 1937–1943: A Comprehensive Survey of Major Developments in China in Six Years of*

War (New York: The Macmillan Press, 1943), pp. 1–2. The actual compilation of the book was carried out under the auspices of the Chinese Ministry of Information.

17. Interview with Chung Li-jieh, former resident of Longnan (d.o.b: 28 Sept. 1912), 22 July 1993 in Taipei.

18. On the settling of Jiangxi and the formation of social relationships and structure which were later to play a role in the political events of the region, cf. Stephen C. Averill, 'The Shed People and the Opening of the Yangzi Highlands', *Modern China*, 9/1 (Jan. 1983), pp. 84–126.

19. Interview with Wang Sheng, 13 July 1993 in Taipei.

20. Interview with Chung Li-jieh, 22 July 1993 in Taipei.

21. During his lifetime, Wang Sheng was to author a number of publications, most significantly *The Theory and Practice of Political Warfare*, first released by *Fu Hsing Kang* College in 1959, and *The Thought of Dr Sun Yat-sen* (Taipei: Li Ming Cultural Enterprise Co., 1981). His actual authorship of these works has been questioned by some. See e.g. Chiang Nan [Henry Liu], '*Wang Sheng hsien-sheng che-ko-jen*' ['Wang Sheng the Man'], *Ch'i-shih Nien-tai Yueh Kan* [*The Seventies Monthly*], No. 103 (Aug. 1978), pp. 52–4, where he writes at one point [original in Chinese]: 'The words "high office and wide learning" as applied to Wang became something of a joke'. Nonetheless, that Wang Sheng actually wrote the works credited to him seems sure. Drafts of major pieces in his hand do exist. An impressive demonstration of his ability to compose occurred during a lengthy session I held with him on 24 July 1993 in Taipei. At that time, Wang Sheng was unable to speak due to an inflamed throat. To answer my questions, which became increasingly more detailed as we progressed – and were all extemporaneous – he wrote in rapid fashion on a pad of paper, then handed me the responses. They were impressive in both depth and scope, containing a wealth of detail.

22. Interview with Wang Sheng, 25 July 1993 in Taipei.

23. Ibid.

24. Ibid.

25. Even Wang Sheng's foreign models – several Americans have been mentioned earlier in the text – he interpreted in a very particular way, as evidenced in a comment: 'Forty years ago on Chiang Kai-shek's birthday, Chiang Ching-kuo gave me a book, *Autobiography of Benjamin Franklin*. It reminds me of myself, but I doubt I could work as he did. I admire Franklin, as well as Lincoln and Washington. The first two came from very humble beginnings like my own and worked very hard to get themselves up'. (Ibid.)

26. Philip C.C. Huang, 'The Jiangxi Period: an Introduction', in Huang, Lynda Schaefer Bell, Kathy Lemons Walker, *Chinese Communists and Rural Society, 1927–1934*, Chinese Research Monograph No. 13 (Berkeley, CA: Center for Chinese Studies, 1978), pp. 1–4.

27. *Baowei tuan*: literally, 'safeguarding corps'; generally translated as 'official militia'.

28. William Wei, 'Law and Order: The Role of Guomindang Security Forces in the Suppression of the Communist Bases during the Soviet Period' (note 7), p. 44. Wei is the basic source for all of the organizational details contained in this discussion of the evolving KMT security apparatus. See also Hung-mao Tien (note 15).

29. For military particulars and maps see William W. Whitson with Huang Chen-hsia, *The Chinese High Command: A History of Communist Military Politics, 1927–71* (New York: Praeger, 1973), esp. pp. 268–91.

30. Wei, 'Law and Order...', (note 7), p. 47.

31. Cf. Wei, 'Warlordism and Factionalism in the Guomindang's Encirclement Campaigns in Jiangxi' (note 7).

32. Cf. Wei, 'Five Encirclement and Suppression Campaigns (1930–1934)' (note 7).

33. Cf. Wei, 'The Guomindang's Three Parts Military and Seven Parts Politics Policy' (note 7).

34. Cf. Eastman, *Abortive Revolution* (note 9), pp. 66–70.
35. Wei, 'Law and Order' (note 7), p. 50.
36. Considerable confusion exists in the literature concerning the inspiration for this successful approach. As correctly ascertained by Wei, 'The Role of the German Advisers in the Suppression of the Central Soviet: Myth and Reality' (note 7), the operational particulars were not drawn from foreign advice but rather from historical precedent, particularly the suppression of the Nien Rebellion in the mid-nineteenth century. Cf. Mary C. Wright, *The Last Stand of Chinese Conservatism: The T'ung-chih Restoration, 1862–1874* (Stanford UP, 1957); Teng Ssu-yu, *The Nien Army and Their Guerrilla Warfare, 1851–1868* (Paris: Mouton & Co., La Haye, 1961); Chiang Siang-tseh, *The Nien Rebellion* (Seattle, WA: U. of Washington Press, 1954); and Elizabeth J. Perry, *Chinese Perspectives on the Nien Rebellion* (Armonk, NY: M.E. Sharpe, 1981).
37. Wei, *Counterrevolution in China* (note 7), p. 137. The actual text reads, 'One the eve of...'; this is clearly a typographical error.
38. *Gan* is the region south of the Poyang Lake, or the province of Jiangxi; *nan* is 'south'. Cf. R.H. Mathews, *Mathews' Chinese-English Dictionary*, rev. American ed. (13th printing), 1975 (Shanghai: China Inland Mission and Presbyterian Mission Press, 1931), p. 487 (character no. 3239).
39. To avoid confusion, the districts will be delimited as they were eventually constituted, a time which included all key periods of this narrative (refer to Map 2). The Fourth District, or what came to be called simply 'Gannan', had in it the counties of: Ganxian, Nankang, Shangyu, Chongyi, Dayu, Xinfeng, Qiannan, Longnan, Dingnan, Xunwu, and Anyuan. The Eighth District included the counties of: Huichang, Yudu, Xingguo, Ningdu, Ruijin, Shicheng, Guang Chang, and Nanfeng. Interview with Wang Sheng, 3 July 1994 in Carmel, California.
40. Jonathan D. Spence, *The Search for Modern China* (New York: Norton, 1990), p. 437.
41. For a far more hostile appraisal of Chiang Kai-shek's wartime role, cf. Sterling Seagrave, *The Soong Dynasty* (New York: Harper & Row, 1985), *passim*.
42. Counties were the basic geographic unit for recruiting into the army. Each had a training depot at which the 'strong youths' – draftees – were taught the rudiments of soldiering before being delivered to the provincial level, where a regimental administrative area was located ('corps' is also, in the present context, translated as 'regiment', since it is the next echelon to which 'battalions' would report). Thus there could be as many as 81 such units as that for which Wang Sheng was clerk (no actual count has been found in my research), assuming one per county. He would have become a part of the training base cadre. Details have been derived, in part, from an Interview with Wang Sheng, 3 July 1994 in Carmel, California.
43. For a discussion of particulars, to include the nature of instruction, cf. Jane Lois Price, *The Training of Revolutionary Leadership in the Chinese Communist Party, 1920–1945*, Columbia University PhD diss., 1974, esp. pp. 218–62. A list of prominent KMT individuals included in the first class may be found on p. 237. On the departure of the KMT contingent, Price notes (pp. 238–9): 'While many of the Kuomintang students were able to hurry back to China, those who had not left Vladivostok by December 15, 1927 ['The date when China and the USSR severed relations'] were detained indefinitely. As guests of Russian hospitality, they found themselves in prison, Siberian labor camps or on tours of duty with the Red Army. Several, such as Lin Hsieh and Kao Ju-ch'en ended their lives there. Others were released when Sino-Soviet relations had improved and a number were detained permanently'.
44. In a letter to a Moscow newspaper, Chiang Ching-kuo is quoted as writing: 'Chiang Kai-shek was my father and a revolutionary friend. He has now become my enemy. A few days ago he died as a revolutionary and arose as a counter-revolutionary. He used fine words about the revolution, but at the most convenient opportunity, he betrayed it...Down with Chiang Kai-shek! Down with the traitor!' See Seagrave, p. 233.

45. Cf. Chiang Ching-kuo, 'My Days in Soviet Russia', repr. in Ray S. Cline, *Chiang Ching-kuo Remembered: The Man and His Political Legacy* (Washington, DC: US Global Strategy Council, 1989), pp. 148–87.

46. Li Yun-han, 'Chiang Ching-kuo's Struggles During the War of Resistance Against Japan', *Chin-tai Chung-kuo*, No. 76 (30 April 1990). The article is the text of a presentation made by Li on 12 April 1990 at the National Central Library (orig. in Chinese; trans. Edward A. Suter). *Chin-tai Chung-kuo* is a bimonthly publication of the Central Historical Publishing House, Taipei.

47. Interview with Wang Sheng, 25 July 1993 in Taipei.

48. F.F. Liu, *A Military History of Modern China 1924–1949* (Princeton UP, 1956), p. 148: '...190,000 officers were trained [by all sources] during the war years. China's wartime officer strength was estimated by the Japanese at roughly 180,000 men. To maintain this strength in the face of heavy casualties (perhaps overestimated by the Japanese at 54,000 officers annually) the training schools of wartime China graduated between 42,000 and 43,000 officer cadets each year, while 12,000 junior officers were commissioned each year from the ranks. Between 1929 and 1944 the Whampoa and Central Military Academies graduated a total of 146,449 cadets in 19 classes, an average of about 7,700 a class'.

49. Interview with Lin Jung-chu, CMA Class 16 member, 16 July 1993 in Taipei.

50. Interview with Sha Chi-liang, CMA Class 16 member, ibid.

51. Interview with Tai Ch'i-hung, CMA Class 16 member, ibid.

52. Interview with Liu Ch'i-hsiung, CMA Class 16 member, ibid.

53. Interview with Lin Jung-chu, CMA Class 16 member, ibid.

54. Interview with Sun Hwa-chieh, CMA Class 16 member, ibid.

55. Interview with Liu Ch'i-hsiung, CMA Class 16 member, ibid.

56. Interview with Ch'en Shen, CMA Class 16 member, ibid.

57. Interview with Tsai Ping-jung, CMA Class 16 member, ibid.

58. Interview with Sun Hwa-chieh, CMA Class 16 member, ibid.

59. Interview with Lin Jung-chu, CMA Class 16 member, ibid.

60. Paul M.A. Linebarger, *The China of Chiang K'ai-shek: A Political Study* (Boston: World Peace Fdn, 1941), p. 343.

61. Hsu Hao-jan as told to Wu Shih-ts'ang, Wang Sheng in Gannan', in 'Chiang Ching-kuo in Southern Jiangxi (Gannan)' section of *Jiangxi Historical Records Selections* [Nanchang], No. 35 (Aug. 1989), pp. 366–7; trans. Edward A. Suter.

62. Interview with Wang Sheng, 25 July 1993 in Taipei.

63. Ibid.

64. The remaining members of the class were posted to counties throughout Jiangxi to lay the groundwork for that provincial branch of the *San Min Chu-i* Youth Corps. Wang Sheng has since noted, almost wistfully: 'I wanted to go to the front as a platoon leader. I liked the machine-gun. I even had dreams at night of being the best machine-gunner!'. (Interview, 25 July 1993 in Taipei.) Liu Ch'i-hsiung, a CMA Class 16 classmate, adds: 'He [Wang Sheng] was most interested in automatic weapons, especially the machine-gun. He was always the fastest in the class where we had to disassemble and assemble the machine-gun while blindfolded to simulate night combat'. (Interview, 16 July 1993 in Taipei.)

65. Cf. Lo Hsuan, *The Saga of Chiang Ching-kuo in Jiangsi* (Canton: South China Press, 1988), esp. pp. 42–60 (trans. Edward A. Suter).

66. For greater discussion of this matter, cf. the benchmark work by Mary C. Wright, 'From Revolution to Restoration: The Transformation of Kuomintang Ideology', *Far Eastern Qtly*, XIV/4 (Aug. 1955), pp. 515–32.

67. On Chiang Kai-shek's intentions *vis-à-vis* the Youth Army, cf. Ch. 4, 'Politics Within the Regime: The Youth Corps', in Eastman, *Seeds of Destruction* (note 9), pp.89–107. He states e.g. (p. 90): 'In creating the Youth Corps, Chiang Kai-shek hoped to provide a framework within which all true supporters of the revolution and the war of

resistance could set aside their differences and work together in a common effort'. Later (p. 92) he writes: 'In sum, Chiang's purpose in forming the Youth Corps was to form a new revolutionary organization that, by eliminating the divisive quarrels of the past and by attracting the nation's youth, would take up the revolutionary tasks the Kuomintang had forsaken'. That he was forced to alter the Corps' role is also noted by Eastman (p. 94): 'So serious did the situation become that by March 1939, just one year after the official decision to form it, Chiang Kai-shek completely altered his conception of the Youth Corps. Whereas he had originally conceived it as assuming a leading – if not the leading – political role in the Nationalist regime, he now reduced it to indoctrinating and controlling the youth and preparing them for future membership in the Kuomintang'. For Chiang Kai-shek's views on behavior, structures, and values, see Robert E. Bedeski, 'Pre-Communist State-Building in Modern China: The Political Thought of Chiang Kai-shek', *Asian Perspective* [Seoul], 4/2 (Fall–Winter 1980), pp. 149–70. Bedeski expands upon this effort in *State Building in Modern China: The Kuomintang in the Prewar Period*, China Research Monograph No. 18 (Berkeley: Center for Chinese Studies, 1981).

68. Basic works include: W.F. Elkins, "Fascism in China: The Blue Shirts Society, 1932–1937', *Science and Society*, 33/4 (1969), pp. 426–33; Lloyd E. Eastman, 'Fascism in Kuomintang China: The Blue Shirts', *China Qtly*, 49 (Jan.–March 1972), pp. 1–31; Eastman, *Abortive Revolution* (note 9), specifically Ch. 2 (pp. 31–84), 'The Blue Shirts and Fascism'; Maria Hsia Chang, *The Chinese Blue Shirt Society: Fascism and Developmental Nationalism*, Chinese Research Monograph No. 30 (Berkeley, CA: Center for Chinese Studies, Inst. of East Asian Studies, 1985); and Eastman, 'The Rise and Fall of the "Blue Shirts": A Review Article', *Republican China*, XIII/1 (Nov. 1987), pp. 25–48.

69. Most sources have the Fourth District administering 11 counties; e.g. Li Yun-han (note 96), p. 33. Upon occasion, however, the figure 12 is used, apparently when Ganzhou town is considered as a separate administrative entity.

70. Cf. *Report From Xunwu* (note 7).

71. Cf. Hsu Cho-yun, 'Historical Setting for the Rise of Chiang Ching-kuo', in Leng Shao-chuan (ed.), *Chiang Ching-kuo's Leadership in the Development of the Republic of China on Taiwan*, Vol. III in the Miller Center Series on Asian Political Leadership, U. of Virginia (New York: UP of America, 1993), pp. 1–29. More colorfully, Liu Jing-shing, Gannan Finance Section Chief under Chiang Ching-kuo, puts the goals as: 'for all the people to have work; to have something to eat; to have clothes to wear; to have houses to live in; and to have books to read' (Interview, 22 July 1993 in Taipei).

72. Li Yun-han, (note 46), p. 33.

73. Hsu Cho-yun (note 71), p. 6. See also pp. 350–1 in Chang Su, 'Chiang Ching-kuo and Chang Ya-juo', in 'Chiang Ching-kuo in Southern Jiangxi (Gannan)' section of *Jiangxi Historical Records Selections* (note 61).

74. Chang Su (note 73), pp. 350–4. This, it should be noted, is a mainland source of uneven quality. The translation provided is not literal but true to the sense of the original. There is little cause, in the matter at hand, to doubt its veracity.

75. For a brief discussion cf. Li Yun-han (note 46), pp. 34–5.

76. Liu Jing-shing, *Wo Sheng You Shing – Liu Jing-shing Chi- Shih Sheng-chen-chi (I Was Fortunate in my Life – Recollecting the Past on my Seventieth Birthday)* (Taipei: private imprint, Quan Qing Color Printing Co., 11 Nov. 1989); see subsection 1 of Ch. 4 (pp. 66–80; orig. in Chinese). Liu has further explained (Interview, 22 July 1993 in Taipei) that his means for approaching Chiang Ching-kuo was neither unique nor unusual: 'We [others who joined 'the team'] knew of Chiang Ching-kuo only due to his five goals. We had heard of him but had never seen him. As youngsters, though, we thought these were lofty goals for which to strive, so we wrote to Chiang Ching-kuo and said we wanted to join. Our loyalty came from the patriotism in our hearts. We wrote and received letters back from him saying to show up. You have to understand

the situation. People were very poor, and he offered hope. We treated him as a savior'.

77. Lo Hsuan (note 65), see pp. 52 and 59.

78. Two readily available sources for this important work are: *Chiang Ching-kuo Shensheng Yen-lun Chu-shu Hui-bien* [*Collection of Speeches and Writings of Mister President Chiang Ching-kuo*], Vol. 1 [of 26] (Taipei: Li Ming Cultural Enterprises, 1981), pp. 215–33; and *Chou-yige Gang-tei Hao-han* [*Be an Iron Man!*] (Taipei: Li Ming Cultural Enterprises, 1978), pp. 204–18. 'Be an Iron Man!' comes from the title of one of the selections; the work contains what are judged to be the 20 most important speeches given by Chiang Ching-kuo during his Gannan years.

79. Lo Hsuan (note 65), p. 59.

80. Interview with Wang Sheng, 25 July 1993 in Taipei.

81. Wang Sheng, *What I Know About President Chiang Ching-kuo* (Taipei: Li Ming Culture Enterprise Co., 1980), p. 28.

82. Wei, *Counterrevolution in China* (note 7), has noted (pp. 149–50), speaking of the former soviet areas in general: 'Widespread or persistent peasant resistance failed to appear because of the political apathy of those left in the former soviet areas, the government's relatively mild treatment of the people, and the depressed state of agriculture'. Given the amount of information which flowed in from the populace to the security forces once the communists had been displaced, there would seem to be more to the picture than just this. In particular, CCP repression – which Wei correctly notes as a cause for bringing the gentry off the fence onto the government side – also seems to have been an important factor in alienating much of the population. Once able to work with government forces, people proved more than willing to inform upon those who had been in the covert CCP infrastructure.

83. It should come as no surprise that 'the German-made Maxim gun, 30-caliber, water-cooled' figured prominently in Wang Sheng's scheme of weapons training! (Interview with Wang Sheng, 25 July 1993 in Taipei.) It may be further noted, that while technically only the Political Officer for the battalion, he was, in fact, its ultimate superior by virtue of his position as district chief.

84. In his *What I Know About President Chiang Ching-kuo* (note 81), Wang Sheng presents slightly different numbers (pp. 28–9): four companies and a hundred men. The figures I have used come from ibid and were confirmed in an additional Interview, 2 July 1994 in Carmel, California.

85. Ibid.

86. Ibid.

87. Ibid. There is again a different version, though not significantly so, in *What I Know About President Chiang Ching-kuo* (note 81), where Wang Sheng has Chiang Ching-kuo saying (p. 29): 'You must know that for the suppression of bandits, we should not rely completely on bullets, but should rely on culture and economy'.

88. Figures for 1940 list all of Jiangxi as having, in 1940, 2,381 villages (*hsiang* or *chen*) with 23,853 *bao*; and 226,564 *jia*. Given the decimal nature of the *baojia* system, operating as it did in multiples of ten, these figures work out reasonably well. See *China Handbook 1937–1943*, p. 2.

89. Cf. Wei, *Counterrevolution in China* (note 7), pp. 140–1.

90. Liu Jing-shing (note 76), see subsection 3 of Ch. 4 (pp. 66–80).

91. Interview with Wang Sheng, 25 July 1993 in Taipei.

92. See e.g. Barbara W. Tuchman, *Stilwell and the American Experience in China, 1911–45* (New York: Macmillan Press, 1971), *passim*. Spence (note 40), p. 478, writes: 'Other Americans, including General Stilwell himself, were equally horrified at the campaigns of enforced conscription carried out by the Guomindang armies, and at the sight of ragged, barefooted men being led to the front roped together, already weakened almost to death by beriberi or malnutrition. Random executions of recruiting officers, occasionally ordered by Chiang Kai-shek, did nothing to end the abuses. It was estimated that of 1.67 million Chinese men drafted for active service in 1943, 44

percent deserted or died on the way to join their units. Those draftees who died *before* seeing combat between 1937 and 1945 numbered 1.4 million, approximately 1 in 10 of all men drafted'.

93. Wang Sheng himself feels this demand sprang from a desire to embarrass Chiang Ching-kuo. Though he does not know the instigator, he observes that the very success of the 'New Gannan' plan had aroused considerable jealousy and animosity from those officials who suffered by comparison. An effective way to fight back was to claim that development was occurring at the expense of the war effort, that Chiang Ching-kuo's counties were not fulfilling their recruiting quotas. Interview with Wang Sheng, 3 July 1994 in Carmel, California.

94. Interview with Wang Sheng, 25 July 1993 in Taipei.

95. Ibid. Hsu Hao-jan and Wu Shih-ts'ang (note 61), paint a different picture. While lauding Wang Sheng's fairness – 'every able-bodied young man, no matter what his status, had to serve in the army' – and his incorruptibility – 'over 200 young men whose status was unclear were arrested and sent into the army' – they nonetheless emphasize the coercive aspects of his campaign – 'All able-bodied men were enlisted. Those who did not go willingly were seized and forced to go to army camps. Thus the atmosphere in Gannan suddenly became more tense'. There can be no doubt that the entire recruiting structure in China during the Second World War was a nasty business. Looking at the big picture, however, is to miss the point that Wang Sheng in his small world appears to have been attempting to come up with an approach which was different, at a minimum more carrot than stick.

96. Source for Chiang Ching-kuo's assumption of his national Youth Corps position at this time is Li (note 38). The judgement of Chiang Ching-kuo's early influence, however, is mine. It expands upon, and advances by some years, the hypothesis of Eastman, *Seeds of Destruction* (note 9), p. 91: 'In 1940, General Chang Chih-chung took over as secretary-general [of the Youth Corps]. Effective leadership of the corps, however, probably fell to lesser cadres. K'ang Tse seems to have been the dominant personality in the corps until about 1944; thereafter, at least according to some reports, Chiang Kai-shek's son, Chiang Ching-kuo, took a leading role'. The Sec.-Gen. until 1940 was Chang Chih-chung's predecessor as head of the Political Department, Gen. Ch'en Ch'eng; but, as Eastman correctly notes (also p. 91), he, too, had so many additional positions that acting Sec.-Gen. was Chu Chia-hua.

97. Though we agree in certain particulars, this is a different version of events than that presented in Joseph J. Heinlein, 'Political Warfare: The Chinese Nationalist Model', American University PhD diss., 1974. Heinlein, in my opinion, greatly oversimplifies what was occurring. He has a 'Central Training Center' – which I take to be the Central Political Institute, a KMT school established in 1928 – being closed down in favor of a 'political operations research class', which would be the Central Cadre Academy. He has the faculty from the former transferring to the latter. Yet, as per Li, (pp. 39–40), the Central Cadre Academy and the Central Political Institute both existed in 1945 at war's end, and it was at that time that they were merged to become National Chengchih (Political) University. Li would appear the more credible source. In fact, there seems to have emerged a parallel system of schools. This would make sense given the competition between the Youth Corps and the KMT. Heinlein is incorrect in his assertion that the Youth Corps was an integral part of the Kuomintang, responding to its orders. Accepting this chain-of-command creates in his rendition a smooth evolution from the Central Political Institute to the Central Cadre Academy as part of a KMT effort to produce 'commissars'. Not only is 'commissars' a value-laden (and incorrect) translation of 'political officers' – a position to be considered later in this work – but there are inherent problems to any approach which minimizes the chaotic inner workings of Chiang Kai-shek's push to form a *revolutionary* effort. Finally, Heinlein is much taken, as have been any number of scholars since, with 'Blue Shirts' involvement in the cadre structure. Eastman, *Seeds of Destruction* (note 9), in

his chapter on the Youth Corps (pp. 89–107), discusses the often overstated degree to which the 'Blue Shirts' influenced the Youth Corps, to include formation of the Central Cadre Academy. That the 'Blue Shirts' were a faction in Kuomintang politics is without question; that this has any particular interest to our discussion of the Youth Corps results from the debate over whether the 'Blue Shirts' was a Fascist body. As Eastman notes (p. 96), there are those who contend outright 'that the corps was simply a metamorphosis of the Blue Shirts. In fact, however, the Blue Shirt faction was never able wholly to dominate the Youth Corps...Actual operations of the corps, nevertheless, were in large part directed by cadres associated with the former Blue Shirts'. Be all this as it may, comparison of the evidence (contained in the sources cited in note 68 above) demonstrates that the 'Blue Shirts' was 'Fascist' only in as much as it sought to divine the secrets whereby the Fascist movements – in particular, of Italy, Germany, and Japan – were able to tap nationalist passions for the purposes of unity, independence, and development. Eastman, in the paperback edition of *Abortive Revolution* (note 9) (Cambridge, MA: Harvard UP, 1990), has attached an appendix (unpaginated; facing p. 374), 'Formation of the Blue Shirts', which discusses the new material he earlier presented in 1987 (see note 68 above).

98. Thus I have rendered the name as Central Cadre 'Academy', because the more normal translation of 'School' simply does not convey the envisaged scope of the institution.

99. Some sources put the number at about 250. This is not a major discrepancy. It may be added that to stand for the exam, it was not necessary to be a Youth Corps member. Membership became mandatory, however, once an individual was accepted at the Academy (both men and women attended).

100. Ch'i Hsi-sheng (note 9), p. 80. For further analysis cf. Ch'i's entire section on *Ichigo*, pp. 68–82. He includes tables detailing the extent to which central government units were mangled in the campaign.

101. Li Yun-han (note 46), pp. 40–1. Quite accurate also is *Shuei-sheng Juen-hsiung Wu-shr Nien* (*Fifty Years of Student Military Training*) (Taipei: Military Training Dept of the ROC Ministry of Education, 1978), pp. 73–9. Again, I find myself at odds with the account of these events provided in Heinlein (note 97), pp. 437–42. His version of the Youth Army's formation will be dealt with more fully later in my text. For now suffice to say that I consider his rendition a Machiavellian assessment of Chiang Kai-shek which depends heavily upon biased American sources. For certain particulars his account can be useful; it must, however, be used with caution. The heart of our disagreement would appear to lie in the manner in which we have used our sources, with Heinlein relying upon what he terms 'primary sources' – that is, US and Taiwan government-sponsored histories. These works vary considerably in reliability and, while they may have enhanced access to certain materials not normally subject to academic scrutiny, are secondary compilations which must be judged accordingly. American histories, *in particular*, even where well-meaning, often reflect a definite institutional and cultural bias which leaves the Chinese coming across as straw men in *ex post facto* resolution of the debates of the time.

102. Li Huan, 'Chiang Kai-shek and Chinese Youth' (p. 684) in *Proceedings of Conference on Chiang Kai-shek and Modern China*, Vol. III: *Chiang Kai-shek and China's Modernization* (Taipei: China Cultural Service, 1987).

103. Interview with Wang Sheng, 25 July 1993 in Taipei.

104. Interview with Liao Kuang-hsun, 22 July 1993 in Taipei.

105. Interview with Wang Sheng, 25 July 1993 in Taipei.

106. Ibid.

107. Liao Kung-wei remarried but has since passed away. For a time after the divorce, she kept Wang Hua with her, then gave her to her mother (i.e. Wang Hua's grandmother) to be raised. Wang Hua obtained some education and is now a deputy to the PRC National People's Congress. She has four children, two boys and two girls. She is aware that Wang Sheng is her father; they met once in Hong Kong and continue to correspond.

108. Interview with Wang Sheng, 25 July 1993 in Taipei.
109. For a discussion of gender trends, several works are available. A sense of historical perspective, together with the approaches of the KMT and CCP, can be gained from: Colleen S. She, 'Toward Ideology: Views of the May Fourth Intelligentsia on Love, Marriage, and Divorce', *Issues & Studies* [Taipei], 27/2 (Feb. 1991), pp. 104–32; Norma Diamond, 'Women under Kuomintang Rule: Variations on the Feminine Mystique', *Modern China*, 1/1 (Jan. 1975), pp. 3–45; and Chi-hsi Hu, 'The Sexual Revolution in the Kiangsi Soviet', *China Qtly*, 59 (Sept. 1974), pp. 477–90.
110. Allen Whiting, 'Mystery Man of Formosa', *Saturday Evening Post* 12 March 1955, cited in Chiang Nan [Henry Liu], *Chiang Ching-kuo Zhuan* (*A Biography of Chiang Ching-kuo*) (Montebello, CA: *Mei-guo Lun-tan Bao* [*The American Tribune*], 1984), Ch. 10 [trans. excerpts, np].
111. Interview with Kung Chiu-Chuan, 12 July 1993 in Taipei.
112. Two accounts of the relationship may be found by consulting Lo Hsuan (note 65), and Chang Su (note 73). Both appear to be informed largely by gossip but are useful for some particulars. In recent years there has been an upsurge of interest in Chang Ya-juo herself, and two biographies have appeared, one in Taiwan, the other in China: Chou Yu-kou, *Chiang Ching-kuo yu Chang Ya-juo* [*Chiang Ching-kuo and Chang Ya-juo*] (Taipei: Lien Ching, 1990); and Hu Shin, *Jiang Jing-guo yu Zhang Ya-ruo Chih Lien* [*The Affair of Chiang Ching-kuo and Chang Ya-juo*](Changchun, Manchuria: 'Literature of the Times' Publishers, 1993). Significantly, both authors are women and give the subject the sensitive treatment it deserves. Neither attempts to be sensational. Chou, a journalist, writes as a reporter, basing her story largely upon interviews. Hu, a writer and teacher, uses a style reminiscent of her novels, even to the extent of imagining dialogue between the principals. Particularly useful in Chou's book are a chronology of Chang's life (Appendix 1, pp. 249–53) and a foldout chart (App. 2, p. 255) showing her lineage (i.e. family tree). Chang Ya-juo is also discussed in Yang Tsun's treatment of Chiang Ching-kuo's early life (note 2).
113. This was most likely their initial meeting. The version given by Chang Su (note 73), pp. 350–1, that Chang Ya-juo was already smitten with Chiang Ching-kuo due to his Gannan policies, does not ring true.
114. Lo Hsuan (note 65), in rather contradictory fashion, discusses the military regimen of the students (p. 45), then has Chiang Ching-kuo giving Chang Ya-juo a ride 'home' on his motorcycle, staying the night – 'thus began their love affair' (p. 51). To the contrary, claim course participants, to include Wang Sheng (Interview, 25 July 1993 in Taipei), all students lived in a compound, though certainly the women had separate quarters. Similarly, Chang Su (note 73), has Wang Sheng as the go-between – 'seeing that Chiang and Chang Ya-juo were attracted to each other, Wang decided to help their relationship along' – which is even more unlikely, given his relationship with Chiang Ching-kuo as described previously in my text. It may be further recalled that Wang Sheng did not actually know Chiang Ching-kuo on a personal basis at this stage in their own relationship.
115. Both became prominent citizens in Taiwan. Chang Hsiao-yen, a former Vice-Minister of Foreign Affairs, is now head of the Commission for Overseas Chinese; Chang Hsiao-chih was the president of Soozhou University in Taipei but died in March 1996 (see the *Daily Telegraph*, 2 March 1996). Chang Hsiao-yen is listed in *The Republic of China Yearbook 1993* (Taipei: ROC Govt Info. Office), p. 527. His birthdate is given as 2 May 1941, which would be correct in the sequence I have constructed. A somewhat later date, however, as provided by Chou (note 112), in her chronology of Chang's life (Appendix 1: she puts the date of birth as 27 January 1942) would not alter the narrative. She does not give a date of death in 1942 but has Chang Ya-juo as 30 years of age when she suddenly grew ill and passed away. Blood or food poisoning is the most often cited cause. The two sons by her first marriage were raised by their grandmother. Chang Ya-juo's tomb was refurbished by the local branch of the United

Front Department of Guilin, Guangxi municipal government; it was repaired at the twins' commission. Apparently, Chang Hsiao-chih subsequently visited it several times. Chang Hsiao-yen, as a government official, has yet to be able to do likewise.

116. According to Chou (note 112), Chang Ya-juo was married at age 15 or 16 and widowed at 22 or 23.

117. Interview with Kung Chiu-chuan, professor at Tamkang University, 12 July 1993 in Taipei.

3 Civil War: Competing Revolutions

Momentary setback: Chiang Ching-kuo (left) and Wang Sheng (center rear) during June 1952 visit to offshore islands. Hands point to the lost mainland.

WORLD War II's end, though welcomed by all, found a China on its knees, its society so thoroughly ripped asunder that there was no dominant locus of order. In effect, a period of resurgent warlordism was in full sway, for the Nanjing government (the capital was moved back to that city from Chongqing) held power in name only. Its position as the leading contender among many, a dominance which was firm, in any case, only in the single 1927–37 decade normally associated with the Republic, had ended with the repeated decimation of its troops in battle with the Japanese. *Ichigo* had been the final blow. Ironically, Chiang Kai-shek's plans for fostering national unity through various programs and designs only served to undercut his position still further, because they fostered resistance from his rivals, who saw them as thinly disguised stratagems for strengthening the Kuomintang's hand.

Far from being ruses, though, the programs were the essence of what Chiang Kai-shek saw himself to be about. He had a vision, arrived at through his association with Sun Yat-sen, of what the new China should be like. Where Chiang fell short, as is by now well known, was in the details. It is perhaps an oversimplification – but only just – to say that his problem was not that for which he is frequently condemned, his ruthlessness, rather the opposite, an inability to be ruthless enough.[1] He fully recognized that the wounded Chinese society which he was endeavoring to lead into a new era lacked both the local leaders and the behavioral particulars which would allow 'modernity' to flourish. He could have acted in the manner of the wrathful God of the *Old Testament*, who time and again tore down that He might rebuild. Instead, Chiang consistently endeavored to *reform* China. His most well known efforts – the New Life Movement and the 'Blue Shirts' again come immediately to mind – stemmed from this orientation. Their failure is laid at Chiang's door but was certainly as galling to him as it has been tautologically comforting for his critics.

China's difficulties cannot be underestimated. Simultaneously, however, it must be noted that the actual dimensions of even the land problem are yet the subject of scholarly debate.[2] What is without question is that the need for national integration was a pressing concern, one, ironically, which both Chiang Kai-shek and Mao Tse-tung saw as central to their programs for dealing with all other issues. In this they were *both* unlike their warlord rivals, with the term being employed here to mean not only the regional, stereotypical *satraps* but expanded to include the myriad locally-oriented figures such as the gentry. It was Chiang and Mao who articulated a national view but were constantly bedeviled by two problems: *factionalism* and *incompetence* among their subordinates. Thus both found themselves fighting on multiple fronts. Even while combating the forces pressing for regionalism and localism, they were forced to deal with those within their own nationally-oriented efforts who continued to represent those very forces. Simultaneously, they had to grapple with the more prosaic problem of finding capable individuals who could carry out instructions and were motivated to do so; on a higher plane, such competent individuals having been found, they needed to be driven by the ideals of the revolution. Historically, this cut across the grain, because the very nature of Chinese culture was to emphasize and reward those who interpreted loyalty in personal rather than national terms.[3]

Chiang Kai-shek, guiding force behind the Kuomintang revolution following the death of Sun Yat-sen (Wang Sheng at right).

Where Chiang and Mao differed was in their grappling with this multi-faceted conflict. Mao purged; Chiang tried to convert. Always the key, as Chiang Kai-shek saw it, was the value of the individuals concerned. It is in this light that the ongoing effort to develop a core group committed to the revolution, as best exemplified by initiation of the Youth Corps and setting up of the Central Cadre Academy itself, should be interpreted. Chiang Kai-shek harped on the topic relentlessly throughout his life.[4] Such efforts have frequently been portrayed as little save a means for Chiang Kai-shek to create a loyal following, his own faction; but there is little in the manner these personnel were *employed*, as discussed in Chapter 2, which would buttress such a contention. We may even, as mentioned previously, factor into this argument Chiang's various personal and leadership shortcomings without in the slightest detracting from the essential rectitude of his conclusion that competent, right-minded officials were the indispensable element. If such were to be had, the issues of factionalism and incompetence would be eliminated, and the revolution could go forward. The riddle of this era of Chinese history, then, becomes not whether various problems were addressed but rather whether they were addressed adequately. The issue has salience, because a particular, if unstated, theme in the scholarship of the Chinese Revolution has been the *moral* failure of the KMT to grapple with the plight of the populace. Ergo, continues the logic, Nanjing *deserved* to lose. The dangers of such an orientation for accurate assessment of what actually occurred should be apparent.

The dominant approach in the historiography of modern China has been to dismiss the KMT interregnum (between the imperial and communist eras) as one which was doomed to failure because it ignored the pressing issues of the day. Yet the Gannan efforts under Chiang Ching-kuo, in which Wang Sheng played such an important role, were intended specifically to experiment with a model, based upon the *San Min Chu-i*, for dealing with them. The CCP developed an alternative. Significantly, it was the KMT approach which was successful in Gannan. It mobilized an effort which routed the CCP, an effort which was intended for implementation elsewhere in China. To claim that this was only due to superior KMT power is actually to make the very point that personnel and their ability to mobilize resources were a decisive factor. Ultimately, the communists were successful in China as a

Chiang Ching-kuo, son of Chiang Kai-shek and increasingly the day-to-day manager of KMT affairs (Wang Sheng behind right shoulder).

whole only when this KMT power was destroyed through
external, Japanese, intervention.[5] This left the KMT as but another
player in the renewed drama of 'warlord' competition. That the
CCP could emerge the strongest contender, able to seize the
Chinese mainland, was because of its mobilization capabilities,
capabilities which rested upon an able cadre. There was, in other
words, more than one avenue to mobilization, though all were
rooted in the structural realities of China.

None of this discussion should be taken as dismissing the rough
edges of the Nanjing regime. Whatever his vision, Chiang Kai-shek
was also a player in the rough and tumble, day-to-day realities of a
political game waged for keeps. He did what was necessary to
survive. Much, for instance, has been made of his associations with
underworld elements, especially in the early days when he needed
manpower and financial support. How much less has been said of
communist resort, especially as concerns Mao and other CCP
organizers in the countryside, to the same sort of fringe elements

to breathe life into their own movement. Chiang Kai-shek, in other words, may have had his Dai Li, the Whampoa graduate who headed his 'dreaded' secret police apparatus, the so-called Bureau of Investigation and Statistics; but whatever Dai Li and his minions did had its counterpart on the other side in CCP campaigns of land distribution and ideological rectification. 'Civil wars are anything but', as the play on the oxymoron goes. Mao recognized this directly, but he is incorrectly credited with engaging in hyperbole when he wrote of the reign of terror which had to accompany revolution. To the contrary, he knew what he was about.

Rather than the 'bean counting' inherent to a focus upon tactical action, more fruitful is to examine strategic goals and operational implementation of the contenders. Chiang Kai-shek sought a revolutionary break with the decayed imperialist past, his national revolution as we have already identified it; Mao Tse-tung sought the same revolutionary break through social revolution dragging the national revolution along. Both engaged in perhaps expedient tactical moves which do not stand up well to the light of day. The Chinese Civil War could not have been a case of Gandhi mounting a campaign of nonviolence, for there was no side in China to play the principled role of the British. Where the KMT and the CCP parted company dramatically, however, was in strategic approach. Chiang Kai-shek sought an order rooted in a nativistic vision of a righteous past; Mao Tse-tung opted for an order tied to a utopian vision of a socialist future. Operationally, this caused Chiang to focus upon restoration of traditional values and structures, Mao to work for the implementation of a new society. Where the CCP sought to construct what came to be called 'the New Maoist Man', the KMT sought a return to the correct orientation and behavior embodied in traditional Chinese culture, albeit as modified to take cognizance of the modern industrial and political world. Actual implementation suffered from abuses on both sides. But where these were tactical excess on the KMT side and not a part of strategic design, for the CCP they were expressly that and inherent to Marxism as interpreted by Mao. Therein lay the future tragedy of the mainland following the communist takeover – and the ability of Taiwan to blossom under KMT rule. For KMT excess could be ended because it was peripheral to the design; for the mainland it could only grow worse, as it did in the CCP's 'People's Republic', because it was integral to the blueprint.

Aftermath of War

For those caught in the winds of the Second World War, these considerations could not have been further away. When the enormous conflict ended, Wang Sheng, like everyone, was very happy. Still, he felt a sense of unease:

> I was going shopping with my wife when we heard the news that the Americans had dropped the atomic bomb and that the war was over. We were all very excited. But I was worried – people were not paying enough attention to the communist threat. In Jiangxi I realized that they could attract people with their message. They did all the bad things but cloaked them in good words. They were like opium: it makes you feel good, but deep down it damages you. I read a lot of books and realized that the communists were not just bandits but a serious threat. From self-study, I realized that this was not the way to go.[6]

Wang Sheng had come far in his understanding of China's problems and its internal enemies as he judged them. Fundamentally he realized what would loom increasingly larger: that mobilization of the masses was the CCP aim, but mobilization only so that it could carry out a Marxist revolution. Hence, as it had demonstrated time and again, both in its activities in the field and in its negotiations with the government, the CCP would do whatever was necessary *tactically* to assure itself of *strategic* success. This success, Mao himself knew, could only be based upon military power deployed to protect the Leninist party structure intended to guide the masses through to successful completion of the revolution. Thus the war had been a boon, because Yenan had been a safe haven from both the Japanese and the KMT. After the August–November 1940 Hundred Regiments Campaign, the CCP was not again to launch a major operation, content instead to build up its guerrilla forces behind Japanese lines (in the process eliminating Kuomintang units and any other rivals), its mobile forces and party structure in Yenan. Potentially divisive redistributive policies were downplayed in favor of 'united front' appeals. The New Fourth Army incident in early 1941 ended whatever potential had existed for actual cooperation; thereafter it was a contest of mobilization for the ultimate reckoning.

Certainly the KMT had the tougher time of it, for not only did it have to maintain some semblance of a functioning state in order to continue receiving important foreign aid, but its forces were consistently mauled by the Japanese even as the regime was cut off from its power base in occupied China. This left Chiang Kai-shek in an ever more precarious situation. The war's sudden conclusion caught him virtually flat-footed. In the rush to accept the surrender of the more than one million Japanese troops who remained on Chinese soil, emphasis was given to reclaiming the traditional centers of KMT support along the coast. Poor conduct by the liberating forces, though, cost the government much of the good will it might have reaped had its representatives behaved with a modicum of civility and grace. Standing in stark contrast to such behavior was the deportment of the CCP's soldiers as they, too, moved to take advantage of the vacuum created by Imperial Japan's collapse.

Their prime goal, however, was Manchuria, occupied by the Soviets in the closing August days of the war.[7] Soviet forces were not particularly helpful to the CCP due to Stalin's suspicions of Mao's independent bent – as well as his pragmatic judgement that the CCP had little chance of emerging victorious. Still, they allowed large amounts of surrendered weapons to be seized and stuck to their business of looting, giving the Chinese communists full reign to mobilize the countryside. This they did behind a Soviet shield which refused access to KMT forces and did not depart until April 1946. By that time the CCP had built up a truly formidable position, consisting of numerous picked troops which had forced marched into the region immediately at war's end, as well as guerrillas now 'regularized' into more conventional units. So solid were the communist preparations that the government, despite airlifting (on American planes) to Manchuria some half a million of its best troops (few of whom were from the region), was never able to dislodge the CCP from the area north of the Sungari River (with its main urban center of Harbin). Instead, as at least some American advisors realized, the move greatly overextended the KMT's lines of supply and communication. They became more attenuated than even the Americans anticipated when the full extent of CCP guerrilla force organization in former Japanese-held areas was appreciated. It was these very areas, concentrated in north China, which sat astride the lines of communication necessary to support the troops in Manchuria. Additionally, the troops themselves added to their isolation by behaving poorly towards the population and hugging the urban areas. The results, once battle was joined in earnest in mid-1947, were predictable. By late 1948 Chiang Kai-shek had lost the cream of the only forces remaining to him which could really be considered 'government'. Thereafter, Nanjing was forced to rely upon less loyal, less well-trained units which collapsed like a deck of cards in some of the most massive conventional battles ever seen in the history of warfare.

Crucial to CCP success, of course, was the mobilization which allowed it to field forces capable of besting the Nationalists. This process, however, has occasioned no little analytical confusion. True, solution to 'the land problem' was the element upon which the communists were able to build their power base. Yet their 'solution' was not that called for in their dogma; neither did it occur in competition with other alternative mobilization efforts. Rather, shielded by the Soviet military presence, the CCP had the field to itself and could adopt a divide-and-conquer approach which pitted some elements of the community against others to the extent necessary to achieve inroads. Skillful use of cadre and an absolute preponderance of force – with a substantial percentage comprised of outsiders, particularly Koreans – gave the communist campaign a self-sustaining quality once it was underway. The point is that whatever worked in Manchuria due to the peculiarities of that former Japanese puppet state did not necessarily have anything to do with 'the land problem' – or any other structural dilemma – in China itself. What resulted, though, was that the CCP was able to build a potent martial instrument in a very particular post-colonial vacuum, and with it destroy the linchpin of what remained of the KMT military institution.[8] Those KMT units which were yet to join the battle, while they were impressive in sheer numbers, were unimpressive in every other respect and scarcely put up credible resistance.[9]

That even many good units performed poorly could hardly be surprising. The disastrous financial trends mentioned earlier reached such a state[10] that anyone on a fixed income, such as officers and men, was in an impossible situation.[11] Morale was further broken by fragmentation on the home front. Large numbers of students and intellectuals deserted the regime. A virulent peace movement pressured the government, fanned by communist infiltrators. Factionalism within the government itself was serious. Small wonder, therefore, that of the 4.9 million men reportedly lost by the Nationalists between mid-1946 and the end of 1948, three-quarters had either defected or been captured. Entire armies simply broke. 'Equally devastating, some 105 of 869 Nationalist generals defected to the Communists'.[12] It was later revealed that even the Nationalist Deputy Chief of the General Staff, Wu Shih, was a longtime communist agent.

As might be anticipated from the turn his career pattern had taken, Wang Sheng was to experience this betrayal. Yet as also befits his progress, he was to experience it in a very unique manner, one which would solidify his backing for the Republic and for Chiang Ching-kuo, while simultaneously convincing him of the utter ruthlessness with which the communists were prepared to act.

Initially, he would seem to have been forgotten in the welter of events which accompanied the end of the war. 'Peace' found Wang Sheng still at the Southeast Branch Training Base in Jiangxi as its Political Officer. Though the Youth Army was not immediately ended in a formal sense, recruiting specifically for it did halt. Those units which were already in being were integrated into the regular army force structure. The nine divisions (numbered 201st to 209th) were grouped into three corps (numbered 6th, 9th, and 31st). Wang Sheng subsequently accompanied the two divisions from his base, the 208th and the 209th (recruited principally from Guangzhou and Jiangxi) – which had become part of the 31st Corps – to the city of Hangzhou on the coast of Zhejiang (Chekiang) Province, south of Shanghai, in November 1945. There, they were charged with garrison duty and maintaining order. As a Section Chief in the Political Department of the Corps, Wang Sheng became a full colonel. His First Section was responsible for political education, cultural affairs, and propaganda. He was to serve in this capacity until June 1946.

There is another way to read these mundane events. Joseph Heinlein, for instance, citing US sources, feels that the Youth Army – which in his text is called the Youth Expeditionary Force – was nothing less than an effort by Chiang Kai-shek to recreate the 'party army' which had been the original intent of Sun Yat-sen in pushing for a military academy, Whampoa. In Heinlein's telling: By manning the nine divisions completely with students, all of whom were members of the Youth Corps, which itself was a KMT organ – and officering it with his most battle-tested and loyal subordinates – Chiang Kai-shek would have a Praetorian Guard armed, equipped, and trained by the Americans but completely loyal to himself and the revolution.[13] Heinlein continues:

> Chiang's scheme was frowned upon by [his US advisor, Major General Albert C.] Wedemeyer who argued vehemently against it. The compromise reached called for student recruits to be trained as separate 10,000 man divisions after which, Wedemeyer insisted, they would be distributed throughout the army in groups of a few thousand each. Chiang never did keep the bargain and the Youth Expeditionary Force remained intact as an élite force.[14]

There is a certain logic to this analysis. It does, after all, accord well with the effort we have hitherto seen by Chiang Kai-shek to foster revolutionary consciousness in his personnel. Further, the creation of a new military derived from the Whampoa model, dovetails neatly with the Youth Corps experiment itself, which Heinlein sees as an integral part of the KMT effort. Yet just as he has overstated the relationship between the KMT and the Youth Corps, so would he seem to have overplayed the Youth Army card. In particular, there is no evidence that the Youth Army was ever used in the manner one would expect of a force envisaged as an élite. Chiang Ching-kuo, for instance, whom Heinlein does not mention in his account, was still Political Warfare Chief in Youth Corps Headquarters, effectively the leading figure in that organization.[15] Yet at war's end he was concurrently placed in charge of a newly created Demobilization Bureau of the Youth Army, hardly an office one would expect to appear for a just-formed body intended to be an élite force! Furthermore, rather than working with this purportedly hand-picked group, Chiang Ching-kuo's energies were occupied with his tasking as a special KMT representative in Manchuria and the Soviet Union.[16] The three Youth Army corps, in any case, were not kept together, as one would expect of an élite force, but used as were any other units. Wang Sheng, we have noted above, soon found himself with the 31st Corps on garrison duty in Hangzhou.

What Chiang Kai-shek seems to have intended, then, was again to provide a *model*, just as Gannan was to be a model. That he did *not* use this model more to his advantage hardly does credit to the Chiang-as-Machiavelli school of thought. Yet Heinlein, unwittingly, is on to something. For a military man, and one who was reasonably successful in his days as a revolutionary leader, Chiang Kai-shek does seem, time and again, to demonstrate a quite extraordinary lack of organizational acumen. His dissatisfaction with the lack of character and revolutionary zeal of his subordinates was frequently entirely justified. Still, having made this judgement, and launched programs to set the situation right, he repeatedly overextended himself, dissipating his effort and bringing it to grief. The Youth Army, whether intended as model or Praetorian Guard, would be an ideal illustration. It was used effectively as neither. Further, once an idea such as the Youth Army or Gannan took root, Chiang Kai-shek's tendency was to rush the best personnel involved off to the next brushfire, rather than keeping them *in situ* and expanding from this secure base.[17] It was an erroneous approach; significantly, Mao Tse-tung did not make the same error.

Unlike Chiang Kai-shek, Mao was able to avoid strategic and operational distraction, and to see that a solution which worked needed to be pressed home, regardless of the events, external and internal, which demanded otherwise. This is what gives Maoist insurgency, in retrospect, its inevitable quality, when, in reality, it was anything but that. Chiang Kai-shek, in sharp contrast, continually expressed his frustration to achieve perfection by endeavoring to come up with new organizations and approaches, even while leaving the old in place. Mao saw the disastrous implications of such clutter and so kept his lines of command and implementation clean and concentrated. The results were a CCP responsiveness, in the end, which was the very quality Chiang Kai-shek sought from the KMT.

Chiang Kai-shek, to look at the problem from another angle, was a bad Leninist. As he pointed out any number of times, it was he who had urged adoption of the 'political officer' system after his three-month visit to Russia in late 1923 and early 1924.[18] Sun Yat-sen was already working with Moscow to strengthen the Kuomintang – it was at the behest of Russia's chief representative, Michael Borodin, for example, that the First Congress was called on 20 January 1924.[19] Chiang Kai-shek convinced Sun Yat-sen that the Russian system of 'commissars', instituted to insure the loyalty of military commanders in a Red Army which still contained many 'Whites', could help a KMT revolutionary army grappling with similar problems of internal cohesion and fealty. Consequently, a Party Representative had been made co-equal with the Whampoa

Academy Commandant (Liao Chung-k'ai and Chiang Kai-shek, respectively). A Political Department had been established (the most famous head of which was Chou En-lai, appointed in April 1925), and a system of party representatives had been established in the military. For some decades this system of party oversight in the units culminated in a Political Department under the KMT Military Committee; later the system was shifted to the Ministry of Defense under the 1944 American-inspired reorganization (the same impetus behind the plan to reconstitute 39 divisions, to which the Youth Army contributed nine). American distaste for Soviet forms meant the Political Department was redesignated the Information Bureau with a more narrow responsibility.

The innumerable permutations through which the system went were of little consequence save one: unlike its Maoist equivalent, the KMT structure of political officers remained haphazard, incomplete, and quite ineffective.[20] As with the Youth Army, Chiang Kai-shek never saw the project through to fruition by steadily building unit upon loyal unit. Instead, he attempted to push the political officers into the already existing system without backing them up with the coercive power they enjoyed in the communist system. To the contrary, he repeatedly emphasized the primacy of his military commanders – even while denouncing their lack of revolutionary spirit. In individuals such as Chiang Ching-kuo and Wang Sheng, he sought to gain the best of both worlds. Thus it was that as early as the fourth Whampoa class, which began in 1926, functional specialization within the corps of cadets included the choice of becoming a political officer. Likewise, a special class of 120, trained at the same time as the fourth class by the Whampoa Political Department, consisted entirely of military officers, especially returned graduates from Whampoa's own second and third classes. The KMT political instruction courses which followed were also military-dominated. Though civilians were included, it was only in the Youth Corps that a system of political instruction, as comprehensive as that available in the military, was attempted for party members at large.

That Chiang Kai-shek should adopt this approach stemmed from his constant disappointment with civil society as opposed to its military counterpart. His emphasis upon values and correct conduct leading to institutional probity took, in his judgement, its most concrete form in the revolutionary military. 'Now the party is about to complete the second phase of the revolution and establish a new China', he told the assembled students and staff at the 5 May 1944 official opening of the Central Cadre Academy. 'What is necessary for completion of this second phase is military discipline'.[21] What he constantly sought was a society which would match the military in its commitment and sense of mission. When this proved impossible, as we have noted above, he tended to lose heart and interest. By contrast, Mao knew that he had the key and so was willing to endure any degree of internal turmoil and momentary ineffectiveness to achieve his end. It was precisely these lapses, during which the system was being purged and righted, which Chiang Kai-shek never felt he could afford in the world of dog-eat-dog warlord politics. Given the fate of CCP efforts at popular mobilization when they were actually subject to the brunt of KMT military power – Canton, Shanghai, Jiangxi – Chiang may well have been correct.

There is, however, the nagging suspicion that in units such as the 31st Corps of the Youth Army, where Wang Sheng was an important element, lay the seed which should have been nurtured so as to germinate into something more substantial. Was that not precisely what had been done in Gannan with the 'model' approach to counterinsurgency (though it was not called this)? As Heinlein has noted, 'Into this élite force was placed an élite Political Department'.[22] Allowing for hyperbole, it is true that not only did each Youth Army corps have a political department, but so, too, did the major component units. Even each company had a political officer. For all of the political officers, roles were far more broad than their title implied. In addition to representing the KMT – Wang Sheng himself had become a party member when he entered the Central Military Academy – they also looked after a wide variety of functions ranging from counterintelligence to civic action to putting out a corps newspaper. Such duties as these had been brought together in *The Political Warfare Manual*, issued in 1941.[23]

What could not be brought together was the Kuomintang itself, which continued to be riven with debilitating factionalism. The KMT had copied the *form* of a Leninist party; but it never implemented the most important element, the principle of democratic centralism, whereby decisions reached through democratic debate (at least in theory) were enforced through party discipline so that the body presented a unified face, both theoretically and actually. Consequently, while Mao Tse-tung was building a dedicated, disciplined body to implement his strategic approach, Chiang Kai-shek presided over an amorphous, fractious mass and concentrated upon fostering individual discipline. Needless to say, it was the former which made the more potent weapon. James Harrison has perceptively summed up the situation:

> Given the diversity and limitations of all the Nationalist groups and the problems they faced, it is perhaps understandable that no effective Nationalist government could be realized in China after the war. Many individuals in the Kuomintang and the independent groups were extremely able, but they were not backed by effective organization.[24]

One of the consequences of this, as we have noted, is that those individuals who proved themselves very able were increasingly in demand as tasks arose. They held multiple positions and shuttled from spot to spot, serving as the government's fire brigade. Though this could be quite good for their careers if they were consistently successful, it deprived an already weak system of whatever stability it might have been able to gain from competent individuals remaining in position long enough to make a significant impact.

End of the Youth Army

It was not surprising, therefore, that after just six months as a colonel in the 31st Corps Political Department, Wang Sheng was in July 1946 pulled out and given a sensitive posting as the Director of Student Affairs at the Chia-hsing (Jiaxing) Youth Middle School. He was thus effectively in charge of a large institution created specially to meet the needs of the demobilized members of the Youth Army. Since many of them desired to resume their studies, disrupted due to their enlistments, Youth Army members were placed in what in essence was a government-run preparatory school. There, their academic skills could be refurbished to the extent necessary to return them to the normal educational flow. Using two schools within its compound, a vocational and a high school, Chia-hsing's mission was to ready the students for a return to civilian life or to prepare them for further education, if they so chose. Wang Sheng had been brought in because the effort had not been going well.

The Youth Army, it will be recalled, had been enlisted to fight the Japanese. Consequently, once the war was over, it was difficult to convince the educated manpower of the body that it should remain in, of all things, the army. Most wanted nothing more than to resume their studies and to begin moving up in life. The problem was that China was in no shape to absorb them, or the countless other ex-servicemen whom the government returned to the market. Keeping them in 'middle schools' – there were seven altogether – solved several problems simultaneously. It created others, though, and at Chia-hsing the 2,000-member student body had become restless. Its lack of discipline had affected not only the functioning of the school itself but also the larger community.

Wang Sheng arrived as a whirlwind; he was not yet 31. Chiang Ching-kuo, as before, was still his ultimate boss and had personally directed that he be detailed to the assignment. In addition, Chiang Ching-kuo was nominally the head of the school. None of this could help Wang Sheng on the ground. As he recalls:

> While I was Director, I was very strict. Since the students had been soldiers, they were very wild. They were now civilians, but the military was running the school. They felt they had served and deserved accolades. They would catch the train and not pay; they would eat at restaurants and not pay. I kept telling them to study hard, that if they didn't or if they bothered civilians, they would be expelled. I kept threatening to get rid of some. Finally, I did – some who were very bad. Once we did so, the rest of the school became well-behaved. People thought these students would come back and hurt me, but they did not. To the contrary, some wrote letters saying that they had missed their chance. My students did very well. Most got into college. Many came to Taiwan.[25]

Matters, of course, did not proceed quite so effortlessly, but the results were as Wang Sheng has related. His first act exemplified a political officer's approach to the problem. He placed posters throughout the campus stating the reasons for his coming. Then he paraded the student body and laid down the law. The effects were immediate. Chang Tsun-wu, a member of the education staff at the time, relates that previously stealing had become a problem which the faculty had been unable to control. 'No one was afraid of us', he observes. 'Because Wang Sheng was military and from the Youth Army, he had credibility. At a very young age he already acted very experienced and sophisticated. His loyalty to duty was unwavering'.[26]

That loyalty extended to a higher calling. Wang Sheng demanded of the students precisely what he expected of himself. 'He was very strict and cautious in his behavior', notes James C.C. Chan. 'He did not smoke or drink or gamble. He was a very industrious person. He asked the same behavior from us'.[27] Adds Ju Chong-huang, 'He detested gambling and severely punished those who did it. He carried on in the Gannan tradition'.[28] When a group of students was caught stealing coal, 'he scolded us and said we were acting like bandits. The way he said it frightened us. He was very authoritative'.[29] Chang Shr-jieh recalls the same incident:

> One time some students stole coal to cook dog meat. Wang Sheng inspected the kitchen and reprimanded them: 'You look like bandits!' The students ran away. He had dignity despite his young age. He kept after us in an effort to foster our own dignity.[30]

Perhaps more than anything else which has been said, this observation by Chang Shr-jieh summarizes Wang Sheng's approach to himself and to leadership: he sought to foster *dignity*. He accepted completely the message of his traditional Chinese education that the essential element for a just society was righteous conduct stemming from individual perfection. In the teaching of Sun Yat-sen – as further explicated and amplified by Chiang Kai-shek – he felt he had found a tap into the wellsprings of Chinese culture and order. After he had taken the difficult admissions examination for the Central Cadre Academy, Wang Sheng had finished in the bottom 20 of the 300 selectees (and this only after six months of previous preparation at the civil servant's school). As he began classes, he was but a KMT 'member of convenience' – 'you just joined when you became a cadet at the Central Military Academy'.[31] Suddenly, in that first term, he was to discover that the essence of the KMT, that which Chiang Kai-shek endeavored to build the party around, was Sun Yat-sen's *San Min Chu-i*, the 'Three Principles of the People'. The more he learned, the more excited he grew. In Sun Yat-sen he felt he was dealing with one of the great sages; in Chiang Kai-shek there existed a student of Sun who had first hand knowledge. Chiang's own teachings he found equally stimulating. Wang Sheng, guided and challenged by his Central Cadre Academy philosophy teacher, Fang Tung-mei, threw himself into expanding his knowledge. By the end of the term, he was in the top 20 of the class.[32]

It was this centrality of *learning* which Wang Sheng emphasized to his young charges, that through knowledge would come dignity – individual success and systemic redemption. Knowledge could only be gained through disciplined pursuit, though, by mastering one's more base impulses. Says Chung Ming-fung, 'Wang Sheng looked very mature. He used his will to revive himself. He was not very book-schooled but was very diligent in pursuing knowledge, eager to learn. Since he was eager to learn, he required us to study all the time'.[33] Adds Ju Chong-huang, 'He was a man of diligence, simple honesty; frugal and honest – a very pure leader'.[34]

Such intensity might have been expected to slide into an autocratic nature. One mainland source, written by a former student, asserts as much:

> His first act was to post 'Rectify School Spirit Announcements' saying that he came under orders from Chiang Ching-kuo to correct the situation at the school, and that those students who did not attend his lecture the next morning would be expelled. The next morning, the students gathered on the drill field. Unit commanders sported submachine-guns, and machine-guns were placed around the field, creating a tense atmosphere. The commanders reported that more than ten of the students were missing; and, after a short lecture, Wang Sheng announced that those missing students would be expelled and escorted back to their hometowns. No one dared oppose Wang, as he acted under Chiang Ching-kuo's authority. In this way, the situation was rectified.[35]

It is the peculiar mix of fact and fancy which makes a recounting such as this so difficult to judge. The use of posters, for instance, is accurate, as is the expulsion of the ten students. Yet all sources interviewed recalled the ten students as being expelled later, when they refused to mend their ways, not initially to make a point. Further, none recall the threat of violence, though it would seem doubtful that Wang Sheng would have avoided taking elementary precautions for security (again, we see machine-guns coming into play in Wang Sheng's life!). Quite the contrary, former Youth Army participants at Chia-hsing are overwhelming in their agreement that their Director attempted to lead by example and understanding. Says Hwa Lee-jin:

> The school was run in a military way. Yet Wang Sheng, who was the Director of Student Affairs, was very flexible. When once we boycotted classes, he could have handled the matter according to military discipline. Instead, he handled it in a very low key manner. He was very empathetic, tender. He listened to our complaints. The school emphasized honesty. Before I joined the Youth Army, I was a graduate of Peking University. I had been accepted by all seven of the leading universities of China. Wang Sheng was totally sincere with us. When we were attending school, we had the boycott I've just mentioned. It was an English class we boycotted. I was the class leader, so this incident had serious implications. Though Wang Sheng was the Director, he came over, understood the whole situation, and forgave me. He used a softer approach.[36]

This description would seem more in accord with Wang Sheng's approach than machine-guns 'around the field'. What is not in question is that Wang Sheng consistently got the job done in a manner which justified his superiors' faith in him – especially Chiang Ching-kuo. Wang's next assignment, therefore, brought him again into direct contact with Chiang. In July 1947 he went to work as an inspector in the Bureau of Preparatory Cadres of the Ministry of National Defense – the 'renamed and reorganized' Demobilization Bureau of the Youth Army folded into yet another reorganization undertaken to bring the Nationalist military structure in line with that of the United States. Chiang Ching-kuo was now the Director, and the task at hand was to continue with the transition of Youth Army personnel into civilian life, as well as to recruit replacements. For Wang Sheng it was another step up, though he remained a colonel.

Events proceeded at such a breakneck pace, however, that he soon found himself thrust again into the fray. Negotiations with the communists, pushed strenuously by the Americans under the guidance of 'Special Representative to China' General George C. Marshall, had gone on throughout 1945 and 1946, with heavy fighting breaking out from mid-1946.[37] Conflict occurred amidst the soaring inflation detailed earlier[38] and a concerted CCP effort to infiltrate all groups which it thought could be useful to its own campaign. In particular, these were student, youth, and intellectual bodies, together with labor unions. These groups, of necessity, were concentrated in urban areas, those most affected by inflation and already swollen in population due to the continued presence of refugees. Taking advantage of the declining purchasing power which reduced students and faculty virtually to the point of beggars, the CCP was able to use them to spearhead a variety of 'peace' campaigns, to include a 'GIs Leave China' movement.[39] The alleged rape of a university girl in Peking by an American serviceman proved an issue sufficient to support widespread youth protest in December 1946 and January 1947, combined with denunciation of US support of the government and Nanjing's alleged insistence upon waging civil war. These protests increased still further when, on 4 July 1947, a general mobilization was decreed to fight the communists.

Ironically, in the effort to deal with these events, which were so centered in youth activity, the government was seriously hampered by its decision to disband the Youth Corps by merging it with the Kuomintang. This ill-timed fusing of the two bodies, which had been recommended by Chiang Kai-shek on 30 June to the Standing Committee of the KMT's Central Executive Committee (the party's supreme body), but which went on throughout the crucial 1947 year of student strife, was the culmination of the long battle which had pitted the Youth Corps against the KMT ever since the former's founding in July 1938. We have already noted that Chiang Kai-shek's long-range intent, all tactical considerations aside, seems to have been to start again from scratch, to grow a new party from the revolutionary soil while allowing the disappointing KMT plant to wither and die. Yet he proved unable to bear the pressure which party stalwarts, his crucial KMT allies, were able to muster. Frustrated with the resulting squabbling and factionalism, he took his fateful course, merging the two organizations into a whole. Perhaps naively, he seems to have thought he could turn this situation to his advantage, solving two problems simultaneously, that of the squabbling and that of his disappointing KMT. Hence Chiang Kai-shek took steps which indicate he believed the amalgamation would reinvigorate the KMT at no loss to the youthful, revolutionary spirit of the Youth Corps. Thus:

> The agreement finally arrived at – ratified on 12 September 1947, by the Fourth Plenum of the Kuomintang's Central Executive Committee – carefully protected the political positions of Youth Corps cadres by assuring them comparable positions within the Kuomintang structure. Corps cadres at the *hsien* level, for example, would be reassigned to party headquarters at that level, and members of the corps' Executive Secretariat would receive appointments to the party's Central Executive Committee. The total number of staff positions would not be decreased, therefore, unless a cadre voluntarily resigned. In the wake of the merger, too, the Kuomintang would be radically reorganized. All corps and party members would have to re-register for party membership. This, in effect, would purge all undesirables from the party, including those who engaged in factionalism, were corrupt, or spoke or acted against the party. To deter further corruption, party members would have to record their property and wealth with the authorities. The merger plan also called for implementation of land reform.[40]

Instead of rescuing the party and stilling factionalism, the merger, in the event, exacerbated the problems. The hostility of former Youth Corps members towards their mainline KMT counterparts remained intense, so much so that it affected the ability of the KMT to present any sort of unified effort against the communists at this important time. More significantly, the Youth Corps spirit was lost, as many members resisted the merger with the KMT altogether and quit outright.

That these events hampered Wang Sheng's current assignment is undoubted. That he personally was not affected by them says a good bit about his relationship with the Kuomintang itself. He, after all, as any number of Youth Corps members, already held dual status. He had been recruited as a Youth Corps cadre by Chiang Ching-kuo after he had already joined the KMT at the Central Military Academy. Thus the organizational distinction between the two bodies was in his life meaningless. His career, though it included some Youth Corps assignments, had been based principally upon filling functional positions which were 'Youth Corps' only incidentally. It was as though, by being a KMT and Youth Corps member, Wang Sheng was a member of a select group of those who were certified 'truly revolutionary'. He was still young enough – 31 in mid-1947 – and junior enough so that he had no organizational stake either way, and no role in the machinations of those fighting for power and influence at higher levels. In his world, the KMT meant commitment to a body which ideologically was committed to Sun Yat-sen's *San Min Chu-i*; a body wherein he consistently was asked to perform important tasks for Chiang Ching-kuo, a dedicated revolutionary who was the son of the senior living KMT revolutionary figure and Chinese philosopher, Chiang Kai-shek. The fundamental point was that in commitment to Sun Yat-sen's dreams for China, Wang Sheng had found his identity. He was linked to political and party structures, because he judged them to be likewise committed. Entirely in keeping with his traditional ethos, this was a matter of personal calling. That the KMT might contain 'impure' elements was something to be struggled against and overcome but in no way diminished his own role or argued for his non-participation. It meant only that he had to struggle that much harder to realize the revolutionary goal. If such an orientation may be judged pathetic when part of a losing cause, it is nonetheless considered quite the opposite when displayed on the winning side

And for Wang Sheng, even as China's circumstances deteriorated, he continued to win. Each task with which he was charged was performed successfully; each involved the application of what he saw as a revolutionary approach, what we would call a restoration – a return to the 'true values' of China. Speaking to the heart of the matter as concerns Wang Sheng's character formation, the signal feature of his postings was that in each he was able to engage in behavior, *at the behest of official KMT representatives* (notably Chiang Ching-kuo), which further reinforced his conviction that he was in the revolutionary service of the Chinese people and working for their betterment. Had he ever been placed in a position where the conduct of his ultimate superiors created a conflict between his value structure and them, there is no doubt he would have opted for his beliefs over loyalty to individuals. It was this very fact – his *sincerity* is the term used universally by sources, even his enemies – which made him such a formidable individual. Time and again he put his world view into play, each time to have his faith in it validated by the response of those for whom he was responsible, whether villagers in Gannan or restless Youth Army members. His true enemies were not those who had not yet seen the revolutionary way; they were simply misguided. Rather his enemies were those who adopted false gods and who were not sincere. It was such people who were communists.

Always for Wang Sheng the essence of communism was duplicity. The CCP was not *sincere*, because it knew the message it preached was false. Its members would adopt whatever tactical position was appropriate to the moment, so long as it served the operational purpose of mobilization into the CCP infrastructure. The party's strategic goal, that of a Marxist society, was known to its trusted members but was rarely, if ever, presented in its true form to the masses. Instead, tactical resolution of their grievances was held up to be what the CCP was all about strategically. Wang Sheng, from his study, knew this was not the case. In a prominent example:

> Mao Tse-tung used his education to take advantage of the peasants. He convinced them that when they were landless, the communists would give it to them. They took land from those who had it and gave it to the landless – then they took it all. They destroyed the country even as we fought the Japanese. They were cruel people, and all the means they employed were cruel.[41]

Undoubtedly, the KMT had its share of 'cruel people'. Yet they were not individuals with whom Wang Sheng came into contact. More importantly, since he was dealing, in a sense, with the actual wellsprings of KMT doctrine, with Chiang Ching-kuo, hence Chiang Kai-shek – and through him the deceased Sun Yat-sen himself – he was convinced that the KMT revolution was precisely what its public face said it was, pursuit of *San Min Chu-i*. KMT 'cruel people', then, were not a part of the sanctioned order; they were aberrations. Such conduct could be dealt with. In contrast, as Wang Sheng judged them, for the communists the aberration *was* the sanctioned order. They knew they could never appeal to the Chinese on the merits of the communist argument, so they lied. 'Cruel people' were not CCP outlyers; they were the very essence of the ideology. To be righteous was to be a true follower of *San Min Chu-i*; to be duplicitous was to be a Marxist-Leninist.[42] Wang

Sheng's work with the Bureau of Preparatory Cadres only served to confirm his belief.

Faced with the turmoil on the campuses, the KMT was aware that it would need a counter. Consequently, Wang Sheng was shifted within the Bureau, which was still headed by Chiang Ching-kuo, to become the Deputy Section Chief in the Kuomintang Youth Department, the new body which had taken the place of the Youth Corps. His direct supervisor, the Section Chief, was Liu Cheng. Their overriding mission was to organize campus Youth Department branches, drawing, in particular, upon former Youth Army members.

Based in Nanjing, Wang Sheng travelled to universities all over China, setting up KMT anti-communist organizations.

> I found many professors and many youths behaving like drug addicts – wanting to be anti-Kuomintang, anti-Republic of China, anti-US – but having very little knowledge of the issues involved. In this period I learned a lot about communism, how they organized youth to cheat other youth.[43]

The episode which made most impression upon him was his experience at Nanjing Central University, because it seemed such a classic illustration of united front tactics at work. 'It was like an Ivy League School then', Wang Sheng observes. 'It had a very strong staff and good students. In the whole school there were only twelve-and-a-half communists – the one-half, because he wasn't sure! They were good kids and didn't break the rules, but they were behind the communist activities on campus'.[44] Taking advantage of the dire straits in which many students found themselves due to soaring inflation, the communists set up a Student Assistance Movement. Their meetings were normally attended by less than a hundred students (of a student body estimated at more than 10,000), but the organization would work to assist any who were in need. Just as important, it would inquire as to the well-being of their families and then have CCP cadre contact them, also. It endeavored to foster a sense of personal participation by working on group projects designed to generate funds for the organization. At the beginning and the end of each such outing, meetings would be held in which personal situations were linked to the need for structural revolution. From these meetings issued demands directed at the university administration, demands which mobilized support because they were directed at particular issues of concern to the student body in general. At no time did the organization which was actually behind the formulation of these demands label itself as communist, but its key members were CCP operatives.

A university crackdown which banned the organization simply caused the Student Assistance Movement to switch tactics. It became a weekly newspaper rather than a direct action group. Its activities remained the same, and it continued to organize the discontent on campus through its distribution network. Analyzes Wang Sheng:

> It was pure communist propaganda. This is a very typical way in which the communists operated. In the CCP setup, they would use practical experience to train their members. Of those who went through such an experience, about 50 per cent became cadre; 30 per cent said no; 20 per cent were not quite sure. The strength of the system is that the CCP didn't have to spend any money from beginning to end but got its people trained.[45]

Finally, the Department of Student Affairs of the university banned the newspaper, too, as part of a government crackdown on dissent in late October (the legal opposition, the Democratic League, for instance, was banned on 28 October). What happened was predictable:

> The President was a scholar, and the Dean was a generous sort, not experienced in dealing with communists. They just put out the order. The students involved were mad and wanted to create disturbances. They surrounded the Office of Student Affairs, together with onlookers. Someone threatened to beat the Dean, so he ran off. No one was running the place, so the communists took over the school. They did so easily by striking right at the center. And this was what happened to a very good university of thousands – turned into a communist base by a handful of communists.[46]

He continues, drawing upon his Chia-hsing experiences to analyze the situation:

> If I had been Dean, I would have used different methods to

solve these problems. First, I would have taken the CCP newspaper and put it next to the Student Assistance Movement
newspaper to have the students compare. I would ask them
what they want. I would have asked the paper's staff to
explain their purpose: Is the university a place for study or a
place at which to conduct a political movement? Did they
want a communist-run newspaper to disturb the campus? I
would expose their organization. This time, I would say, the
newspapers must only be banned or seized immediately. Next
time, I'll expel you.[47]

His authority, however, was only to organize a group to counter
the communist front organization, not to lead the reclaiming of the
campus. In campus after campus he saw the technique of the
united front at work. It was a crucial lesson: 'The communists
organize two groups, those who believe and those who don't. By
using fronts they are able to get the second to help the first. Chou
En-lai was a master at this. It is the most successful way to recruit
members'.[48] Increasingly, there was no shortage of willing recruits.

'Fighting Tigers' in Shanghai

By early 1948 the Chinese economy was in such serious shape that
any hope the government had in restoring order, whether on the
campuses, where Wang Sheng was active, or elsewhere, had
disappeared. As prices had continued to soar throughout 1947, a
wave of communist-instigated strikes had rolled over major urban
centers. The government promised wages indexed to the cost of
living but, in reality, could do little save keep its printing presses
running. Hyperinflation reached such an extent that ordinary
transactions could not be carried out. In early 1948 a point was
reached at which notes could physically not be created fast enough
to keep up with price increases. Many shops simply closed down.
For all practical purposes, China had become a barter economy.[49]
    Desperate measures were called for. At the heart of the problem
was lack of faith in the existing currency, the *fabi*. Consequently,
though badly split over the wisdom of the measure, the
government decided to replace the *fabi* with a new gold *yuan*
(*chin-yuan ch'uan*) at a rate of 3,000,000 to one. Though it would
not be freely convertible into gold, it was to be issued only to the

extent that it was backed by the precious metal. This was announced on 19 August 1948 as part of a package, the Financial and Economic Emergency Measures (*Ts'ai-cheng ching-chi chin-chi ch'u-fen ming-ling*). The other part of the program was a series of controls on hoarding and speculation. These necessarily were to be applied most stringently in the areas of greatest concern, the major cities, especially Shanghai, Canton, and Tientsin. In each an Economic Supervisor's Office was set up. The official designated to take charge of Shanghai, China's largest financial center, was Yu Hung-chun; his assistant – and in effect the Supervisor – was Chiang Ching-kuo.[50] He arrived in Shanghai in late August (currency exchange actually began on the 23rd). The man he called for immediately as his right hand was Wang Sheng.

Chiang Ching-kuo had been quick to size up the situation. He was being called upon to bring stability to a massive city, the population of which no one seemed to even know. Some sources put it at 3.6 million, others at as high as 6 million. One thing was clear, he could expect little help from the Shanghai administration, headed by Mayor Wu Kuo-chen (more commonly known, particularly in the West, as 'K.C. Wu'). Recalls Kung Chiu-chuan, who emerged as Wang Sheng's own assistant commander:

> Of course we wanted to use official authority, to go through government officers. But Wu Kuo-chen was mayor, a Western-educated scholar oriented towards the capitalist class. He had little sympathy or interest in seeing the success of Chiang Ching-kuo's work. He hated to see Wang Sheng, this low-ranking officer. So he tried every way to make trouble. If we had followed his way of doing things, we would have had no chance save failure. We could not do that.[51]

Adds Tracy T.S. Cheng, who was to play an important role in the Shanghai events:

> In Shanghai then no one in an official position was supporting the reforms, not even the actual government. K.C. Wu was a free economist. He didn't believe in trying to force anyone to do anything. He said so publicly: 'I don't believe in forcing anyone to do anything'. Even the police didn't support us too much.[52]

Hence with Wang Sheng, Chiang Chiang-kuo brought the 6th

Battalion of the Bandit-Suppression National-Reconstruction Corps (*K'an-luan chien-kuo ta-tui*), of which Wang Sheng assumed command. The 6th Battalion, one of eight such units in the country, had a strength of just 100.[53] All, however, were cadres of at least lieutenant rank or above (most were captains); most were former Youth Corps members. Their unit, like its counterparts, had been formed in 1947 upon the merger of the Youth Corps and the KMT. The unwillingness of the young, idealistic Youth Corps members to belong to the same party organizations as those they saw as having lost their revolutionary enthusiasm, had caused many to quit outright. Concerned lest he lose the very talents he looked to for the rejuvenation of the KMT, Chiang Kai-shek ordered that a three-month Bandit-Suppression National-Reconstruction Institute in Nanjing train 1,000 cadres – most but not all recruited from the Youth Corps – in what can best be termed pacification. Organized as eight battalions, the cadres were subsequently deployed to different parts of the country 'to organize and train the masses' in conjunction with military operations.[54] They were to do, in other words, precisely what Chiang Ching-kuo and Wang Sheng had done successfully in Gannan as a systematic part of government counterinsurgency operations. Unfortunately, by the time the concept was tried, the war had become an all-out conventional contest with little room for the 'revolutionary development' component envisaged for the cadres. Instead, they found themselves in Shanghai.

For just as quickly as Chiang Ching-kuo determined that he needed Wang Sheng and cadres, so did it become evident that a single battalion would not be able to influence the situation. Ergo the other seven battalions were brought into Shanghai and placed under an *ad hoc* command structure headed by Wang Sheng, who was made a major-general.[55] He was just short of 33 years, an age he would reach while in Shanghai. His superior, Chiang Ching-kuo, was 38.[56] That Nanjing would commit all of its pacification battalions available nationwide to the 'gold *yuan* reform' struggle in Shanghai was indicative of just how crucial the battle was viewed. If economic conditions could not be turned around there, in the fiscal heart of China, it was gloomily predicted by experts and laymen alike that financial collapse was certain.

In fact, the initial stages of the reform plan went fairly smoothly. Long, orderly lines of citizens exchanged their notes and turned in their gold, silver, and foreign currency, as called for by the regulations. Ironically, the very fact that Nanjing demanded the submission of precious metals helped stoke a renewal of the very inflationary pressures it was seeking to dampen. Simultaneously, this created incentives to hoard and speculate in commodities. Nevertheless, before all this hit home, there was an easing of the situation. Popular confidence was the key, and to win and keep it, Chiang Ching-kuo and Wang Sheng understood that, above all else, the control measures had to be seen as fair, applicable to all. This was to be the role of the Bandit-Suppression National-Reconstruction units. They were used to organize popular participation in the campaign.

Actually, public response had been quite enthusiastic, particularly when the initial measures seemed to be working and brought some relief to the chaos of only weeks before.[57] Those who had not been enthusiastic were the wealthy and the elements of organized crime, aided by corrupt, hostile, or merely indifferent officials. 'Chiang Ching-kuo and Wang Sheng had to combine two tasks', remembers Kung Chiu-Chuan,

> Reform the monetary system and free the people. They were controlled 'down' by the gangsters, 'up' by the big capitalists. Thus we had to fight on two fronts: first, reform the monetary system, which the capitalists were not exactly for; second, fight the gangsters. They combined to resist us. Therefore, when Chiang Ching-kuo came to Shanghai, he faced a very difficult situation from these two groups. He had to face them in different ways. He had to use special methods. Therefore, he used Wang Sheng's organization to get information on hoarding and profiteering.[58]

As soon as Wang Sheng arrived, he appeared with Chiang Ching-kuo at a press conference. There, Chiang Ching-kuo promised fair and equitable distribution of the burden which came with the reform measures; he promised swift and harsh punishment for those who sought to cheat. It was here that he uttered his noteworthy line: 'I would rather see one household weeping than all of the people along a road' – meaning, better to burn a few to spare the many.[59] Subsequently, with an announcement on 9 September 1948,[60] Wang Sheng called upon the youth of the city to rally to the Greater Shanghai Youth Service Corps (*Ta-Shang-hai ch'ing-nien fu-wu tsung-tui*), which they did in droves. Some 30,000 poured in; after screening, 12,000 were given a week's training, during which time they billeted together, then marshalled on 20 September at a large park in the French Quarter. A public ceremony followed on the 25th, at which Chiang Ching-kuo and Wang Sheng urged them on. In this short span of time, the volunteers had been trained and organized by the cadres of the eight battalions, but they provided their own 'officers'.[61] Constituted as 18 'brigades', their mission was to enforce the reform measures. Within a matter of weeks, a network of part-time operatives was thus created. Patrols were instituted, the volunteers wearing armbands, and drop boxes established for anonymous denunciations of those violating the reforms. The only weapons used were the 45-caliber pistols carried as the personal sidearms by the cadre. 'Chiang Ching-kuo and Wang Sheng were overwhelming and strong', says Tracy T.S. Cheng, who became commander of the largest brigade, the 16th, which had 3,000 youths in it. 'They shocked the businessmen, especially the wrongdoers, the gangsters, and the corrupt officers. All were shocked by these two gentlemen. No one thought they could work so hard!'[62]

Indeed, the two drove themselves. Observes Tracy T.S. Cheng, 'Chiang Ching-kuo worked very hard, all day, all night, no lunch. And several times I was with Wang Sheng for days in his office. He never rested, never went to bed'.[63] It was Gannan all over again. Indeed, both envisaged it as such. The aim was not merely to enforce the reforms as a tactical measure, rather to use them to further the revolution, to free the people. 'Even during chaos', notes Kung Chiu-chuan,

> you still can find people who are willing to take up arms to fight for the good of society. Under Chiang Ching-kuo's orders we launched the '12 September Movement' for social reform. We did so from the bottom, to replace government oppression by popular action. It brought people to our side.[64]

It was this appeal to the spirit of the revolution which caused idealistic young people, even at this late date in the civil war, to rally to the KMT's banners. 'I was the assistant chief', Kung Chiu-chuan states, 'and I was only 29. Wang Sheng himself isn't that much older than I. We were all very, very young. We were working for social reform, for a better society'.[65] Agrees Tracy T.S. Cheng:

We were all very young. I was elevated to the Central Committee of the Kuomintang at 26! During wartime we had great responsibilities. So many of us joined the *San Min Chu-i* Youth Corps, which worked closely with the military. We believed in loyalty, righteousness, national salvation – wisdom, knowledge, and right action. Even girls worked against the Japanese. We were so filled with love of the country. I was a graduate of National Chongqing [Chungking] University in Business Administration and was working in the Youth Corps during the war. After the Yalta Conference, when Vice-President Wallace visited Chongqing [Chungking] in 1945, I was the leader of the student movement that presented him with a protest paper. We threw a lot of stones at the American Embassy – and burned the communist newspaper office in Chongqing [Chungking]. We organized ourselves; my wife was one of them. We were enraged that the Yalta Agreement gave Manchuria to the Russians. They robbed all the industry, and a very important man's daughter was raped to death by Russian soldiers. So we attacked the Russian Embassy also. In Shanghai I was a professor teaching at the Shanghai Institute of Commerce, but I was in charge of the student movement for the party. I became involved, because Chiang Ching-kuo asked me personally to become a brigade commander. I participated in the movement, because I thought this was the way to save our country, to put down those bad businessmen and gangsters and corrupt officers.[66]

The enthusiasm was contagious. At a rally held on 'Double Ten' Day, the 10 October anniversary of the Republic, an estimated 100,000 youths appeared. Again, both Chiang Ching-kuo and Wang Sheng spoke, stressing the concept of service to the people and the country, of social justice and equity. Wang Sheng, just 5ft 3in in height and barely 120 pounds, spoke extemporaneously – 'convincing, very emotional, like a big general', as one onlooker recalls. Chiang Ching-kuo and Wang Sheng – they seemed inseparable, one and the same. Kung Chiu-chuan thought so: 'Chiang Ching-kuo told Wang Sheng his thinking. He took the ideas from Chiang Ching-kuo and put them into the pronouncements we used to inspire the youths'.[67] To which Tracy T.S. Cheng agrees: 'They were very, very close. I think all the policy papers were actually written by Wang Sheng after they talked together'.[68]

The mesh was reflected in the manner in which the operation worked. Chiang Ching-kuo occupied himself with policy, interacting with the individuals high and low, and liaised with his father in Nanjing. Wang Sheng directed the actual operations. Probably the most significant tactical decision they reached was that they needed to go after the big fish, not the innumerable small fry who inevitably seemed to bear the brunt of policy swings. Thus they began by moving directly into the 'jungle' which was the seedy side of Shanghai, there to 'fight tigers' (*da lao-hu*). They raided the warehouses of, and arrested, some extraordinarily powerful individuals. That they were not assassinated remains something of a mystery.

Even as the Greater Shanghai Youth Service Corps was being organized, Chiang Ching-kuo and Wang Sheng arrested 'some of the most famous names in Shanghai'.[69] Among them was Tu Wei-ping, son of Tu Yueh-sheng ('Big Eared Tu') who was head of the powerful Green Gang syndicate. A corrupt official with a record judged to be particularly egregious, Wang Ch'un-che, was executed as a warning to others who abused their trust.[70] And in the most daring move of all, they went after one of the biggest 'tigers', Kung L'ing-k'an ('David'), the 'owner' of the Yangtze Development Corporation. In reality, of course, David was merely the overseer for his family interests; the Kungs themselves being tied into the so-called 'Soong dynasty', one of the richest families in the world at that time (if not the richest).[71] David's father, Kung Hsiang-hsi (H. H. Kung), a billionaire by most accounts, had been ROC Finance Minister during the Second World War and was married to Soong Ai-ling, sister of Chiang Kai-shek's wife, Soong May-ling. Soong May-ling's other sister, Soong Ching-ling, was the widow of Sun Yat-sen himself; and still another brother, Soong Tse-ven (T.V. Soong), also fabulously wealthy, had only recently stepped down as ROC prime minister. There were others, the point being that the two intrepids appeared to many to be suicidal.

Yet Chiang Ching-kuo and Wang Sheng were very calculating in their intent. They knew they had to demonstrate that none were above the law. Recounts Kung Chiu-chuan, no relation to the Kung family involved:

> We knew this was a sensitive matter, very sensitive politically. But without this one effort, we would be unable to do anything. Without making an impression with our fairness,

we could not get the trust of the people of Shanghai. I joined in. It was very exciting. There must have been several thousand people. We knew that if we could not do this raid successfully, we would have to surrender to the combined forces of the capitalist money class and the criminals and the corrupt officers. But we did it, so the people trusted us.[72]

They moved, then, but they did so carefully. Wang Sheng personally directed the raid against a group of Kung warehouses denounced as hoarding sugar. (He was to note later, 'We received 4,000 secret reports concerning people hoarding merchandise on a list of seven controlled items. This was just one of them but certainly the biggest target'.[73]) A combined force of Greater Shanghai Youth Service Corps personnel and cadre, military, police, and Central Bank officials surrounded the warehouses and seized them. A large cache of sugar was indeed found, but it ultimately turned out to be for industrial use (i.e. the manufacture of medicine), so it was returned. Chiang Ching-kuo and Wang Sheng were determined to be scrupulously fair. Yet their honesty in this case caused serious public relations difficulties, because it gave the impression of favoritism. More fancifully, it sparked a spate of sensational stories concerning dramatic confrontations and direct intervention by Soong May-ling and even Chiang Kai-shek. According to Wang Sheng, nothing extraordinary happened, certainly no dramatic rescue mission by Madame Chiang Kai-shek or her husband.[74]

Of more concern to Wang Sheng was that something untoward might happen in the normal day-to-day operations involving the myriad searches, checkpoints, and raids to upset the delicate balance in an already tense situation. David Kung, for example, was to figure in another episode which very nearly became a spark the Shanghai kindling did not need. Stopping a car late at night, a Greater Shanghai Youth Service Corps checkpoint found itself facing an outraged David Kung brandishing a pistol. Since none of the checkpoint volunteers were armed, tempers subsided, and an incident was avoided.[75] Still, it did highlight the dangers inherent in any situation where thousands of minimally trained individuals were working long and tedious hours under difficult circumstances. This was particularly so given the indifference or even hostility of many officials connected with the K. C. Wu mayorship. Thus there occurred the anomaly of some officials working openly with the Economic Supervisor's Office while others tried to sabotage its efforts. Astonishingly, given this environment, there seem to have been few complaints of any kind, no doubt because the volunteers were not armed. This, of course, exposed them to a certain amount of risk, and several were killed, particularly as the communists became more aggressive in infiltrating the city.

For Shanghai did not exist in a vacuum; and the initial success of the price controls caused the cost of goods to fall below those in surrounding areas. Thus there was an influx of outsiders – including CCP cadre – coming in to buy. This only created artificial shortages which further undermined the reforms. What is perhaps most surprising is that there is no evidence for corruption ever becoming a factor in cadre and volunteer operations. Certainly both Chiang Ching-kuo and Wang Sheng were offered bribes regularly, the gifts ranging from meals to houses and wealth. Strong-willed enough to turn down the bribes himself, Wang Sheng left nothing to chance where his men were concerned:

> I called my cadre together and told them, 'Shanghai is a difficult place. If you find that I have taken so much as a dollar, you have your pistols and know what to do. If any one of you takes a dollar, I won't even waste a bullet. I'll put you in a potato sack and throw you in the river'.[76]

His words may have worked, but no amount of effort could make the gold *yuan* reform work. Shortages came back, as did galloping inflation, driven by Nanjing's inability to limit its issues of banknotes to finance deficit spending. On 27–28 October 1948 key figures in the government met to reconsider the entire scheme. Chiang Ching-kuo was one of the few arguing in favor of continuing with the plan. Ironically, even as he fought, his cadres waited for him to deliver a scheduled address. Finally, when he did not appear, Wang Sheng telephoned him in Nanjing, only to receive the bitter news that the campaign was over. Wang Sheng returned and gave an impassioned, extemporaneous speech which ended with a version of a page from his past lessons on the American republic, 'This is the time for those of patriotic spirit and strength to rally to the defense of their country'.[77]

It was indeed. On 31 October price controls were lifted, and Chiang Ching-kuo returned to Nanjing. Wang Sheng and the

Bandit-Suppression National-Reconstruction Corps units, however, were asked by the general charged with the defense of the city to remain there to turn their organizing skills into mobilizing the populace as the communists pressed forward. Furthermore, because they had not abused their positions during the control campaign, the cadre continued to have credibility and could work to maintain order as events spun out of control.[78]

End of the Old-Regime

By this time there was no saving the old-regime, as the social science literature would call it. On 8 November 1948 the communists launched the battle for Hsu-chou, the key to the Yangtze and the approaches to Shanghai and Canton themselves. As the Nationalist armies crumbled, so, too, did the country's finances, fatally undermining morale and purchasing power.

> In just two weeks [following the unfreezing of prices] the wholesale index rose over sixteen times...Early in 1949 the gold yuan began to depreciate uncontrollably...By April, the price index stood at over 3,000,000 and the National Government – now having fled to Canton – desperately attempted yet another currency conversion, replacing the gold yuan with a new silver yuan. In just eight months, therefore, the gold yuan had lost virtually all value, just as the fa-pi [*sic*] before it.[79]

Given this dismal end to the 'gold *yuan* reforms', it would be hard to imagine that any good could come out of the experience. Nevertheless, 'Shanghai' profoundly affected the youths who took part. Paramount, there was the shared sense of purpose, the feeling of fighting for a just cause against overwhelming odds – and actually winning for a time. Furthermore, the nature of the 'loss' was such that it hardly seemed to the cadre to have anything to do with *them* so much as factors and individuals beyond their control. Analyzed Kung Chiu-chuan: 'To build up a new society, you must have a new people with a new heart. A new world must be built by new men'.[80] Lack of success, then, further reinforced the world view of young stalwarts such as Kung and Wang Sheng: the people had not been revolutionary enough. Despite their best efforts, they had not been able to reach the hearts and souls of too many 'bad elements'.

In this realization, too, there were practical lessons to be drawn. Kung puts it simply, 'We learned in Shanghai that what is most important is that the economy cannot be controlled by any particular authority or any one force'.[81] Tracy T.S. Cheng notes this same point and elaborates :

> The lessons we drew from our Shanghai experience have been fundamental to what we have done here on Taiwan. First lesson: Economic activities cannot be controlled by political measures. Attempting to control and plan the economy is no good. Economic activities can only be built up by incentive, not by control. As a result of his experience, Chiang Ching-kuo understood this very well, and he was the main influence on Chiang Kai-shek. That's why [on Taiwan] Chiang Kai-shek handed over all economic decisions to economists. The second lesson Chiang Ching-kuo learned was the value of youth. From this time on, we see a new emphasis upon them. It was General Wang, himself then a young person, who invented the political warfare system to inspire the people. The 'Shanghai spirit' was a very important part of this. In Shanghai, Chiang Ching-kuo had no organization, no people, because the government organization did not support him. He had only Wang Sheng and a few others, no others but these. But he needed to implement the controls. What could he depend upon? Only the revolutionary spirit, the mass movement organization – and his will to struggle [for justice]. This is what I mean by 'youth', not just young people. Third, we learned all about the personnel system. To carry out any policy you must have people. These people must be trained. And their promotion, decoration, and assignment must be very fair. Finally, the need to avoid corruption was also a lesson. The big families tried so many times to bribe Wang Sheng, but he refused. And when Kung's warehouse was taken over, it was Mr Wang who also stood by it to make sure nothing was stolen.[82]

Implementation of these lessons learned, however, would have to wait for another day. In the Republic on the mainland, it was but a matter of time before the end came. Massive battles in the north during autumn and early winter 1948–49 had already decided the military issue.[83] Fruitless negotiations made clear that the CCP would settle for nothing short of unconditional surrender and the punishment of leading 'war criminals', to include Chiang Kai-shek himself, his wife, and leading members of the Soong and Kung families.[84] On 21 January 1949 Chiang resigned the presidency and retired to his native town, Chikow in Fenghua county of Zhejang (Chekiang) Province, south of Shanghai. He was succeeded by his vice-president, Li Tsung-jen, who sought to revive peace talks. The next day, the 22nd, the Nationalist forces in Peking surrendered. In Chikow, Chiang Kai-shek's security was provided by elements of Wang Sheng's 6th Battalion, which remained under his direct control.

Wang Sheng, despite his decade of association with Chiang Ching-kuo, had never met Chiang Kai-shek. Even while providing his security, at the behest of Chiang Ching-kuo, no relationship was struck. Indeed, the only time Wang Sheng actually came face to face with the elder Chiang was apparently on 12 February 1949. Wang Sheng was talking with Chiang Ching-kuo when Chiang Kai-shek entered the room. He only greeted Wang Sheng before being informed by Chiang Ching-kuo that his longtime political associate, T'ai Ch'i-tao, had died due to an overdose of sleeping pills the night before. 'He walked around the courtyard', Wang Sheng remembers. 'He was very unhappy'.[85]

Yet Chiang Kai-shek did not let his unhappiness interfere with his plans for continued resistance. Already, he had decided upon Taiwan for a last stand and was having it fortified. KMT headquarters was transferred there in August 1949. In addition to preparations for its defense, Chiang Kai-shek had transferred to it numerous government records, art treasures, and the gold accumulated in Shanghai during the 'gold *yuan* reform'. The latter was to become the basis for Taiwan's monetary system, the former for a continued Nationalist government; given the devastating results of the various iconoclastic episodes which followed in the decades of communist rule on the mainland, the art treasures were to concentrate much towards preserving China's artistic heritage. It is the gold, of course, an estimated $300 million, which has captured the imagination of some.[86] Neither Wang Sheng nor his men played any role in its transfer.[87]

Meantime, Li Tsung-jen's efforts to negotiate with the CCP had come to nothing. He gave in to some communist demands, among them that the Bandit-Suppression National-Reconstruction Corps be disbanded, but there was no middle ground to be had.

On April 21, Liu Po-ch'eng's Second and Ch'en Yi's Third Field Armies crossed the Yangtze on a 300-mile-wide front and took Nanking [Nanjing] on 27 May, Foochow on 17 August, and Amoy on 17 October. On 16–17 May, Lin Piao's Fourth Field Army captured the Wuhan cities and moved south, taking Changsha on 5 August, Canton on 14 October, Kweilin on 22 November, Nanning on 4 December, and, finally, in April 1950, Hainan Island, which since the 1920s had been partly controlled for the Communists by Feng Pai-chu.[88]

This irresistible progress (see Map 6 for some guidance) was met with feeble countermeasures. As refugees poured south, communist operatives mingled with them and hampered what resistance the Nationalists could still mount. Ironically, the communists themselves played a hand in snatching Wang Sheng and his 6th Battalion – now 'reorganized' as a Political Work unit – from the jaws of fate in Shanghai. Under the reorganization scheme, they were ordered to Nanchang, where they arrived in March 1949. There, the former 6th Battalion was folded into the also-reorganized Rebellion-Suppression National-Reconstruction Brigade operating in Jiangxi. Its tasking was essentially that under the previous name, pacification. Wang Sheng, still with the acting rank of major-general, became the commander of this new 3rd Political Work Brigade, though his formal position was as the KMT's Jiangxi Provincial Secretary.[89] It was a throwback to his Gannan days when, as political officer and inspector, he had maneuvered the militia battalion so successfully. His chief of general provincial security was none other than Liu Jing-shing. Yet now circumstances had changed radically, and the Nationalist forces were in full retreat. Internal security became increasingly difficult to maintain. Only days after he entered Nanchang, Wang Sheng saw his headquarters sabotaged, destroyed by fire. Finally, after a month in Nanchang, the Ministry of National Defense ordered him to fall back to Ganzhou with his brigade and the Jiangxi KMT personnel.

After just two weeks, in April, new orders sent them all to Canton, where the Nanjing government moved as the communists attacked across the Yangtze River. First, however, 3rd Political

MAP 6
CIVIL WAR IN SOUTH CHINA – 1949

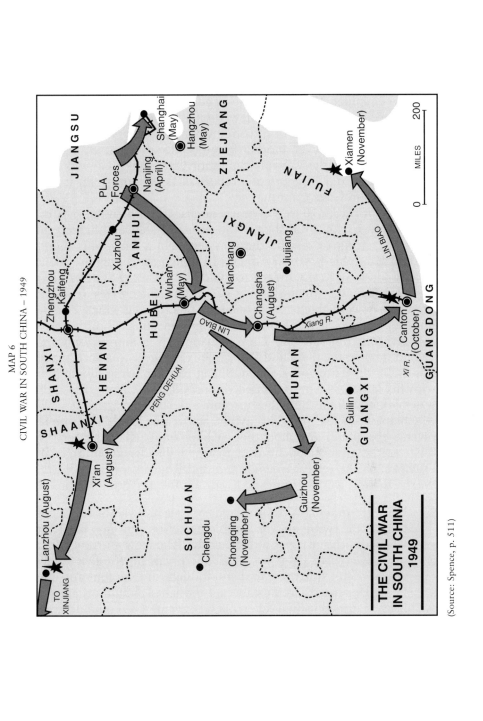

**THE CIVIL WAR
IN SOUTH CHINA
1949**

(Source: Spence, p. 511)

Work Brigade had to assist in the evacuation from Nanjing, assigning a cadre to each hundred families for organization of their movement. Using rail and truck, it was able to get everyone out, then to organize Canton for absorption of the influx. A brief respite occurred before the renewed CCP assault made it obvious that Canton would be cut off from the rest of China (refer again to Map 6). This led to yet another long-distance evacuation, in June by truck, back to the wartime capital of Chongqing (Chungking). The 3rd Political Work Brigade repeated its Nanjing role; it was the last unit to leave Canton.

The political situation was nearly as chaotic as the military rout. Eventually, Chiang Kai-shek, who was on Taiwan, agreed in November 1949 to resume the presidency. In a dangerous flight, he returned to his 1940–45 capital of Chongqing (Acting President Li flew to Hong Kong, thence to exile in the United States). Thus Wang Sheng and Chiang Ching-kuo found themselves reunited again. They were able to have one long talk, during which Chiang Kai-shek walked in while breaking from a meeting with his corps and division commanders. They exchanged pleasantries, only the second time on the mainland Wang Sheng was ever to meet Chiang Kai-shek.[90] In Chongqing, Wang Sheng found Chiang Ching-kuo with his father. Having resumed the presidency, Chiang Kai-shek was talking with all the military commanders of the area.[91]

Chiang Kai-shek's presence, while heartening, could do little to reverse the situation. Chongqing (Chungking) fell in November 1949 as the government moved to Chengdu, deeper in Sichuan Province. In the retreat, the 1st and 2nd Brigades of the Political Work Division were cut off and captured. Relates Wang Sheng:

> We were moving further inland. My brain was not sufficient to grapple with all the problems. I lost all my hair! At Chengdu, the city was in total chaos. The New Currency [i.e. the 'silver *yuan*'] was no good; there was no food. It was a very difficult situation. Yet I still thought the Kuomintang had hope. Under the circumstances, I thought I should organize a brigade armed to fight guerrilla war against the communists.[92]

In quintessential Wang Sheng fashion, he made his proposal to do just this; first, in writing to the Ministry of National Defense; then, receiving no response, in person. His battalion commanders continued to press him. Returning to the relocated Central

Military Academy in Chengdu, he attempted to see Chiang Ching-kuo or Chiang Kai-shek. They were not there, having already gone to Taiwan. Instead, he was met by General Shu Huan-shen, later to become head of the ROC Air Force but then commanding the local air base, who delivered Chiang Ching-kuo's handwritten orders that he was to follow him to Taiwan.

It was an agonizing moment. Wang Sheng was not concerned about his family – by this time his wife had given him a daughter and three sons – because he had sent them to Taiwan when the government left Nanjing.[93] Rather, he was worried about his unit. They had not only been together a long time. He carefully briefed the deputy brigade commander on possible overland escape routes, then obeyed his orders. He went to Taiwan via Hainan island. Shortly afterwards, communist forces occupied all of Sichuan (Szechwan). His narrow escape was small comfort for Wang Sheng:

> I understood Chiang Ching-kuo's intentions: if I was caught, I was a dead man. We had always been involved in rear area work, and I was well known to the communists by this time. But on my way to Taiwan I felt awful, because I couldn't bring my cadre with me. Many later waged guerrilla war, as we had planned, and a majority got out, especially through Burma. I couldn't know that then. I felt depressed, gloomy, sorry, that I couldn't bring my soldiers. I felt I couldn't face my country. I thought I would give up government work. My wife would teach high school. I would teach college – study, teach, write.[94]

It was not to be. Wang Sheng had become too valuable to the Republic and to Chiang Ching-kuo.

NOTES

1. Robert E. Bedeski has recognized this irony. See e.g. his *State-Building in Modern China: The Kuomintang in the Prewar Period*, pp. viii-ix: 'The historical dilemma of the KMT was that in creating a State it had to assemble a monopoly of force. Until a State exists as a unified coercive apparatus, it lacks political substance. A government in exile is not a State, nor is it a national liberation movement. One might even argue that civil rights have no political status without some sort of State apparatus to guarantee and adjudicate those rights. Lenin, Kropotkin, and Weber attributed a monopoly of legal force to the State. Those who exercise force without the express consent of the State (i.e., criminals, bandits, and rebels) do so illegally. In the case of KMT China, the incompleteness of the monopoly of force – not the misuse of force – was the major cause of failure'.

2. See e.g. Kenneth E. Shewmaker, 'The "Agrarian Reformer" Myth', *China Qtly*, 34 (April–June 1968), pp. 66–81; Joseph W. Esherick, 'Number Games: A Note on Land Distribution in Prerevolutionary China', *Modern China*, 7/4 (Oct. 1981), pp. 387–41; Randy Stross, 'Number Games Rejected: The Misleading Allure of Tenancy Estimates', *Republican China*, X/3 (June 1985 sp. issue), pp. 1–17; David Faure, 'The Plight of the Farmers: A Study of the Rural Economy of Jiangnan and the Pearl River Delta, 1870–1937', *Modern China*, 11/1 (Jan. 1985), pp. 3–37; and Linda Gail Arrigo, 'Land Concentration in China: The Buck Survey Revisited', *Modern China*, 12/3 (July 1986), pp. 259–360. Also useful is K.C. Yeh, *The Chinese Communist Revolutionary Strategy and the Land Reform Problem, 1921–1927*, Memorandum RM-6077-ARPA (Santa Monica, CA: Rand Corp., April 1970).

3. This line of inquiry, it is recognized, is fraught with peril. While we may debate the extent to which factors uniquely 'Chinese' influenced events, we ignore this dimension altogether at our peril. Lloyd Eastman has dealt with the subject sensitively, also placing emphasis upon the degree to which loyalty was directed towards persons or factions rather than abstract principles, in his *Abortive Revolution*, pp. 295–311. Also useful is Eastman as discussed in review by Susan Mann Jones, *Comparative Politics*, 72/1 (March 1978), pp. 309–10.

4. See e.g. Chiang Kai-shek as explained by Eastman, *Abortive Revolution*, pp. 1–30. Several typical analyses by Chiang Kai-shek: 'The Chinese revolution has failed. My only desire today is to restore the revolutionary spirit that the Chinese Kuomintang had in 1924' (in 1932; p. 1); or 'The reason [revolutionary forces had been unable to take Hopei and Shantung] is that the revolutionaries have become degenerate, have lost their revolutionary spirit and revolutionary courage. And the basic reason is that, after those individuals got to Nanking, they developed erroneous thoughts of struggling for power and profit, and are no longer willing to sacrifice' (p. 5)

5. In Ch. 2, I have highlighted the military decimation of the KMT, while mentioning the critical role played by the regime's losing access to its resource base. Just how critical was such loss has been discussed by several sources; e.g. Arthur N. Young, *China's Nation-Building Effort, 1927–1937* (Stanford, CA: Hoover Instn. Press, 1971). Therein, he illustrates (for a telling summary, see his chart on p. 73, 'Distribution of Revenues, 1929–1937') how the Republic almost completely depended on the manufacturing and trade sectors for its revenue. Having lost these virtually entirely to the Japanese, yet nonetheless forced to fight a war, the regime found itself unable to solve its fiscal problems.

6. Interview with Wang Sheng, 27 July 1993 in Taipei.

7. Cf. Steven Levine, *Anvil of Victory: The Communist Revolution in Manchuria, 1945–1948* (New York: Columbia UP, 1987).

8. James Pinkney Harrison has put this well in his *The Long March to Power: A History of the Chinese Communist Party, 1921–72*, p. 394: 'Reliance on activists among the people for recruits, supplies, intelligence, and general support had been a basic feature of Communist strategy since the mid-1920s, but the propaganda, organizational, and military techniques for "people's war" that had been worked out over two decades really bore fruit in the "third revolutionary civil war". Naturally, they did so unevenly and primarily in certain areas where the Communists were able to consolidate their support. In most of the country, traditional practical concerns continued to prevail, but in crucial areas in the late 1940s, especially in North China and Manchuria, the Communists were able to use the "mass line" as a decisive weapon'.

9. Numerous sources are available for the military particulars of the civil war, among them: Whitson (Ch. 2, note 29); Liu (Ch. 2, note 48); E.R. Hooton, *The Greatest Tumult: The Chinese Civil War 1936–49* (New York: Brassey's [UK], 1991); and Trevor N. Dupuy, *The Chinese Civil War* (New York: Franklin Watts, 1969).

10. The discussion on inflation in Jonathan D. Spence, *The Search for Modern China* (New York: Norton, 1990), pp. 498–504, is quite useful, esp. the tables. They demonstrate

that between Sept. 1945 and Feb. 1947, the Shanghai wholesale price index went from 100 to 3,090; pegged again at 100 in May 1947, it reached 11,100 by July 1948; returned to 100 in Aug. 1948, it was 40,825 by Feb. 1949. For the long-term consequences, see Chang Kia-ngau, 'War and Inflation' in Pinchon P.Y. Loh (ed.), *The Kuomintang Debacle of 1949: Conquest or Collapse* (Boston: D.C. Heath, 1965), pp. 23–6. Therein he provides startling figures, 'based on statistics compiled by Directorate-General of Budgets, Accounts and Statistics' (see esp. Table 27 on p. 24). The Shanghai index, for example, with January–June 1937 pegged at 100, had reached 4,635,700 by Sept. 1947 ('the last month for which the wholesale price indexes of major cities were published by the government'). In a city such as Tsingtao, it was at 6,304,000. Principal causes of this spiral were uncontrolled government spending financed in the main by the printing of bank notes. For the war years specifically, cf. Arthur N. Young, *China's Wartime Finance and Inflation, 1937–1945* (Cambridge, MA: Harvard UP, 1965).

11. Young (supra), pp. 318–20. Observations for 1937–45 are appropriate in a discussion of the civil war, as well, when the trends he identifies became still worse. He notes, in part (pp. 318–19): 'The heaviest burden of inflationary finance fell upon those receiving salaries or payments that were more or less fixed; and first and foremost of these was the army...The effect on the army's morale and value as a fighting force was grave...About 20 officers *monthly* were deserting from one division [observed by two European Red Cross doctors 1941–42] for economic reasons' [emphasis added].

12. Harrison (note 8), p. 424.

13. Heinlein, 'Political Warfare' (Ch. 2, note 97), pp. 437–43. Though he relies upon various sources, the particular 'take' he gives to events comes from Charles F. Romanus and Riley Sutherland, *The History of the China-Burma-India Theater*, 3 vols. (Washington, DC: Dept. of the Army, 1959), esp. pp. 247–49 in vol. 3, *Time runs out in CBI*. These volumes, part of the US Army's official history of the Second World War, are presented by Heinlein as a 'primary source', which patently they are not. It would also seem, given the strained relations which prevailed throughout the war between Chiang Kai-shek and the American advisory effort (to put the matter in its best light), that a more skeptical weighing of the official history's evidence would have been in order.

14. Ibid., p. 438. The source of this information, again, is the US Army's official history (see note 13 above).

15. Interview with Wang Sheng, 27 July 1993 in Taipei.

16. Chiang Ching-kuo's command of the Russian language caused him to be used extensively in the negotiations with the Soviets concerning both their intentions towards Manchuria and the details of the Sino-Soviet Treaty of Friendship and Alliance signed in 1945. The latter, lengthily negotiated in Moscow, was from the Chinese perspective not sufficient but improved on the Yalta terms – many details of which had been kept from China but were revealed by Stalin in secret talks. The central point upon which no Soviet-Chinese agreement could be reached was the status of Outer Mongolia; it remained in the Soviet orbit. See Li.

17. What Chiang Kai-shek should have done, in other words, was adopt the French 'oil spot' technique of pacification: focus upon particular regions and secure them completely before moving on, thereby avoiding dissipation of effort and resources. Cf. Douglas Porch, 'Bugeaud, Gallieni, Lyautey: The Development of French Colonial Warfare', Ch. 14 in Peter Paret (ed.), *Makers of Modern Strategy from Machiavelli to the Nuclear Age* (Princeton, NJ: Princeton UP, 1986), pp. 376–407.

18. See e.g. Chiang Kai-shek's 16 April 1926 speech at Whampoa as related in Heinlein (Ch. 2, note 97), pp. 172–4.

19. Cf. Dan N. Jacobs, *Borodin: Stalin's Man in China* (Cambridge, MA: Harvard UP, 1981).

20. Heinlein (note 13), devotes the bulk of his work to demonstrating this very fact; but then, in important parts of his analysis, reaches conclusions which could only be so if

there was a degree of competence and focus that his own evidence suggests the KMT did not possess.

21. Cf. Chiang Kai-shek, '*Chung-yang kan-hsiao ch'eng-li tian-li chi yen-chiu-pu ti-yich'i k'ai-hsueh tian-li hsun-tz'u*' ('Address at the Ceremony Establishing the Central Cadre Academy and First Research Class') in *Chung-yang kan-pu hsueh-hsiao yen-chiu-pu ti-yi ch'i pi-yeh shih-chou-nien chi-nien t'e-k'an* (*Special Issue Commemorating the Fortieth Anniversary of the Graduation of the First Research Division of the Central Cadre Academy*), pp. 11–14.
22. Heinlein (note 13), p. 441.
23. Ibid., pp. 395–6: 'The manual served as a basic reference document for the political officer, listing in one place the many regulations and the background material pertinent to his job. It contained an exposition of Sun Yat-sen's philosophy, subsequent interpretations of Sun's theses by Chiang Kai-shek, current rules and regulations, and a chapter on examples of practical experiences of political workers in the past'.
24. Harrison (note 8), pp. 369–70.
25. Interview with Wang Sheng, 27 July 1993 in Taipei.
26. Interview with Chang Tsun-wu, former Youth Army member, 26 July 1993 in Taipei.
27. Interview with James C.C. Chan, former Youth Army member, ibid.
28. Interview with Ju Chong-huang, former Youth Army member, ibid.
29. Interview with Chang Tsun-wu, former Youth Army member, ibid.
30. Interview with Chang Shr-jieh, former Youth Army member, ibid.
31. Interview with Wang Sheng, 2 July 1994 in Carmel, California.
32. Cf. 'Paying Homage to a Man of Lofty Virtues – Philosopher Fang Tung-mei's Impact on General Wang', 1; typescript in translation, nfd.
33. Interview with Chung Ming-fung, former Youth Army member, 26 July 1993 in Taipei.
34. Interview with Ju Chong-huang, former Youth Army member, ibid.
35. See p. 370 of Fang Ch'ing-yen, 'Wang Sheng during the Pre-Taiwan Period', in 'Chiang Ching-kuo in Southern Jiangxi (Gannan)' section of *Jiangxi Historical Records Selections* [Manchang], No. 35 (Aug. 1989), pp. 369–74 (orig. in Chinese; David A. Suter trans.). As with much of the material from the mainland, this selection contains some useful data while simultaneously slanting its presentation to place the subjects in an unfavorable light. The consistency with which the phrase 'created a tense atmosphere' appears in mainland accounts dealing with KMT figures is revealing.
36. Interview with Hwa Lee-jin, former Youth Army member, 26 July 1993 in Taipei.
37. For details cf. Harrison (note 8), Ch. 18 ('The Third Revolutionary Civil War Begins'), pp. 366–93.
38. Ibid., p. 391: 'Some seventy per cent of the Nationalist budget was still going to military expenses, and, by the end of 1946, the government had lost one-half of its gold reserves. During the same year, prices rose 700 per cent'.
39. In the immediate aftermath of World War II, the US had some 113,000 troops in China, 53,000 of whom were Marines. Most were concentrated in the north pursuing missions connected with the surrender and repatriation of Japanese armed forces, which in China alone numbered more than a million men. Throughout the conflict, American involvement with and support of the established government had been extensive. It was not surprising, then, that by mid-1946 the CCP had initiated direct attacks against US forces. In the most well-known incident, in July 1946, a small Marine convoy was ambushed between Tianjin and Peking, resulting in four Marine dead (three on the scene, one later of wounds). Less well-known was the assassination on 25 Aug. 1946 of John Birch, after whom the right-wing society was named. Aside from residual contingents, however, all American forces had been withdrawn by early 1947. Cf. ibid., p. 391; Spence (note 10), pp. 488–91.
40. Eastman, *Seeds of Destruction* (Ch. 2, note 9), p. 106.
41. Interview with Wang Sheng, 13 July 1993 in Taipei.
42. An excellent – and absorbing – discussion of the interplay between CCP tactical and

strategic concerns may be found in Harrison (note 8), pp. 394–420 (Ch. 19: 'The Party and the North China Land Revolution').

43. Interview with Wang Sheng, 27 July 1993 in Taipei.
44. Ibid.
45. Ibid.
46. Ibid.
47. Ibid.
48. Ibid.
49. Eastman (note 40), p. 173 states: 'The economy of Nationalist China during 1947 and much of 1948 was in a terrible state: the fabric of rural society was faltering; the transportation system was in a state of continual disrepair (largely owing to Communist sabotage); and inflation was daily eroding the value of the fa-pi, the national currency..'.
50. The best account of the larger events in this episode is Eastman, *Seeds of Destruction* (note 40), Ch. 8 ('Chiang Ching-kuo and the Gold Yuan Reform'), pp. 172–202. Though many of his details may now be corrected and expanded upon, this in no way detracts from the masterful job he has done in piecing together a very complicated episode. An alternative look, far more colorful and designed to appeal to a mass audience, is to be found in Seagrave (Ch. 2, note 41), pp. 425–29. It must be used with caution but contains some shrewd insights.
51. Interview with Kung Chiu-chuan, now professor at Tamkang University, 12 July 1993 in Taipei.
52. Interview with Tracy T.S. Cheng, now professor at National Taiwan University, 14 July 1993 in Taipei.
53. Eastman, *Seeds of Destruction* (note 40), p. 184 translates the 6th Battalion as the 'Sixth Large Corps'. This stems from his misinterpretation of the term *ta-tui* (see his character listing on p. 304). He translates it literally, when in reality *ta-tui* is the equivalent of the military unit *ying*, or battalion. While *ying* is used to refer to a field unit, *ta-tui* is used for administrative or school units. Thus today the cadet battalions in ROC military schools are *ta-tui* rather than *ying*, but they are decidedly not 'large corps'. The same problem can arise in translating *K'an-luan chien-kuo ta-tui* (Bandit-Suppression National Reconstruction Corps), because in some circumstances the *ta-tui*, being the headquarters element for several battalions, could become 'regiment'. In the present context, however, Eastman is correct in opting for 'corps'. He is incorrect in asserting that there were six *ta-tui* nationwide; there actually were eight.
54. Interview with Wang Sheng, 5 July 1994 in Carmel, California.
55. It is uncertain whether this promotion, which was made by Chiang Ching-kuo, was ever recognized officially in orders. Wang Sheng himself is not clear on the point: 'I was promoted to major-general and just called 'general'. Usually you're known by your position, not by your rank. I was still the 6th Battalion Commander, but I had been tasked with coordinating the activities of all the battalions. MND [Ministry of National Defense] might not even recognize the promotion I received'. (Interview with Wang Sheng, 27 July 1993 in Taipei.) It may be further noted that the rank Wang Sheng received, 'major-general', would be in the US system a one-star equivalent, or a brigadier general. The Nationalist system had no brigadier-general, however. From colonel an officer became a major-general, entitled to wear one star; subsequently a lieutenant-general, entitled to wear two stars; finally, a general second grade followed by a general first grade, both of whom wore three stars (refer to note 1 of Ch. 1). Only Generalissimo [Field Marshal] Chiang Kai-shek had four stars. Confusion is minimized by bearing in mind that the Nationalist structure, as with most armies, had five grades of general, regardless of actual title and insignia of rank.
56. Eastman, *Seeds of Destruction* (note 40), p. 180 lists Chiang Ching-kuo as 39; but if his birthdate is correct as utilized in this study, 18 March 1910, he would have been 38-and-a-half in Sept. 1948. Wang Sheng, as per Ch. 2, has a birthdate of 28 Oct. 1915, so he would have turned 33 during the Shanghai campaign. The point, of course, is that

they were both very young yet already quite experienced.

57. Ibid., pp. 173–4: 'During just the two and a half months from late May to mid-August [1948], prices in Shanghai increased approximately ten times. Rice, which had sold for Y6.3 million on May 26, sold for Y63 million on August 18; peanut oil during the same period increased from Y18.5 to Y195 million; and soap rose from Y7 to Y83.5 million'.

58. Interview with Kung Chiu-chuan, 12 July 1993 in Taipei.

59. Interview with Wang Sheng, 27 July 1993 in Taipei. A different version of the same phrase, apparently a clumsy translation, appears in Wang Sheng, *What I know about Chiang Ching-kuo*, 32: 'Let one family cry, instead of having all the people crying on the road'. The meaning is the same.

60. This is the date used by Eastman, *Seeds of Destruction* (note 40), p. 184. Tracy T.S. Cheng, however, recalls it being on 10 Sept. (Interview, 14 July 1993 in Taipei). Eastman appears to have arrived at his date through use of newspaper accounts, so I have given it precedence.

61. Ibid., p. 184 has the numbers right but has misconstrued their relationship. He apparently did not realize that the Bandit-Suppression National-Reconstruction Corps battalions were comprised of cadre, who were used to mobilize, organize, and train the volunteers of the Greater Shanghai Youth Service Corps. Hence he puts the Bandit-Suppression National-Reconstruction Corps strength at 30,000, which is actually the number of volunteers who appeared; he has correct the 12,000 youths who were actually inducted into the Greater Shanghai Youth Service Corps. Again, his date of 25 Sept. appears to have been gained from press clippings, so I have used it instead of 20 Sept. which Tracy T.S. Cheng recalls as being the date of the induction (Interview, 14 July 1993 in Taipei). Eastman further identifies Wang Sheng, the overall commander, as 'a longtime close friend of Chiang Ching-kuo', which I would claim overstates the relationship as per my earlier discussion in Ch. 2.

62. Interview with Tracy T.S. Cheng, 14 July 1993 in Taipei.

63. Ibid. In another portion of the same interview, Cheng observed: 'Wang Sheng had been well trained by the military. He was very spartan and worked very, very hard. Sometimes he could not even sit down to eat. The same with Chiang Ching-kuo. I cannot work that hard. I'm not a military man'.

64. Interview with Kung Chiu-chuan, 12 July 1993 in Taipei.

65. Ibid.

66. Interview with Tracy T.S. Cheng, 14 July 1993 in Taipei.

67. Interview with Kung Chiu-chuan, 12 July 1993 in Taipei.

68. Interview with Tracy T.S. Cheng, 14 July 1993 in Taipei.

69. Cf. Eastman, *Seeds of Destruction* (note 40), p. 188; Seagrave (note 50).

70. Apparently some other individuals were executed after trials. Military courts martial were used for a list of special crimes; elsewise, a suspect, if a civilian, was tried in the regular courts. Interview with Wang Sheng, 5 July 1994 in Carmel, California.

71. Cf. Seagrave (note 50), *passim.*

72. Interview with Kung Chiu-chuan, 12 July 1993 in Taipei.

73. Interview with Wang Sheng, 27 July 1993 in Taipei.

74. Interviews with Wang Sheng, 27 July 1993 in Taipei and 5 July 1994 in Carmel, California. For a highly dramatic version, cf. Seagrave (note 50).

75. Interview with Wang Sheng, 5 July 1994 in Carmel, California.

76. Interview with Wang Sheng, 27 July 1993 in Taipei. Wang Sheng further noted, in the same interview: 'Of the 15,000 youth we had under us, not one was corrupt. No one reported a case. No Chinese complained about our troops. One guy dropped a pistol, which discharged and hurt someone. Some of these individuals later became Political Warfare officers. They made very good officers. Some did all sorts of heroic things. Many were killed after the communists took over'.

77. Ibid.

78. Ironically, it is in discussing the Shanghai episode that Fang Ch'ing-yen, *op.cit.* is most

credible and accurate in particulars. This is understandable when one considers the language used by many of those interviewed in this work (e.g. Wang Sheng himself and Kung Chiu-chuan). It is apparent that the communists and the youth fighting on the government side shared a mutual animosity towards the 'big capitalists' they saw as indifferent both to the suffering of their own people and to the revolution.

79. Eastman, *Seeds of Destruction* (note 40), pp. 194–5.
80. Interview with Kung Chiu-chuan, 12 July 1994 in Taipei.
81. Ibid.
82. Interview with Tracy T.S. Cheng, 14 July 1993 in Taipei.
83. Cf. Harrison (note 8), pp. 423–4.
84. Spence (note 10), p. 510: 'Mao's eight points were stark: (1) punish all war criminals; (2) abolish the invalid 1947 constitution; (3) abolish the Guomindang's legal system; (4) reorganize the Nationalist armies; (5) confiscate all bureaucratic capital; (6) reform the land-tenure system; (7) abolish all treasonous treaties; (8) convene a full Political Consultative Conference to form a democratic coalition government'.
85. Interview with Wang Sheng, 28 July 1993 in Taipei. In this interview, Wang Sheng related the incident. I have based the date on the time of the T'ai Ch'i-tao suicide given by Seagrave, *op.cit.*, 442.
86. See e.g. Seagrave (note 50), pp. 440–1.
87. Interview with Wang Sheng, 27 July 1993 in Taipei.
88. Whitson (Ch. 2, note 29), p. 426.
89. Interviews with Wang Sheng, 28 July 1993 in Taipei and 6 July 1994 in Carmel, California.
90. Interview with Wang Sheng, 28 July 1993 in Taipei.
91. Circumstances surrounding both Chiang Kai-shek's stepping down from the presidency and his resumption of power are discussed in Sidney H. Chang and Ramon H. Meyers (eds.), *The Storm Clouds Clear Over China: The Memoir of Ch'en Li-fu 1900–1993* (Stanford, CA: Hoover Instn Press, 1994), pp. 209–11. Ch'en Li-fu, of course, was at one time Chiang Kai-shek's personal secretary and rose to hold important positions prior to 1950.
92. Interview with Wang Sheng, 28 July 1993 in Taipei.
93. Wang Sheng does not recall how he learned that Taiwan 'was the goal of our retreat', but it would seem logical to presume that Chiang Ching-kuo informed him during Chiang Kai-shek's 'retirement' from government. Wang Sheng, after all, was providing the security for the Chiang household.
94. Interview with Wang Sheng, 28 July 1993 in Taipei.

4 Taiwan: Revolution in Exile

Leadership of a revolution in exile: Chiang Ching-kuo at center, Wang Sheng at right, during a 1952 inspection of offshore islands.

EVEN AS resilient a man as Wang Sheng could be expected, under the circumstances, to ponder the hand fate had dealt him. Hardly past 35 years old when he arrived in Taiwan in early 1950, he had already experienced as much as many men would know in a lifetime. Certainly the KMT's enemies knew who he was. 'In Chengdu', writes Fang Ch'ing-yen, a mainland writer who claims to have served with him, 'Wang Sheng continued his secret police work. He had his few remaining subordinates arrest, interrogate, torture, and bury alive suspected communists'.[1] The compliment lay not in the doctored history but in the fact that the CCP saw the need to discredit him at all. He had obviously been a thorn in their side.[2] Now, a brigade commander without a unit, he could do little save watch his world turn upside down.

This it did rapidly. Chiang Kai-shek, who had returned to Taiwan on 10 December 1949 with Chiang Ching-kuo, resumed the presidency formally on 1 March of the new year. Less than a week later the first communist troops landed on Hainan Island. Fighting for this last major KMT 'mainland' redoubt went on throughout that month and the next, with the evacuation of the last Nationalist forces from there occurring on 2 May. By 16 May another 150,000 troops had also been brought to Taiwan from the Chousan Islands. They joined those already there and the hundreds of thousands of refugees who had poured in. Ultimately, somewhere between one and two million displaced persons – most sources put the figure at 1.2–1.5 million – crowded into a space not even twice that of Jiangxi (35,834 sq. km. instead of 23,000 sq. km.), which already had a population of 6.8 million.

Conditions were both precarious and difficult. Taiwan had still not recovered from the dislocation of the Second World War, particularly the disruptive effects of the Japanese departure after a colonial interlude of half a century.[3] To this had been added the chaos of 'liberation' itself, when a multitude of factors, notably corruption and misunderstanding, had culminated in widespread disorder and repression which left at least 8,000 dead in 1947. Remembered thereafter simply as '*er-er-ba*' ('two-two-eight', or the 28 February Incident), it had been anything but an auspicious beginning to a new era of Taiwan's history and opened up wounds which fester to the present.[4] In the wake of the KMT's collapse on the mainland, though, the most pressing issues were those of livelihood and imminent invasion.

Amidst such chaos and uncertainty, Wang Sheng was not even

sure where his family was. He eventually located them, only to learn that tragedy had struck. As Wang Sheng had worked in the April 1949 evacuation of Nanjing, he had sent Hu Hsiang-li to take the children to Taiwan through Ningbo, the Zhejiang (Chekiang) city linked to the port at Zhenhai. Units were using Zhenhai to retreat to Taiwan. Struggling to make her way amidst a crush of movement, Hu Hsiang-li had her three sons – Kung-tien, Pu-tien, and Hsiao-tien, the eldest of whom was just five, the youngest but a month. Her sister had the only daughter, Po-er, who had been born after the eldest son.[5] The family became separated, and Po-er was left, to be raised, first by the aunt, then by Hu Hsiang-li's mother.[6]

Indeed, tragedy had nearly been visited upon the family twice. The strain of the ordeal upon Hu Hsiang-li, still not recovered from Hsiao-tien's birth, was multiplied when the ship they were on could not immediately land in Keelung (also rendered as Chi-lung or Jilong; see Map 7). Exhausted, trying to control a fidgety Kung-tien, she gladly accepted the help of a soldier who took Pu-tien off her hands for a moment. A swell, an awkward plunge of the ship; Pu-tien and the soldier found themselves thrown overboard even as the vessel plowed ahead. The soldier and a fishing boat saved the day. Pu-tien was restored to a frantic Hu Hsiang-li. Finally allowed to land, the family attempted to reach their regroupment area in T'ai-chung (Taizhong) by rail. Their adventure was not yet ended, because an exhausted Hu Hsiang-li, sick and very weak, did not awake as the train rolled through their destination. Far off the mark, they stepped down in Chia-i (Jiayi) and took another train back to T'ai-chung. There they stayed until word finally came that Wang Sheng, too, was alive.[7]

In the months ahead, more bad news was to follow. It had been a brutal civil war, fought between contending visions of revolution. Victory for the CCP on the battlefield, though, was just the beginning of its effort to transform society. Many cadre from the Youth Corps, Youth Army, and Greater Shanghai Youth Service Corps were identified and executed. Longnan itself was caught in the whirlwind. Wang Sheng's teacher at Nanfang Institute of Chinese Literature, Liao Cheng-pu – the man who had been so influential in forming his young pupil's world-view – was killed. So, too, was the anchor of Wang Sheng's youth, his eldest brother:

MAP 7
TAIWAN PROVINCE

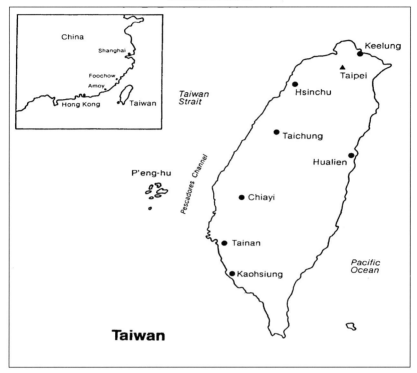

(Source: Copper, p. xi)

After the communists took over, my brother was tortured to death. He was generous, plain spoken, and upright. When the communists came, they classified him as a counter-revolutionary. They also knew that his younger brother, I, was an anti-communist element. So he was put on a work crew and sent up into the mountains to make charcoal. But there were neither trees nor food. He was worked to death. The death of my brother...[unable to continue]. I did not resist the communists simply because our national leadership said to do so. I saw at first hand what they did. People such as me could not even receive a good education, because the communists caused turmoil. They ruined areas where they were and forced people to lead hard lives. The communists were behind our [national] ruin.[8]

Still, there was good news, too. The other surviving members of his family, elder sister Wang Hsiang-feng and younger brother Wang Chien-hu, were not harmed. Furthermore, as units sorted themselves out and rosters were compiled, it became clear that any number of his former associates had made their way to Taiwan. There were compatriots from the Central Military Academy's Class 16 and the Central Cadre Academy, to include the philosopher Fang Tung-mei; from the Gannan campaign, men such as Liu Jing-shing and Kung Chiu-Chuan; from the Youth Corps and the Youth Army, among them Li Huan and a good many who had been at the Chia-hsing Middle School; from the Greater Shanghai Youth Service Corps, Kung Chiu-chuan and Tracy T.S. Cheng headed a list of survivors;[9] and from his 3rd Political Work Brigade there were men who had come out through Burma.[10] As the KMT struggled to bring order to the mass inflow, Wang Sheng helped all those he could. Recalls Central Military Academy classmate Lin Jung-chu, who eventually became a lieutenant-general, 'He helped all he had known to find work. He even took money from his own pocket for them'.[11]

For all who knew him, such action was typical of Wang Sheng. He was absolutely loyal to all those, superiors or subordinates, who were loyal to the ideals of the revolution. Now, in exile, he was again to be called into its service.

Reorganizing the Revolution

Chiang Ching-kuo called Wang Sheng in March 1950 and said that he wanted him to assume a position in a new 'Political Work Department' he had been tasked by his father to set up. A reconstitution of the previous 'political warfare' apparatus which had long existed in the Chinese military, the body was to breathe life into a system of 'political officers' which had been allowed to languish. Renamed the Political Work Department in 1950 – and ultimately the General Political Warfare Department (GPWD) in 1963 – it was to have six divisions (see Figure 1).[12] Chiang Ching-kuo asked Wang Sheng to become the Deputy Director of the Fifth Division, or P-5, that concerned with 'Civil-Military Programs, Welfare, and Services'. To do so, he was to revert to his official rank of colonel and work under a major-general.[13] As one of several such deputy directors in his division, Wang Sheng's specific task was laying the foundation for a Chinese Youth Anti-Communist League (CYACL), or simply the China Youth Corps, as it came to be termed. This was the *San Min Chu-i* Youth Corps reborn, but its essence was to be directed far more towards mobilization and youth development than party work. Wang Sheng did his task successfully and consequently was moved by Chiang Ching-kuo in September 1950 to the First Division, P-1 (Organization, Training, and Personnel), as a Deputy Director. It was a crucial assignment, for what Chiang Ching-kuo had underway was nothing less than the retooling of the entire KMT apparatus, both civil and military.

FIGURE 1

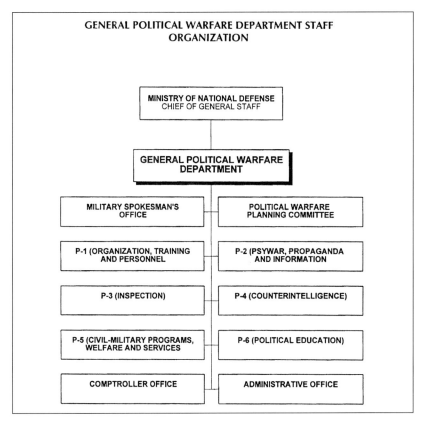

GENERAL POLITICAL WARFARE DEPARTMENT STAFF
ORGANIZATION

MINISTRY OF NATIONAL DEFENSE
CHIEF OF GENERAL STAFF

GENERAL POLITICAL WARFARE
DEPARTMENT

MILITARY SPOKESMAN'S OFFICE

POLITICAL WARFARE PLANNING COMMITTEE

P-1 (ORGANIZATION, TRAINING AND PERSONNEL)

P-2 (PSYWAR, PROPAGANDA AND INFORMATION)

P-3 (INSPECTION)

P-4 (COUNTERINTELLIGENCE)

P-5 (CIVIL-MILITARY PROGRAMS, WELFARE AND SERVICES)

P-6 (POLITICAL EDUCATION)

COMPTROLLER OFFICE

ADMINISTRATIVE OFFICE

Source: *General Briefing on Political Warfare System in the Chinese Armed Forces,* p. 4. as modified.

This, of course, was not solely his doing but also that of his father, Chiang Kai-shek. It has long been known that the elder Chiang's 'retirement' to Chikow was in reality a stepping away from the day-to-day business of running the government and that he continued to be involved in party matters, even to the detriment of Li, the acting president. What has been far less understood is precisely what Chiang Kai-shek saw himself as doing during those months. The most common explanations combine personal pique and Machiavellian calculation for a future recall upon his terms. These could well have been factors. Yet such analyses ignore Chiang Kai-shek the *revolutionary*. His demands upon those engaged in the great Kuomintang endeavor with him, the quest for a nation ruled and prospering in accordance with the *San Min Chu-i*, had never wavered. His displeasure as his would-be followers failed to measure up had been equally consistent, vocal and explicit. By early 1949, he had already decided that the mainland phase of the civil war was lost. Further, he felt he knew precisely the reason: lack of revolutionary commitment, of *sincerity*, which showed itself in myriad ways, ranging from corruption to factionalism to simple incompetence. This most traditional of analyses was virtual tautology: we have failed, because we are weak; because we are weak, we have failed. He had made this point in his famous 1932 utterance, 'The Revolution has failed. My only desire today is to restore the revolutionary spirit that the Chinese Kuomintang had in 1924'.[14] He had never stopped believing this. What Chiang Kai-shek did in Chikow, though, was to work out, apparently in close consultation with Chiang Ching-kuo, the mechanics of restoration. On Taiwan, these were put into operation.

Writes Bruce J. Dickson:

> Few political parties have the opportunity to make a fresh start in a new location. An organization is rarely able to leave the environment in which its lessons are learned and apply them in a new one. However, the Chinese Kuomintang (KMT) encountered this situation after its defeat on the Chinese mainland and retreat to Taiwan. From 1950 to 1952, the KMT underwent a thorough organizational restructuring.[15]

Chiang Kai-shek wasted no time. As outlined by Dickson,[16]

Chiang Ching-kuo (left) and Wang Sheng (center) talk to members of the China Youth Corps during summer training.

by 20 September 1949 a formal announcement on party reform had already been issued in Taiwan, the product of a small, ten-man working group of KMT leaders who in mid-June of the same year had been instructed by Chiang to begin examination of rectification. There followed, in January 1950, the setting up of a reorganization study group which worked out details of implementation. Their plan was approved by the Standing Committee of the Central Executive Committee, the KMT's highest organ, on 22 July 1950.[17] The timing was fortuitous, because the outbreak of the Korean War on 25 June, followed by President Harry Truman's 'neutralization' of the Taiwan Straits with the US Seventh Fleet, ended emphatically the danger of immediate invasion from the mainland. So precarious, in fact, had been the Nationalist position, that Washington – which had played such a key, though to the Chinese frustrating, role in the civil war – had effectively written off the Chiang regime.[18] Now effectively sealed off, it could test its reform program as in a laboratory. In a sense, it was a return to Gannan, and many participants who had been through both were later to articulate their experience in such terms.

In one sense, the level of the residual 'bandit' threat, the two situations were not comparable. Yet neither was Taiwan a clean slate as concerned the population. Pacification of a recently liberated populace, many members of which remained sullen and resentful; severe problems of social disorder and economic dislocation; and a shattered administrative structure; these were all elements which would have been recognized by any of the cadre who had served with Chiang Ching-kuo in Gannan. There also remained at large numerous communist infiltrators and agents, thousands of whom would either be detained or give themselves up in the years ahead. Most fundamentally, morale was low and defeatism rampant. It was clear to Chiang Kai-shek that his course was the correct one: he would change the values of individuals so that they would act virtuously through institutions of service. Always his fear had been that the very act of refashioning would expose his position to a mortal thrust from his opponents. The US Seventh Fleet became a key intervening variable which allowed him to proceed.

On 5 August 1950 a Central Reform Commission (*Zhongyang gaizao wei-yuanhui*, or CRC[19]) was formed, comprised of 16 members, all relatively youthful. It 'took over all administrative functions that had previously been invested in the Central Standing Committee and the Central Executive Committee. These two bodies were disbanded with the explanation that their formal terms of office had expired.'[20] Led by the original Youth Corps Secretary-General, Ch'en Ch'eng, a Whampoa faction leader, the CRC set to work on a multitude of fronts, all directed at forging a viable KMT capable of functioning in a revolutionary manner. Party members, for example, were required to re-register within 20 days, and they were then investigated and evaluated. Undesirables were expelled. To lift the party itself out of the realm of virtual honorary fraternity to functioning organization, members were assigned to cells – the workplace was the basic organizational block, though different life circumstances (e.g. the countryside) resulted in different 'basic-level organizations'. Meetings and courses of instruction became mandatory. Through a disciplined, indoctrinated cadre, the KMT was to dominate the institutions of the state and society.

This, at least, was the model, and it was nothing less than an effort to establish a Leninist party in the fashion Chiang Kai-shek had originally envisaged when he recommended adoption of the *form* to Sun Yat-sen. There was a crucial distinction, however, which went to the heart of how the Nationalists saw themselves as distinct from the communists, despite the outward similarity of their Leninist infrastructures. In the Soviet Union the party, though it did serve as a means for the propagation of communist ideology, was principally a means of political control. Such could hardly be otherwise, because the core of the Marxist persuasion was not a prescription for politics but a socio-economic analysis. *Leninism* gave this analysis its political shape and practices. In contrast, in the exiled Republic, the KMT served for the propagation of a core argument, *San Min Chu-i*, which itself already espoused not only a socio-economic philosophy but also a scheme of political organization justified by a complete political philosophy. In reality what Sun Yat-sen had set down, in numerous works, only one of which was *San Min Chu-i* (itself a series of lectures), was an all-encompassing philosophy which discussed the entire socio-economic-political universe of China at the time he wrote. It was to be implemented through *democracy*. Though the democracy of the KMT vision was certainly élitest, it was neither vague nor unspecified. It was articulated through both a governmental framework – which, in addition to the usual Western tripartite division of executive, legislative, and judicial, added 'control' and 'examination' functions[21] – and a schedule for implementation – a period of military administration, to be followed by those of, first, political tutelage, and, finally, constitutional government.[22] Moreover, since it rested upon popular sovereignty – as given power through a system of electoral, oversight, and recall mechanisms – it was bound to be capable of both subversion and regeneration, if these terms are considered in their broadest definition. It was precisely this quality which made it 'revolutionary'.

What Chiang Kai-shek sought, then, was not 'commissars' but 'clergy'. Again, one realizes that Chiang Kai-shek's own personal inadequacies, particularly his lack of organizational finesse, were quite irrelevant to the philosophical thrust of his approach. What was more important, as had been demonstrated time and again on the mainland, he felt, was to build into the system mechanisms for producing pragmatic sages, those both versed in *San Min Chu-i* and capable of carrying out the tasks necessary for any modern nation-state to function. That he, as Sun Yat-sen's heir, would have to direct the task at hand he undoubtedly did not question; he was the *heir*. Yet it is unlikely that he ever interpreted this role in a distinctly *political* sense. This was important, for it brought to a Leninist political system a socio-economic value structure rooted in a quest for individual perfection and social justice as opposed to the mere exercise of power. Placed in historical context, it was the 'mandate of heaven' reified in democratic mechanisms which were designed to allow the ouster of the new mandarinate. Even if judged imperfect in implementation, such a philosophy surely carried the seeds of destruction for a Leninist system which sought to perpetuate its hold on power or to abuse its mandate.

This was the manner in which Wang Sheng, among others, interpreted his political reality. His son, Pu-tien, was to observe, 'My father told me once that as long as Chiang Ching-kuo works for the country, for the people, I will die for him. But if he works only for himself, I will not follow him'.[23] It was this *conditionality* of loyalty which was unique for a Leninist party. It was actually latent in KMT ideology. Thus there was no doubt in Wang Sheng's mind that it was indeed the revolution which the reform of the party was designed to serve. Every mechanism, even the key personnel, echoed the vitality and sincerity of the Youth Corps, that particular aspect of the Kuomintang experience which had fired the imagination of so many young people.

As the reform proceeded, the local representatives of the process became the party, just as the Youth Corps had been used in Gannan to revitalize the weary and dysfunctional elements of the system. As concerned Wang Sheng directly, not only was Chiang Ching-kuo (now 40 years old) himself on the CRC, he was also the head of the crucial Cadre Training Commission (see Figure 2). It was he who was charged with designing the particular mechanisms for insuring that KMT cadre lived up to the expectations of his father and the party's ideology, *San Min Chu-i*. To assist him, he selected for the actual membership of the commission a small group, one of whom was Wang Sheng.[24] Together, they launched an ambitious training program whereby all civilian and military cadre were reindoctrinated, beginning with the most senior and working down to the lowest levels. These courses were anywhere from two to twelve weeks; their content depended upon both the level of personnel being taught and their functional specialties. Always, though, the emphasis was upon political content as laid out in *San Min Chu-i*. For comparison, communist materials were used; more directly, so were certain CCP methods such as self-

FIGURE 2
ORGANIZATION OF THE CENTRAL REORGANIZATION COMMISSION

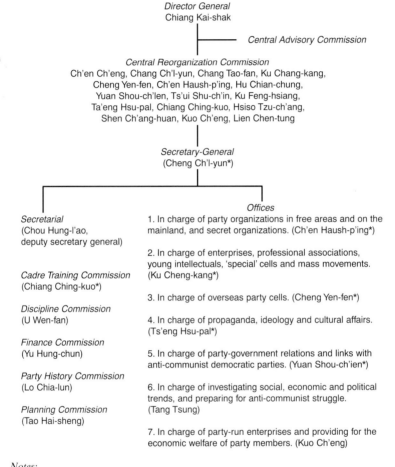

Notes:
Heads of offices and commissions in parentheses; * indicates concurrent membership of CRC.
Sources:
Adapted from Xu Fuming, *Zhongguo Guomindang de gaizao, 1950–1952 (The Reorganization of the KMT, 1950–1952)* (Taipei: Cheng Chung Book Co., 1986), p. 65; names of heads of offices and commissions from Qin Xiaoyi [Ch'in Hsiao-yi] (ed.), *Zhongguo Guomindang jiushi nian dashi nianbiao (A 90-Year Chronology of the KMT's Major Events)* (Taipei: KMT Central Committee, Party History Commission, 1984), p. 443.

(Source: Dickson, p. 66).

criticism. Simultaneously, permanent centers were created to institutionalize the training procedures and course contents. The capstone for civilians was the Revolutionary Practice Institute (*Geming shixian yanjiuyuan*) at Yangmingshan,[25] which continues today. Similarly, an Officers Training Institute, which later became the Armed Forces Staff College, worked with all officers of middle grades and above. This effort was distinct from that designed to retrain the military's political officers themselves. Comments Wang Sheng:

> We were putting Political Warfare cadre through two-week training cycles. It took us almost one year to retrain all who made it to Taiwan, just to get them ready for current requirements. We trained the company-grade Political Officers in their units. All battalion and above cadre were brought in to Tansui [near Taipei] to be retrained. We built an assembly hall and four battalion buildings. Thus our first job was to train existing Political Warfare cadre, then to train new cadre, for which we started a new school. I said we needed a proper staff and buildings. So we got this place and started to set things up. Chiang Ching-kuo was the Class Director. I was the Deputy Director. Chiang Kai-shek came in to look. He said nothing, but then came the order that they wanted our base for 'the Western company' – the CIA – to train the people to go back to the mainland. So we moved to Beitou [also in present Taipei]. We took the name *Fu Hsing Kang*, which means 'Restoration Hill Base'. The site we got had been a horse racing track. According to local lore, it was where the Japanese tortured prisoners during the Second World War. How to start such a school? We had no model, no money, no teachers, no doctrine. There was no such school in the world, so the difficulty you can visualize.[26]

What was founded on 1 July 1951 was called the Political Staff School, which in October 1970 would be renamed the Political Warfare College or '*Fu Hsing Kang* College'.[27] Its mission was to produce 'political officers' who, assigned to military units and other designated positions, would perform a multitude of functions – ranging from counterintelligence to dependent welfare – normally divided, at least in foreign armies, such as the American, amongst numerous proponent agencies (see Figure 3).

FIGURE 3
US – ROC POLITICAL WARFARE STAFF COMPARISON

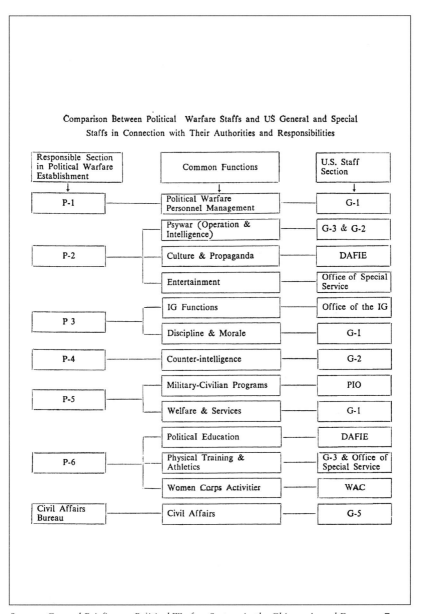

Comparison Between Political Warfare Staffs and US General and Special
Staffs in Connection with Their Authorities and Responsibilities

Responsible Section in Political Warfare Establishment	Common Functions	U.S. Staff Section
P-1	Political Warfare Personnel Management	G-1
P-2	Psywar (Operation & Intelligence)	G-3 & G-2
	Culture & Propaganda	DAFIE
	Entertainment	Office of Special Service
P 3	IG Functions	Office of the IG
	Discipline & Morale	G-1
P-4	Counter-intelligence	G-2
P-5	Military-Civilian Programs	PIO
	Welfare & Services	G-1
P-6	Political Education	DAFIE
	Physical Training & Athletics	G-3 & Office of Special Service
	Women Corps Activities	WAC
Civil Affairs Bureau	Civil Affairs	G-5

Source: *General Briefing on Political Warfare System in the Chinese Armed Forces*, p. 7.

Given the turbulence which had attended the entire 'political' structure throughout its history, particularly during World War II and the Civil War, the only recent example was possibly the use of political officers in Youth Army units. Regardless, Chiang Ching-kuo, as the head of the General Political Warfare Department (hereafter, GPWD, a label which enjoys wide usage in Taiwan today), forged ahead. He appointed air force Lieutenant-General Hu Wei-k'e as the commandant of *Fu Hsing Kang.* Beneath him was an assistant commandant, or Provost (also translated as Dean), overseeing four directors responsible for, respectively, general affairs, education, student affairs, and troop command. Chiang Ching-kuo transferred Wang Sheng from GPWD to the school as the Director of Student Affairs. He was 36 and still a colonel.

Taken at face value, this would seem a strange assignment for a 'right hand man'. Yet it reveals much of the Taiwan milieu, both organizationally and culturally. One facet of the environment was the sheer chaos which prevailed. Consequently, anyone who could perform competently was tasked to his limits, as we have seen was the case previously when the KMT was on the mainland, regardless of his formal position. Wang Sheng's entire career illustrated this principle. His latest move to *Fu Hsing Kang* was no different: 'At that time a lot of people knew that Chiang Ching-kuo was paying attention to the project, so they wanted to become involved. I told them to go for it, but Chiang Ching-kuo told me to do it. Thus I had to come up with everything'.[28] Yet such tasking could not always be recognized through the formal awarding of rank and position, both for cultural reasons of face and for the very practical consideration that Taiwan was a closed system. Where were discards to go, save perhaps to fester as malcontents who might ultimately endanger national security or internal stability? A delicate balance thus had to be maintained between systemic efficiency and personnel considerations colored by all that was 'Chinese'.[29] Certainly there was a degree of operational inefficiency introduced, but it was considered a necessary price to pay for social harmony. Thus, for Wang Sheng:

> Chiang Ching-kuo assigned me this division [Student Affairs], because he considered it the critical position. The spirit of the students was the most important thing. I had to come up with a complete set of procedures for making this a reality. Things were very difficult, because the mainland experience had left

Chiang Ching-kuo personally calls roll at the Political Staff School, later to become the Political Warfare College, *Fu Hsing Kang*. Wang Sheng, Director of Student Affairs, is at right.

Wang Sheng leads celebration of *Fu Hsing Kang*'s second anniversary in 1952.

us in terrible shape. We had nothing but obstacles. Yet this
made morale very high, because we had to make everything
ourselves. Initially, the first commandant of the school was an
air force general. This was a particularly difficult period,
because he knew little about political warfare or education.[30]

Political Warfare versus Intelligence

Difficulties, though, came in more than one form. Physically and
intellectually, Wang Sheng was tasked to the limit. Even prior to his
transfer, Wang Sheng had been assigned by Chiang Ching-kuo to
the effort to revamp the intelligence services. Another oxymoron,
the 'intelligence' community on the mainland was a further
reflection of KMT factionalism, neither a community nor devoted
entirely – if even in the main – to the production of intelligence
through analysis of information gathered. Instead, there were two
main bodies, both termed in the literature 'Bureau of Research and
Statistics', but one, *Chung-t'ung*, connected to the KMT's
Organization Department, which itself fell under the Central
Executive Committee (and hence the normal term, the Central
Bureau of Research and Statistics); the other, *Chun-t'ung*,[31] to the
Military Affairs Commission of the government (hence termed the
Military Bureau of Research and Statistics). From the scanty
evidence available, it would appear the former engaged in more
intelligence work than the latter, which quickly became deeply
involved in 'direct action' under the Dai Li referred to several
times previously. It was incorrect, however, to impute too much
significance – in an organizational, factional, or functional sense –
to this split, because at the apex of the very short chain of
command for each was Chiang Kai-shek. Thus the two
intelligence services were arms of the same body. Nonetheless, they
had become competitive to the detriment of efficiency and product
quality, a situation which had to be remedied.[32]

Wang Sheng, by virtue of his position, rank, and age, should
have remained outside such considerations. That he was involved
at all was because Chiang Ching-kuo had asked him to be his
deputy in the effort; that Chiang Ching-kuo was involved was
because he had been charged by his father with rectifying the
problem. Chiang Kai-shek was well aware of the sensitive nature
of security services. The 'father' of KMT intelligence, if anyone is

Political Warfare remained quite distinct from the organs of internal security. On the contrary, it emphasized the fostering of allegiance. Here, Wang Sheng inspects an artistic works brigade.

to be labelled as such, was Ch'en Li-fu, the younger half of the 'C.C. Clique', who in certain respects had served Chiang Kai-shek in much the same fashion as Wang Sheng was called upon to do for Chiang Ching-kuo. Beginning as Chiang Kai-shek's personal secretary, his competence and energy gradually cast him as the elder Chiang's premier troubleshooter in a series of increasingly responsible and sensitive positions. These included taking the post of Secretary-General of the Kuomintang Central Executive Committee, as well as forming the original, untitled intelligence organization which ultimately became the unit called Combined Reporting on Investigation and Statistics. It was this which had split in 1938 into the *Chung-t'ung* and the *Chun-t'ung*.

As often happens, however, there could not always be eye-to-

Chiang Ching-kuo
(right) and Wang
Sheng (left) reorga-
nized and retrained
the ROC intelligence
services, but Wang
Sheng declined to
become their head.

eye agreement on all matters. Increasingly, as the situation on the mainland became ever more difficult throughout the Anti-Japanese and Civil Wars, and as Ch'en Li-fu became a figure in his own right, he found himself at odds with Chiang Kai-shek in subtle, often unstated ways. These may have been as much in Chiang Kai-shek's mind as in reality, for Ch'en Li-fu continued to serve as a loyal subordinate in task after task. Indeed, it was he who had done the initial legwork in getting the Central Reform Commission off the ground – and who, together with his brother, had offered to step aside because they had been important in the unsuccessful defense of the mainland. Yet he does not appear to have anticipated Chiang Kai-shek's decision to marginalize him completely. He was not even listed as a member of the Central Advisory Commission to the CRC, though his brother Kuo-fu was. Neither does he seem to have grasped that his 'faction' was being cleared away so that KMT unity could be established. He went into voluntary exile in the United States but remained on good terms with Chiang Ching-kuo, with whom he had long been friendly. He was to return to Taiwan in 1970 at the invitation of both the Chiangs and thereafter remained active as a senior KMT advisor and promoter of Chinese culture.[33]

The parallels to Wang Sheng again loom large. For the amalgamation and retraining of the intelligence services eventually went so well that Chiang Ching-kuo asked Wang Sheng if he would assume control of them. 'I said', Wang Sheng relates, 'that to do such a job, I would have to have 100 per cent loyalty to the country and the people – and 100 per cent ruthlessness. I felt I couldn't be ruthless in that manner. I'm too forgiving. So I went back to Political Warfare'.[34] Years later, too, Chiang Ching-kuo, dissatisfied like his father with the performance of the Kuomintang, would ask Wang Sheng, who then had risen to much higher heights, to become Secretary-General of the party. Again, Wang Sheng would refuse. His reasons were illuminating: 'I said no, because [if I accepted the position] people would think Political Warfare was involved with intelligence. I wanted it clean. [By then] Political Warfare people were known as able, competent, as very just people who had not been corrupted'.[35]

Extraordinary about this statement is that the reality, as it developed under Wang Sheng, matched the sentiment. He may indeed have been summoned repeatedly to perform key tasks for the KMT as embodied in Chiang Ching-kuo – who, it should be clear, was emerging at this time as the heir apparent and as the party linchpin – but he marched to his own drummer. In making him the linchpin of Political Warfare, first behind the scenes and, finally, directly, as we shall see in the pages ahead, Chiang Ching-kuo was putting into play a man with very distinct philosophical views of his own. These would profoundly affect the shape of modern Taiwan. Where Chiang Kai-shek saw the new Political Warfare scheme as a means to guarantee the loyalty of a military which had only recently demonstrated the contrary (and its incompetence), Wang Sheng, working with Chiang Ching-kuo, envisaged something a step beyond, an organization which insured loyalty by winning allegiance rather than merely guaranteeing it through oversight. For this an élite cadre of virtual knights was needed, Jesuits armed on a quest for a Grail, missionaries of *San Min Chu-i* issuing forth from *Fu Hsing Kang* College, figures who would serve as the embodiment of all that was best in the KMT. To do this they had to remain monastically apart, at least in structure. Hence, while Wang Sheng would accept any task given to him, he did not want his troubleshooting to entangle his new cadre organizationally in other functional components. It was a principle he would adhere to religiously. He was never to become either a Ch'en Li-fu or a Dai Li.

He could well have been, had he chosen to be. There was ample opportunity for able individuals to rise as the Republic was rebuilt and direct conflict still continued with the communists. True, the American security blanket ended the immediate threat of invasion, and Washington had declined Chiang Kai-shek's offer of troops to fight in the Korean War. Yet the US had agreed to open up a second front using the KMT personnel in the Golden Triangle area of Southeast Asia, where they had been driven at the culmination of the Civil War. Reinforced, these remnants of two divisions were not particularly effective at causing military concern for Peking but did succeed in providing useful intelligence. Inevitably, they also became involved in the drug trade of the region, which created a peculiar mix of sanctioned and unsanctioned activities carried out by personnel directly under Taipei's control and others who had long ceased to respond to orders.[36] It was the resulting 'gray', the blending of right and wrong, which Wang Sheng wanted no part of. The Intelligence Bureau of the Ministry of National Defense (IBMND), that organization which had grown out of *Chun-t'ung*,[37] was in the field with the KMT remnants; and ROC welfare programs were directed by Political Warfare personnel rotated into the area. Yet it was doubtful Taipei (or the CIA, for that matter) ever 'controlled' the situation on the ground.

Regardless, it was an operational effort which was not in what Wang Sheng increasingly took to be his area of specialty: Political Warfare.

This he defined thus:

> War is basically an act of violence in which both sides exert maximum efforts for the purpose of defeating, subjugating and rendering the other side helpless. During the course of the conflict both sides employ violence and weapons to seek victory. In addition, they use every means at their disposal to develop the maximum efficiency of this violence. At times, they *resort to nonviolent activities* and are able to achieve victory. Political warfare is this type of warfare [my italics].[38]

If the role of the officer, then, as traditionally conceived, was the management of violence,[39] the political warrior was to be the expert in the management of non-violence in the pursuit of military aims. His sights were to be trained upon six possible target audiences: civilians in friendly areas; civilians in enemy areas; his own forces; enemy forces; overseas Chinese; and foreigners. The techniques and the content of Political Warfare tools would be slightly different for each. Always, though, the central focus was to remain upon multiplying combat power.[40]

To cite several examples: As the Northern Expedition (1926–27) led by Chiang Kai-shek moved to unify China, its way was smoothed by teams of propagandists and agitators, acting under the control of Political Departments at the major command level headquarters. The Political Departments were further charged with insuring the loyalty of the armies themselves. Ironically, the key individual in this effort – the KMT representative in the Front Political Department, the apex body for this field testing of Political Warfare – was at the time none other than the CCP's Chou En-lai, who was working with the KMT as part of the first united front. The KMT 'army', to recall, was but an alliance of rival groups. Only certain units were 'KMT'. Most came from warlord allies. Hence only those KMT units with non-communist Political Officers were considered totally reliable by Chiang Kai-shek, which highlighted still another facet of 'political warfare' – a commander had no units if they were loyal to another cause. Interestingly, while the ideological message of KMT and CCP propaganda and agitation teams might differ, the methodology they used was fairly standard. And the goal was the same, to multiply combat power. In still another example, one brilliant in its simplicity of design but operationally overwhelming in its impact, revolutionary agitators would foment labor unrest amongst railway workers so that opposition warlord troops could not join the battle. There were innumerable other tactical gambits which could be played, limited only by the imagination.[41]

Wang Sheng built upon this legacy. He conceptualized the field by noting that 'political warfare included warfares of strategy [how to outwit the enemy at the strategic level], ideology [how to promote one's own ideology and discredit that of the enemy], organization [how to foster the growth of organizations within society so as to make them resistant to enemy penetration and exploitation], psychology [how to use propaganda to change the attitudes and behavior of the enemy], intelligence [how to collect information about the enemy and prevent him from doing the same] and mass [how to mobilize the masses to fight against the enemy]'.[42] The point, therefore, was: 'Military warfare alone cannot achieve sustained power and victory. The integration of the six warfares is the decisive factor'.[43] A discipline such as economics, of course, was also critical for battlefield success, but its study and implementation had advanced to the point that it had its own body of specialists – economists. Likewise, what Wang Sheng termed 'offensive intelligence' had become such a 'science and art' that it had its own practitioners and had spawned independent *intelligence* agencies. *Counterintelligence within the military*, in contrast, was still within the realm of Political Warfare; it was the only aspect of 'intelligence warfare' with which Political Officers would be involved. Intelligence officers would have their own chain of command.

While intelligence operations – as the term is commonly understood – were not a part of Political Warfare, nevertheless Political Warfare could certainly influence the practice of intelligence. Disunity within the intelligence community, for instance, or even disloyalty, would render it impotent. Hence Wang Sheng, acting throughout 1951 and into 1952 in response to Chiang Ching-kuo's orders, oversaw the rectification of the 'spiritual orientation' of the intelligence apparatus, while simultaneously implementing organizational rationalization. 'Shih-pai was the location, near where the Veteran's Hospital is today', he recalls. 'Since I was an outsider, setting up this school was very hard. In the morning, I'd be raising the flag at *Fu Hsing Kang*, then having breakfast at Shih-pai. Neither I nor Chiang Ching-kuo had any intelligence training'.[44]

It was not necessary. The lessons to be learned were of the mind:

> The training program taught them four things: First, to think alike, to consolidate into one stream. Second, to accept that people could transfer within units and between units. Third, to understand the danger the country was in: 'Your every intention must be that you are here to serve the country'. Intelligence people are not to start rumors, to cheat others, or to lie to them. Fourth: You don't fight against your own people. This is very shameful and not moral.[45]

To absorb this message, the 'Shih-pai class', as Wang Sheng referred to it, was broken down into eight terms of four weeks each. All intelligence personnel were rotated through one term each. 'We were instructors', says Wang Sheng, 'but in classes we didn't teach about intelligence techniques'. What was desired was a transformation of the spirit, not an enhancement of technical expertise. 'Only a few of the faculty came from the Political Warfare Institute', he continues. 'Most came from local universities. We also got government officials and senior members of the party who were knowledgeable and had good morality'.[46]

Predictably, such exhortations could not eliminate factionalism altogether, but certainly the training given to the intelligence personnel helped. Just as fundamentally, organizational lines of command, authority, and communication were greatly simplified, and the rival organizations and functions were consolidated in a manner which had hitherto been the case, at least in twentieth-century China, only with the CCP.

Reconstructing a Revolutionary Weapon

Chiang Kai-shek closely studied his adversary and, we have noted, even adopted some of its methodologies. Yet he did not intend that the Kuomintang become a CCP clone. This would be impossible, because while he admired the sense of *revolutionary* commitment displayed by CCP cadre, he saw their organization as built upon deception. In contrast, he wanted KMT cadres who were equally committed but whose organization was built upon a foundation of Chinese core values. This would be the true revolution. Thus organizational flaws stemmed from the failure to embrace core values. The reasons for the revolution's defeat on the mainland, Chiang Kai-shek pointed out to KMT listeners, did not stem from any source save its own internal weaknesses. It was a theme he returned to repeatedly in public and private utterances throughout and after the Civil War period. Eastman, for example, has recorded a telling January 1948 speech by Chiang Kai-shek:

> To tell the truth, never, in China or abroad, has there been a revolutionary party as decrepit (*tuitang*) and degenerate (*fubai*) as we [the Guomindang] are today; nor one as lacking spirit, lacking discipline, and even more, lacking standards of right and wrong as we are today. This kind of party should long ago have been destroyed and swept away.[47]

In a similar analysis, written eight or nine years later, Chiang Kai-shek hammered home this message:

Admittedly, many factors contributed to our defeat. The mortal blows to our anti-communist struggle when we were still on the mainland, however, did not come from administrative shortcomings alone. As a matter of fact, similar political and social shortcomings, unavoidable during and after a long war, occurred in other countries, too. *The mortal blows sprang from serious defects in organization and technique, from serious errors in policy and strategy, and, above all, from the weakening of our national willpower at the time when it most needed to be strengthened* [emphasis added by Eastman].[48]

These points surfaced, too, in the formal analyses that Chiang Kai-shek had individuals and organizations make of the 1921 to 1951 struggle against the communists. One, in particular, put together by the consolidated Bureau of Investigation, was extraordinarily frank. The KMT, it noted throughout the report, had never come up with 'an organizational strategy'.[49] Chiang Kai-shek would speak in the same vein when he addressed the 200 delegates of the KMT's Seventh National Congress held in October 1952:

Our party has been engaged in the struggle with the Communists for thirty years. By now, we should have acquired enough experience to fight the enemy successfully. At such a critical moment should we still be preoccupied with factional conflicts among ourselves instead of focusing our attention upon the foe? Why did some of the party members, who could not distinguish enemies from friends, shamelessly go over to the Communist side? Such failure shows that the party's discipline was ignored and the party's organization slackened. These weaknesses gave openings to the Communist bandits to infiltrate our party and divide us. Shame on all of us for this failure! Under no circumstances should we endeavor to excuse ourselves by putting the blame on our effort to enforce the Constitution.[50]

What has perplexed scholars and participants alike – and convinced more than a few that Chiang Kai-shek was Machiavellian or devious, or both – was the apparent divergence between word and deed, a divergence which lasted a lifetime. If

In 1955, at 40 years of age, Wang Sheng, shown center with Chiang Ching-kuo left, became Commandant of *Fu Hsing Kang*.

Cadets at *Fu Hsing Kang*: Wang Sheng conceived of Political Officers not as commissars but as examples of revolutionary virtue.

Wang Sheng addresses *Fu Hsing Kang* cadets in August 1956.

the man could so accurately analyze KMT shortcomings, then why did so little ever seem to change? And if factionalism was at the heart of the matter, then why did he seem so assiduously to promote it? Further, why did he seem, publicly, to blame external factors, such as a lack of American aid or the duplicity of the Soviet Union?

Judgements of ulterior motives place the blame on character flaws, the simplest statement being that the man had a dark side. A similar explanation, and the one which continues to enjoy the greatest currency, is that which has Chiang as a 'military man' who never truly understood politics and economics. Both approaches seem off the mark. More in accord with the evidence would be to recognize Chiang Kai-shek for what he was: the talented follower of a sage who had charged him with certain military tasks for which he showed a flair but which were not his true calling. If anything, his tactical skills in political maneuvering were greater than those he displayed on the battlefield. His principal strength, though, lay in neither of these areas but in his tying the past to the present in a vision of what China could become. He was, in other

FIGURE 4
POLITICAL WARFARE OPERATIONAL UNITS AND SERVICES

POLITICAL WARFARE OPERATIONAL UNITS AND
SERVICES SUBORDINATE TO MND

M N D
Chief of General Staff

GENERAL POLITICAL
WARFARE DEPARTMENT

- POLITICAL STAFF COLLEGE
- CIVIL AFFAIRS BUREAU
- GENERAL WELFARE SERVICE
- PSYWAR GROUP
- YOUTH & WARRIOR DAILY
- NEW CHINA PUBLICATION SERVICE
- DISTRIBUTION CENTER
- MILITARY INFORMATION SERVICE
- MILITARY BROADCASTING GROUP
- CHINA MOTION PICTURE STUDIO
- SPECIAL SERVICE GROUP
- COUNTER INTELLIGENCE GROUP
- MILITARY INFORMATION COMMUNICATION GROUP
- WAC BATTALION
- PRINTING SHOP
- 1ST CIVIL AFFAIRS GROUP

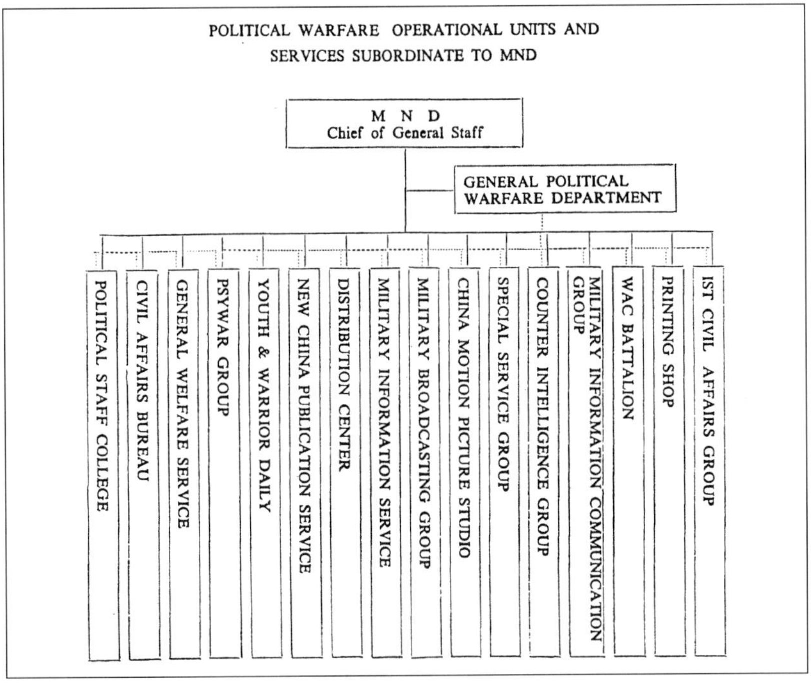

(Source: *General Briefing on Political Warfare System in the Chinese Armed Forces*, p. 8).

words, a sage out of place. His principal weakness lay not in the area, politics or economics or military, but in implementation in general. As Ch'en Li-fu was to write, after Chiang Kai-shek's death, 'Chiang was a Confucianist and influenced by the Wang Yang-ming [Wang Shou-jen] philosophy of the unity of knowledge and action [*Chih-hsing ho-i*]. I never doubted his sincerity and unselfishness in serving the country'.[51]

Chiang, then, was strong in the 'knowledge' portion of the equation, weak in the 'action'. Though the precise directions or understandings are not yet in the public domain – if even there exists such evidence – it is plain that on Taiwan he turned to his son, Chiang Ching-kuo, to fill this gap, to *manage* the revolutionary endeavor in response to broad directions, to become an efficient chief of staff for a philosophical commander weak on details. The entire reform was designed to produce a framework and personnel who would respond to these new arrangements. The collapse on the mainland was not to be defeat but only a setback. Victory could be gained by learning from the past and strengthening the revolution in exile.

Wang Sheng threw himself into this effort. His contribution to the revolutionary arsenal would be Political Warfare, because it alone addressed those crucial elements of the battlefield where the KMT had been found most lacking. And the necessary first ingredient for the non-violent weapons system to function was properly trained personnel posted to positions where they could serve as combat multipliers. That is, they were to insure that the military itself would function in the manner it was intended.

In the Political Warfare scheme, all military units, down to company level, were to have Political Officers. Additionally, there would be 15 supporting or operational units under the direct command of the Ministry of National Defense and supervised by GPWD to carry out political warfare activities (see Figure 4), units to carry out functions as diverse as troop welfare or radio broadcasting and motion picture production.[52] All of these positions would have to be filled with Political Officers, all of whom would have to be trained at *Fu Hsing Kang*. In his position as Director of Student Affairs, it was Wang Sheng's task to formulate not only the training framework but the institution itself. Recounts Wang Sheng:

> Everyone wanted to do something, but no one wanted to write things down. So I wrote it all out, putting everything that should go into Political Warfare, the ten departments and their missions. I took the school draft plan to my superior in the Administrative Office of GPWD. He was under Chiang Ching-kuo, yet he had his eyes on being the head of the school, so he gave me a lot of resistance. (Later, when I became important, he always helped me.) He threw the papers on the floor. I picked them up, folded them, and put them into my pocket. Because education in the military is under the Ministry of National Defense's Fifth Department, who was a Jiangxi person, I sent my plans up there. There was no answer, though, so I took a copy up myself. I waited for twenty minutes, but he didn't recognize me. He said, 'You know nothing about organization, do you?' I said, 'That's right, Colonel, that's why I wear the same rank as you. I've

been standing here for twenty minutes waiting for your assistance'. He looked at the plans again and told me to do what I wanted but that I would get no money from MND. But Chiang Ching-kuo wanted the school. He was a great person. Everything I proposed, he gave us. We called it the Political Staff School then. The only thing Chiang Ching-kuo did not agree to was that I wanted it to be a four-year school. He wanted it to be two years. He thought it should be a revolutionary melting pot rather than an institution on an academic footing.[53]

It was a key point for Wang Sheng. He, with others in GPWD, but principally Chiang Ching-kuo, had developed a comprehensive scheme for training the necessary number of Political Warfare officers (see Figure 5). Most of this cadre, it was recognized, would have to come from traditional sources; for example, regular officers who would receive a Political Warfare Basic Course designed to qualify them to carry out their duties, or reserve officers who would perform their time in service as Political Officers following attendance at the same Basic Course. Yet to serve as the skeleton for the system, its brains, Wang Sheng was looking for his superior men: 'In my heart the school would never be complete until it became a four-year school. The students would take regular military training, as at the military academy, *and* Political Warfare training. I wanted my people to have the double training, to be superior officers'.[54]

To that end, what Wang Sheng had in mind was a full-fledged academic, degree-granting institute, the academic majors at which would be in fields appropriate to Political Warfare. It was the fundamental debate between 'education' and 'training' which has had to be addressed in the military establishments of virtually all nations. While training drills the student in specific skills, physical or mental, education endeavors to develop the higher order cognitive processes. Training, in other words, centers on *execution*; education centers on *conceptualization*.

Initially at *Fu Hsing Kang*, training won out; but soon the year-and-a-half curriculum at least expanded to the two-year Special Course alluded to by Wang Sheng above. Graduates received an Associates Degree. The specialty areas, as reflected in Figure 5, were rather less comprehensive than Wang Sheng desired; but in the years ahead they would expand to the conceptual breadth he

FIGURE 5
POLITICAL OFFICER TRAINING

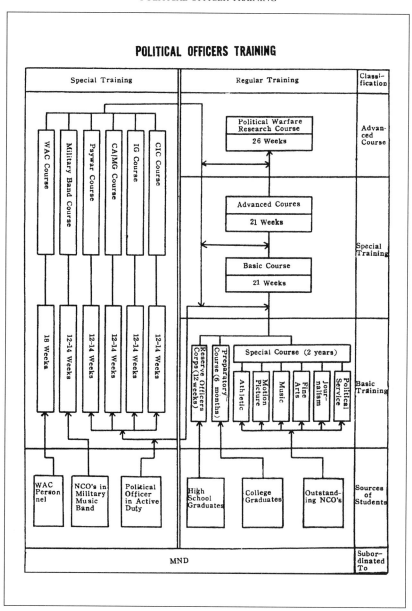

(Source: *The Political Establishment in the Chinese Armed Forces*, p. 114).

had envisaged (see Figure 6), and *Fu Hsing Kang* would become a four-year college from which would issue the cream of the Political Warfare officer corps. Simultaneously, on the same campus, the full array of training courses appropriate to any military 'branch' were held, such as the Advanced Course and the Staff Course. Just as fundamentally – offering that which he had never been able to gain because of the Anti-Japanese War – Wang Sheng saw his reconstituted 'Research Course' grow into a graduate school offering both MA and PhD degrees in certain majors, the most important of which was Political Science.

The need for such well trained, superior individuals stemmed from the role, discussed above, which Wang Sheng saw for them as exemplars of the Kuomintang and *San Min Chu-i*. Though KMT membership was not mandatory for officers, it was for any key position, which meant that most officers became party members during the rectification period. This eliminated any distinctive position for the Political Officer as the party representative organizationally. In a fundamental departure from the Soviet system upon which it had originally been modelled, the Nationalist armed forces codified the superiority of the unit commander in any and all circumstances. Just as GPWD was a staff function of the Chief of General Staff, so Political Officers were staff officers working for their commanders. This was made explicit by KMT directives which designated that the unit commander, rather than the Political Officer, would be the head of the KMT cell in each unit or command element. The latter's principal function, then, as Wang Sheng envisaged it, was to be the commander's assistant for the maintenance of unit probity, morale, and loyalty. Such a charge would include preventing enemy infiltration and checking for corrupt practices, with reports to be forwarded through an independent GPWD reporting chain (Political Officers were also rated by their GPWD superiors). Yet this reporting fed not into party organizations but those of the military, culminating in the office of Chief of General Staff. Political Officers, in other words, were not 'the party's eyes and ears in the military', as so many sources have held, because all individuals in positions of influence would themselves already be KMT members.[55] GPWD, to point out one explicit omission of a control mechanism, had no direct veto power over promotions.[56]

For Wang Sheng, his success in bringing *Fu Hsing Kang* to fruition would result in his own promotion. Moved up in early

FIGURE 6
POLITICAL WARFARE COLLEGE

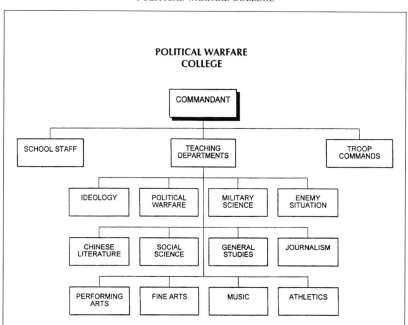

(Source: *The Political Establishment in the Chinese Armed Forces*, p. 112).

1953 to become Assistant Commandant, or Provost (with the restored rank of Major-General effective 1 January 1954), he served under a new Commandant, Wang Yung-shu, the same man who had commanded a regiment of the 208th Division of the Youth Army while Wang Sheng was the 31st Corps Political Officer – and who had captured Jiang Tse-min, only to turn him loose. The two Wangs, having worked together previously, got on well. Chiang Ching-kuo and Wang Yung-shu turned effective control of *Fu Hsing Kang* over to Wang Sheng, who moved ahead vigorously with his plans to turn it into a first class institution of learning. When Wang Yung-shu rotated to become a corps commander in December 1955, Wang Sheng became Commandant. He was 40 years of age.

He would remain in the position of Commandant for the next five years – the most illustrious of the 16 commanders the school would have up to the present. Remarkably, *none* of the these individuals were to be *Fu Hsing Kang* graduates. Instead, emphasizing the position in the Nationalist system of Political Warfare as a staff function, they were all, like Wang Sheng himself, line officers of varying backgrounds. Lieutenant-General Hu Wei-ke, for instance, the first official Commandant and an air force officer, was a graduate of Sandhurst, the British military academy. Wang Sheng's immediate predecessor, Wang Yung-shu, was an infantry officer.[57]

Trials in the Quest for Perfection

Gradually – under Wang Sheng's guidance, first as Provost and then Commandant – the college took shape. In front of the main gate, he directed that a sign be placed: 'Enter only if you are willing to devote and sacrifice yourself to your country'. Similarly, each newly admitted student received a letter which stated, 'If you seek wealth, power, and status, do not enter'.[58] These slogans symbolized Wang Sheng's commitment to perfection and the commitment he demanded of his charges. He was determined that *Fu Hsing Kang* would be as close to perfect as he could make it. Thus no item seemed too insignificant – or too immense – for his attention. He was everywhere. 'He was always working', remembers Liao Kuang-hsun, who had first met Wang Sheng in Jiangxi and later been one of his students at Chia-hsing Youth Middle School – in Taiwan they had maintained contact. 'All he talked about was schooling and the need to work'.[59] Adds Liu Jing-shing, who had also worked with Wang Sheng since Jiangxi, 'He was ready to sacrifice at any time for the country, whenever it was necessary. He would work 24 hours straight, without even going home. The spirit of devotion he brought to his work was exceptional. I could never work like that'.[60] It was as though all the hopes and dreams of Wang Sheng's youth, his quest for an education and for a revolutionary future for China, could be channeled into his creation. He, too, recalls the intensity:

> During the ten years I was at the school, every morning at reveille, I would be there to see the students get up, to see them take their jobs seriously, to clean up. At night after 'taps', I would finish my office work, then go again to check

on the students in the dorms. Finally, I would bicycle home. In those ten years, I never took a day off. Sometimes, on Sunday afternoon, I would go into town to serve as a guarantor at a wedding. Most of these were my graduates, colleagues, instructors. I took no vacations. It is always the case in such positions that you lead a solitary existence.[61]

In fact, Wang Sheng appears to have had no close friends beyond his wife, Hu Hsiang-li. She was his confidant, his support. Yet 'his work was his life'.[62] Driving him was the specter which continued to hang over Taiwan. Order had been restored and external security improved. The economy was moving, built upon a successful program of land reform, efforts at industrialization, and substantial American aid.[63] Life nevertheless remained difficult for most. 'Free China' could not have appeared to many as much of an alternative to its mainland rival. Both were in sorry straits, but for decades the veneer of revolutionary enthusiasm which Peking threw over its programs blinded observers to the staggering human cost of its designs.[64] The KMT's attempts to claim that it was the true custodian of China's past and its future seemed laughable. Taiwan continued to hold the 'China seat' in the United Nations and to be recognized by a majority of UN members, but in all other respects had become something of a backwater.

Like their new home, Wang Sheng's own family had little, even though a daughter, Wang Hsiao-li, had been born on 15 August 1953 to enlarge the household. A government-managed distribution system insured that official personnel had subsistence rations. Beyond that, there was nothing. 'When General Wang commanded *Fu Hsing Kang*, he only wore the khaki uniform', relates Lin Jung-chu, himself a retired general officer with Political Warfare experience. 'But once there was a meeting at which, on orders from the Ministry of National Defense, the Class A [dress] uniform had to be worn. But he didn't own one, so he didn't attend the meeting!'[65] Wang Pu-tien, the second son, who was six when his sister was born, has similar memories:

> Our family was very poor. The children were shoeless. For our birthday we had a boiled egg with sugar on top, one for each of us. Whoever had the birthday got two eggs! We lived at *Fu Hsing Kang* and ran around with bare feet. Mother was so popular that she always had visitors. She had little time to rest.[66]

Indeed, Hu Hsiang-li was not only mother to her own four children but to the school as a whole. She was the soft edge of the Wang team. Many turned to her for assistance. Much like her husband, she set a punishing pace for herself. She was still in the military and, in uniform, taught at *Fu Hsing Kang*. Yet her health had never recovered from the blows it suffered during the evacuation. The strenuous conditions of service life in Taiwan did not help the situation. In 1955, after a miscarriage, Hu Hsiang-li collapsed while going to the market on her bicycle. Rushed to the hospital, she lingered for several days, then passed away when treatment was unable to arrest the complications of infection. She was only 33. Before she died, unable to speak due to a tracheotomy, she motioned to Wang Sheng that she wished to see her children. He was unable to comply.

It was as if the bottom had dropped out of his world. 'That was the most emotional time I can remember', says Liao Kuang-hsun.[67] Pu-tien adds, 'The family, of course, didn't think mother was dying. Father made us stay home. He went to the hospital each day. He came back one day, and he was sobbing, being supported by many people. Everyone was crying – we didn't know what was happening'.[68] The sheer force of the moment would hit them all only later. What she had meant to those around her was brought home to Pu-tien in an incident a decade later:

> My mother was very, very kind. Her heart was very soft. For instance, one of the young students who came from the mainland to Taiwan had nothing. He was in tears. She gave her wedding ring to him. Ten years after her death, he came and told me this story. She was kind to everyone, which is why she had many friends.[69]

The friends tried to be of assistance. For a time, Wang Sheng's work habits changed. He would bring his papers home at night and labor at a small desk, stopping to talk to the children when they sought attention.[70] It was especially hard on the youngest two, daughter Wang Hsiao-li, who was not quite two, and son Wang Hsiao-tien, just six.[71] Friends offered to introduce Wang Sheng to suitable women who might ease his burden, which became all the more intense when he formally became school Commandant in December.[72] Of particular concern, the needs of the children weighed heavily on his mind. Soldiers helped him look after them, but it was an unsatisfactory arrangement. Eventually, acting through an intermediary, he met Hsiung Hwei-ying, daughter of a military veteran of the Jiangxi period. She herself, during her youth, had spent five years in Jiangxi. In Taiwan, she was a kindergarten director who had rapidly made a name for herself as an educational innovator. (She would go on to found her own institution, *Kwei San* Middle School, which continues in operation.) In manner she was outspoken and intense. Obviously, Wang Sheng felt he had found a facsimile of Hu Hsiang-li. They were married on 17 November 1956. It was to prove a stormy union.

For the children, it was to be more than that – it was the loss of their father only shortly after the departure of their mother. They were never to adjust to the change. Again, it is Pu-tien who has the most accurate recollections of what occurred:

> Stepmother is very strong-willed. She never changes an opinion. She and my father would argue all the time. He didn't want to do this, so he just ignored her. She was very hard on us. I was nine when they got married. We could not get along with her, so we went out when we were very young – went to school and lived there or lived at a friend's house. It was hard on father, because he loved us very much. He tried to check on us, but he had to choose. My father had an important position. It was very sensitive, and he had enemies. He didn't want his family problems to be public, so he tried to make some sort of peaceful arrangement. If we could have good schooling, good friends, he thought all would work out. But he missed us. I knew we were most important to him. I don't think he liked her very much, but he decided to persevere. He doesn't worry about what people think, so I asked him, 'Why don't you divorce her?' He was very patient; he was convinced things would work themselves out.[73]

As the years would pass, however, what occurred was just as Pu-tien has remembered it. Little changed. And as his family life drifted, Wang Sheng resumed his punishing work schedule; the children, already in a sense gone, would leave home in fact at their earliest opportunity, beginning with the eldest, Kung-tien. Significantly – to leap ahead for the sake of clarity – all would eschew politics, pursuing careers in other fields, particularly the sciences. All would earn advanced degrees in the United States, relying mainly upon their own means to put themselves through school.[74] Pu-tien discussed the situation with Wang Sheng at times, but the results were inconclusive. So 'we lived at friends' homes', he states.[75] A new brother, Wang Li-tien ('Mao Ti'), who would be born four years after the marriage, on 1 September 1960, did not help matters. Instead, it isolated them still further. Remarkably, Mao Ti would follow in their intellectual footsteps, earning his own advanced degree;[76] but for the moment that was in the future. In the present Wang Sheng did what he could under trying circumstances. Wang Hsiao-tien relates:

> The best thing my father gave to me was his own personality. He showed me how to be a true person. He did a lot of great things, became very famous. I hear things from people, things I didn't even know. All I know is that he devoted his life to the country, worked so hard. He always accomplished his task. Whenever he was given a job, he wanted to do his best. When he finished a job, anyone could take over without difficulty. First understand your work [was his philosophy], then make decisions. Build a firm foundation; start at the base. Don't just show results when you finish but leave something lasting. He knew how to do his job! He had a love of knowledge. He didn't spend much time with us, because he worked so hard. He was always at work by five in the morning, and he would come home very late. But whenever he had time, he would try to let us know that you have to work, target your future knowledge. Our stepmother was also very busy. For a period of time, I was not a 'good boy'. I didn't study very hard. About middle school, I was always in trouble. In senior high school, I became interested, so I did well when I went to the university. The best thing my father did was to show his own example to us, to influence us. He didn't give us the details. I tried to figure out how he was.[77]

Wang Hsiao-li has similar memories:

> Father had to work so hard as an official. He should not have had trouble with his family. But we did have problems. When I was a teenager, I was very bad. I matured very late. I hated all the studies. I was a very bad student. Thinking back, I remember my father saying, 'No matter how hard it is, I'll put

Hsiung Hwei-
ying.

Wang family portrait at wedding of eldest son, Kung-tien (right front). Center
front are Wang Sheng and Hsiung Hwei-ying; to left, the bride, now deceased.
Back row, from left: Hsiao-tien, Hsiao-li, Li-tien ('MaoTi'), and Pu-tien.

you through college, even if I have to beg'. I wondered [then] why he talked like that. I knew we were successful. Now I realize that this was how he set a goal for us – how he was, how he talked – what he wanted – how hard his own family life had been with my grandfather, how he had to study. He wanted to give us better. Because he was very busy, my father was not that close to us when we were kids. My stepmother was also very busy. Thus our family didn't do much together. For me, my friends at that time were more important. Yet whenever he had time, he talked about what a person should be, how hard the family and the country had it. Or he would talk about traditional lessons – for example, from Confucius – things such as, 'Don't think any job is too small to do'. You can't tell that to a kid! I wanted to play all the time. How do you expect a kid to listen to such a conversation? Study hard, hardships of the country, Confucius? Basically, he was setting goals for us. All the kids when I was growing up had little choice. We were just expected to study. All my friends had this sort of father – they went through hard times and were hoping their children would have more opportunities. My brothers at least considered my father's position but not me. My friends were never from our circle. Most ended up never going to college. Even when I was with those who were very bad, though, such as some of my friends who were fighting all the time on the streets, there were some things I wouldn't do, such as drugs. I steered clear of the really bad influences. Father didn't really push us on the grades. I got punished for behavior but not grades. I think he was very worried.

He had to put up with a lot of things. My stepmother started a school when I was in first grade. She is like a career woman: strong personality, not very tolerant, [traits which became more pronounced as] she became more and more religious. At first she was a Buddhist. She would go get the Chinese writing from the spirit temple. Then around junior high, she had all sorts of religious people come talk to her school. She herself was open to all. At that time she decided upon Christianity. This is a local, non-denominational Protestant group, testimonial. It is worldwide. Previously, we had still practiced ancestor worship, but she stopped him from going. Put altogether, it wasn't a fun life. So all I could do was to take off.[78]

In her analysis, Wang Hsiao-li displays many of the character traits his associates came to associate with Wang Sheng himself: an ability to analyze the situation, appreciation for all sides of an issue, tenacity sliding off into stubbornness, and a bluntness which often bordered on the painful. He was not loud or overbearing, but would not let go of an issue once he had fixed upon it. And his mind ranged near and far in its effort to grapple with the issues. In the effort to save the revolution, there were so many matters which needed to be addressed. His rocky home life did not create his driving force but surely must have given it an added edge. All of his bridges had been burned, so to speak, and there was nowhere to go but forward. Though he still reached out to his children, whenever possible, the lack of a safe harbor in which to anchor meant that, like the hero in 'The Rhyme of the Ancient Mariner', he was doomed to sail the seas forever.

It was this quality which many over the years were to interpret as rigidity. It was anything but. In his day-to-day dealing with people, in his willingness to look for any solution to a problem, and in the institutions and programs he created, Wang Sheng demonstrated amazing flexibility. Yet all of these were operational and tactical designs dedicated to the goal of strategic victory. Thus, when pressed orally on any subject, especially by foreigners, Wang Sheng's responses often came across as a veritable 'Newspeak' of hackneyed anti-communist phrases. He may well serve as an early example of a figure fundamentally ill-suited to the 'sound bite', the tremendously quotable line which will fill a slot on the evening news. With its roots in classical Chinese, his prose, either verbal or written, was eloquent but required a cultural Rosetta Stone. It fared poorly in English translation, as does much in Chinese.[79] Still, it was never his prose which singled out the man. Rather it was the use to which he put it, to the monuments he built, to play upon Wang Hsiao-tien's words. Wherever he focused his prodigious energies, organizational edifices of substance resulted which were fundamentally sound in design and function. *Fu Hsing Kang* and, ultimately, the entire Political Warfare system were eloquent enough testimony.

Perhaps, to continue the metaphor a moment longer, it is useful to hold Wang Sheng the builder in counterpoint to what he was not, Wang Sheng the artist. Even he would never claim to have been the creator of that for which he was responsible. 'I worked in the Political Warfare system for a long time', he was to say, when analyzing *Fu Hsing Kang* and GPWD, which he would eventually head, 'but I'm not the person who contributed the most. That was the person who set up the foundations. That was Chiang Ching-kuo. It was he who was able to reform the military and lay the basis for the Political Warfare system within a very short ten years. People give me the credit, but it belongs to Chiang Ching-kuo'.[80] He was, then, both in his own mind and in reality, a builder – an architect even – but not an artist. He had in mind precisely the edifice he wanted to construct; and he was willing to do as much work as required, alone if necessary. Further, he was willing to show astonishing flexibility in the particulars, such as the plans and the nature of the materials and furnishings. Yet he would not, could not, contemplate a different end product.

His quarrels with his mentor, Chiang Ching-kuo, were along just such lines:

> If Chiang Ching-kuo's decision was not viable, I would continue to argue until we reached agreement. We often had fights when I wasn't willing to implement an order, when I still thought there was something wrong with it. We had some big fights. Chiang Ching-kuo would get so angry that he'd be ready to kill me. His face would get very red for forty minutes or so. One time he threw the papers on his desk at me. I jumped up and said, 'If you want to shoot me, do so! I'm not going to do it!' Sometimes the result would be that Chiang Ching-kuo would not see me for three or five months. It was like the Cold War. You might wonder, if we fought so often, how could I [ultimately] serve him for fifty years? The secret was that I had my own principles in dealing with him. First, I decided early on that Chiang Ching-kuo was truly a person who loved his country, who also had true revolutionary spirit. He was 100 per cent behind these ideas. I felt I could give my heart to such a person and be very sincere in dealing with him. I could be totally frank with him. Second, [I reasoned] as long as Chiang Ching-kuo was ready for revolutionary reform and sincere, I shall be proper and behave well. My guiding principle was to be proper, to be honest, to be very sincere. Even if there are misunderstandings [I felt], as long as I'm honest and sincere, in the end Chiang Ching-kuo will find out I'm right. He'll go back and think about the matter and realize the correct course.[81]

In all of this give and take, there were only two issues which
Wang Sheng considered of major importance. The first was the
ongoing debate over whether *Fu Hsing Kang* was to emphasize
training or education. Critics simply could not see a need for
Political Officers to have their own, degree-granting institution.
For Wang Sheng, it was central to his design for safeguarding the
revolutionary ethos. On the theoretical side, there was the need for
an academy of the revolution, a place where appropriate fields of
knowledge essential to the survival of the revolution would be
taught to an élite corps. On the pragmatic side, who, in a modern
world, would pay attention to any member of this élite corps if he
did not have at least a bachelor's degree? It was just the sort of
farsighted argument which many could not see. Even Chiang
Ching-kuo resisted making an issue of a matter he initially viewed
as peripheral. 'So Classes One through Seven earned no
[bachelor's] degree', observes Wang Sheng. 'I fought with Chiang
Ching-kuo on this point. There were bad endings after several
briefings. Gradually, he came around and finally approved. This
shows his greatness. He would always go back and think about an
issue, re-evaluate'.[82]

The second such issue was the procedure by which the Political
Officers would be rated. Wang Sheng insisted that the evaluation,
promotion, and assignments of Political Warfare officers should be
recommended by the Political Warfare Director at each level.
Chiang Ching-kuo said they should be the prerogative of the Chief
of Staff at each level. Relates Wang Sheng, 'Chiang Ching-kuo
insisted that the *power* belonged to the Chief of Staff, but I said the
Chief of Staff could not be completely familiar with all Political
Warfare officers. It was a matter of *responsibility* rather than
control'.[83] Wang Sheng's point was that officers had to be under the
control of those they served. So recommendations on rating,
assignment, and promotion went through a chain which ultimately
reached the GPWD Director, where they remain today, though
final approval is exercised by the Chief of General Staff.[84] Thus,
while the reports filed by Political Officers fed into the chain of
command – with all follow-up action the responsibility of line
officers – the independence of the officers themselves was
guaranteed. The corruption, malfeasance, disloyalty, and enemy
infiltration which had destroyed the armed forces of the revolution
on the mainland would not again take root, because it would be
reported. 'It took me more than ten years [on the mainland] to

learn the principles I was trying to stand for', summarizes Wang Sheng. 'As soon as we got to Taiwan, we were prepared to switch!'[85] This the 'builder' would not do, even for Chiang Ching-kuo.[86]

Political Warfare versus Internal Security

Wang Sheng knew what he wanted to build. It was his astonishing capacity for work and ability to get the job done which his superiors, above all Chiang Ching-kuo, found attractive. Regardless of their disagreements – which, whatever their intensity, were minimal within the overall scope of their relationship – Chiang Ching-kuo was well pleased with Wang Sheng. The graduates of *Fu Hsing Kang* had lived up to expectations. The military had become a far more cohesive, effective body; corruption had been reduced to the point that the ROC armed forces had become, and would remain, among the least corrupt of any in the Third World. Just as importantly, the military had served as an important tool for the *socialization* of the young people who entered its ranks under the requirements of universal service. Political officers looked to their welfare and emphasized the concepts of national unity and citizenship.[87] These were lessons which were also presented to youth through a variety of extracurricular and school-based programs, all of which were run by the Youth Corps (which Wang Sheng had worked to institute). The Youth Corps, in turn, fell under GPWD and thus was also at this time staffed by Political Officers. The importance Chiang Kai-shek attached to the effort was illustrated by the fact that Chiang Ching-kuo was the Youth Corps head from 1952 until 1973 (and was to be followed by Li Huan, 1973-77). That the military itself was chosen to head the effort stemmed both from Chiang Kai-shek's personal belief in its professional ethos (at least in the ideal) and from its being one of the most cohesive, responsive tools available to him in a field of limited options. Though eventually formal training in civilian schools was transferred to the Ministry of Education in July 1960; and the Youth Corps, which had increasingly civilianized its cadre, would become an independent body in 1969; close working relationships with GPWD would continue.[88]

Additionally, GPWD would play a crucial role in the

socialization campaign directed at society at large. The lack of a common core of knowledge, Chiang Kai-shek believed, had allowed the communists to exploit divisions, real and contrived, within the polity. There had been very little sense of citizenry. The military worked to create such a sense through its actions in five areas, as identified by Monte Bullard:

> (1) Establishing close relationships between military units and civilian authorities in the areas where units were stationed; (2) Dispatching mobile 'culture' groups to travel throughout the island(s) promoting various nationalist themes; (3) Teaching the equivalent of adult education classes, particularly the Chinese Mandarin language; (4) Organizing a civil defense system; and (5) Exposing citizens to nationalist mass media messages.[89]

In such activities, 'military' should not be equated with GPWD, but key elements, such as the mobile 'culture groups', did come from the department and were staffed with Political Officers. In particular, GPWD provided the ethos which suffused the effort as a whole, the emphasis upon socialization rather than oversight or control. 'My philosophy is plain', Wang Sheng was to state. 'People say Political Warfare emphasizes brainwashing, controlling people's thinking. But you can't wrap paper around fire. We are [principally] educating young people. We try to educate them. We cannot control their thoughts. We're educators, not brainwashers'.[90] At the same time, there was no doubt that Political Warfare was anti-communist and put out an uncompromising message to that effect within the military and through the organizations and activities for which it had responsibility. It was a view shared by those in the official hierarchy and the organs of state power. As the final bastion of Sun Yat-sen's revolution, Taiwan was a society and a nation-in-all-but-name locked in a battle to the death with Peking. Even as the island and its associated territories were molded into a model province, into a self-sustaining entity capable of independent action – with individuals using many of the lessons they had taken from their mainland experiences, particularly Gannan, Shanghai, and the Youth Corps – national security continued to be of overriding concern. This was demonstrated by the September 1954–55 and 1958 crises involving the offshore islands.[91] In the first episode,

Political Warfare works to shape the mind of the enemy. Wang Sheng inspects US-supplied psychological warfare systems during exercises on Taiwan.

1954–55, communist bombardment of Quemoy (Kinmen), in what appeared to be preparation for an invasion of that island and neighboring Matsu, resulted in a December 1954 'Treaty of Mutual Defense' between the US and the Republic, followed by the January 1955 'Formosa Resolution', which essentially enlarged upon the American commitment. In the second episode, 1958, which came to be termed 'the Taiwan Strait(s) Crisis', a similar communist methodology, highlighted by an intense pounding of Quemoy and an attempted blockade, the US Seventh Fleet itself became involved.[92] Both of these attacks were apparently launched by the CCP with the political intent of testing the American commitment to Taiwan's defense; and while the allies saw them through successfully, the episodes strained Taipei–Washington relations. In return for the 1954–55 commitment to the defense of Taiwan, the US demanded (and assisted in) the evacuation of the exposed Tachen island group, as well as the adoption of a defensive posture *vis-à-vis* the mainland. More seriously, the 1958 crisis – had the Seventh Fleet been unable to force the blockade – threatened to involve the US in an escalation which many saw leading to possible use of nuclear weapons.[93] Chiang Kai-shek's obstinacy in heavily fortifying Quemoy and Matsu, and thus exposing nearly one-third of his effective ground forces, was viewed by Washington as making little military sense. That, of course, was beside the point in Chiang's mind, where the struggle was one of *legitimacy*. Who had the right to represent the Chinese revolution, the KMT or the CCP? Possession of the offshore islands symbolized the KMT determination to return from exile.

Yet this very determination called into question methodology. That Taiwan and its associated minor territories were to serve as the jumping off point for 'the return' was self-evident. Less so was how long the wait would be. As the years passed, the second facet of the role the KMT had staked out for Taiwan – that of serving as an example of what Chinese society would look like under *San Min Chu-i* – began to loom much larger. This necessarily pushed forward issues of internal policy, which in turn necessarily brought into play the relationship between ideology and praxis. For Wang Sheng, this would involve not just the theoretical positioning of Political Warfare within the national strategy but also operational designs and tactical decisionmaking. This was even more the case when, in May 1960, he was elevated to the post of Deputy Director-General of GPWD. He recalls:

> After ten years at the school [*Fu Hsing Kang*], one day I received a call from Chiang Ching-kuo asking me to transfer to GPWD. I tried to get out of it, because I had lots of things yet to do. Some days later, Chiang Ching-kuo came to my office. He said Chiang Kai-shek had decided I would move to GPWD. I asked again if such a move was absolutely necessary. I wanted to stay and make the school a real going concern. We had come so far but had so far to go. Obviously the matter

had been settled, though, so I became Deputy Director-General of GPWD. There were three Deputy Director-Generals. The senior one was like the Chief of Staff of GPWD, or the Executive Deputy Director-General. I became this in July 1961 and was promoted to lieutenant-general. Chiang Ching-kuo was no longer head of GPWD. He had stayed there only four years or so before moving to the National Defense Council.[94]

His position as Deputy Secretary-General in the National Defense Council, a key body for both national and internal security (it was to become the National Security Council in 1967), was only one of Chiang Ching-kuo's many tasks. In terms of functional power, it went hand in hand with his designation as a Minister without Portfolio (1958–65). Simultaneously, as we have already seen, he was head of the China Youth Corps; he was also Chairman of the Vocational Assistance Commission for Retired Servicemen (1957–64) and Vice-Chairman of the Council for International Economic Cooperation and Development (1965–69; CIECD dealt, in particular, with US aid monies). Later, while still serving as Deputy Secretary-General of the National Defense Council (he would leave in 1967), he would first become Deputy Minister of National Defense (1964–65), then Minister of National Defense (1965–69). Finally (1969–72), he would rise to Vice-Premier (also translated as Deputy Premier or Deputy Prime Minister), simultaneously with becoming chairman of CIECD; he became Premier in 1972. He would become President in 1978 and serve as such until his death in 1988 aged 78. Giving continuity to the whole, beginning with the reform in 1952, he was a member of the KMT Standing Committee.[95] Though it gradually expanded from its original ten members in 1952, it was still just 22 individuals when its 11th iteration met in November 1979 and increased the membership to 27.[96] Thus it was the locus of decisionmaking, all the more so since the Central Committee, which theoretically was the most important body, was to expand significantly. From its 1952 strength (established by the Reform Committee) of 32, it was to reach 150 (with another 75 alternate members) by the KMT's Twelfth National Congress in March–April 1981.[97] Membership in this became an honor, bestowed much in the manner of knighthood in Britain. Central Committee meetings were held but once a year; the Standing Committee met *weekly* on Wednesday.

It was the Standing Committee, therefore, which met to discuss broad national policies. Assisting them was a Central Committee for Deliberation and Consultation (*Chung-yang p'ing-i wei-yuan hui*), comprised of party elders, who were consulted at important times and at the pleasure of the active leadership.[98] As matters actually worked, however, even the Standing Committee invariably took its lead from the KMT Director-General. Until his death in 1975, aged 87, this was Chiang Kai-shek, who had the title *tsung-ts'ai*, so as not to infringe upon the memory of Sun Yat-sen, who had been *tsung-li*. Subsequently, it was Chiang Ching-kuo, who aged 65, upon his father's passing away, took the title *chu-hsi*, the previous designations being reserved out of reverence for their holders.[99] Hence it was Chiang Ching-kuo who, as he moved up the ladder of succession, was the linchpin of decisionmaking. No concentration of power could emerge in government institutions themselves due to KMT control. Until he actually had power, though, Chiang Ching-kuo's position was never firm, because he, too, had to defer to his father, whose intimates continued to dominate the membership of both the Central Committee and Standing Committee until Chiang Kai-shek's actual departure. Thereafter, Chiang Ching-kuo could move to name his own men.

Certainly the most significant point as concerned Wang Sheng and where he fitted into the system was that he was not named to the Standing Committee until the December 1979 increase to 27 members. Though he had been elected to the Central Committee as early as October 1957 by the KMT's Eighth Party Congress, he had declined the appointment in deference to a more senior officer. He therefore became the first among the Alternate Members and moved up to become a full member on 19 May 1959. By this time, as we have already seen, the body had ceased to have any real decisionmaking purpose. Wang Sheng's tenure on the Standing Committee, to be discussed ahead but already mentioned in Chapter 1, was likewise brief. He was, in other words, for all his importance in reconstituting the party and formulating the Political Warfare system, not moved into the inner circle until very late, and even then under exceptional circumstances.

This had considerable effect upon the influence Wang Sheng could actually bring to bear beyond those matters under his direct control. The Leninist structure of the KMT, for instance, designed to insure that *San Min Chu-i* would inform the operations of all bodies where party cells were present, fell under ultimate control of the Standing Committee, of which Wang Sheng was not a member (at least until 1979). Likewise, as a member of the staff group of the Chief of General Staff, he had no command authority over any units save those operational elements of GPWD itself (e.g. *Fu Hsing Kang*). Indeed, having been made Deputy Director General and then Executive Director-General, Wang Sheng was to remain in the latter position for 15 years – serving four different directors, Generals Chiang Chien-jen, Kao Kuei-yuan, Tang Shou-chih, and Lo You-lun – before finally becoming Director-General in April 1975. During the long interim, though he was promoted to general in June 1970, aged 55,[100] he did not even have command authority over GPWD operational elements. Finally, GPWD, a staff unit, was not linked in any command sense with either the intelligence structure or the mechanisms of internal security.[101] Neither did the Political Warfare elements of those bodies, if they were military (e.g. IBMND or Garrison Command), have command authority. The actual commander was in every case supreme – and also a KMT member.

How then to account for the reputation Wang Sheng began to acquire, which reached its peak once he had actually become GPWD Director, a reputation which labelled him not only as a key figure in the hierarchy of power in the Republic but also as something more odious, as the mastermind behind repression? Surveying the literature, there are few references to Wang Sheng which are not adverse and which do not use terms such as: 'security chief';[102] 'the premier's closest military assistant';[103] 'hardline security czar';[104] 'the powerful head of Taiwanese Security Bureau';[105] 'considered by many to be the second most powerful man on Taiwan because of his close association with the government's many security and intelligence agencies...the chief spokesman for hardline security forces';[106] or worse.[107] Even the evenhanded Maria Hsia Chang is seriously deficient; for example: 'A careful study of Wang's authority within the security system indicates that, at best, he may have wielded authority over three of the ten organizations that together with their superordinate organization, the National Security Bureau, constitute the island's security system – (1) the General Political Warfare Department, (2) the Taiwan Garrison Command, and (3) the Bureau of Investigation'.[108]

The answer to the query as to Wang Sheng's reputation lies in the type of organizations Chang has listed; it is both a simple and detailed response. That is, even as Wang Sheng was promoted, his very competence carried him to the heart of the anti-communist struggle, a *revolutionary* struggle which necessarily had two components, the external and the internal. He considered his crucial contribution to be safeguarding the integrity of the revolutionary effort through nonviolent means, through maintaining the spirit and ethos of *San Min Chu-i*. As had been his belief in Gannan – and those of others working with him – he felt that if the values of each individual were correct, organization and actions of a just nature would follow. As a soldier, though, Wang Sheng's principal charge and instrument for realizing his ideals was the military. And there is no doubt that what were ultimately *his* Political Officers, both in theory and in fact, were exceptionally successful in all but wiping out the vices of old, in particular corruption and disunity. Simultaneously, they reached out to other segments of the populace through youth and educational programs, both of which, we should add, became independent efforts even before Wang Sheng became actual GPWD Director. Yet Wang Sheng's Political Officers were not the only players in the game. If his effort was principally *socialization*, there were others whose function was *control*. The most notable of these was the Taiwan General Garrison Command.

A regular military command falling under Chief of General Staff, General Garrison Command was the Taiwan reincarnation of a standard command procedure which had been used by Nanjing to garrison all major urban centers on the mainland even well before World War II. It was, in other words, a military unit charged with maintaining law and order in cities or regions. In Taiwan, in a situation of continued civil war (i.e. the KMT versus the CCP), the General Garrison Command was charged with the same function, which, in the broadest terms, meant enforcing the martial law enacted in 1949 according to the relevant provisions of the Chinese Constitution of 1947.[109] The term itself was something of a misnomer, since 'martial law' in the Chinese context was actually a variant of the civil law 'state of siege'.[110] Civilian government, in other words, continued to function, as did the courts; but certain crimes – in the main, those labelled sedition or espionage[111] – fell under military jurisdiction and were tried by military court martial. The apparatus both for investigating and prosecuting these crimes, as well as imprisoning those found guilty, was contained within General Garrison Command. Avenues for appeal of actions and sentences lay within the military and, ultimately, specific government and party organs.

While the mechanisms for detention and trial did become more open with the passage of time, they were not only military but built upon the inquisitorial precepts of civil law of those countries upon which Republican China had based its own legal reforms.[112] Predictably, as would be expected in circumstances of conflict wedded to mechanisms of authoritarianism, military or otherwise, abuses occurred.[113] These were magnified by a peculiar confluence of circumstances. Most particularly, the United States, as Taiwan's security guarantor, was a democracy; further, it was a democracy going through a very particular moment in its own history, an upheaval in values which culminated during the Vietnam War years. Circumstances outlined earlier had already produced an embittered Taiwanese exile community (i.e. those who saw themselves as ethnically distinct, particularly as concerned language and culture).[114] This community lived mainly in Japan and the United States, where it was further exposed to both Anglo-American concepts of democracy and adversarial law, as well as burgeoning concepts of social freedom and human rights. Its efforts were not unified, ranging from 'Taiwan independence' to 'democratic rights', but all points of view to some extent came together around the notion that the system which was in place in Taiwan was repressive. Incidents consequent to General Garrison Command activities, therefore, real and imagined, were invariably presented through a very particular filter – and, more often than not, packaged for a Western audience, since such support, signally American, was viewed as the linchpin of the KMT position. Similarly, as increasing numbers of Taiwan students went abroad to study, America was the favored destination. Invariably, there were those who, like the expatriate community, were influenced by Western concepts of social justice and also rebelled.

Paradoxically, within Taiwan itself, there was no groundswell of support for rebellion of any stripe,[115] particularly not in favor of what became the umbrella group for opposition exile sentiment, the Taiwan Independence Movement (most elements of which, but not all, were committed to nonviolence). This indifference at home, which stemmed from successful socialization[116] and continued economic success,[117] was exasperating to the exile community, which sought the explanation by claiming that order was maintained only through dictatorship and terror – a dictatorship of the Kuomintang, and terror perpetrated by 'secret police'.[118] As the most visible anti-communist figure in Taiwan, and as a man known to be linked to Chiang Ching-kuo, the son of 'dictator' Chiang Kai-shek and the emerging KMT leader, it was Wang Sheng who attracted dissatisfaction with the system. Most significantly, since Wang Sheng, even when he was Deputy Director of GPWD, was the acknowledged 'soul' of the department, he was naturally enough connected with 'commissars', who, in turn, were connected with repression.

In reality, Political Officers were less closely connected with Taiwan General Garrison Command than they were with normal military units. First, in the table of organization, Taiwan General Garrison Command was on a level equal to that of the Army, Navy, or Air Force, reporting directly to the Chief of General Staff – as did the Military Police, in another significant difference from the procedures normal to most armies. It was commanded by a line officer who had all the prerogatives and command authority that go with a major command. If anything, the sensitive nature of his work gave him even greater independence than would accrue to a normal line unit. In any case, Taiwan General Garrison Command's commander, like all those operational units, was not within GPWD's span of control.[119] Second, the Garrison Command commander had two deputy commanders. One was superior to the Director of the command's own Political Warfare Department (every regiment or higher unit had such a staff), which had a Director and a Political Warfare Staff organized in the P-functions (refer again to Figure 8); the other oversaw the Chief of Staff, who supervised the normal G-functions (present in all military units of battalion or higher, though their precise designation changes). These functions supervised those Garrison Command units involved in internal security, an array of police and civilians. A special Security Preservation Department (*pao-an-chu*), reporting directly to the Taiwan General Garrison Command Chief of Staff, performed the counterintelligence function within the command's geographic area. The Political Warfare counterintelligence personnel, assigned to the P-4 section of the Command's own Political Warfare establishment, were charged with performing this function *only as it concerned the military personnel assigned to Garrison Command*. They were, in other words, charged with insuring the integrity, loyalty, and indoctrination of the military personnel assigned to Taiwan General Garrison Command. They took no part in operational aspects of counterintelligence *per se*. This was not unlike their role in other units. What insured a further degree of detachment was the classified (i.e. secret or restricted) nature of much of the work, as well as its performance by civilian elements, especially the police, whom Taiwan General Garrison Command was also charged with coordinating for the internal security mission.

If GPWD was thus, in one sense, organizationally separated from the internal security role, it was, in another sense, integrally involved. For it was GPWD, at Wang Sheng's direction – and, through *Fu Hsing Kang*, his creation – which worked ceaselessly to instill anti-communism in all military personnel and to inform them of enemy methodologies. *San Min Chu-i*, to emphasize the point, was the revolutionary alternative to communism within the Chinese environment. It was not intended for universal application; neither were the specifics of Political Warfare, though the basic principles involved in Political Warfare were thought to have more general application, as we shall see in the next chapter. Anything which helped communism, therefore, was antithetical to the revolution; thus counterrevolutionary, or subversive. The very prominence which 'united front' activities had played historically in communist strategy and tactics – and continued to play – heightened the sensitivity to activities which created division, or faction. This attitude insured that certain modes of conduct, most particularly dissent aimed at attacking the system, were invariably seen as subversive and described as such. Demands for 'Taiwan independence', for instance, because they necessarily caused factionalism, were subversive and of benefit to the communists. There was obviously some tautology at work – if it helped the communists then it must be a communist ploy – with the distinctions left to the individual.

Simultaneously, however, Political Warfare put out a very definite message of redemption. As perhaps best exemplified by Wang Sheng's own traditional philosophy, it was believed that through education any individual would eventually see the rectitude of the *San Min Chu-i* philosophy, particularly its superiority to others which might be offered as alternatives within the Chinese environment. Thus, even as Taiwan General Garrison Command put its emphasis upon control – that, after all, was its charge – GPWD put its emphasis upon education. Those convicted under martial law provisions, for instance, were incarcerated in the Garrison Command's own prison system. Within these, Political Officers took charge of rehabilitation programs.[120] Since the prison system itself remained a constant problem for the authorities, in that too many of its personnel were wedded to traditional notions of prisoner treatment (e.g. beatings), the resulting conflict of philosophies was well illustrated. Under even the best of circumstances, this would have resulted in a considerable psychological battle on a *personal* level. At times when the ongoing struggle between the KMT and CCP intensified, as it would do periodically (e.g. in the years following the 1978 'derecognition' of Taiwan by Washington), the compulsion to 'get tough' must have been overwhelming; at others, a distinct mellowing of approach was evident.

None of this analysis could have been even small comfort for those who found themselves on the wrong side of the authorities. Nevertheless, if one accepted the premise that there was a war situation, martial law could be deemed acceptable, with only the methods of implementation – especially their inconsistency – becoming the issue. But if one did not accept that there was any justification for martial law at all, then any actions which followed were doubly damned, especially those which violated the most common precepts of human rights. Torture, for instance, though it, too, gradually diminished (and much that was normal in any police environment was routinely deemed 'torture' by human rights advocates), nevertheless remained an ongoing problem and issue. To the extent that such abuse occurred, it was blamed on the system. The system's very success in cloaking its organizations in secrecy (a predictable deception measure in time of war), only contributed to the anger and the need to single out identifiable culprits. As the ideological basis for the whole, Political Warfare and its director (ultimately), Wang Sheng, became the accepted resolution of the enigma. In reality, this was wide of the mark.

More fundamentally, it missed the very essence of both Political Warfare and Wang Sheng, which was a belief that popular *allegiance* could only be won through establishment of regime *legitimacy*. Critics, particularly those in exile, started with the premise that the Kuomintang regime was illegitimate. All else followed naturally. Yet this ideological stance ignored the realities of what was occurring within Taiwan. This was that the KMT, simply by attempting to live up to *San Min Chu-i*, as well as to its role as 'Free China', necessarily created the conditions for the undoing of authoritarianism in whatever degree it was present. The constant need to work for the citizenry, especially its economic well-being, as well as to offer all that the CCP on the mainland could not, led to a plethora of activities which resulted in nothing less than the creation of civil society, those patterns of association which stand outside the state.[121] This trend assumed added salience due to the growing complexity and urban nature of Taiwan society, which generated diverse pressures for everything from veteran's rights to pollution controls. The very success of economic development, carried out in such manner as to insure relative equality of income distribution,[122] pushed class considerations aside and channelled popular demands, which were necessarily voiced by a majority which was both educated and middle class, into social movements (especially those built around consumer issues) and local politics (which, from the beginning, featured elections, even if flawed).[123] This process, in turn, created its own pressure for further democratization. Simultaneously, ideological emphasis upon preserving and developing Chinese culture and the arts (which the CCP was attacking), necessarily resulted in additional forms of association and modes of unregulated conduct.[124]

Overlying the whole was another trend which thoroughly undermined the Taiwan Independence Movement argument, this being the demographic fact that the principal beneficiaries of these developments were Taiwanese. Though the exile community would continue to claim discrimination, the very passage of time meant that increasingly every sector of society, to include the government and the KMT, had a growing 'born in Taiwan' complexion, whether Taiwanese or Mainlander.[125] Even the military, it should be pointed out, had always been overwhelmingly Taiwanese in its manpower, as were the police; gradually the officer ranks, as well, began to reflect this reality.

Ironically – when one considers the negative role assigned to GPWD and Wang Sheng by their critics – Political Warfare can be judged to have played an important role in facilitating all of these developments. In the largest sense, its very success in providing for troop welfare, together with developing cohesion and loyalty to established authority, meant that Taiwan never suffered military intervention in political affairs. Considered from another angle, the unity it helped engender in society at large, both through socialization of military recruits and through direct programs, aided in the emergence of issue-oriented social movements rather than those focused more narrowly upon ethnic concerns. Indeed, through its own pronounced cultural emphasis – Wang Sheng, for instance, had been a key figure in the restoration of Chinese opera in Taiwan – Political Warfare reinforced the very pluralism which was surfacing. Pronounced, as well, was Political Warfare's emphasis upon *service*, of which *Fu Hsing Kang* graduates were to be the revolutionary models. Safeguarding the revolution from threats within certainly was crucial – 'Overall, Garrison Command did a very important job', Wang Sheng was to state[126] – but his facet of such an effort was to be on a higher plane, as well illustrated in the handwritten, classically poetic mottos he had drawn up for his departments (and still in use today):

- Political Science: To lift up the cross of humanitarian politics and march into the paradise built of ethics, democracy, and science.
- Music: Sing out the voice of justice from the bottoms of our hearts and inspire the echo of humanity.
- Fine Arts: Dip with tears, blood, sweat, and paint a perfect world living in harmony.
- Physical Education: To have tough exercise of one's physical body, to have arms as strong as steel, to save our fellow compatriots who have now fallen behind the Iron Curtain.
- Drama: Make benevolence into a stage made of bread to feed the hungry souls of mankind.
- Foreign Languages: Combine the merits of Chinese and Western cultures together to carry out the idea of the *San Min Chu-i*.
- Journalism: Hold a righteous pen to tell right from wrong.
- Chinese Literature: Take up the sacred sword of Chinese culture to eradicate the devils grown out of the communist heresy.
- Social Work: Put problems and tough jobs on one's shoulders and devote charity and love to the people.
- Psychology: To have a thorough understanding of one's passions and seize the critical moment to overwhelm the enemy at first strike.[127]

Summarizes Wang Sheng:

> I think outsiders intentionally want to distort what goes on at *Fu Hsing Kang*. Political Warfare includes counterintelligence,

which gets confused with internal security. Yet my handscript on the contents of our curriculum is on display in the museum for all to see. When I set up _Fu Hsing Kang_, I saw it as having five missions: foster understanding of Chinese culture; foster an understanding of Western culture and Western democracy; research on Marxist-Leninism and studies on communism in general; teach how we should fight against communism, together with military training; and foster revolutionary spirit, to sacrifice yourself for the country. This is why it takes four years. The only real question is whether the curriculum jibes with the mission. Thus far, the record established by our graduates in serving the country would show that our sincerity has been rewarded.[128]

Taiwan had surely been rewarded, as well. For as the years passed, order and development resulted in increasing prosperity and a gathering trend towards democratization. Wang Sheng, still working his 'morning to morning' schedule, could look with satisfaction at what the revolution in exile had been able to accomplish. In other lands, however, would-be revolutionary efforts were having a far more difficult time. It was to Taiwan that they looked for assistance; and, predictably, it was Wang Sheng who was given the task of exporting Political Warfare and the KMT revolution.

NOTES

1. Fang Ch'ing-yen (Ch. 3, note 35), p. 374.
2. Cf. This selection, as noted before, contains some useful information but is clearly intended to discredit Wang Sheng. The author, writing on the mainland, claims to have been a member of a secret society with Wang Sheng and to have watched him operate; e.g. (pp. 373–4): 'Wang would occasionally laugh, boasting that the Shanghai Communist Party considered him the top spy for the Kuomintang. In Chongqing [Chungking], Wang was responsible for ferreting out communists and was empowered to use ruthless methods to do so. In a short period of time, many leftists were secretly arrested, and more than ten of them were executed'; and (p. 373) 'Wang Sheng said that he wanted to cooperate with me secretly to gain Chiang Ching-kuo's trust. I was disgusted with this idea, believing it to be ridiculously childish, since anyone could see that the Kuomintang was on its last legs. Outwardly, though, I agreed'. Wang Sheng himself does not recall a Fang Ch'ing-yen (Interview, 6 July 1994 in Carmel, California.) It is possible that he was a member of the unit who was left behind; and it is the use of contextual detail which causes me to judge that the CCP had, in fact, identified Wang Sheng as an important target and gathered information on him before he became a prominent figure in Taiwan.

3. For details on the colonial period cf. Ramon H. Myers, 'Taiwan as an Imperial Colony of Japan: 1895–1945', *Jnl of the Inst. of Chinese Studies of the Chinese Univ. of Hong Kong*, 6/2 (1973), pp. 425–53; and Myers and Mark R. Peattie (eds.), *The Japanese Colonial Empire, 1895–1945* (Princeton: Princeton UP, 1984). Interesting is Yosaburo Takekoshi, *Japanese Rule in Formosa* (New York: Longmans, Green, & Co., 1907).

4. Efforts to deal with the 28 Feb. 1947 Incident have been hampered by both the unavailability of relevant materials and the central role the bloodshed has assumed in the mythohistorical view of modern Taiwanese politics adopted by advocates of an 'independent Taiwan' (to be considered in greater detail in the text of this work). The most impressive effort to date is Lai Tse-han, Ramon H. Myers, and Wei Wou, *A Tragic Beginning: The Taiwan Uprising of February 28, 1947* (Stanford UP, 1991). For three reviews, listed in order of favorable to hostile, see: John Watt in *American Asian Review*, X/2 (Summer 1992), pp. 152–9; Harry J. Lamley in *The Jnl of Asian Studies*, 51/3 (August 1992), pp. 652–4; and C.L. Chiou in *The Australian Jnl of Chinese Affairs*, 28 (July 1992), pp. 206–9.

5. Wang Kung-tien was born 18 March 1944; Pu-tien on 7 Aug. 1947; Hsiao-tien on 3 March 1949. Thus at the time of the evacuation Kung-tien was five, Pu-tien not yet two, and Hsiao-tien less than two months.

6. Wang Sheng observes: 'From my second marriage, my second eldest child was a daughter. That daughter was hurt more than the others because of me. She was left behind on the mainland during the flight. She was raised by her grandmother, my wife's mother. When the grandma was getting old, there was no money with which to live. Eventually, she became a scissors sharpener, thousands [of pairs] per day. I feel very sorry about how this turned out. It took me a long time, but I found her. She has a boy and a girl. In 1992 I brought her with her daughter to Taiwan for three months to visit. I showed them around everywhere. Both are fine women, very filial, pious [if translated more closely but awkwardly: 'deeply practice filial piety']'. (Interview, 25 July 1993 in Taipei.)

7. Interview with Wang Pu-tien, second son of Wang Sheng, 24 July 1993 in Taipei.

8. Interview with Wang Sheng, 13 July 1993 in Taipei. Author's note: apparently, Wang Chien-kang died in 1951, though the actual date (and even year) has yet to be determined.

9. Apparently, as late as 1968 there were at least 70–80 individuals still in Taiwan who had been members of this body.

10. As best I can discern, of those who had worked with Wang Sheng and escaped to Taiwan, the largest single group – though they did not move as a unit – were former Youth Army students at Chia-hsing Youth Middle School. This is intuitively satisfying when one considers that these highly motivated young people were demobilized in a coastal area and thus had both the desire and the means to continue the fight. These two characteristics of location and motivation, in fact, appear to be the common denominator amongst those who arrived in Taiwan as individuals rather than as members of organizations which moved en masse (e.g. certain military units). Certainly a case could be made that the KMT simply took care of its own and saved those deemed most valuable (or who were most corrupt, if we take the extreme side of the negative interpretation). Yet this does not seem to have been what actually happened, judging by my interviews, though I am unaware of any study which actually details the nature of the exodus. Rather, highly motivated individuals sought to get to Taiwan where they knew the battle against the communists would continue. Indeed, for years afterwards small groups surfaced who had held out and made their way to safety. There are apparently several hundred CMA Class 16 graduates in Taiwan, as well, though the breakdown by 'campus' is unclear.

11. Interview with Lin Jung-chu, 16 July 1993 in Taipei.

12. The functions of the sixth section would later be consolidated with those of the fifth section, thus giving the system a total of just five sections. This is the structure 'Pol

War' retains today, though some of the precise duties performed by each P-section have been modified somewhat. Two additional sections, one for psychological warfare and the other for military dependents, have also been added, but they are not organized at the P-level.

13. When tables of organization are compared at this high level, the 'major-general' who was Wang Sheng's superior would be equivalent to a major-general in the US system. As the Political Work Dept head, Chiang Ching-kuo was a lieutenant-general.

14. Eastman, *Abortive Revolution* (Ch. 2, note 9), p. 1. For further discussion of the context, as well as an empathetic review of KMT shortcomings, cf. Eastman's first chapter, 'The Revolution Has Failed' (pp. 1–30).

15. Bruce J. Dickson, 'The Lessons of Defeat: The Reorganization of the Kuomintang on Taiwan, 1950–52', *China Qtly*, 133 (March 1993), p. 56 of pp. 56–84.

16. Ibid., pp. 65–8. In the published literature, this work is among the most comprehensive dealing with the KMT reform. It does contain minor errors, not the least of which is its mistaken assertion (p. 75) that the political system in the military was done away with after the Northern Expedition; but these do not detract from an exceptional piece which has made superb use of source material. It was able to fill key gaps in my own narrative.

17. Dickson in Ibid., p. 65, calls this the 'CSC', or Central Standing Committee. We are talking about the same body. Prior to the reform under discussion, it was the Standing Committee of the Central Executive Committee; after the reform, terminology adopted was the more practical Central Standing Committee (i.e. the Standing Committee of the Central Committee). To avoid confusion, I shall, like Dickson, use Central Standing Committee (CSC) throughout.

18. See e.g. Jim Mann, 'Taiwan Thriving Four Decades After CIA Predicted its Fall', *Los Angeles Times*, 6 Nov. 1993, A3. Background on US policy towards Taiwan may be found in June M. Grasso, *Truman's Two China Policy* (Armonk, NY: M.E. Sharpe, 1987), with informative reviews: Claude A. Buss, *Jnl of Asian Studies*, 47/2 (May 1988), pp. 346–7; Sandra Penrose, *Australian Jnl of Chinese Studies*, 22 (July 1989), pp. 197–9; and David Chen, 'What Was Truman's China Policy?', *Free China Review* (July 1988), pp. 24–5.

For discussion of the evolution of both American and Chinese communist plans concerning Taiwan, cf. two works by Jon W. Huebner: 'The Americanization of the Taiwan Straits', *Asian Profile*, 13/3 (June 1985), pp. 187–99; and 'The Abortive Liberation of Taiwan', *China Qtly*, 110 (June 1987), pp. 256–75. These are fairly comprehensive but must be used with caution. They perform a useful service in placing the Taiwan situation within the context of larger events and policies but at times strain to establish linkages. Thus conclusions are not always substantiated by the data presented, with sources of widely differing provenance given virtually equal weight. Particularly in the former work, this can lead to some strange twists. Noisome is the insistence upon a 'Korean civil war' framework, presented with none of the subtlety or nuance of, say, Bruce Cumings (e.g. *The Origins of the Korean War: Vol. II The Roaring of the Cataract, 1947–50* [Princeton UP, 1990]). Two other excellent manuscripts by David M. Finkelstein have come to my attention, though their availability in the published literature is not known: 'Acheson in Opposition: United States Policy Towards Formosa, 1949–1950' (dated 27 April 1983) and 'Crisis and Confusion: United States Policy Towards Formosa, June–November 1950' (dated March 1984).

19. Dickson (note 15) translates this as Central Reorganization Committee. This is not incorrect, but 'reform' conveys a greater sense of what the KMT thought it was doing. The changes were not to be mere organizational tinkering but a transformation, a *reform*.

20. Dickson (note 15), p. 65. He observes (pp. 65–7): 'All 16 members were hand-picked by Chiang Kai-shek to guarantee they would serve his interests... The CRC members

were young (average age 47, oldest 54, youngest 38) and highly educated (all received college degrees or its military equivalent; nine had studied abroad and two had a PhD from an American university). They represented virtually all important interests in the Party: military, security organization, propaganda, news media, education, youth, government and administration, representative bodies and foreign affairs. All had experience in several sectors. Five came from Chiang Kai-shek's home province of Zhejiang; the only member born in Taiwan (Lien Chen-tung) had extensive experience on the mainland. Many were already prominent in the Party: seven had belonged to the Central Executive Committee elected in 1945 (which had 223) and five to the Standing Committee of the Central Executive Committee (which had 50). Above all, Chiang had personal connections with most members, either as a teacher or as a superior officer'.

21. The function of the Control Department (or *yuan*) was oversight; it monitored the other branches of government to insure there was no abuse of power. Its role was similar to that of imperial 'censors', those whom the emperor sent to check on the functioning of the system. The Examination Department was charged with developing and implementing criteria for government personnel recruitment. The goal was that the best and the brightest would be drawn into official service.

22. Wang Sheng, *The Thought of Dr Sun Yat-sen* (Ch. 2), p. 170: 'In the *Chien-kuo Ta-kang* (*Guidelines for National Construction*) published in the same year [1924], Dr Sun laid down the three-stage procedure for China's nation-building, namely, the period of military administration, the period of political tutelage, and the period of constitutional government. The *Guidelines* also included the concrete measures for establishing the five-power constitutional system and local self-government'. Wang Sheng's work is a comprehensive treatment of Sun Yat-sen's entire corpus. For his actual *San Min Chu-i* lectures, there are numerous sources. Readily available is an abridged edition of the translation by Frank W. Price, *The Three Principles of the People* (Taipei: China Publishing Co., 1981). For a useful discussion of Sun Yat-sen's conception of democracy, see Monte R. Bullard, 'Taiwan and Democracy', draft used with permission; and Thomas A. Metzger, 'Did Sun Yat-sen understand the Idea of Democracy? The Conceptualization of Democracy in the Three Principles of the People and in John Stuart Mill's "On Liberty"', *American Asian Review*, X/1 (Spring 1992), pp. 1–41. For the actualization of Sun's philosophy, see David Wen-wei Chang, 'Political Development in Taiwan: The Sun Yat-sen Model for National Reconstruction', *Issues & Studies*, 25/5 (May 1989), pp. 11–32.

23. Interview with Wang Pu-tien, 24 July 1993 in Taipei.

24. Dickson (note 15), p. 67: eventually the CRC staff, which numbered 250 at the start of the campaign, would total 414 when it came to a close in Aug. 1952.

25. Even the location is instructive of the all-encompassing determination to build anew. Formerly Grass Mountain, it was renamed Yang Ming Shan (*shan* is 'mountain') after a renowned philosopher of the Ming Dynasty who emphasized putting philosophy into practice. The name stuck and is now in general usage.

26. Interview with Wang Sheng, 28 July 1993 in Taipei.

27. Dickson (note 15), p. 68 uses 'Political Work Cadre School', which is the literal translation, rather than the better Political Staff College; he uses the literal 'Political Warfare School' rather than the better Political Warfare College. The renderings I call 'better' – and have used in my text – are those generally accepted and which appear in official ROC publications. The English translations are chosen to convey a better sense of what is involved in the Western context (e.g. 'college' versus 'school', a college being a degree-granting institution, whereas a military school generally is not).

28. Interview with Wang Sheng, 28 July 1993 in Taipei.

29. It is worth repeating the point noted previously: I am well aware that this is an area fraught with peril. Disagreement is strong concerning not only the role played by culture in behavioral modification but even cultural content. Lucien W. Pye has

explored Chinese culture and personality in at least three works; e.g. *The Spirit of Chinese Politics* (Cambridge, MA: MIT Press, 1968); *The Mandarin and the Cadre: China's Political Cultures* (Ann Arbor, MI: Center for Chinese Studies, Univ. of Michigan, 1988); and, more recently, 'The State and the Individual: An Overview Interpretation', *China Qtly*, 127 (Sept. 1991), pp. 443–66. The debate in general has recently again burst into the open with the exchange embodied in two works: Gananath Obeyesekere, *The Apotheosis of Captain Cook: European Mythmaking in the Pacific* (Princeton UP, 1992); and Marshall Sahlins, *How Natives Think: About Captain Cook, For Example* (Univ. of Chicago Press, 1995). Extracts of the latter are available in Sahlins, 'How 'Natives' Think', *Times Literary Supplement*, 2 June 1995, pp. 12–13.

30. Interview with Wang Sheng, 28 July 1993 in Taipei.

31. In Ch'en Li-fu, (pp. 64–8) this term is rendered as *Chun-tung* [italics added]. Since the word in question originates in the *t'ung-chi-chu* of the full title (see following footnote), this would appear to be an error (i.e. the slip of an apostrophe in the transliteration).

32. Chinese intelligence services have figured prominently in recent popular works. Unfortunately, their enthusiasm has not been coupled with accuracy. See e.g. Seagrave (Ch. 2, note 4), *passim*; David Kaplan, *passim*; or Richard Deacon, *The Chinese Secret Service* (London: Grafton Books, 1989). Two of the better sources are Tien Hung-mao, esp. pp. 45–65 (wherein intelligence organs are discussed within the context of KMT factionalism); and Ch'en Li-fu, esp. pp. 64–71. Ch'en, as one of the two brothers who *were* the so-called C.C. Clique, was the founder and first head of what may be termed 'KMT intelligence'. In his memoirs he notes that in April 1927 he was ordered by Chiang Kai-shek to assemble 'a unit without any formal name' within the Organization Department headed by Ch'en's brother, Kuo-fu: 'The section's main task was to monitor and suppress communist activities' (p. 66). Similarly, Chiang Kai-shek also had Dai Li set up another agency 'only in reality but not in name' (p. 67). After two years, in April 1929, Ch'en Li-fu became Sec.-Gen. of the KMT Central Executive Committee. Finally, in May 1935, Chiang Kai-shek asked him 'to take charge of a unit called Combined Reporting on Investigation and Statistics'. Its First Branch, under Hsu En-tseng, specialized in community communist affairs; its Second Branch, under Dai Li, communist activities in the military; its Third Branch, under Ting Mo-tsun, handled the unit's organizational affairs (p. 67). When Ch'en Li-fu was moved again on 'New Year's Day of 1938' to become the Minister of Education, the unit gradually fragmented: 'My old unit collapsed, and the first branch became *Chung t'ung*, the Bureau of Investigation and Statistics of the Central Executive Committee of Chung-kuo Kuomintang [*Chung-kuo kuo-min-tang chung-yang chih-hsing wei-yuan-hui tiao-ch'a t'ung-chi-chu*], with Chu Chia-hua as head and Hsu En-tseng as deputy. The third branch was dissolved. Later, Ting Mo-tsun joined Wang Ching-wei and performed investigation and statistical work with Wang's puppet government. From that time onward, the operations of the former first and second departments working in the Japanese-occupied areas rapidly deteriorated because of bad management' (p. 67; all italics added). The Second Branch under Dai Li went on to become *Chun-t'ung*, the Bureau of Investigation and Statistics of the Military Committee of the National government (*Kuo-min cheng-fu chun-shih wei-yuan-hui tiao-ch'a t'ung-chi-chu*). 'In 1938, when I became minister of education, these two bureaus, *Chung-tung* and *Chun-tung* [sic], separately continued to investigate communist activities. In the twenty years of the National government's rule on the mainland, the two bureaus coexisted, underwent many reorganizations, and performed intelligence-gathering work' (p. 68; italics added).

33. Information in this paragraph has come in part from Ch'en Li-fu, esp. pp. 218–21; the judgements are my own.

34. Interview with Wang Sheng, 29 July 1993 in Taipei.

35. Ibid.
36. Cf. Bertil Lintner, 'The CIA's First Secret War: Americans Helped Stage Raids Into China From Burma', *Far Eastern Economic Review*, 16 Sept. 1993, pp. 56–8. The article was written, it is noted therein, 'as part of a larger research project conducted under the auspices of the John D. and Catherine T. MacArthur Foundation'. That project has now borne fruit in Lintner, *Burma in Revolt: Opium and Insurgency since 1948* (Boulder, CO: Westview Press and Bangkok: White Lotus, 1994). The drug aspects remain the inspiration for a veritable cottage industry of plot construction; see e.g. Seagrave (note 32), *passim*; and Kaplan, *passim*. In a typical passage, Kaplan (p. 228) writes: 'Before long, the region had become the source of much of the world's heroin, with KMT wholesalers selling to Chinese crime syndicates who in turn marketed 'China White' worldwide. This much has been widely reported. What has escaped public attention is the consistent, institutional commitment of the government of Taiwan to the heroin trade. Since the 1950s, the poppy fields of the Golden Triangle have served as a cash crop for the KMT's military intelligence branch'.
37. IBMND is normally viewed as comparable to the US Defense Intelligence Agency (DIA), in that its specialization is military intelligence. Like DIA, it is an organ of the military, not the entirety of the military intelligence function embodied in the Staff-2 section at various unit levels (e.g. S-2, G-2). Whereas IBMND focuses upon information collection and intelligence production, especially at the strategic level, with some capacity for direct action, the Staff-2 sections are dedicated principally towards providing tactical intelligence in response to the operational designs of the unit commander. The ROC Army, however, unlike the American, does not have a Military Intelligence *branch* in which officers spend their entire careers, rotating amongst intelligence assignments. Thus those who fill 'intelligence' positions – i.e. Staff-2 positions – will frequently have only rudimentary skill levels compared to professionals; e.g. many in IBMND. *Chung-t'ung*, though it apparently did not become so directly, is the predecessor of the National Security Bureau (NSB), a 'civilian' body which is the functional equivalent of the US Central Intelligence Agency (CIA). Like the CIA, the NSB has many active duty military personnel assigned to it. Unlike the CIA, however, it is normal for the NSB to be headed by an active duty military officer. There is also another civilian agency, the Investigation Bureau, which is under the Ministry of Justice and is the ROC counterpart of the US Federal Bureau of Investigation (FBI).
38. Interview with Wang Sheng, 29 July 1993 in Taipei. This is a passage from his book *Political Warfare*, 1963 ed. (trans. Wen Ha-hsiung), p. 3, which he pointed out. Yet the words I have italicized were translated in the text as 'do not need to resort to violence'. This, Wang Sheng clarified, does not convey the complete sense of his meaning. He is not advocating passivity or nonviolence in a Gandhian sense but rather active measures which are other than military. A more complete appreciation of the historical antecedents in the Chinese context may be found in the work of Sun Tzu, wherein he states: 'The supreme art of war is to subdue the enemy without fighting'. (Letter from Sir John Duncan to B.H. Liddell Hart, Spring 1927, quoted by Hart in his Foreward [see p. vii] to Samuel B. Griffith (ed. and trans.), *Sun Tzu: The Art of War* [London: OUP, 1963].) Griffith's own translation of the passage (p. 77) is: 'To subdue the enemy without fighting is the acme of skill'. For other readily available texts dealing with Sun Tzu, see Ralph D. Sawyer, (ed. and trans.), *The Seven Military Classics of Ancient China* (Boulder, CO: Westview Press, 1993), pp. 145–86; and J.H. Huang (ed. and trans.), *Sun Tzu: The New Translation* (New York: Morrow and Co., 1993).
39. For further discussion on this point, see the seminal work, Samuel P. Huntington, *The Soldier and the State: The Theory and Politics of Civil-Military Relations* (Cambridge, MA: Harvard UP, 1964), *passim*.

40. A military concept, the multiplication of combat power refers to those measures which may be taken so that weapons systems or unit operations increase in efficiency and/or lethality. An infantry unit of low morale, for instance, is not the equal of an infantry unit of motivated soldiers. Likewise, one well-trained soldier may be worth a dozen untrained, and so on. The emphasis in Political Warfare is upon active measures which can be taken to facilitate conditions such as enemy low morale or lack of training, thus multiplying the effect of whatever force is possessed by the friendly side.

41. Illustrations are drawn from Heinlein (Ch. 2, note 97), pp. 70–86.

42. Wang Sheng, *Political Warfare*, p. 5. The parenthetical explanations have been adopted, with permission, from Monte Bullard, 'The Soldier and the Citizen: Taiwan's Military in Political Socialization', draft MS, pp. 93–4.

43. Ibid., 19..

44. Interview with Wang Sheng, 29 July 1993 in Taipei.

45. Ibid.

46. Ibid.

47. On p. 658 in Lloyd E. Eastman, 'Research Note: Who Lost China? Chiang Kai-shek Testifies', *China Qtly*, 87 (Sept. 1981), pp. 658–68.

48. Ibid., pp. 666–7. Eastman cites the quotation as having come from Chiang Kai-shek's own *Soviet Russia in China: A Summing-Up at Seventy* (Taipei, 1969), p. 256. In my own copy (New York: Farrar, Straus and Cudahy, 1957), the quotation may be found on p. 242 and is slightly different from that used by Eastman. Nevertheless, the changes are not substantial and do not alter the meaning in any way.

49. Discussed in Hu Kuo-tai, 'The Struggle Between the Kuomintang and the Chinese Communist Party on Campus During the War of Resistance, 1937–45', *China Qtly*, 118 (June 1989), pp. 300–23. He identifies it as: *Sanshinian lai bendang yu zhonggong zhanzheng de jiantao* (*Review on the 30 Years of War Between the Kuomintang and the Chinese Communist Party*)(n.p., 1951), stored in the Library of the Bureau of Investigation, Ministry of Justice, Taipei.

50. Cf. Chang Chi-yun, *The Rebirth of the Kuomintang (The Seventh National Congress)*, trans. Nee Yuan-ching; rev. and ed. Tsao Wen-yen (Taipei: China Cultural Service, nd/offprint), p. 19.

51. Ch'en Li-fu, p. 235. It is worth noting that in the same passage, the author observes, 'I also consider Chiang a product of his era, a military-political leader of modern China. His talents were more military than political. Chiang possessed considerable intelligence and courage'.

52. General Political Warfare Department (GPWD), *General Briefing on Political Warfare System in the Chinese Armed Forces* (Taipei: Ministry of National Defense, npd [c.1960]), p. 8.

53. Interview with Wang Sheng, 28 July 1993 in Taipei.

54. Ibid.

55. This misunderstanding of the Political Officer role is one area where Dickson, *op.cit.* (p. 75) is in serious error. He draws his material on this matter almost exclusively from Tien Hung-mao, *The Great Transition: Political and Social Change in the Republic of China* (Stanford, CA: Hoover Instn Press, 1989), p. 68. In an important passage, Tien states: 'Party reorganization was also carried out in the armed forces, where Chiang Ching-kuo was instructed by his father, Chiang Kai-shek, to establish a system of political commissars. These political commissars were charged with forming and supervising party cells, conducting political indoctrination, and serving as the party's eyes and ears in the military'. At a minimum, these lines overstate the case; taken as a whole, they are inaccurate.

56. Certainly Political Officers had *indirect* veto power over promotions. They were specifically and openly charged with counterintelligence. A report judging that an officer was not ideologically suitable would undoubtedly have spelled the end for his career. What is significant, though, is that any such report would be placed in an

officer's file to be considered *by other officers* within the chain of command as one criterion among many. The process was established openly and subject to command review.

57. Interview with Wang Zong-han, *Fu Hsing Kang* Director of Communist Affairs (Enemy Studies), 21 July 1993 in Taipei. It may be further noted that the present Commandant, Lt.-Gen. Teng Tsu-lin, is also an infantry officer whose career has been spent principally with airborne units. He has never been a Political Officer. (Interview with Teng Tsu-lin, 21 July 1993 in Taipei.)

58. Interview with Lin Tzon-zu, former *Fu Hsing Kang* Director of Student Affairs, 21 July 1993 in Taipei.

59. Interview with Liao Kuang-hsun, 22 July 1993 in Taipei.

60. Interview with Liu Jing-shing, 22 July 1993 in Taipei.

61. Interview with Wang Sheng, 28 July 1993 in Taipei.

62. Telephone conversation with Wang Kung-tien, eldest son of Wang Sheng, 26 July 1994.

63. Excellent discussions of Taiwan's economic background and progress to the present may be found in Stephen Haggard, *Pathways from the Periphery: The Politics of Growth in the Newly Industrializing Countries* (Ithaca, NY: Cornell UP, 1990), esp. pp. 76–99; and Robert Wade, *Governing the Market: Economic Theory and the Role of Government in East Asian Industrialization* (Princeton UP, 1990). For a shorter term historical overview see Samuel P.S. Ho, *Economic Development of Taiwan, 1860–1970* (New Haven, CT: Yale UP, 1978). Peter P.C. Cheng – in an article as interested in attacking its subject as in delivering analysis – stresses the importance of American aid in his often overstated but useful 'Taiwan Under Chiang Kai-shek's Era: 1945-1976', *Asian Profile*, 16/4 (Aug. 1988), pp. 299–315 (see esp. pp. 306–9). Further discussion of the American role may be found in T.H. Shen, *The Sino-American Joint Commission on Rural Reconstruction* (Ithaca, NY: Cornell UP, 1970); and Joseph A. Yager, *Transforming Agriculture in Taiwan: The Experience of the Joint Commission on Rural Reconstruction* (ibid., 1988). A discussion of the land reform itself, within a comparative framework, is provided by Tuan Chia-feng, 'A Comparison of the Land Reform Programs in the Republic of China on Taiwan and Communist China', *Issues & Studies*, XVIII/12 (Dec. 1982), pp. 62–83. A comprehensive discussion of the important early period is Walter Galenson (ed.), *Economic Growth and Structural Change in Taiwan: The Postwar Experience in the Republic of China* (Ithaca, NY: Cornell UP, 1979).

64. The best review of the figures involved, as well as the literature publishing these figures, is the comprehensive series by Rudolph J. Rummel on genocide and government mass murder, or what he terms democide. To date four volumes have appeared. See in particular R.J. Rummel, *China's Bloody Century: Genocide and Mass Murder since 1900* (New Brunswick, NJ: Transaction Press, 1991); and *Death by Government: Genocide and Mass Murder since 1900* (New Brunswick, NJ: Transaction Press, 1994). This said, it must be noted that Rummel's dependence upon secondary sources dictates that his discussion is most credible where there is a plethora of data; i.e. when discussing China under communist rule. In contrast, his sections dealing with the Nationalist era, which he places as 1921–48, are simply inadequate. For a quick summary of figures see John Omicinski, 'Earth's Deadliest Century', *Honolulu Advertiser*, 11 Dec. 1994, B1.

65. Interview with Lin Jung-chu, CMA Class 16 member (retired LTG, former Political Officer), 16 July 1993 in Taipei.

66. Interview with Wang Pu-tien, 24 July 1993 in Taipei.

67. Interview with Liao Kuang-hsun, 22 July 1993 in Taipei.

68. Interview with Wang Pu-tien, 24 July 1993 in Taipei.

69. Ibid.

70. Ibid.

71. I base this conclusion on the material I gathered in Taipei during my interviews with Wang Hsiao-li (25 July 1993) and Wang Hsiao-tien (13 July 1993).
72. Says Wang Pu-tien: 'Some were rich, some were beautiful, some were overseas Chinese from the Philippines'. (Interview, 24 July 1993 in Taipei.)
73. Ibid.
74. Wang Kung-tien earned a PhD in Engineering from Tennessee Technical Institute; Wang Pu-tien an MS in Electronics from University of Tennessee (Knoxville); Wang Hsiao-tien a PhD in Fluid Mechanics from University of Tennessee (Knoxville); and Wang Hsiao-li a MFA (Theater) from Trinity. All are bilingual and work in either the US or Taiwan.
75. Interview with Wang Pu-tien, 24 July 1993 in Taipei.
76. At the time of writing, Wang Li-tien was completing the dissertation for a PhD in Computer Science from Stevens Institute of Technology. He is a university instructor in the United States.
77. Interview with Wang Hsiao-tien, 13 July 1993 in Taipei.
78. Interview with Wang Hsiao-li, 25 July 1993 in Taipei.
79. Lt.-Gen. (Ret.) Wang Yeh-kai, a bilingual officer with an excellent command of English (from 1982–84 he was ROC Army Attaché in the United States), notes: 'His [Wang Sheng] presentation is superb. I was his interpreter [while Chief of the Information Division, GPWD], but I had a hard time conveying the richness of his thought'. (Interview, 28 July 1993 in Taipei.)
80. Interview with Wang Sheng, 29 July 1993 in Taipei.
81. Interview with Wang Sheng, 24 July 1993 in Taipei.
82. Ibid.
83. Ibid.
84. An excellent reference, showing organizational structures and chains of command for Political Warfare, is *The Political Establishment in the Chinese Armed Forces* (Taipei: Political Dept, Ministry of National Defense, Feb. 1960).
85. Interview with Wang Sheng, 24 July 1993 in Taipei.
86. This determination by Wang Sheng, that the Political Warfare cadre would serve as the independent guardians of the revolution is ill-understood, as is their relationship to the command structure. It is worth comparing my own data with a typical passage of purple prose in the popular press, in this case David Kaplan (Ch. 1, note 24), p. 61: 'The Political Warfare Cadres Academy had been planned by Ching-kuo as early as the fall of 1950. The academy was CCK's chance to apply what he had learned in Moscow about Communist thought control. Through a system of political commissars placed in every military unit – and personally loyal to him – Ching-kuo could ensure his control over the military. At the same time, the academy graduates would give him an élite intelligence force, allowing him to move away from the KMT's traditional use of underworld figures and thugs to college-educated operatives trained in research, analysis, and modern espionage. He had borrowed the best, it seemed, not only from his training in Moscow but from his work with the CIA'.
87. See esp. Ch. 4 ('Target Audience: Military') in Bullard (note 42).
88. Best single source on these relationships and the programs involved is Ch. 5 ('Target Audience: Youth') in ibid. A pictorial look at typical China Youth Corps activities following the organization's establishment as an independent body may be found in 'Challenge: Students Flock to Vacation "Battle Camp"', *Free China Review* (April 1983), pp. 36–43.
89. See Ch. 6 ('Target Audience: Civilian Populace') in Bullard (note 42).
90. Interview with Wang Sheng, 28 July 1993 in Taipei.
91. Cf. Melvin Gurtov, 'The Taiwan Strait Crisis Revisited: Politics and Foreign Policy in Chinese Motives', *Modern China*, 2/1 (Jan. 1976), pp. 49–103; Kwan Ha-yim (ed.), *China and the US 1955–63* (New York: Facts on File, 1973); Tang Tsou, *The Embroilment Over Quemoy: Mao, Xhang, and Dulles*, International Study Paper No.

2 (Ogdan, UT: Inst. of Int. Studies, Univ. of Utah, 1959); Sukhumbhand Paribatra, *The Taiwan Straits Crisis of 1958: A Study of the Use of Naval Power*, Asian Studies Monographs No. 030 (Bangkok: Inst. of Asian Studies, Chulalongkorn Univ., 1981); Allen S. Whiting, 'New Light on Mao – 3. Quemoy 1958: Mao's Miscalculations', *China Qtly*, 62 (June 1975), pp. 263–70; and Kenneth S. Chern, 'The Ideology of American China Policy, 1945–1960', *Jnl of Oriental Studies* [Hong Kong], XX/2 (1982), pp. 155–72. Tang, in particular, provides a wealth of data but must be used with care, as his analysis is strongly influenced by the 'Chiang Kai-shek as Machiavelli' school of thought.

92. A useful recapitulation, with photos, is Wang Chien-hui, 'Anniversary: Bombardment of Quemoy', *Free China Review* (Aug. 1988), pp. 32–41. An estimated 25,000 artillery rounds struck Quemoy during the first two hours of bombardment, with some 57,000 fired by the communists the first day alone. Chiang Kai-shek, Chiang Ching-kuo, and Wang Sheng all visited the islands, to include several outlying points, during the crisis.

93. See esp. Tang Tsou (note 91).

94. Interview with Wang Sheng, 28 July 1993 in Taipei. Wang Sheng's lieutenant-general rank in the ROC system was now equivalent to lieutenant-general in the American system as judged by span of control.

95. Numerous versions of Chiang Ching-kuo's official and unofficial positions exist. The one I have used, which I find accurate, is drawn from *Republic of China Yearbook 1989* (Taipei: Kwang Hwa Publishing Co., 1989), X–XI. The version given in Cline is also generally correct, though several positions are translated confusingly (e.g. the use of 'National Security Council' for years when it was still the 'National Defense Council'.

96. The official title is the Standing Committee of the Kuomintang (KMT) Central Committee. It is the equivalent of the Politburo in a communist Leninist system. The Nov. 1979 Fourth Plenary Session of the KMT Eleventh Central Committee, at which this increase was made, is discussed (and the entire Standing Committee listed, with new members indicated) in Yang Ming-che, 'Kuomintang on the Move for the 1980s', *Free China Review* (Jan. 1980), pp. 13–22. In Feb. 1984 the body was expanded to 31 members; see p. 90 of James C. Hsiung, 'Taiwan in 1984: Festivity, New Hope, and Caution', *Asian Survey*, XXV/1 (Jan. 1985), pp. 90–6. A complete list of the 31 members is contained in Tien, pp. 78–80 (Table 4.2).

97. See pp. 48–9 in James Franklin Cooper, 'Taiwan in 1981: In a Holding Pattern', *Asian Survey*, XXII/1 (Jan. 1982), pp. 47–55.

98. For fascinating insight into this body, cf. Ch'en, pp. 239–41, which discusses the actions which occurred upon the death of Chiang Kai-shek.

99. The present holder of the position, President Lee Teng-hui, was named in July 1988 following the death of Chiang Ching-kuo. Cf. Thomas Ching-peng Peng, 'President Lee's Rise to Power and His Reform Program', *Issues & Studies*, 28/6 (June 1992), pp. 59–69.

100. Though this would be but the third rung in the general officer progression of the Nationalist armed forces, due to span of control exercised, the American equivalent would be four-stars. On official visits to the US, this was the rank used by the hosts for protocol purposes.

101. GPWD does have command authority over its own, organic counterintelligence (CI) regiment (or brigade), which is charged with performing the 'CI' function within the military.

102. See p. 486 of Edwin A. Winckler, 'Institutionalization and Participation on Taiwan: From Hard to Soft Authoritarianism?', *China Qtly*, 99 (Sept. 1984), pp. 481–99.

103. See p. 619 of Tien Hung-mao, 'Taiwan in Transition: Prospects for Socio-Political Change', *China Qtly*, 64 (Dec. 1975), pp. 615–44.

104. See p. 114 of Gold (Ch. 2, note 1).

105. Testimony of Mrs Helen A. Liu before Congressional sub-committee hearings regarding House Congressional Resolutions 49 and 110, 7 Feb. 1985. See *The Murder of Henry Liu: Hearings and Markup before the Committee on Foreign Affairs and its Subcommittee on Asian and Pacific Affairs, House of Representatives (99th Congress, 1st Session)*(Washington, DC: US Govt Printing Office [hereafter GPO], 1985), p. 48. In the same statement (p. 46), Mrs Liu claims her husband, murdered journalist Henry Liu, while attending *Fu Hsing Kang* as a student, met both Chiang Wei-kuo (Chiang Ching-kuo's half brother) and Wang Sheng. The case of Henry Liu will be discussed later in the text. Suffice it to say here that it is doubtful any such acquaintance occurred. Wang Sheng himself states that he has no recollection of ever meeting Henry Liu, who was, in fact, a cadet but did not graduate. There are hundreds of cadets per class. (Interview with Wang Sheng, 28 July 1993 in Taipei).
106. Testimony of Martin L. Lasater before Congressional subcommittee hearing regarding House Congressional Resolution 129, 31 May 1984. See *Political Developments in Taiwan: Hearings and Markup before the Subcommittee on Asian and Pacific Affairs of the Committee on Foreign Affairs, House of Representatives (98th Congress, 2nd Session)*(Washington, DC: US GPO, 1984), p. 81.
107. Cf. Kaplan (note 112), *passim*.
108. See p. 434 of Maria Hsia Chang, 'Political Succession in the Republic of China on Taiwan', *Asian Survey*, XXIV/4 (April 1984), pp. 423–46.
109. One of the best readily available sources is the Congressional hearing held on 20 May 1982, *Martial Law on Taiwan and United States Foreign Policy Interests: Hearing before the Subcommittee on Asian and Pacific Affairs of the Committee on Foreign Affairs, House of Representatives (97th Congress, 2nd Session)*(Washington, DC: US GPO, 1982). See also Peng Ming-min, 'Political Offences in Taiwan: Laws and Problems', *China Qtly*, 47 (July/Sept. 1971), pp. 471–93.
110. Cf. the excerpts from Chiu Hung-dah, 'Law and Justice', in James C. Hsiung (ed.), *Contemporary Republic of China: The Taiwan Experience 1950–1980* (New York: Praeger, 1981), pp. 328–30, 336–7; contained in App. 4 ('Material Submitted by A. James Gregor') of ibid., pp. 193–8. Chiu is possibly the best (and certainly the most dispassionate) discussion of the legal aspects of martial law. His comparison of the different martial law expectations and powers in civil as opposed to common law countries is revealing. For a comparative framework, cf. Franz Michael, 'The Role of Law in Traditional, Nationalist and Communist China', *China Qtly*, 9 (Jan.–March 1962), pp. 124–48.
111. As pointed out by Wang Yu-san in his Congressional testimony contained in Ibid, pp. 80–9, while in theory there were 106 kinds of offenses, in reality these amounted to four categories: '(1) Sedition and espionage; (2) Theft or purchase or sale of military equipment and supplies; (3) Stealing or damaging military communication or communication equipment; and (4) Stealing, damaging, transporting, or warehousing pipelines, telegraph, telephone, broadcasting, television, underwater cables which are in violation of "Communications and Electronic Equipment Protection Statute during War Time"' (p. 83).
112. John Kaplan, *The Court-Martial of the Kaohsiung Defendants*, Research Papers and Policy Studies No. 2 (Berkeley: Inst. of East Asian Studies, Univ. of California, 1981), p. 21, perceptively points out: 'The legal system on Taiwan is the product of seventy years of rapid change. It not only retains remnants of the Imperial legal system of ancient China but contains elements of the inquisitorial and adversary systems as well. During the early twentieth century, in its drive for Westernization, China attempted to reform itself upon European lines. The particular Western model selected for the legal system was Germany, the nation whose criminal process was the closest to a pure inquisitorial system in Europe. Indeed, many of the law professors in Taiwan's universities today received their legal training in Germany. Lately, however, under the influence of America and Anglo-American law, the criminal procedure on Taiwan has

become more adversary, and greater attention has been given to protecting the autonomy of the individual'. He continues: 'Though reams have been written about the differences between the inquisitorial system and the adversary system, the basic definition lies in the way the proceedings are regarded. In the Anglo-American adversary system the procedure is conceived of as a dispute between two parties, the State and the individual, a dispute which must be resolved by an independent, impartial judge or jury, after hearing both sides. In the inquisitorial system the proceedings are perceived as an investigation by the State, conducted by impartial judges, into the question of whether or not a crime has been committed, and if so, by whom'.

113. For a typical example see Edel Lancashire, 'Popeye and the Case of Guo Yidong, Alias Bo Yang', *China Qtly*, 92 (Dec. 1982), pp. 663–86.

114. Early sources include: Maurice Meisner, 'The Development of Formosan Nationalism', *China Qtly*, 15 (July–Sept. 1963), pp. 91–114; George Kerr, *Formosa Betrayed* (Boston: Houghton, Mifflin, 1965); and Douglas Mendel, *The Politics of Formosan Nationalism* (Berkeley: Univ. of California Press, 1970). For further historical background on the pre-Nationalist era, see Kerr, *Formosa: Licensed Revolution and the Home Rule Movement, 1895–1945* (Honolulu: UP of Hawaii, 1974).

115. One effort of which I am aware that attempts to go beyond the impressionistic to explore this subject in a systematic manner is Chang Wen-lung, 'A Study of Political Coercion in Urban Taiwan', Northwestern Univ. PhD diss., 1972. For all its promise, the study is disappointing due to flawed methodology. It equates any actions by a government entity, such as the police, with *political* coercion. Consequently, dissatisfaction among blue collar workers with police harassment, to cite but one prominent selection, becomes equated with *systemic* disaffection. Yet the evidence provided in this – and other cases – would seem to demonstrate precisely the opposite, unfocused disaffection with abuse of authority resulting in the subjects' verbal abuse of the system. This would appear to be a response not particularly unique or related to political coercion as the term is most usefully understood.

116. See e.g. Sheldon Appleton, 'Taiwanese and Mainlanders on Taiwan: A Survey of Student Attitudes', *China Qtly*, 44 (Oct.–Dec. 1970), pp. 38–65, together with the exchange between the author and Gordon Bennett in ibid., 46 (April–June 1971), pp. 353–7; Richard W. Wilson, *Learning to be Chinese: The Political Socialization of Children in Taiwan* (Cambridge, MA: MIT Press, 1970); Roberta Martin, 'The Socialization of Children in China and on Taiwan: An Analysis of Elementary School Textbooks', ibid., 62 (June 1975), pp. 242–61; Jeffrey E. Meyer, 'Teaching Morality in Taiwan Schools: The Message of the Textbooks', ibid., p. 114 (June 1988), pp. 267–84; and Jau-shieh Joseph Wu, 'Analysis of Individual Level Transformation in Taiwan: A Note on Development Theory and the Implications for Third World Communism', *Issues & Studies*, 26/11 (Nov. 1990), pp. 116–33.

117. In addition to the several sources cited earlier, one may profitably consult, for insight into this period: Thomas W. Robinson (ed.), *Democracy and Development in East Asia: Taiwan, South Korea, and the Philippines* (Washington, DC: American Enterprise Institute Press, 1991); Lin Ching-yuan, *Industrialization in Taiwan, 1946–72: Trade and Import-Substitution Policies for Developing Countries* (New York: Praeger, 1973); Ramon H. Myers, 'The Economic Transformation of the Republic of China on Taiwan', *China Qtly*, 99 (Sept. 1984), pp. 500–28; John C.H. Fei, 'A Historical Perspective on Economic Modernization in the ROC', Ch. 4 in Ramon H. Myers (ed.), *Two Societies in Opposition: The Republic of China and the People's Republic of China After Forty Years* (Stanford, CA: Hoover Instn Press, 1991); Andrew B. Brick, 'The East Asian Development Miracle: Taiwan as a Model', *Issues & Studies*, 28/8 (Aug. 1992), p. 1–13; and Samuel P.S. Ho, 'South Korea and Taiwan: Development Prospects and Problems in the 1980s', *Asian Survey*, XXI/12 (Dec. 1981), pp.

1175–96. A source which attempts to relate economic and political development, with particular note taken of repression, is Gold. Useful reviews, which contribute in their own discussions, are: J. Bruce Jacobs in *Australian Jnl of Chinese Affairs*, 16 (July 1986), pp. 145–7; John R. Watt in *American Asian Review*, IV/3 (Fall 1986), pp. 110–14; Lin Ching-yuan in *Pacific Affairs*, 60/2 (Summer 1987), pp. 331–2; and Dennis Duncanson in *China Qtly*, 112 (Dec. 1987), pp. 678–9. Though all of these reviews are generally impressed with Gold's attempt to use a fresh methodology, several note problems with data. This has been my own experience when dealing with those portions directly applicable to my subject. Another such attempt at economic and political synthesis is James C. Hsiung, *Contemporary Republic of China: The Taiwan Experience, 1950–1980* (New York, Praeger, 1981).

118. Any of the Congressional hearings previously cited (notes 105 and 106) may be used to gain details of such accusations, together with considerable details of individual cases. The close relations between Washington and Taipei have insured the regular examination by the US Congress of the specifics of Taiwan's internal security mechanisms. The high level of interest notwithstanding, the subject matter has guaranteed that testimony has generally been long on emotion and short on substance. A good exchange on 14 June 1977, one of the more low key, is contained in *Human Rights in Taiwan: Hearing Before the Subcommittee on International Organizations of the Committee on International Relations, House of Representatives (95th Congress, 1st Session)* (Washington, DC: US GPO, 1977).

119. In a peculiar note (n. 51), Maria Hsia Chang, 'Political Succession in the Republic of China on Taiwan', p. 435, observes: 'According to Huang Hsin (in CSNT, p. 39), in 1979 Chiang Ching-kuo removed the Garrison Command from the jurisdiction of the National Security Bureau and placed it under the command of the Ministry of Defense in order to place the Command under the direct influence of Wang Sheng'. Notwithstanding its reliance upon another party for its information, the note contains little that is accurate. Initially, when Taiwan was recovered from the Japanese in 1945, the island's internal security came under the responsibility of the Southeast Executive Administration – which included parts of the mainland, such as the area around Canton. Under this body was a Security Preservation Dept. With the loss of the mainland in 1949–50, the SE Executive Admin. was disbanded, and the Security Preservation Dept became the Taiwan Security Preservation Command (Cmnd) under Peng Meng-chi. It was under the command authority of the Chief of General Staff (CGS). On 1 July 1958, while Wang Sheng was still Commandant of *Fu Hsing Kang*, the Security Preservation Comnd was given service-level status (i.e. made equal to the Army, Navy, and Air Force) and redesignated the Taiwan General Garrison Command (TGGC), its official title (*Taiwan chin-pei tsong si-ling-pu*). Absorbed by this much larger organization – hence the new title – were the previous Taiwan Security Preservation Cmnd, the Taiwan Civil Defense Cmnd, the Taiwan Defense Cmnd, and the Taiwan Garrison Cmnd (a military HQ). The Security Preservation Cmnd itself became a dept under the new TGGC, which in English is normally shortened in Taiwan Garrison Cmnd. These details are accurately related in *Chung-hwa min-kao nien-chien 1958 (ROC Yearbook 1958)* (Taipei: ROC Yearbook Society, 1958), p. 363. The TGGC remained under command of the CGS, who, of course, was ultimately responsible to the Minister of National Defense.

The National Security Bureau (NSB), the Taiwan equivalent of the American CIA, has never had 'jurisdiction' (or any command authority) over the TGGC or its forerunners. Neither was the TGGC ever under any body other than the CGS. A possible mistranslation by Maria Hsia Chang – 'National Security Bureau' rendered rather than 'National Security Council'? [I do not have access to the original Chinese source text] – would not rescue the passage, since the National Security Council also has never commanded the TGGC. The National *Defense* Council, the forerunner of the National *Security* Council (the name was changed on 16 Feb. 1967), was formed on 1 July 1954, with Hwang Shao-ku as its Sec.-Gen. and Chiang Kai-shek as its Chairman. The NSB was under its supervision, but neither body had anything to do with the command relationships of the TGGC. For particulars of organization cf. *Tung-yuan kan-lun shi-chi kao-chia huei-yi yun-tsao kai-kwang pao-kao* (*A Brief Report on the Operation of the National Security Council during the Period of General Mobilization and Rebellion Suppression*), a report by Hwang Shao-ku to the Fifth Session of the First National Assembly, 29 Feb. 1972, bound and catalogued in East Asian Collection of Hoover Instn, Stanford Univ. (No. 4890.231//6748.677). Finally, as explained in the text, even if we allow for a move *which did not in fact occur* – the 'Taiwan Garrison Command' going from 'National Security Bureau' to 'Ministry of National Defense' – the passage collapses in its logic, because Wang Sheng in 1979 was a staff officer serving the CGS and had no power to rate, appoint, or transfer Taiwan Garrison Cmnd. officers other than his own Political Officers posted to its Political Dept. as described in the text which follows.

120. Under the TGGC's Security Preservation Dept. were five prisons, separate from Taiwan's normal system of criminal prisons. Three were designated correctional institutes and were for ideological offenders (e.g. treason). Two were designated vocational training brigades and were for behavioral offenders (e.g. murder). What would generally be termed 'political prisoners' were, of course, in the correctional institutes. These, unlike the vocational training brigades, normally had Political Officers assigned as commanders, because their thrust was rehabilitation. The actual mechanism for assignment involved the Security Preservation Department talking to the chief of staff of its parent TGGC, who in turn dealt with the Political Officer assigned to head the Garrison Command's own Political Dept. A Political Officer assigned as head of a prison was under the command authority of the Security Preservation Dept., but he would coordinate with the Political Officer of the Garrison Command's Political Dept.. Most of the personnel actually working in the prisons, however, had no connection with GPWD. Hence, supervisory problems were ongoing. In addition to the involvement of Political Officers with the TGGC's prison system, the P-3 Dept of GPWD ran two correctional institutes of its own – *Ming Te* (Understanding Virtue) and *Jin Te* (Advanced Virtue) – for military offenders who had committed offenses short of court martial level (the American military equivalent, now abandoned, would be the practice of assigning soldiers to 'disciplinary barracks' for offenses deemed serious but insufficient to invoke the Uniform Code of Military Justice, UCMJ). The emphasis in *Ming Te* and *Jin Te* was on strict discipline and education; those who did not measure up in *Ming Te* were sent to *Jin Te*.

121. The concept is well discussed in an entire issue of *Modern China*, 19/2 (April 1993), pp. 107–239. Though the focus is upon the mainland, the concepts developed have applicability to Taiwan, which is mentioned in several of the essays. See esp. Philip C.C. Huang, '"Public Sphere"/"Civil Society" in China? The Third Realm Between State and Society', pp. 216–39. Another work, which endeavors to apply the concept specifically to Taiwan, is Hsin-Huang Michael Hsiao, 'Emerging Social Movements and the Rise of a Demanding Civil Society in Taiwan', *Australian Jnl of Chinese Affairs*, 24 (July 1990), pp. 163–79. For general consideration of the concept, cf. Adam Seligman, *The Idea of Civil Society* (New York: The Free Press, 1992); and Ernest Gellner, *Conditions of Liberty: Civil Society and its Rivals* (New York: Allen Lane/Penguin Press, 1994). Useful are two reviews of Gellner: Francis Fukuyama, 'The Mystery Deepens: The Persistance and Fragility of Civil Society', *Times Literary Supplement*, 28 Oct. 1994, pp. 3–4; and Alan Ryan, 'Why Democracy? A Scholar Asks if Liberal Democracy Is Really All There Is', *New York Times Book Review*, 1 Jan. 1995, p. 8.

122. Statistically, Taiwan remains a country with one of the most equitable distributions of wealth in the world. Its Gini coefficient in 1989 was 0.303; its ratio of income for the top 20 per cent of households compared to the bottom 20 per cent of households was

just 4.94 (as compared with the U.S. figure, which is on the order of 16). Although recent research has pointed out that these measures have increased since 1980, thus demonstrating a growing accumulation of wealth at the top, they remain low, both in global and temporal perspectives (e.g. the Taiwan figures for 1964 are higher than those for 1989). Cf. Ke-jeng Lan and Jiann-chyuan Wang, 'The Taiwan Experience in Economic Development', *Issues & Studies*, 27/10 (Oct. 1991), pp. 135–57.

123. Cf. Hsin-huang Michael Hsiao, 'The Changing State-Society Relation in the ROC: Economic Change, the Transformation of the Class Structure, and the Rise of Social Movements', Chapter 6 in Ramon Myers (ed.), *Two Societies in Opposition: The Republic of China and the People's Republic of China after Forty Years* (Stanford: Hoover Instn Press, 1991), pp. 127–40; also Tsai Wen-hui, 'Protest Movements in Taiwan in the 1980s', *American Asian Review*, VIII/4 (Winter 1990), pp. 116–34. For a largely impressionistic look at politics below the national level during the early period in Taiwan, cf. Arthur J. Lerman, *Taiwan's Politics: The Provincial Assemblyman's World* (Washington, DC: UP of America, 1978).

124. For the particulars of the artistic movement, see e.g. Edel Lancashire, '*The Lock of the Heart* Controversy in Taiwan, 1962–63: A Question of Artistic Freedom and a Writer's Social Responsibility', *China Qtly*, 103 (Sept. 1985), pp. 462–88; also W. Tozer, 'Taiwan's 'Cultural Renaissance': A Preliminary View', ibid., 43 (July-Sept. 1970), pp. 81–99. The analysis of the systemic consequences is my own.

125. See e.g. the discussion and data in Lee Kuo-wei, 'The Road to Democracy: Taiwan Experience', *Asian Profile* [Hong Kong], 19/6 (Dec. 1991), pp. 489–504.

126. Interview with Wang Sheng, 28 July 1993 in Taipei.

127. The original handwritten sheets upon which Wang Sheng wrote these mottos are on display in the *Fu Hsing Kang* museum.

128. Interview with Wang Sheng, 29 July 1993 in Taipei.

5 Counterrevolution Exported

Wang Sheng and the commander of US forces in Vietnam, General William C. Westmoreland.

IT IS NOW necessary to step back in time. As the 1960s dawned, the KMT revolution-in-exile had been at war with the mainland for a decade. As such, it had become the *counterrevolution* for the reasons we have discussed throughout this work. To go directly to the heart of the matter, the KMT revolution, relatively isolated in its small Taiwan domain, though it ruled over a society increasingly stable and prosperous, was unable to influence directly events on the mainland. There, in the People's Republic of China, the bulk of the Chinese people lived under the CCP version of the national and social revolution. That the course charted by the CCP was something of a disaster was quite irrelevant to the fact that the KMT guardians of Sun Yat-sen's *San Min Chu-i* on Taiwan, for all their determination, could not expect to return home in the foreseeable future. The communist position, though hardly firm, was nonetheless formidable and certainly beyond the capacity of the Nationalists to alter through military means. At best, martial measures were an annoyance for Peking. In contrast, the CCP could continue to threaten the very existence of the KMT regime, as it had appeared to do in the 1958 Formosa Straits Crisis.

Still, this threat did not keep the Nationalists from attempting to strike out. Political Warfare measures were ongoing, with Wang Sheng, in his position as Commandant of *Fu Hsing Kang*, playing a key role by overseeing the training of the Political Officers themselves. Peking's harsh occupation of the Tibetan heartland in 1959 led to the flight of the Dalai Lama to India and, consequently, to a war of resistance – the principal guerrilla forces involved in this 'secret war' were Tibetan Khampa nomads who operated out of the Mustang salient in Nepal to attack communist forces in their homeland – which was a joint effort run by the ROC and US. Additionally, even before the 25 June 1950 outbreak of the Korean War, the CCP had agreed to provide tangible assistance to the Vietnamese communist movement in its struggle against the French colonial power. By early August of the same year the first Chinese advisors were on the ground with the Viet Minh and played a critical role in all major operations thereafter, both as tactical field advisors and as strategic and operational planners.[1]

The conflict, of course, was fought according to the precepts of Maoist 'people's war', as modified so as to be relevant to the Vietnamese environment, and did not end with the collapse of the French position in 1954. Instead, the newly created South Vietnam became a client of the United States as it squared off against North

Vietnam, linked to the Soviet Union and China. Laos and Cambodia, as the other two former French colonies in Indochina, were also involved in the struggle, but South Vietnam, or the Republic of Vietnam (RVN), remained the linchpin in the anti-communist position. Needing allies, it was logical for the fledgling state, under President Ngo Dinh-Diem, to turn to Taiwan in an Asia of limited possibilities. Not only was Taiwan an *Asian* state, but it had long experience in dealing with communist insurgency. Furthermore, though more developed than South Vietnam, Taiwan nevertheless was in the same league economically. The average monthly wage in Taiwan (using 40 NT/dollar) was but $11.50 per month, or $138 per year. Socially and culturally there were many similarities. And at least some key advisors to the fledgling Republic of Vietnam in the 1950s, such as Wolf Ladejinsky, had been active in Taiwan's own development.[2]

On 5 January 1960 Diem – as he is universally referred to in the literature – began a one-week visit to Taiwan. What particularly impressed him was not the sites he inspected, such as military academies, or the troops themselves, but rather the discipline and morale he found. Ascertaining that these were a result of the Political Warfare system, Diem asked Chiang Kai-shek to arrange more in-depth discussions with Chiang Ching-kuo. This was done, with the result that Diem formally requested that Political Warfare officials be sent to Vietnam 'to improve the soundness of the system there', as it was put later by Chen Tsu-yao, then only a captain but later, as a colonel, to become chief of staff of the ROC presence.[3]

Political Warfare in Vietnam

Predictably, it was to then-Major General Wang Sheng that the actual tasking was directed. An order was issued on 3 May 1960, and the 44-year-old Wang Sheng, accompanied by two captains, proceeded to Vietnam 'as visitors' to assess the situation. Both captains were named Chen. The first, Chen Tsu-yao, was a graduate of the 1st Class of *Fu Hsing Kang* College. The other, Chen Ti (who was later to die of liver cancer), was from the 2nd Class of *Fu Hsing Kang* and an English Instructor at the National Defense Language School, distinguished as an English broadcast

Visit to *Fu Hsing Kang* by the South Vietnamese Chief of the General Staff, Nguyen Van-Thieu. As president, Thieu oversaw creation of a political warfare system modelled after that of Taiwan. Wang Sheng is at Thieu's right hand.

teacher. The latter was to insure accurate communication, for only he spoke English. None of the three spoke Vietnamese.

The group was received on 4 May 1960 by Tran Trung-Dung, deputy defense minister, standing in for Diem, who was himself minister of defense. Tran relayed Diem's request that the Chinese examine four areas in particular: how to unify the armed forces; how to boost the morale of the armed forces; how to prevent Viet Cong penetration; and how to strengthen operations in the enemy rear area, behind enemy lines. All four were Political Warfare specialties. As in-processing and orientation progressed, a further message from Diem followed on 9 May 1960, again transmitted by Tran, in which he asked to meet the team after it had first thoroughly inspected the entire country, 'from north to south, at all levels, to assess the situation'.[4] The next two months were spent doing precisely that, and on 6 July the team was summoned to see the president.

Wang Sheng elaborated upon what the group had seen over the

two months and how it related to Taiwan's own experience. He also advanced seven papers containing points of discussion, the most important of which was to emphasize human factors, ideology, to counter 'materialism'. Diem apparently had given this matter much thought himself but had done no further work with it; thus he was receptive. Wang had prepared thoroughly and on the spot presented Diem with the draft of a book of some 200,000 words, authored by the team, elaborating Diem's own ideas. It was in Chinese, which Diem could read, and had his name on it. He was stunned. All they had done, Wang explained, was to piece together the president's own thoughts from his speeches and policy statements. So it was, in fact, authentic Diem. His beliefs had simply been arrayed systematically in such form that they could now offer policy guidance. Not surprisingly, the meeting, which had originally been scheduled for only one hour, went on for three.

As a result, the president instructed his younger brother, Ngo Dinh-Nhu, or Nhu as he was known to the West, to organize a commission to study the Chinese proposals. This, Diem confided, was necessary in a country of Vietnamese beholden to the Americans (he had, in fact, just returned from the US) and defended by a French-trained military – 'coordination' had to be effected before orders were issued. In the interim, he asked Wang Sheng to address certain units to put forth his ideas. This meant remaining in South Vietnam for an additional month; it was not until 7 August 1960 that Wang returned to Taiwan. He had delivered three major speeches in the Saigon area, including one to the Vietnamese Joint Chiefs of Staff.

It was immediately prior to his departure that Wang Sheng had been told by Chiang Ching-kuo that Chiang Kai-shek had decided he should move to GPWD. While Wang Sheng was still in Vietnam, the orders were actually issued, effective 16 May 1960. Yet it was not until his return that the change of command ceremony could take place. Wang Sheng then settled in at GPWD, where he continued to work tirelessly to develop the Political Warfare system.

Only a few months after his return, as the Chinese proposal continued to be 'studied' by the Vietnamese, it received an unexpected boost when, on 20 November 1960, an unsuccessful coup attempt against Diem was led by the RVN air force. Though put down, the uprising included the bombing of the presidential palace compound by several planes. Not only was South Vietnamese government morale seriously damaged, so, too, was there deep concern for armed forces loyalty, one central aspect of the Political Warfare approach advanced in the July report. Hence, just three days after the coup attempt, on 23 November, at Diem's request, Wang Sheng was back in Saigon. On this, his second visit, he came alone. His schedule was heavy as he worked with the Vietnamese, preparing for the implementation of his proposals. On 2 January 1961 another six officers joined him. All went in plain clothes and were called the *Kwei San* Officer Corps. Wang Sheng, on the verge of promotion to lieutenant-general, was designated chief of the mission for the moment. Rear-Admiral Yuan Ch'eng-chang was his deputy. Among the other members – Colonel Liu, two lieutenant colonels (Yang, Chen), and a captain – was again Chen Tsu-yao, by now the group's institutional memory.

By 15 January they were ready to brief President Diem on his most pressing concerns: how to protect the security of the armed forces; how to prevent the armed forces from being penetrated; and how to set up his own 'Political Warfare Research Class', the first step towards an actual Political Warfare Institute. The security and counterintelligence functions could proceed immediately. As for the training of personnel, Wang Sheng suggested that a high-ranking officer be assigned to organize a Political Warfare Research Commission to study the specifics of implementation. On the spot, Diem assigned General Nguyen Khanh, Chief of the General Staff – who later led a coup and then became prime minister – as head of the committee.

In order to make all of the committee members understand how Political Warfare worked, they, to include the chief of staff, visited the appropriate facilities for eight days in Taiwan from 23 February to 2 March 1961. Wang Sheng accompanied them. Back in Saigon, under the direction of Rear-Admiral Yuan, the advisory group worked on plans. On 27 May 1961 a Political Warfare Institute was formally established. The inauguration ceremony was presided over by the deputy defense minister, the chief of staff, and other high ranking dignitaries among which were military attachés from different countries. There were 120 well-selected participants, all lieutenant colonels and colonels, in the first class of 16 weeks. When the class began, Wang Sheng gave a series of lectures on the central role of the human element and 'human-based ideology' in warfare. Then he returned to Taiwan on 12 June.

Left behind to grapple with the intricacies of Political Warfare was the first class. The 'human-based ideology' it studied was based on the 200,000-word draft originally prepared by the Chinese, who actually carried out the instruction. The goal was to establish a common theoretical foundation upon which actions could be based. To give this effort at articulating a national ideology greater circulation, it was placed in all military units and offered for sale in bookstores.

Starting day for the first class was 14 October 1961. Diem himself presided. The course had been held in downtown Saigon, so many dignitaries were there for the morning ceremony. In the afternoon there was a private meeting with the president in his office, at which he individually greeted the trainees and the Chinese staff and the training officers themselves. Diem, growing more animated as he expounded upon the goals of the new political warfare concept and its potential, launched into 'a serious pep talk'.[5]

Quickly, on 30 October, a second class began, an intermediate level for captains and majors. It also had 120 participants but lasted only eight weeks, because the Chinese were on a one-year tour and eight weeks was all that could be squeezed in before their rotation. The same information was presented as had been offered to the first class, but it was compressed to fit the available time. Graduation was 2 January 1962. There, the members of the mission were fêted, as the Vietnamese were quite pleased with the results. Though not a matter systematically studied, it does seem that those who graduated did do quite well in their careers. Perhaps more crucially, Diem felt that he had found other Asians whom he could use as sounding boards for ideas or turn to for advice. This he did regularly. He appears to have particularly valued the assessments of now-Lieutenant-General Wang, who visited Diem several times at his request.

Yet no amount of advice could arrest the declining situation within South Vietnam. As feuding with the Buddhists led to demonstrations, relations with Washington deteriorated, too. Asked to return for consultation, Wang talked with Diem on 21 October 1963 and encouraged him to be tolerant with the Buddhists and to work with the US government. He advised him not to be taken in by communist intrigue: 'They want to divide you, so be cautious. They are using the Buddhist movement to inspire divisions, so don't fall into their trap by cracking down on them. Further, in the anti-communist struggle, you need American assistance. Without it you can go nowhere. You have to have close cooperation with them'.[6] On 26 October he returned to Taiwan after a visit of just six days.

Not a week later, on 1 November 1963, Diem was overthrown in a coup led by his own 'special advisor', General Duong Van-Minh, called 'Big Minh' for his size. Both Diem and his brother Nhu were killed, ushering in a period of instability when governments changed with bewildering rapidity. Ironically, all of the individuals involved were acquaintances of Wang Sheng. And since the war continued, regardless of palace politics in Saigon, so it was on 6 March 1964 that Wang Sheng made his sixth visit to Vietnam to consult with Tran Van-Trung, who was both prime minister and commander of all the armed forces. Key individuals not only knew Wang Sheng but had been part of the Vietnamese group which had visited Taiwan in early 1961. Consequently, lengthy discussions held over a week could quickly turn from concepts to specifics.

It was not until General Nguyen Van-Thieu assumed power, however, that concrete steps were again taken. On 24 August 1964 he invited Wang Sheng to visit, at which time he requested that Taiwan help institute the Political Warfare system within the Vietnamese armed forces. Wang Sheng agreed to make the proposal to the Chinese side but stipulated that support be gained first from the Americans. A series of discussions ensued. At his initial meeting with General William C. Westmoreland, the Military Assistance Command - Vietnam (MAC-V) commander, Wang Sheng was asked about the concept of Political Warfare and consequently briefed Westmoreland in detail on it three days later on 27 August.

Wang Sheng himself wrote the briefing. He made several proposals, the most important being that a Political Warfare system should be established for the Vietnamese Army. Another was that a television station be set up to disseminate news and the government position. General Westmoreland was concerned about the cost of the station. Wang bluntly pointed out that it would cost no more than a B-52 bomber but would be much more powerful. The general laughed at the comparison, and the station was subsequently set up – as was the advisory mission, with the

Americans providing all administrative support as stipulated in the terms of the agreements under which the US facilitated Allied participation in the Vietnam conflict. On 28 August both MAC-V and the Vietnamese government agreed to the establishment of the ROC Military Mission to Vietnam. That day an agreement was signed. Wang Sheng represented Taiwan; the defense minister, Vietnam. Wang Sheng returned to Taiwan on 4 September 1964.

Only a month later, on 8 October 1964, Lieutenant General Teng Ting-yuan was the leader of 15 officers arriving in Vietnam. This time they were in uniform, as the advisory mission had been formally established. In the years that followed, there were to be four mission chiefs. Lieutenant-General Teng served until 1967; between 1967 and 1971, there were Ko Yuen-fen and Hsu Ju-chi; last was air force Lieutenant-General Chiang Hsien-hsiang, who commanded from 1 July 1971 until 12 March 1973. Wang Sheng's associate in 1960, Chen Tsu-yao, by this time a lieutenant-colonel, was among the original 15 officers and in charge of the political warfare training section. As a colonel, he was to be mission chief of staff under Lieutenant-General Chiang in 1971–73.

Later describing the Chinese role, Chen noted:

> An American reporter once interviewed one of your soldiers. 'Who are the VC [Viet Cong]'? he asked him. 'Anyone who fires at me is a VC', he replied. There's your mistake in a nutshell. The Vietnam War was a typical political war, a war without front lines, without boundaries. The enemy was everywhere, even in the major cities such as Saigon. Our mission wanted, first, to teach the Vietnamese armed forces to understand for whom they fought. We didn't want them to be susceptible to propaganda. We didn't want them to be taken in. Second, we wanted to boost their morale, to show them how to keep it in good shape, to teach them to implement orders thoroughly. Third, we wanted to help them maintain the security of the armed forces, to prevent their penetration by the VC. Fourth, we wanted to teach the Vietnamese armed forces how to win the support of the masses, to avoid being separated from them, to keep good relations with the masses. All of those years there, our most important mission was to put across these four points.[7]

To carry out this mission, the small advisory staff was organized in a simple scheme. Above the chief of staff in the mission organizational chart were the Commandant and Deputy Commandant; below were four bureaus, each with two officers: political training, psychological warfare, security, and society. Essentially, the mission functioned as liaison officers who went out to the different units to inspect and offer advice in the bureau areas. There were also two advisors assigned to the army and air force but not to the navy; and each of the four military corps regions had two advisors; there were two advisors to the Political Warfare College itself in Dalat. The chief advisor to the Political Warfare Bureau was also the chief of staff of the mission. Altogether, the small group numbered just 31, though there were other covert operations personnel in-country. At least one special forces team operated with MACVSOG, the élite Special Operations Group which conducted reconnaissance missions deep behind enemy lines.[8]

Though Political Warfare officers played a central role in the effort, which remained under GPWD, personnel were a mix of line and GPWD. Wang Yeh-kai, who was in Vietnam 1966–68, has outlined his selection and role thus:

> When I volunteered for Vietnam, Lieutenant-General Teng said I shouldn't go. I was in guided missiles commanding AA-ACP, the air defense artillery for any command post. He said I should stay and become a battalion commander. I was a line officer, so Political Warfare had nothing to do with my wishing to go. To be a corps advisor you had to have certain qualifications so that you would be able to do a good job. You had to be a line officer, to have been a company commander; you must have English language training; certain types of training in the US. You must be married; for three years you should have received high ratings in your duty performance. We were assigned by twos to the corps areas, a line and a Political Officer, so that we could consult with each other. Political Officers didn't know military measures; the line knows these. Our line officers are US-trained, so we were very familiar with the South Vietnamese situation. I had even been with the 1st Cavalry. We worked together to support a friendly country. The South Vietnamese had counterpart functions to those in our own Political Warfare setup: political education, psychological warfare, troop morale. We were

supporting these. Sometimes, if we had a Chinese-speaking captive, we would act as interpreters, especially if they were CHICOM [Chinese communist] agents.[9]

That the members of the Taiwan group should find themselves interviewing Chinese stemmed from the increasing nature of Peking's commitment to the North Vietnamese side as the war wore on. This went far beyond the better known logistical and diplomatic support efforts and was an integral part of a larger effort by Peking to counter America in Southeast Asia, as well as to assist revolutionary movements worldwide.[10] Throughout the war, for instance, Chinese advisors serving with Viet Cong and North Vietnamese forces in South Vietnam were captured at infrequent but regular intervals. More tangibly, regular Chinese forces were deployed within North Vietnam – these were principally air defense, logistics, engineer, and transportation units – where they engaged in the fighting. Ultimately, some 320,000 Chinese troops served in North Vietnam alone, 'with the annual maximum reaching 170,000'. Casualties were heavy, reaching approximately 20,000 dead and wounded.[11] Additional Chinese forces were deployed to border areas of Burma and Laos.[12]

If Peking, then, offered Southeast Asian communist movements and regimes, especially that of North Vietnam, advice and assistance on how to conduct revolutionary war, what the small Taiwan mission offered Vietnam was a different way of looking at the insurgency problem. While the Americans emphasized military solutions and firepower, the Chinese advocated a political strategy and 'the human approach'. As Rear-Admiral Yuan Ch'eng-chang, who was involved in the ROC advisory process from the beginning, was to describe the process:

> Briefly speaking, Political Warfare is how to shape the battlefield, how to manipulate the playing field. We tried to help Vietnam understand the type of war they were involved in; that the communists apply the same principles everywhere. For example, the communists work to make the war become 'people's revolution'. Take the case of my own father in China. He was a diligent farmer who saved money. We had been poor, but he worked to make our lot better. All around us we could see others who wasted their money, used drugs, gambled. Finally, such people would lose everything, having

to sell even their land to pay off their debts. They didn't work hard and had bad habits, so in the end they lost everything. My father ultimately became rich by acquiring such land, but he tilled it all himself. In this world, some people are diligent, some people are lazy, so there emerges a gap between haves and have-nots. To take advantage of this situation, the communists mobilize the poor farmers. They tell them they will solve their problems, that if they want to become rich all they have to do is turn the world upside down. If you do this, you can become rich overnight. Let's purge the rich farmers, they say. Then comes the so-called 'people's revolutionary war'. Why? Because they manipulate conditions to turn one group against another. There are certain hallmarks of this process. They launch a soft offensive, just planting the seeds of discord. They're very low key, and in the end it is the same. In between they let the people do the dirty work. At the beginning and the end they are in the background. They're very good at it. They applied this same approach in Vietnam. They were able to take advantage of the Buddhist mobilization, for example. It is useful to remember that a monk is not always a communist, but a communist can be a monk. The American people helped Vietnam, but they didn't teach the Vietnamese anti-communist *thinking*. They just gave them weapons, but they didn't help them understand the nature of the communists. We gave the Vietnamese an understanding of the nature of communism. All you did was send people and money. It turned out to be a failure.[13]

Though disagreeing with the American strategic approach, the Chinese members had no trouble interacting with the Americans on the ground. For the bulk of Chinese time and effort was spent in an effort to impart the techniques and operational procedures which made Political Warfare function as a military system. Even if, strategically, the American approach to war fighting drove the conflict, there was much to be done in these areas – and in this effort there was no disagreement. As Lieutenant-General Chiang, final commander of the advisory effort, relates:

> Our Political Warfare and counterespionage experiences were similar to what you yourself had experienced. We performed the same functions, but you divided them all. For example,

counterespionage was placed under your J2, while personnel matters were handled by your J1. In contrast, we simply placed all the functions under political warfare. I made a chart to explain this to your people.[14]

It was a system with which the Vietnamese were comfortable.[15] Indeed, in their Political Warfare Academy, located at Dalat in the central highlands, they sought to build a replica of *Fu Hsing Kang*. Its second-lieutenant graduates, political warfare officers, were used to man a system copied from that of the Chinese. The problem, of course, was that they worked to foster loyalty to a system which was so lacking in stability that at times it was difficult to tell if a government existed at all. In the aftermath of Diem's death, repeated coups robbed the system of the continuity absolutely necessary to personnel development. For in the Chinese analysis, loyalty very obviously needed an object. Only too conscious of the disastrous implications of factionalism, the very factor which they judged to have destroyed their first republic, they would have preferred that South Vietnam use a single party to focus its efforts. This the Chinese themselves had attempted to do with their Kuomintang. The absence of such a strong central rallying point, though, forced them to deal with the military itself, as a surrogate, and to focus their efforts upon the elements of political warfare designed to strengthen military solidarity and loyalty. All they could really do politically was to try to get the government apparatus to exercise greater control over the armed forces.

Thus pushed into a search for 'tactical victories' in an unstable strategic environment, the mission members, as time passed, became in effect troubleshooters. They helped out not only in Political Warfare but in all areas. A significant contribution, for instance, was the Chinese effort to assist with prison reform. The mission found that the Vietnamese did not know how to treat political prisoners. They mixed them with common criminals. 'If you weren't a good communist when you went in', notes a former American advisor with knowledge of the system, 'you certainly were when you came out'.[16] Consequently, the Chinese arranged for a good many Vietnamese prison officials to visit Taiwan to see how the system of rehabilitation worked there, at least four groups of Vietnamese per year, sometimes more. Training included both general orientation and specific instruction for selected individuals. Ultimately, there simply was not time for the

Vietnamese to implement the Chinese system successfully in Vietnam, but the start was made.[17]

As valuable as such 'technical' training was, however, it was in their role as strategic counsellors that the Chinese stood out – a role which assumed increased import as the US withdrawal picked up steam after 1968 and the lack of American enthusiasm about the war effort caused the South Vietnamese to turn for advice to their fellow Asians. Taiwan, despite its relative lack of actual combat experience, was a natural to fill the advisory role once dominated by the Americans. The extent to which this relationship developed was illustrated in 1972 during the Paris Peace Talks. The ROC Advisory Mission prepared a memorandum for the South Vietnamese side, written by Colonel Chen. In it was discussed the Republic of China's own previous – negative – experience in negotiations with the communists. The memorandum was divided into three sections: symptoms, during, after. Within each the mission detailed the strategy applied by the communists, highlighting the integral role played by deception. Chiang Hsien-siang explains:

> We wanted the Vietnamese authorities to understand these things. When [President] Thieu made a statement about the peace talks, 70–80 per cent came from our memo. Of course we weren't credited as the source; that was not necessary. All the ideas were ours, however. We had detailed the communist strategy point-by-point, sometimes more than a hundred points. For instance, we pointed out that when you negotiate with the communists you must be very explicit about what precisely is meant by the terms. We had learned in our own dealings with the communists inside China in the 1940s that this was necessary. If you state that positions must remain the same, for instance, then you must specify that there can be no movement day *or* night. Because what they did in China was to stay put during the day, then move their units at night. The communists were always scheming. We had had bitter experience with them. At that time, three people were negotiating. General Marshall was on your side. He didn't seem to understand these things, so we lost a lot. We were taken advantage of.[18]

As is now fully understood, the South Vietnamese absorbed

these lessons and were quite aware of the inadequacies of the Paris Peace Accords signed on 27 January 1973. Forced to go along with them, Thieu could only make the best of a bad situation. In particular, the ambiguity in the accords' wording allowed North Vietnamese forces to remain within South Vietnam, even as Allied forces departed. Thus on 12 May 1973, in accordance with the terms of the agreement, the ROC Advisory Mission formally withdrew from Vietnam. Its departure was attended by numerous other Allied delegations. Perhaps more significantly, some 5,000–6,000 Vietnamese also appeared to bid them farewell. Only two years later, South Vietnam fell to an onslaught of North Vietnamese armed might.

Had the Chinese political warfare mission been in vain? Wang Sheng observes:

> From 1960–73 our Taiwan mission there had no one killed or wounded. We just used our minds, unlike you, who had so many killed. You devoted a lot of effort, but as a whole the war was a failure. But was this a failure of Political Warfare? I've given serious consideration to reviewing the conflict, especially the political warfare dimension. Actually, it [this dimension] was quite successful. On the whole, the Vietnamese fought very well. In those last years, there were very few surrenders or defections. To the contrary, there were numerous instances of units fighting to the last man and, in the final days, of commanders committing suicide rather than surrender. You can take any number of examples, one of the most famous, of course, being the 18th Division's stand at An Loc [in 1972], where it held out for more than 40 days, surrounded, before being relieved. It would not surrender, and the division commander became a hero. And there was the First Military Region commander who committed suicide after fighting to the last. The point is that the Vietnamese could be as patriotic and steadfast as anyone. They just needed the tools. They had spirit. During the war, I went to Vietnam nine times, staying in that country almost a year in total. As I observed, Vietnamese armed forces personnel overall fought well and deserved our praise, our memories. When I think of those people, some acquaintances killed, some spread out everywhere, I see what a disaster it all was. I feel sorry about the way it ended up. It could have been different.[19]

Political Warfare in Cambodia

Even as the effort to aid the Republic of Vietnam progressed, Wang Sheng looked for ways to expand Taiwan's assistance to the anti-communist forces of Southeast Asia. Training of foreign students in a 'Political Warfare Research Class' had begun at *Fu Hsing Kang* as early as 1968, particularly of students from Vietnam and Cambodia. Yet this early training emphasized psychological warfare techniques. Actual Political Warfare development in Vietnam, as we have seen, was instituted fairly rapidly; but it was not until the 1970 ouster of Cambodian leader Prince Norodom Sihanouk by military head Marshal Lon Nol that such ties with Vietnam's neighbor could expand further.

Wang Sheng visits Cambodia in 1971.

Though much ink has been devoted to an effort to prove that the United States was behind Lon Nol's overthrow of Sihanouk, the coup actually stemmed from a more complex confluence of causes rooted in the internal and personal complexities of Cambodian politics. A key source of discontent with the arrogant, mercurial Sihanouk was outrage at his toleration of a substantial foreign presence in the Cambodian border areas. This presence, of course, was the North Vietnamese/Viet Cong command and logistical infrastructure being used to prosecute the war inside South Vietnam. That Lon Nol and his coterie overestimated their ability to drive the Vietnamese from Cambodian soil is by now well understood. At the time it was not.

Almost as quickly as Sihanouk was ousted, therefore, the new government of Lon Nol found itself on the ropes. Communal strife engulfed the country, with ethnic Vietnamese taking the brunt of the bloodletting. Hapless Vietnamese civilians were butchered by xenophobic mobs. It was another story where the North Vietnamese and Viet Cong were concerned. Feeble Cambodian attacks were brushed aside, and the North Vietnamese pushed into the Cambodian interior, in the process turning the hitherto marginal Khmer Rouge insurgent movement into a going concern. By April, Phnom Penh, the capital, was threatened. Lon Nol, who had frantically backpedalled – attempting to reassert Cambodia's traditional, albeit flawed, neutrality – turned to the Allies for assistance.

Yet he was a fish out of water in the big power stakes of the Vietnam War. Not only was he difficult for the critical player, the United States, to fathom, his own people were never sure what was in his mind. Washington, fearful of leaks, did not bother to consult him when, in late April 1970, President Richard Nixon ordered a massive US military incursion into the communist-held areas across the Cambodian border. Desperate for help, Lon Nol looked to Taiwan. This was not as odd a choice as it might seem. His options were really quite limited. Though inevitably linked to South Vietnam, to the east, by virtue of the anti-communist nature of the struggle, Lon Nol detested the Vietnamese, a traditional Cambodian foe, as much as did his fellow countrymen. To the west, anti-communist Thailand was another problem, perceived as having territorial designs. To the north, Laos could be of no help, either, being possibly the only member of the anti-communist world which was more hapless than Cambodia itself. All now seemed threatened by China, which during the Sihanouk era had been a source of aid and advice. Taiwan, however, had no bones to pick with Cambodia, was not in the neighborhood, and was Asian.

Further, Lon Nol – ironically, given the xenophobia sweeping the country – was not actually Cambodian but ethnic Chinese. He admired Chiang Kai-shek and felt the Nationalists had a great deal to offer in advice appropriate to battling the communists. Indeed, in his office, throughout his presidency, Lon Nol gave pride of place to just two pictures on his wall, one was a large photo of Chiang Kai-shek. Beneath it was a smaller photo of Richard Nixon. The arrangement spoke for itself. Lon Nol could speak only a little Chinese, but his wife was fluent and could write as well. Using personnel already trained in Taiwan as contact points, the Cambodian first family approached the Nationalists.

Normally portrayed as a bit dim-witted, Lon Nol was not a fool. He was shrewd enough to recognize the parallels between his own situation and that of the pre-Taiwan Kuomintang. His request thus was not for military but Political Warfare training. This facet of the Political Warfare approach – the training of foreign personnel – was something which Wang Sheng had already considered. Consequently, in dealing with the Cambodian request, *ad hoc* arrangements were given a formal basis with the inauguration of what was to become the Institute of Political Warfare. A part of *Fu Hsing Kang*, the Institute's goal was to impart to international participants 'a knowledge of fighting communism'. Its first director was Major-General Yu Kuang, who worked closely with Wang Sheng. The first class of 19 students was entirely Cambodian. All returned to Phnom Penh to become either ministers in the government or general officers in the military.

The results of the first Institute training effort had been impressive. Phnom Penh moved to build upon it. Observes Yu Kuang, who was to become head of the ROC Advisory Mission to Cambodia:

> Because President Lon Nol had great respect for President Chiang Kai-shek and deep feelings for our country – America was primarily for weapons and material – he wanted Taiwan to do what it did for Vietnam, send military advisors to help Cambodia. He especially wanted advice in political warfare. Lon Nol realized that the students he had sent to be trained in Taiwan had gained good theoretical knowledge, but what he wanted were more practical techniques. He wanted to set up a thorough Political Warfare system in Cambodia.[20]

Thus it was that Wang Sheng was sent to Cambodia by Chiang Kai-shek to assess the situation, arriving on 4 July 1972. Accompanying him was his chosen small team of three, which

included Yu Kuang and Colonel Chao Chung-ho, who would later
become the head of the Institute of Political Warfare. Already well
versed in the situation, they were able to move much more rapidly
than had been the case a decade earlier in South Vietnam. An
advisory mission was agreed upon, and on 14 September its ten
members arrived. Yu Kuang was appointed head, while Chao
Chung-ho was made chief of staff. Only Yu Kuang was not a *Fu
Hsing Kang* graduate; all had been picked by Wang Sheng.

In one sense, Yu Kuang was an odd choice for commander of
the mission, because he knew no foreign languages. Thus he had to
use any number of translators – English, French, Khmer. In a more
important way, the choice made sense. As head of the international
students' course at the Institute, he knew personally many of the
Cambodian students. His presence had the indirect effect of
further enhancing the influence of Political Warfare tenets, because
the returned students were granted direct access to Lon Nol.
Among his personal staff, key appointments, such as the Public
Relations Officer of the President and the Chief of the Presidential
Security Guard, went to Political Warfare College graduates.

For his part, Chao Chung-ho – whom the others of the mission
referred to as 'Super Chao' in recognition of his two doctorates
and his facility with languages – served as a critical go-between. He
worked with the Cambodians and the Americans. This was crucial
in the mission's work. For regardless of their entrée and
effectiveness, the Chinese had to exist in a world controlled by the
US war effort. Chao, then, with his US schooling, proved
invaluable. Throughout the three years the Taiwan group
functioned in Cambodia, relationships between the Chinese and
the Americans were close. Certainly the inability of the Americans
to deploy in Cambodia the massive military machine they had set
up in South Vietnam worked to Chinese advantage. It was a
shoestring war which placed a premium upon individuals and their
ability to generate solutions to pressing problems. In short,
political solutions had to come to the fore, because there were few
other options. This enhanced still further the Nationalist influence.

The position the Political Warfare personnel were to hold
became clear immediately. Upon their arrival, Lon Nol threw a
great welcoming party for them, personally opening bottles of
champagne and toasting the group. On the spot he appointed
several members of his inner circle to implement plans to be
worked out jointly. These contacts included the president's

brother, Lon Non, the Chief of the Security Bureau, Ek Preung, and the Psychological Warfare/Intelligence Director, An Rong. Yu Kuang, like his Cambodian Political Warfare students, was granted direct access to Lon Nol. He comments:

> Our direct access to Lon Nol had an unexpected, very surprising result. Originally, we thought only the military would build a Political Warfare system, but Lon Nol was more visionary. He believed the entire government – the entire government! – should have such a system. Thus it had to come right out of the president's office, not just the military. Of course you can't compare this with what goes on in democratic countries. Lon Nol had direct control over the Pol War system under him. It came right out of the Presidential Palace. In the military he had started a General Political Warfare Department; in the Presidential Office he had a Directing Committee for Political Warfare. Because Taiwan sent a military advisory group to help, and because the office was under the president, and therefore located in the palace, we became direct advisors to the president on all matters. This was very unexpected. Some other countries were jealous of this, but not America. Especially upset was France. They felt they had a privileged position in Cambodia and had been involved with it longer, so why did the Taiwanese have such access?[21]

Why, indeed: because the Cambodians, like the Vietnamese, felt that they could relate to the Chinese, their fellow Asians, in a manner they never could with the Americans, despite the latter's best intentions. In fewer than a dozen Chinese Political Warfare officers, Lon Nol felt he had found those who could comprehend – and empathize with – the plight of his small country adrift on a raging sea. He turned to them constantly for advice. And what the Chinese offered was advice on a scale and level Cambodia could absorb.

To accomplish this, according to Yu Kuang, the Chinese advisory effort focused upon five major areas: (1) organizational affairs – 'strengthen unity among officers and men'; (2) education and psychological warfare – 'one of our main roles'; (3) inspiration – 'maintain the purity of the armed forces'; (4) counter-espionage – 'security'; and (5) civil affairs – 'you know the communist saying about the guerrillas being the fish and the people being the sea, so in this area we were involved with what would work to win hearts and minds. This area includes organization of the masses and providing welfare services'.[22] Above all, the Chinese emphasized the central role of ideology. The fight against communism, they stated, was a human struggle. It did not rely upon use of weapons. 'We had developed this concept in Taiwan in the form of Political Warfare', analyzes Yu Kuang. 'We felt it was a more advanced form of warfare which could help Vietnam and Cambodia. That is why we have remained close to these two countries, even now, spiritually'.[23] Adds Chao Chung-ho:

> They were involved in an ideological struggle, so the theory of ideological warfare was crucial. Without this they could not fight. It is like the saying in your country: for what and for whom do you fight? Generally speaking, the educational level in Cambodia was very low, so we concentrated on educating them on the why/for whom they fought. That was very important.[24]

Lon Nol, as the Chinese discerned, understood this point far better than he was given credit for by the Americans. That was why, throughout the struggle, the Political Warfare School belonged directly to the presidential palace. As he articulated many times, a speech that went beyond mere verbiage, Lon Nol had the idea that the whole government should be trained in Political Warfare. He even wanted, he would say, 'the whole people to understand it'.

Faced with such a task, the Chinese began immediately by conducting briefings on the Political Warfare concept not only to military personnel but also to civil servants. They concentrated upon the classes then undergoing training in the various civil and military schools, for these were the people who could make an immediate impact when they went into the field. Simultaneously, they prepared the instructors needed to begin producing the personnel necessary to staff the new system. This work progressed quickly, because the individuals previously trained in Taiwan had already laid the foundation, particularly by expanding their own psychological warfare system. What in Vietnam had been a very lengthy process could in Cambodia proceed at all but breakneck speed because of the rudimentary framework already in existence when the Chinese mission arrived.

As the basis for all instruction, a 'national ideology' was drawn up for the Cambodians by the Chinese using the numerous speeches and policy pronouncements which were floating about in disconnected and unrelated fashion. Written by Wang Sheng himself in a year, with input from his staff, the product was staffed and edited by the Cambodians, then published as a book translated into Khmer, French, and English. It was delivered to all units and government levels and used in classes. The content was based on the special situation of Cambodia.

To serve as the medium in which this national ideology would exist, the Chinese struggled to improve the chaotic political situation. After decades of autocratic rule by Sihanouk, followed by the cauldron of civil war and foreign invasion, no coherent organizational structure had been able to develop. Instead, personalism was the order of the day. A strong leader in time of crisis was essential, the Chinese mission felt, but he had to have behind him a strong, unified political party to mobilize support. This Lon Nol did not have. Rather, his rudimentary Socialist Republican Party, fractious and divided, was opposed by equally chaotic opposition bodies. Various leadership figures seemed interested only in power, even as the country floundered. Only a few of the upper leadership, the Chinese judged, seemed to have any understanding of democratic process *per se*.

As matters deteriorated, Lon Nol finally asked Wang Sheng to visit personally. This he did in June 1973, when he brought the factions of the ruling party together for face-to-face talks. The solution to the leadership struggle was to make the prime minister, Han Tao, also the Socialist Republican Party leader. Additionally, Lon Nol, rather than standing above the fray, was briefed on the crucial role he had to play in making the organization a mass base rather than elite phenomenon. 'In other words', notes Yu Kuang, 'General Wang was trying to make it a 'real' party instead of just a facade'.[25] That this effort was overcome by events should not detract from the fact that a start was made.

Similarly, at more operational levels, the Chinese struggled to make progress. At times they felt all but overwhelmed by the sheer magnitude of the task before them, because virtually everything had to be built from scratch amidst cultural practices which often served to undo whatever progress was made. To propagate the government's views, for instance, a comprehensive psychological warfare effort was instituted, with specialists teaching both approaches and techniques. Besides simple means such as leaflets and theater troupes, the mission oversaw the setting up of a radio station. As one psychological warfare specialist, Major Sung Chien-yeh has wryly observed, 'All of our ideas came from the Political Warfare School, but all material – even the toilet paper – had to come from America'.[26]

Yet no amount of psychological warfare finesse could undo the harm done in the field as government troops matched the brutal approach of the Khmer Rouge with atrocities of their own. States the chief of staff, Chao Chung-ho:

> Cambodia had many illiterate but brave fighters. They were not so refined. After killing an enemy, for instance, they would cut off body parts to demonstrate their bravery. It was savage behavior. Our group suggested that it was very important, if they were to win the battle, to also win the enemy's heart. We suggested that they no longer engage in such practices. To win the support of the masses they would have to win their hearts. This meant, among other things, treating prisoners well, not cutting their legs off and things such as that.[27]

Corruption was another major problem, one to which the Chinese were quite sensitive due to their own experiences with its debilitating effects on the mainland. In Cambodia, thrust as it suddenly was into war and the US aid pipeline, corruption was endemic. Furthermore, it was systemic. Opines mission chief Yu Kuang:

> So low were official salaries that officeholders did not have enough money for personal expenses. A basic level civil servant, for example, got no pay. How was he to survive? The people were to support him by paying for his services, such as issuing a marriage certificate. This was how all the local officials lived. Cambodia as a whole was very poor. This meant that corruption and bribery were common. An officer would have 120 men on the payroll, for instance, but he would actually have only 70–80 present for duty. The difference went into the leader's pocket. They had inherited a weak political structure from the monarchy. Since bribery and corruption prevailed, we suggested that they reduce this phenomenon or it would be harmful to the country as a whole. We were not naive. Knowing that it was the structure

of the country which caused bribery and corruption to flourish, we suggested that it be done openly: *allow* commanders to add a certain percentage but force them to turn in the actual fighting strength so that we would know what was going on. Our suggestion was not carried out as a whole, but in one military region, where the commander was one of our students, the idea was adopted. I don't know about other regions.[28]

Difficulties such as these were ultimately to prove intractable. There simply was not enough time to set them aright. More successful were the 'technical adjustments' carried out under the Political Warfare program. A major effort, for example, was made to prevent enemy agent penetration and to prevent government secrets from falling into their hands. Though not totally successful, the program got results. Cambodia was never penetrated to the extent South Vietnam was by enemy spies. In similar fashion, the expected communist efforts to infiltrate and manipulate labor and student movement activity led to a large Chinese effort in working with the Cambodians to counter such activity. Throughout the war, such subversive movements scarcely appeared.

Limited successes, however, were but stop-gap measures. Phnom Penh was simply overwhelmed and could do little in the face of communist might. At the end of 1974, Wang Sheng made his third visit to Cambodia to assess the situation. He knew the situation was grim. Regardless, Yu Kuang had asked to remain when his normal two-year tour of duty was over, as had others with him. Consequently, it was an experienced Chinese advisory group which labored on. Their efforts were for naught. As the situation disintegrated in the first half of 1975, Lon Nol left on 2 April for Indonesia on a planned visit. He had no idea that the United States had decided to fly him into exile. Only the day before his departure he had consultations with Yu Kuang and gave no hint that an abdication was imminent. Only when he arrived in Indonesia was he told that he would be taken to Hawaii.

Taipei, though, rapidly read the omens: the situation was irretrievable. Immediately after Lon Nol's virtual kidnapping, the Nationalist government sent a charter to Vietnam from Thailand to take out the diplomatic mission chief, Lieutenant-General Kung Ling-cheng, who later became the Marine Commandant – and later chief of police at the time of the Kaoshiung riots in 1979 –

together with Yu Kuang, still the head of the military mission. They were the last two to leave, the rest of the mission having been evacuated earlier. Immediately after their departure, Khmer Rouge rocket fire closed down the airport. The charter landed first in Saigon, then went on to Bangkok, where Yu Kuang remained pending developments. The chance to return never came.

Though Lon Nol, even in exile, remained hopeful that Asian anti-communist countries, such as Indonesia and Taiwan, would fill the gap being left by the departing Americans, no tangible aid was forthcoming. Plans for internal resistance, too, foundered. On 17 April Phnom Penh fell to the Khmer Rouge. Yu Kuang summarizes the end:

> There is an ancient story you probably know, *Romance of the Three Kingdoms*. In one episode, the strongest kingdoms are Wei, Wu, and Shu. Wei took over Wu, helped by Shu. At that time their military advisor, Shang Hwei of Shu, designed a phony surrender. At the same time he tried to get the general of Wei to become king of Shu. But this piece of intelligence was revealed. Wei killed the general. Shang Hwei himself, the military advisor, died in the fighting. Lon Nol liked this story very much. He couldn't read it himself, but he heard it from translators, together with other ancient Chinese stories. Before Lon Nol left, I met with him and asked with whom I should work in his absence. He gave a very simple answer, a one name answer, 'Lon Non', together with a look which said, 'Why are you asking me this?' So before he was leaving, he went and said goodby. When he said goodbye he told me this story. I realized what he meant: under the circumstances, Lon Non might have to be Shang Hwei. At the time, there were still several thousand troops under him. When the US departed, he sent someone to contact secretly the Cambodian communists. He said he wanted to arrange to surrender. When the Cambodian communists entered Phnom Penh on 18 April, they encountered no resistance. Lon Non and the chief of staff surrendered together. He thought he was doing the same thing, that he was making a fake surrender, that the communists didn't know. But the first thing they did was to kill his whole family. They hung them on trees, one by one, in front of Lon Non, then killed him. That was the final act. You know what happened afterwards.[29]

It was a nightmare which was to end only when the communist Vietnamese, grown weary of Khmer Rouge provocations, invaded Cambodia in December 1978. Lon Nol himself was never to see his homeland again. Yet he retained deep feelings for Taiwan, requesting of the Americans, at least several times, that he be allowed to visit the island as a private citizen, something he had been unable to do during the war. Each time, Washington refused, fearful lest he become involved in a scheme to liberate his homeland. Ironically, to the end, Taiwan and Cambodia never did have formal diplomatic relations.

It is for Wang Sheng, as with Vietnam, to make the final analysis of the role Political Warfare played in the conflict:

When more advanced democratic countries want to try to help underdeveloped countries, they need to examine the local situation first. Then they must design a specific system for it rather than trying to implement their own. The US tries to help other countries but enters the situation based on its own criteria which are not necessarily relevant. We were able to be quite effective in Cambodia because we made our advice appropriate to the situation; thus it was better received. In aiding other countries during this struggle, we cannot say that Political Warfare is omnipotent. It can only help a situation. America is in a better position to more consistently help materially. Had it done this in Southeast Asia, there would have been a basis for Political Warfare. The two must go together. This was particularly so in Southeast Asia where the communist forces had two larger countries behind North Vietnam with consistent assistance. We lost the war because we didn't understand adequately the political warfare dimension. By the time we realized what was lacking, we were one step too late. Had US material support stayed longer and more consistently, Political Warfare could have stayed longer and perhaps been effective. You need the hammer and the anvil. A fist with holes in it can't pound a nail. It's like a fist trying to pound ants. Political Warfare itself is but one system in the struggle against the communists. I feel sorry for the people of the US that your government is incapable of carrying through with what you start when you play the role of international high priest. Once you commit yourself, you must carry through to victory. When you help someone, you must stick through to the very end, not back out in the middle. In Political Warfare you don't see immediate results. You must get cumulative results through ideology and education.[30]

Political Warfare in Strategic Context

It was to better pass on its own 'lessons learned' in adopting this philosophy that Chiang Ching-kuo, in consultation with Wang Sheng, ordered the setting up of the Institute of Political Warfare in 1971, as noted above; the first formal class had been entirely Cambodian. The Institute was to be but one part of a larger approach aimed at safeguarding Taiwan's international position and striking against the CCP. Agricultural assistance, for instance, first extended in 1959 with the dispatch to the Japanese Ryukyu islands of a technical mission specializing in agronomy, had been followed in December of that year by another agricultural team's work in South Vietnam. Success led to other missions to South Vietnam, and the effort was formalized and expanded worldwide as Operation 'Vanguard', established in 1961, and later to be renamed the International Technical Cooperation Program.[31] As with all such foreign aid efforts, irrespective of the state undertaking them, altruism was mixed with self-interest. In Taiwan's case, the latter component loomed much larger with the 25 October 1971 decision by the United Nations to exclude the Republic (ROC) in favor of the People's Republic (PRC). There followed, with increasing momentum, a trend towards derecognition of Taipei in favor of Peking.[32] Development assistance was seen as one weapon with which to counter this development. In this sense, it was viewed as strategic Political Warfare. Likewise, while the actual training of foreign personnel at the Institute of Political Warfare had operational and tactical value for the students concerned, in a larger sense, the training, too, was strategic Political Warfare. So were other initiatives in the diplomatic and social arenas (e.g. sponsorship of cultural groups sent abroad or foreign groups brought to Taiwan).

Thus Wang Sheng, to a greater or lesser extent, depending upon the particular program and its proponent agency, was concerned with any number of activities not directly within his purview – which were themselves then turned to the service of the revolution. He played a central role, to cite but one prominent illustration, in bringing public television and educational programming to Taiwan through initiation of the China Television System (CTS) in a joint project of the Defense and Education Ministries. Wang Sheng's argument, which he saw as an exemplar of Political Warfare thinking, was that the electronic media could play an important part in expanding opportunities for education.[33] This, in turn, would strengthen the country. It was a message he took every opportunity to see passed on to foreign students who marvelled at the strides Taiwan had made in its development process.

It was just the sort of forward-looking thinking for which Wang Sheng became known. And looking to the fate of CTS serves again to highlight what Wang Sheng and the KMT saw as the essential distinction between the *San Min Chu-i* manner of doing things and that of the CCP's communist philosophy. Certainly use of a television channel by a government entity (whether in Taiwan or elsewhere), for whatever reason, educational or otherwise, presupposed an element of control over content. Yet CTS was not stacked with government operatives.[34] And as it developed into a semi-private enterprise, it battled for market-share with the other two, officially-owned channels. Since actually viewing the content was an optional exercise as concerned the public, this introduced the element of competition. With semi-privatization, the trend toward marketing the product advanced still further, such that the channel invariably found itself among the front-runners in audience ratings. In other words, it had to compete to attract its audience, then fight to maintain its loyalty. As he articulated time and again – and has pithily illustrated in his observation cited previously, 'You can't wrap paper around fire'[35] – this was precisely Wang Sheng's philosophy of Political Warfare.

It was the philosophy which informed the instruction at the Institute of Political Warfare. This fact looms large, because as Taiwan's diplomatic ties contracted, the personnel attending Institute courses came from a shrinking circle of states, not all of them known for their attention to human rights. Countries such as Guatemala and El Salvador, for instance, which were engaged in often brutal counterinsurgency campaigns of their own, sent numerous individuals to Taiwan for training. That some of these same individuals later became associated with alleged abuses – repression – did not help the reputation of the Institute. One trenchant critic, for instance, David E. Kaplan, has written:

But what impressed visitors to the academy was not merely Taiwan's growing prosperity; the KMT's ideology of political warfare found real converts. Among them was Lieutenant-Colonel Domingo Monterrosa of the El Salvadoran military. Monterrosa explained his 1978 training there to the Anderson brothers. 'What we really admired in Taiwan', he said, 'was the way the government was organized and the control they held over the people. It was like Communism of this side....We were taught war of the masses'. The techniques of political warfare, which the KMT employed against its enemies in both China and America, were thus exported to the volatile republics of Latin America. The consequences, predictably, were disastrous. Another academy graduate was Roberto D'Aubisson, an ambitious young officer from the Salvadoran National Guard. D'Aubisson returned from his 1977 course to become mastermind of El Salvador's death squads, the man, say U.S. officials, who ordered the 1980 assassination of Archbishop Oscar Romero. Former US ambassador to El Salvador Robert White would call D'Aubisson 'a pathological killer'. D'Aubisson later credited the Political Warfare Academy with opening his eyes to the true structure of Communism, and with inspiring him to create an underground security force. His course there, he said, was 'the best class I ever studied....In political warfare, everybody participates.[36]

Though Kaplan's hunt for scandal has led him astray in his analysis, there is a thread of reality in what he has written. This is the enthusiasm with which many students greeted the course and its emphasis upon organization. The reasons are illuminating. Unlike Kaplan's expectations, these have nothing to do with 'underground security forces' or a philosophy centered about assassination and torture. Instead, they center about the *political* in warfare, the realization that conflict was a multidimensional phenomenon which went beyond violence. In particular, in the revolutionary wars many Third World students were involved with, the nonviolent aspects – 'winning the hearts and minds' would be the common expression – had not only rarely been taught to them to any extent but had never been tied explicitly into an organizational framework. 'In Political Warfare the first thing to win is the will of the people', comments David Panama, a founding

member of El Salvador's ARENA Party (which has won the
country's last two elections), a 1983 student at the Institute, and
an associate of d'Aubuisson. 'Political Warfare allowed us to build
up a political institution which had not been doing very well. Our
party is still the best organized institution in El Salvador'.[37]
    What Political Warfare emphasized, then, was those lessons
about which Political Warfare itself had been built, in particular the
need for a political ideology of service to the masses to drive all
decisionmaking. Yet all the good intentions in the world, said the
Institute message, were useless if they were not married to effective
organizations, and if the guardians of those organizations were not
versed in the principal means of assault to be used by the enemy.
These means were nothing less than the six types of Political
Warfare articulated by Wang Sheng and discussed in Chapter 4. In
contrast, therefore, to *Fu Hsing Kang*'s courses for the ROC's own
Political Officers, instruction on *San Min Chu-i* was not central to
the international course; teaching about communist methods of
warfare was. The standard curriculum for 240 hours of
instruction, spread over two months, was structured thus
(military/civilian hours): (1) Studies of Political Warfare, 96 hours
(40.0 per cent)/78 hours (32.5 per cent); (2) Briefing on the ROC,
46 hours (19.2 per cent); (3) Trends in World Political Thought, 24
hours (10 per cent); (4) Issues of Communism, 28 hours (11.6 per
cent/11.65 per cent); (5) National Security and Social Order, 0/16
hours (0/6.65 per cent); (6) General Topics, 46 hours (19.2 per
cent)/48 hours (20.0 per cent).[38] The 'Studies of Political Warfare'
block, the most important, used as its principal texts Wang Sheng's
The Theory of Political Warfare and a more detailed follow-on,
compiled by the *Fu Hsing Kang* faculty, *A Study of the Six Types of
Political Warfare*.[39] Therein, case studies were all historical
examples derived from the long KMT versus CCP struggle.
    San Min Chu-i was not emphasized (it was included in the 10
per cent of instruction devoted to 'Trends in World Political
Thought'), because it was recognized as a uniquely *Chinese*
ideology, a philosophy appropriate to China's specific historical
circumstances. This aside, course content for international
students was not markedly different from that offered their
Chinese counterparts, except that ROC Army procedural matters
were omitted as superfluous. Foreigners competent in Chinese,
especially Americans, did learn these procedures, in any case,
because they were placed in the regular courses. Elsewise,

international students were expected to be able to function in either Spanish or English, with two Institute tracks taught in these languages (with identical curriculae). The Nationalists were understandably sensitive about making public a list of countries whose personnel had attended the school – those states having no formal relations with the ROC, for instance, had their students enter the country inconspicuously and attend classes in mufti – but there was little else covert about the operation. There certainly was not, as Kaplan claims, 'a practice ground for parachute drops, and a training center operated by the IBMND, the military intelligence bureau'.[40] Even counterintelligence as a subject was framed within the Political Warfare scheme of employment; that is, for guaranteeing loyalty amongst military personnel.

In fact, the closest thing to a common denominator, in ideological terms, taught to the students was the very antithesis of clandestine activity: 'the Four Opens'. This was a program instituted in April 1950 by Chiang Ching-kuo within the military which insured that personnel affairs, financial and quartermaster matters, 'merit and demerit' actions of all types, and discussion of issues would be open. A fairly simple concept, in reality the program stipulated a wide range of procedures directed towards insuring that abuses of the system could not take place behind closed doors. The goal was to prevent corruption, the element which had so sapped the strength of the Chinese military on the mainland. And it was *corruption*, the Institute emphasized, which was the most salient factor in giving the communists an issue with which to win popular support. The solution, therefore, was not to conceal it but to institute procedures to prevent it from ever taking root.

Certainly there was no means to guarantee that Institute students took away all of the appropriate lessons. El Salvador again provides an excellent case study, because the name of the late Major Roberto d'Aubisson has been so publicly linked to 'death squads'.[41] Numerous Salvadorans, both civilian and military, were trained by Taiwan. Many returned to assume important positions in the country. The Institute's benefit was subject-dependent, but on the whole the response was enthusiastic.[42] That individuals, subsequent to their training, may have participated in abuses, seems clear enough. That those abuses had nothing to do with the specifics of the training they received also seems clear enough. What is more important is the obvious role Political Warfare played in ameliorating the violence in El Salvador by channelling counterinsurgency efforts into political organizing. As David Panama has noted, an observation worth quoting in full:

> In discussing Political Warfare, what we are really talking about [in El Salvador] is building the ARENA Party. I came [to *Fu Hsing Kang*] at a very hard time [1983] for our country. We had to go around armed. We were fighting against the terrorists, even against part of the military. Coming here showed me there were two types of war, the clean war and the dirty war. Political warfare is the clean war; the other is the dirty war. Either way you have to face the enemy. The Political Warfare allows you to do so effectively. When you are fighting 12 years of war, dirty war, this is not a conflict where everything makes sense. I believe the people who went in with us [to form ARENA] wanted to find a way out [of the violence]. We even had a very big split in our group, because in 1980 we decided we would save the country the political way. There was a group that said, 'No way, we must use our weapons!' They didn't want to be involved in the politics. But our analysis showed that armed force could not win. The US wouldn't stand for it, and the country was exhausted. It was a very tense time for our people [in the group]. We started working with d'Aubisson from 1979. In his work he was a military man, but from him we started learning about the existence of Political Warfare. Once I criticized him about his approach, thinking it was too soft. But soon we became a political force all around the country, everyone speaking the same line. We loved our country; we didn't want communism. We had to convince the people that the most powerful weapon they had was the vote. When we came to the first election, there was a great deal of disinformation spread about our party. We did not do so well. Our propaganda, for example, had not been very good. We built up a new constitution and elected a new president. The principles of Political Warfare are simple. You don't have to be in the military to practice them. The members of our original group were never in the military. When d'Aubisson came into our group, in fact, I was very upset. I said I didn't want this military man there and that we should send him to Hell! But he was better than we were on the political side. My batch

was the first civilian group sent to *Fu Hsing Kang* College. Later, many more were sent. I believe we were sent at d'Aubisson's request through the Taiwan Embassy. But nobody cares about us. They just want to think about the death squads. There is nothing in the Political Warfare doctrine that we learned which would call for adopting death squads. If someone shoots at you, of course, you shoot back. But shooting cannot be a *strategic* approach. Yet there is always a moment when you must be willing to fight. The frustration of not having an adequate response produced the death squads. ARENA gave us a response. I don't know how Chiang Ching-kuo used it here, but for us who came to Taiwan to learn it, Political Warfare helped us to save our country. We stopped them [the communists]. If we didn't have Political Warfare, we would have lost.[43]

The feeling was shared by individuals in any number of countries, though few were as directly threatened by communist revolutionary warfare as El Salvador. Thus Taiwan's involvement there was more coordinated and multifaceted than in most other states. Economic and technical assistance complemented Political Warfare measures. Training was conducted for Salvadorans both in Taiwan and in their own country, with several Political Warfare teams spending periods of up to three months in-country working with the Salvadoran military. Ironically, given El Salvador's frequent ostracization due to alleged human rights abuses, Taiwan – which increasingly found itself marginalized as country after country derecognized it – was cast in the role of encouraging diplomatic support for the Salvadoran fight against communism.[44]

Such were the dictates of Taiwan's precarious diplomatic position, in fact, that as the years went on it increasingly found itself with some strange bedfellows. Its connections with Panama, for instance, were of longstanding,[45] predating that country's enmeshment in the international drug trade and various other activities which have lowered its standing in the world community. Consequently, Taiwan's reaction to the depredations of General Manuel Noriega was to try to influence his conduct. Though he himself had not attended *Fu Hsing Kang*, numerous Panamanian officers and civilians had. In their training, as with that of all other students, the dangers of corruption and failure to work towards democracy were central. In a final effort, Taiwan sent Admiral

Soong Chang-chih, its former Chief of General Staff and, subsequently, Defense Minister, to Panama upon his retirement. He was named ambassador, because he knew Noriega personally, having hosted him several times during state visits. 'Chiang Ching-kuo asked me to go', he relates. 'I didn't want to, but our diplomatic situation was so sensitive that I had to go – and I didn't make a penny!'[46] Once there, he met with Noriega regularly and tried to reason with him. 'I told him he was in a very dangerous situation', Soong continues, 'that *he could not alienate the U.S.* If General Noriega had accepted my ideas, things could have worked out better [speaker's emphasis]'.[47] That they did not had little to do with the appropriateness of the effort made. Taiwan, through its activities, had contributed something positive in a negative situation. It certainly did not condone Noriega's activities. To the contrary, Soong pointed out their dangerous consequences.

Such methods were the hallmark of the cautious Taiwan approach to its relations with flawed states. It did not necessarily approve but neither did it publicly condemn, noting instead that each country's internal arrangements were a matter which had to be decided by its indigenous forces. This belief nonetheless was a foreign policy orientation that did not affect the course content at the Institute of Political Warfare. Its message, it seems plain, was actually quite subversive, setting forth an anti-communist approach which built upon the development of democracy and clean government. Even considering the particular slant embodied in the Chinese conception of democracy, the central belief which held governmental legitimacy to be rooted in service to the people could not help but reflect poorly upon a venal, repressive system. We have no examples of individuals who, fired by their lessons at *Fu Hsing Kang*, claim to have rushed back to overthrow authoritarian systems. What does exist, however, is ample testimony, such as that of David Panama above, that the Political Warfare message started foreign students thinking about *political* options within their particular national setting.

Paraguay, for instance, with which Wang Sheng would become more intimately familiar – in a manner he never anticipated (to be discussed in Chapter 8) – was another example of a dictatorial regime with a political system of less character than Taipei might desire, but which was crucial in a foreign policy sense to Taiwan's diplomatic position. Consequently, numerous Paraguayans of all levels received training in Taiwan, and Taipei maintained an active aid mission in the country. Though its political system was authoritarian, Asuncion did have a functioning, albeit corrupt and inefficient, single party system which could be used as a basis for a reform effort. Hence, Paraguayan students seemed to recognize the potential in the political message they were receiving at the Institute. Comments former Institute student Bernardo Antonio Aponte Carballo, a Paraguayan law student simultaneously pursuing an MA in Political Science:

> The *Fu Hsing Kang* course is based on the difference between communism and democracy. First, they gave us general concepts of difference. From this base, they opened up our minds, [urging us] to investigate, to know more about political science. They gave us new ideas, encouraged us to go into new areas. What we learned there was how to distinguish between the two systems, how the communists grab power, how democracy works. Because of this trip, my mind was opened, my curiosity was piqued to know more about political science. It was because of this trip that I started studying political science. In fact, we did lots of studies on and analyzing how communists took power. We did quite a bit of research on how they got their way. We also learned about democracy. For that we used Wang Sheng's book on Sun Yat-sen.[48]

It is worthwhile to compare this quotation with another found in Kaplan which purports to describe the same training:

> The academy's 'ideological strengthening' painted a black-and-white world of pro-Communist and anti-Communist, in which anything was justified to protect one's country from the red menace. Visitors were given crash courses in unconventional warfare, interrogation, and counterterrorism; other classes dealt with indoctrination and psychological warfare. Also stressed was the importance of creating the kind of Leninist political structure that the KMT had found so effective, with a military wing subservient to a single, dominant party.[49]

Obviously a mixture of fact and fancy,[50] the passage nevertheless does again serve to bring to light a very particular aspect of Taiwan's message – it was unapologetically anti-communist. Indeed, this was its purpose. Contrary to Kaplan, however, the thrust of the instruction was precisely the opposite of his 'anything was justified' assertion. To the contrary, said the instructors, *abuses* of the populace, immediate or structural, would be exploited. The only defense was to eliminate such abuses. The only manner in which to do this was through *democracy*. To go from disorder or dictatorship to democracy, however, was difficult; and in making such a transition, a national, *revolutionary* party was an invaluable tool. Thus the Kuomintang could provide a model. It had worked singularly well for Taiwan and had, in fact, prevented military intervention into civilian affairs. Still, it had to be recognized that it was a very particular model.

Here, the use of *San Min Chu-i* to provide the appropriate readings, as mentioned by Aponte Carballo, is instructive, because therein 'democracy' is presented as an inseparable element of a larger framework – the other two principles being 'nationalism' and 'people's livelihood'. The value of that portion of the work in a political science sense is that it makes a tour de force of philosophies for popular rule, examines their philosophical and sociological roots, and finally discusses the various organizational options available for putting theory into practice. A particular solution is given for China, the division of government into five branches rather than the common three used in the West, but it is made clear that this 'solution' derives from China's unique historical circumstances. The Republic, then, offers illustrations, but it cannot provide the 'answers'.

It was a philosophy which echoed that of Taiwan's foreign policy outlook generally, particularly the use of Political Warfare as a diplomatic tool. Thus relations were maintained with international pariah South Africa for reasons of national security centering on access to strategic minerals and technology transfer, but Taiwan made no open attempts to involve itself with the particulars of Pretoria's internal arrangements. South African military missions visited Taiwan and vice versa, including in the latter case visits by Political Warfare personnel to explain their system. Yet the approach taken by GPWD representatives reflected their doctrinal view of the world. To wit, South Africa was a non-communist country of geostrategic significance; by virtue of being non-communist, it possessed the *potential* to become democratic. Says Wang Sheng bluntly, 'We were there to help them fight the communists, not to support *apartheid*'.[51] He adds:

We had to assist in the effort to make sure that South Africa became a democratic country. Occasionally, South Africa sent its military or its representatives to visit Taiwan. They told me their black people had the highest standard of living in all of Africa (which was in many respects true) and that they did not violate their human rights (which we know to be probably not totally true). I told them that the next time they fight the communists, with the Cubans, in Angola, they should not fight only with military force. For example, they should have civic action operations conducted as their forces advance to win over the people. Further, within their own country [I told them], they should provide education for the blacks to build them up. They understood my points. All of our conversations were held privately, however. Publicly, I never interfered in their internal affairs.[52]

Such logic some critics found exasperating; a way of thinking, though, from which Wang Sheng was never to deviate. It was based on a particular analytical framework integral to his traditional education. It was, to return to a point which has been made several times, the value structure which was the crucial ingredient. The world was necessarily an imperfect place; if only the correct philosophy were adopted, all else would eventually follow, even as practitioners made mistakes. That philosophy, of course, in a Chinese context, was *San Min Chu-i*, and Wang Sheng worked relentlessly to hone his knowledge and understanding of it. Throughout his career, he returned time and again to listen to the lectures of his former Philosophy instructor, Fang Tung-mei. Furthermore, beginning in 1958 he taught one of the *San Min Chu-i* courses at the National Chengchi University.[53] His course was popular. Recalls Wang Yao-hwa, who was Wang Sheng's aide after 1964, 'His way of expressing his ideas is very fascinating. A class of 30 would always have 70 or 80 people'.[54] Even as his own insight into *San Min Chu-i* increased, however, Wang Sheng did not lose sight of its distinctly Chinese character. Thus it was not presented to foreign students at the Institute as *the* answer to their own national concerns; it *could* be useful in finding an indigenous approach.

It was this low key approach, married as it was to Taiwan's own example of development, political and social, which was so attractive to certain countries. Anti-communist South Korea, for example, though limited by its own cultural pride in the extent to which it was willing consciously and publicly to adopt any foreign system,[55] was quite interested in the manner Political Warfare worked. Wang Sheng thus visited several times in various capacities – he was, at one point, given an honorary doctorate by Yuang Kuo University – but was questioned most closely regarding the manner in which Political Warfare was used to strengthen national unity. The South Korean military, unlike the South Vietnamese, never did copy the actual Political Warfare system; but a training institute was set up for cadre which endeavored to impart techniques of 'spiritual fighting power' even while avoiding institutionalizing a GPWD-like structure.[56] Such would have been unthinkable given the extensive US involvement with Korean defense.

For the Americans themselves – Taiwan's principal defenders – even while sending students to *Fu Hsing Kang*, remained as ambivalent about Political Warfare on Taiwan as they had been about it on the mainland. It was ill-understood by all but a handful of US officers and smacked of 'Soviet influence'. Indeed, early on in its existence, *Fu Hsing Kang* was visited by a skeptical group from the American advisory mission. Contrary to their own expectations, they came away impressed with the high state of morale and the manner in which the Political Warfare system has addressed, in a single staff function, considerations spread throughout the American structure. Wang Sheng was subsequently invited to visit the US, with one of his stops being the United States Military Academy. (West Point remains a useful template for understanding the actual structure and procedures of *Fu Hsing Kang*.) He did not make any particular converts to Political Warfare as an integral part of the military staff, but the Americans liked the cohesion, loyalty, and high spirits which resulted in units. This was ultimately to be one of the principal reasons they were willing to have the Nationalists try their luck at working with the South Vietnamese, whom so many Americans viewed as hopeless pupils. The Chinese, at least, never saw them as such.

Instead, for Wang Sheng and his fellow Political Officers, all systems were flawed and ever in a quest for perfection. The important thing was the individual and his willingness to *educate* himself. This was at the heart of the message Political Warfare took to countries such as South Vietnam and Cambodia. Though in one sense these efforts may be judged failures, the analyses provided earlier in this chapter demonstrate that the Nationalists were quite insightful in their recognition of the reasons why. Moreover, they were quite philosophical about their inability to overcome certain structural and procedural dilemmas they found deeply rooted by the time they were, late in the game, called on to the field. They were far more pointed in their analysis of the US role in these two cases, which they felt repeated in so many particulars the previous, disastrous American involvement in China's internal politics. Ironically, both the US and Taiwan were to join in a partnership which led to victory in what will surely remain one of the most controversial of the attempts to export counterrevolution, the civil war in El Salvador. More ironically still, it is doubtful the Americans ever appreciated the central role Political Warfare played in orienting key players towards the political processes which ultimately provided for an uneasy but still holding peace in that unhappy country. If such orientation could be achieved in the minds of even a few key students who came through *Fu Hsing Kang*, Wang Sheng was convinced that the seed would grow. The philosophy had worked for the Kuomintang and Taiwan.

NOTES

1. Cf. Chen Jian, 'China and the First Indo-China War', *China Qtly*, 133 (March 1933), pp. 85–110.
2. Anthony Short, *The Origins of the Vietnam War* (London: Longman, 1989), p. 207.
3. Interview with Chen Tsu-yao, retired lieutenant-general and former Political Officer, 17 July 1993 in Taipei.
4. Ibid.
5. Ibid.
6. Interview with Wang Sheng, 28 July 1993 in Taipei.
7. Interview with Chen Tsu-yao, 17 July 1993 in Taipei.
8. Private communication; for information on MACVSOG and related efforts cf. Henry G. Gole, 'Shadow Wars and Secret Wars: Phoenix and MACVSOG', *Parameters*, XXI/4 (Winter 1991–92), pp. 95–105.
9. Interview with Wang Yeh-kai, retired lieutenant-general, 28 July 1993 in Taipei.
10. For the strategic context, as well as many operational particulars, cf. my two works (Ch. 2, note 5): *The Insurgency of the Communist Party of Thailand in Structural Perspective*, esp. Ch. 3, 'Thai Security during the Indochina Conflict', and *Maoist Insurgency since Vietnam*. There is no definitive work on Chinese activities during this period, though release of documentation by the Chinese during their post-Vietnam War dispute with Vietnam has added considerably to our knowledge.
11. See esp. pp. 77–9 of John W. Garver, 'The Chinese Threat in the Vietnam War', *Parameters*, XXII/1 (Spring 1992), pp. 73–85.
12. I discuss these deployments in Ch. 3, *The Insurgency of the Communist Party of Thailand in Structural Perspective*. Available data has been greatly amplified for the Burma case by Bertil Lintner, but the Chinese role in Laos remains largely unexplored. A contemporary, though limited discussion, is provided by the periodic dispatches of

New York Times; e.g. Richard Halloran, 'China Road Force in Laos at 20,000', *NYT*, 16 Oct. 1969, 1. Chinese advisors were apparently also present with the Khmer Rouge in Cambodia.

13. Interview with Yuan Ch'eng-chang, retired rear-admiral and former head of the Bureau of Investigation, 17 July 1993 in Taipei. Wang Sheng has said of him, while discussing personnel assignment policies: 'Take Admiral Yuan. During the war against the Japanese, he was a great hero in undercover work. He was not under Dai Li! To the contrary, most people thought everyone was under him [Yuan]! He was known even to Chiang Kai-shek. *He* told Chiang Ching-kuo to use Admiral Yuan, because he was very talented. Chiang Ching-kuo knew of him through Chiang Kai-shek, not through me. His talents were appreciated, so he was used [as head of the Bureau of Investigation]. While there were espionage cases, he solved most of them. He was certainly qualified to become Taiwan Garrison Commander, but he wasn't placed there'. (Interview with Wang Sheng, 29 July 1993 in Taipei.) For an examination of the clandestine struggle to which Wang Sheng was referring, cf. Hsu En-tseng, *The Invisible Conflict: The Behind-the-Scenes Battle in Pre-'49 China* (Hong Kong: The Green Pagoda Press, 1962).
14. Interview with Chiang Hsien-siang, retired air force lt.-gen., 17 July 1993 in Taipei.
15. Cf. Monte R. Bullard, 'Political Warfare in Vietnam', *Military Review*, XLIX/10 (Oct. 1969), pp. 54–9.
16. Interview with Monte Bullard, retired US Army colonel and PhD (Berkeley), 17 July 1993 in Taipei.
17. Interview with Chen Tsu-yao, 17 July 1993 in Taipei.
18. Interview with Chiang Hsien-siang, ibid.
19. Interview with Wang Sheng, 29 July 1993 in Taipei.
20. Interview with Yu Kuang, former head of the ROC Advisory Mission to Cambodia, 19 July 1993 in Taipei.
21. Ibid.
22. Ibid.
23. Ibid.
24. Interview with Chao Chung-ho, 19 July 1993 in Taipei.
25. Interview with Yu Kuang, ibid.
26. Interview with Sung Chien-yeh, ibid.
27. Interview with Chao Chung-ho, ibid.
28. Interview with Yu Kuang, ibid.
29. Ibid.
30. Interview with Wang Sheng, 29 July 1993 in Taipei.
31. Cf. Wang Yu-san, 'The Republic of China's Technical Cooperation Programs with the Third World', *Issues & Studies*, XIX/5 (May 1983), pp. 64–79. 'Vanguard' itself was originally conceived as an assistance program for African nations, but its potential was soon realized and the effort expanded. See also Betty Wang: 'Foreign Affairs: A Policy of Intensive Cooperation – ROC's Technical Missions Abroad', *Free China Review* (Dec. 1985), pp. 39–49; and 'Technical Exchanges: Forging Ahead in the Dominican Republic – International Cooperation builds Progress, Friendship', *Free China Review* (March 1986), pp. 46–53.
32. In 1971 Taiwan had relations with 68 countries, China with 53; by 1988, 55 countries had switched their allegiance to China, and only nine new countries added to the Taiwan roster. In 1993, there were 29 countries which still recognized Taipei, but many, to include the US and Japan, which maintained 'informal' relations. Cf. Tien, *The Great Transition* (Ch. 4, note 55), pp. 216–27; also *The Republic of China Yearbook 1993*, pp. 758–69.
33. For a factual discussion of actual implementation, see Jin Kai-shin (ed.), *Twenty Years of CTS* (Taipei: China Television Service, 1991), pp. 6–9.
34. Some personnel within the CTS structure, to include the present president and vice-president, are former Political Warfare officers. The vice-president and general

manager, in fact, is Chen Tsu-yao, discussed in the Vietnam section of this chapter. Most
employees, however, are civilians who have had no direct connection with the Ministry
of Education or the Dept. of Defense, the two original owners.

35. Interview with Wang Sheng, 28 July 1993 in Taipei.
36. David Kaplan (Ch. 1, note 24), p. 216. There is little in this phrase, or his book in
    general, which can withstand academic scrutiny. My own negative review of *Fires of the
    Dragon* may be found in 'This Taiwan Exposé sheds More Heat than Light', *Asian Wall
    Street Journal*, 26–27 Nov. 1993, p. 8. Less pointed in its wording but still cognizant
    of serious flaws in Kaplan is Nicholas Eberstadt, 'Who wanted Mr Liu dead?' *New York
    Times Book Review*, 25 Oct. 1992, p. 32.
37. Interview with David Panama, present Ambassador of El Salvador to Taiwan, 15 July
    1993 in Taipei.
38. Publicly displayed at the Inst. of Political Warfare briefing room; confirmed through
    interviews and examination of course syllabuses, 21 July 1993 in Taipei. The failure to
    adhere to the 'significant figures' convention in the percentages nonetheless allows
    them to add up to 100 percent. Though not open to the general public, neither is the
    Institute 'secret'. American officers, for example, have attended both the regular and
    international (i.e. Institute) *Fu Hsing Kang* courses. As such, they have been given access
    to all course materials. I base my comments on the comparative weight given *San Min
    Chu-i*, for example, upon an examination of the complete course syllabus of 'Advanced
    Class 72', which met from Nov. 1967 to 30 March 1968; supplemented by Interview
    with Monte Bullard (course attendee), 27 July 1994 in Carmel, California.
39. Though the several copies in my possession have little publication data (i.e. 'Taipei,
    Taiwan, Republic of China: Compiled by The Fu Hsing Kang College' [*sic*]), those
    obtained over a period of decades show no appreciable differences.
40. Kaplan, p. 215. As best I have been able to determine, neither *Fu Hsing Kang* nor its
    surrounding area has been used for intelligence training other than of an *ad hoc* nature.
    That the former campus might have been so used, given that it was turned over to an
    operation involving the CIA (see comments by Wang Sheng in Ch. 4), cannot be ruled
    out, though it is doubtful that parachute training was conducted even at that location.
    We need not belabor the point, but it does highlight the shortcomings of Kaplan's
    treatment of his subject. The *Fu Hsing Kang* campus – during the mid-1970s, as now –
    is in an urban area and would be singularly ill-suited for such parachuting of any sort,
    much less novice training. Furthermore, *all* regular and rough terrain jump courses were
    moved, quite early on, to the more open spaces of southern Taiwan. They were being
    conducted there in 1974, for example, as were unit mass jumps, a full year before
    Kaplan has parachutists landing in Taipei. For some years, all male cadets at *Fu Hsing
    Kang* were required to become airborne-qualified (as was also the case for a time at West
    Point); but this training, too, was conducted in the south during the summer months.
    As for the use of *Fu Hsing Kang* facilities by other activities, Wang Sheng has
    commented, in addressing another matter: 'There was an institute in the same area and
    sponsored by us, where overseas Chinese were training. There was some unit training,
    and there was the Institute for Political Warfare. There was also a class for youth being
    trained in civic action and civil affairs in preparation for a return to the mainland – it
    prepared local government officials to assume their positions when we go back. There
    was a military band. There were also some outside units which borrowed land from *Fu
    Hsing Kang* to carry out their activities. At one point, the National Security Bureau, our
    CIA, did borrow some area to do something, but this happened after I had left for
    GPWD. Also, there might have been some short-term physical education training in the
    vicinity of the campus. The Ministry of National Defense has to give final approval for
    such use of facilities'. (Interview with Wang Sheng, 29 July 1993 in Taipei.)
41. E.g. see Clifford Krauss, 'US, Aware of Killings, worked with Salvador's Rightists,
    Papers suggest', *New York Times*, 9 Nov. 1993, A1.
42. David Panama has noted: 'About 15 members of our present Congress have been

Counterrevolution Exported   237

through the Political Warfare Academy. Many officers have come here. Some just have a good time the whole two months, but some have gained a great deal'. (Interview, 15 July 1993 in Taipei.)

43. Ibid.
44. See e.g. 'Foreign Affairs: Premier asks Free World Backing for El Salvador', *Free China Review* (April 1982), p. 3.
45. See e.g. Yang Yung-shan, 'Foreign Affairs: Growing with Panama – ROC Mission specializes in Agricultural Diplomacy', *Free China Review* (October 1982), 8-16; and Betty Wang, 'Technical Exchanges: Panama', *Free China Review* (January 1986), 47-53.
46. Interview with Soong Chang-chih, 13 July 1993 in Taipei.
47. Ibid.
48. Interview with Bernardo Antonio Aponte Carballo, 20 Aug. 1993 in Asuncion, Paraguay. Aponte Carballo attended the Advance [Superior] Course of Political Warfare for Foreign Officers for seven weeks from Aug. 1989. At the time Wang Sheng was the ROC Ambassador to Paraguay and no longer involved with GPWD. Course content, however, had remained stable. Wang Sheng's text is that referred to previously, *The Thought of Dr Sun Yat-sen* (Ch. 2, note 21).
49. David Kaplan (Ch. 1, note 24), p. 215.
50. The Institute course for foreign officers is conducted largely on a theoretical level with some operational applications. Techniques *per se* are not taught. As mentioned in Note 39, course content has been remarkably stable over time (some would claim stagnant). Even today there are no classes offered at *Fu Hsing Kang*, to either the Chinese or foreign classes, on either 'unconventional warfare' or 'counterterrorism'. Neither does the course on 'interrogation' deal with mechanics but rather the use of information gained from prisoners, particularly the use in psychological warfare operations. 'Indoctrination' and 'psychological warfare' are established parts of the instruction provided by all major armies, to include the American. There are few *techniques* discussed in the Chinese course, if any, which are unique or unusual.
51. Interview with Wang Sheng, 4 Aug. 1994 in Carmel, California.
52. Ibid.
53. *San Min Chu-i* courses are a mandatory core requirement at high schools and universities in Taiwan. The institutions themselves fall under the jurisdiction of the Ministry of Education, which must accredit courses.
54. Interview with Wang Yao-hwa, 13 Aug. 1993 in Asuncion, Paraguay. It is worth noting, bearing in mind that some sources have spoken of Wang Sheng as 'the most feared man in Taiwan', that, according to Wang Yao-hwa (no relation), Wang Sheng was never armed as he moved about, certainly not when he went to teach his weekly *San Min Chu-i* course. Neither was there seen to be any need for security; his only accompaniment was normally his driver, who might or might not actually proceed with him to the class.
55. A topic I have discussed previously in my 'Korea's Search for Identity Tests US', *Asian Wall Street Journal*, 6–7 July 1990, 10; repr. as 'US must understand a Changing Korea', *The Asian Wall Street Journal Weekly*, 27 Aug. 1990, p. 14.
56. Interview with Wang Sheng, 4 Aug. 1994 in Carmel, California.

6 Strategic Counterrevolution

Wang Sheng visits 'frontline' troops stationed on the offshore islands, May 1981.

EVEN AS Taiwan joined battle directly with the communists by sending advisory missions to South Vietnam and Cambodia – by exporting counterrevolution through its Political Warfare mechanisms – it found the ground shifting from under it.[1] Consequently, the 1970s, and the early 1980s, would be a time of considerable uncertainty and danger for the Republic, marked by a sea-change in the long-time relationship with the United States. That Taiwan was able to survive a near-complete collapse of its international position was a result principally of the success individuals such as Chiang Ching-kuo and Wang Sheng had achieved in building a secure base area, to use the terms of insurgency. From there, after being pressed on to the defensive in the 1970s, they were finally able to counterattack internally and externally in the 1980s with what may be termed strategic counterrevolution.

The years leading up to this dramatic reversal, however, were troubled. The concern that America's anti-communist resolve was weakening, stirred by the pull-out from Southeast Asia, gained substance as relations warmed between Washington and Peking. For despite their extensive history of hostility, the United States and the People's Republic of China gradually moved towards reconciliation. In November 1969 the US terminated regular naval patrols of the Taiwan Strait. Subsequently, the dramatic Nixon–Kissinger moves, leading to President Richard Nixon's visit to Peking and the historic Shanghai Communiqué, re-established relations between the two states and paved the way for a significant shift in American attitudes. The contents of the Shanghai statement clearly indicated that the greatest issue preventing a full reconciliation was the future of Taiwan. On 21 September 1971 the US Senate Foreign Relations Committee recommended repeal of the Formosa Resolution.[2] The vote reflected the shift which had already begun earlier in American attitude in favor of rapprochement with China. In the absence of Washington's leadership, nations which had hitherto backed Taipei wavered. As the US hedged its stand, the United Nations voted on 25 October 1971 to admit the PRC and exclude the ROC. Thereafter, the process took on a momentum of its own. In the aftermath of the UN decision, the American position itself – of standing firmly with the ROC – became more difficult, because the ROC rapidly lost support as a multitude of nations broke relations and recognized the PRC. Thus the Republic found itself increasingly isolated, with the US only remaining as a major though questionable supporter.

What most disturbed the Nationalists was not merely the chain of events themselves but more crucially the manner in which a U.S. lack of resolve appeared to contribute directly to the result. The extent to which the American Congress appeared to be abandoning Phnom Penh and Saigon, not to mention Vientiane, cast grave doubts upon the validity of the US commitment to defend Taiwan in similar circumstances. The impression of a lack of American resolve created pressures for more military self-sufficiency.

Renewed Security Concerns

To move in this direction necessitated a major commitment, both psychologically and in resources. As long as American defense pledges had seemed firm, there had been little incentive for Taipei to press ahead in this direction. Yet with Washington's resolve in doubt, steps had to be taken to shore up the defenses of Taiwan. The ROC leadership began to shift defense priorities towards the immediate defense of Taiwan. This required investment in new weapons, as well as an emphasis upon reorganization. There followed an ambitious military procurement and development program, which aimed at nothing less than military independence from the United States and eventual self-sufficiency.

Even as steps were taken to develop an in-country production capability for weapons systems ranging from surface-to-surface missiles (SSM) to naval vessels, contracts were made with foreign sources to obtain an influx of sophisticated armaments and technology which could be absorbed, reproduced, and eventually improved upon by Taiwan's growing advanced industrial infrastructure. The aim was to bypass whole stages of development which would have been necessary if the nation were to opt for pure self-sufficiency. Thus Taiwan hoped not only to gain an immediately credible defense against the mainland (i.e. by possession of more sophisticated hardware), but also to start its own development process at a higher point on the weapons technology development curve than that to which Peking had progressed.[3] When the United States proved unwilling to provide the systems desired to carry out this plan, Taiwan turned elsewhere. A covert program made some attempt to obtain restricted military technology.⁴ Such activities, however, were minor compared to efforts to deal on the open arms market. Due to Taiwan's increasingly isolated diplomatic status, this proved difficult. Western Europe was one source, but the governments there practiced restrictive export policies. Hence Taipei communicated with the other pariahs of the international order, South Africa and Israel.

This was a controversial course, certainly, though a logical one. It is not clear at what precise point in time extensive contacts between these three states began, but a close working relationship developed, to include the Political Warfare contacts with South Africa already detailed.⁵ Such relations offered certain advantages to each of the states concerned.⁶ For Taiwan, as far as defense was concerned, the advantages were technological (both Israel and South Africa possessed highly developed arms industries) and strategic (South Africa's raw materials). To ensure access to that necessary military commodity possessed by neither Israel nor South Africa – oil – Taiwan strengthened its ties with the anti-communist Arab state of Saudi Arabia (the ROC's anti-communist and technological credentials proved more important to the Saudis than the former's links to Israel).

These contacts yielded quick and tangible benefits to Taiwan. Among the most important was the delivery to the ROCN in late 1973/early 1974 of the first shipments of the Israeli *Gabriel* SSM. Such a missile was essential to Taiwan's naval modernization plans, which called for the construction of a missile-armed fleet of fast patrol craft, for it had no effective long-range anti-shipping capability. The proposed fleet of over 40 small warships, augmented by appropriate larger vessels, would have represented a substantial improvement in the ROC capability to repulse any attempt at invasion or blockade. Yet while the vessels themselves had been procured, both abroad and through indigenous design and production, the United States had refused to sell the desired SSM, the *Harpoon*. The *Gabriel* thus provided a weapon for the vessels and was followed by acquisition, also from Israel, of a long-range system.⁷

With the new strategy well on its way by mid-1975, Chiang Kai-shek died; but whatever momentary dislocation this caused in the leadership of Taiwan was duplicated within a year on the mainland, when both Chou En-lai and Mao Tse-tung also passed away. Thus the ROC shift in defense priorities continued smoothly. The new look was best illustrated by the appointment in mid-1976 of Fleet Admiral Soong Chang-chih, former ROCN Commander-in-Chief, as Chief of General Staff. There followed an emphasis upon the Navy as Taiwan's first line of defense. He moved quickly to insure that Taiwan, the 'model province' and that piece of China in which the KMT revolution continued to exist, was safeguarded. It was to be but the beginning of a long process of reshaping Taiwan's defense posture, for Soong, a decorated veteran who had fought in the civil war and then headed the Navy for six years, would remain Chief of Staff for another six years. Finally, he would spend a further five years as Minister of Defense. The defense posture he implemented was a return to military basics:

> When I became Chief of General Staff, I announced to my subordinates that survival was the key. We must build up our defense capabilities. Most importantly [I said], we need local air superiority and control of the sea. Then we need to be able to communicate outside the island. Once we survive, then we can worry about other options. We were still practicing landings to invade the mainland. This wasn't practical.[8]

Throughout Soong's tenure as Chief of Staff, of course, Wang Sheng was one of his staff officers. They already knew each other and got on well. Soong considered Political Warfare indispensable for what he was trying to do. As he put it:

> The main strategy of our armed forces is to defend itself. We have an enemy army just across the strait and off Quemoy and Matsu. Political Warfare is a system for the security of our armed forces. It teaches them why they fight the communists and how to fight the communists. There are so many parts to the Political Warfare system. One aspect is to teach patriotism. A second is to look out for the welfare of the men and to further their educations. A third is security, counterintelligence. A fourth is anti-corruption. Actually, it is a very natural system. One of the crucial lessons we learned during the civil war was the last one, anti-corruption. You must strictly control corruption within the military and look after the education and welfare of the men. Thus Political Warfare is indispensable for everything else we hope to do professionally.[9]

Sure of the quality and loyalty of his forces, therefore, Soong could press ahead in conjunction with the national leadership. For Taipei, the need to continue such an independent course, as well as the long-range development process of which it was a part, had been highlighted by the disturbing end to the Indochina conflict and the actual repeal of the Formosa Resolution. Then in 1976 several incidents in the technological field convinced Taipei that Washington was more concerned with badgering its friends than with keeping an eye on possible threats to the ROC. In the first of these, the US publicly extracted from Taiwan a pledge to cease the reprocessing of nuclear fuel which might have had application to a nuclear weapons system.[10] In the second incident, the US State Department, as a result of protests organized in America by anti-KMT groups – against the military applications of a Massachusetts Institute of Technology (MIT) program, in design and production of aircraft navigation systems, being conducted for 15 ROC engineers – instigated the cancellation of the contract. Faced with such apparent hostility, Nationalist officials increased their contacts elsewhere, particularly with Israel. Again an effort was made in Western Europe. In late 1976 a ROC purchase commission solicited offers in London from Western European arms dealers for filling a substantial shopping list designed to remedy some basic flaws in Taiwan's air and ground defenses.[11] The weaponry, had it been acquired, would have significantly altered the regional military balance and made Taipei's forces an exceptionally tough nut to crack.

Although acquisition did not materialize for various reasons but due mainly to policy decisions made by the proposed exporting nations, the weaponry desired reflected how the ROC intended to push its technology development program. In any case, other purchases proceeded. From the United States were purchased a completely automated air defense system (at a cost of US $34 million), a battalion of 24 improved *Hawk* surface-to-air missile launchers (SAMs), and the right to build an additional 60 F-5E fighters. All of the ROC Navy's 18 destroyers were refitted with modern electronic and fire control systems, which included linkage of the new central computers for shipboard command and control to heliborne radar. From Israel the new *Gabriel* II was obtained, both in round form for existing launchers as well as mounted on Israeli-produced fast patrol boats. Talks began on the possible co-production of the anti-ship missile, while the ROC Air Force analyzed the Israeli-produced *Kfir* fighter as a possible addition to its inventory.[12] Within the ROC Army (ROCA) a major retrofit and upgrade program of the armored arm began, concentrating principally on self-propelled anti-aircraft units. For the individual soldier American M-16 rifles were procured. The only dent in the momentum of the effort was the blockage by the British government of the sale of 'a considerable number' of *Rapier* SAMs.

Hand-in-hand with procurement went the drive toward self-sufficiency. Unlike many states, the ROC was able to overcome some difficulties in absorbing advanced weapons technology, for Taipei had the infrastructure needed to deploy, maintain, and train forces to use military equipment provided by outsiders. This same technical, logistic, and management capability infused the start of an indigenous arms production capability. In the naval area, for example, great strides were made in the development of anti-ship missiles, influence mines, an effective anti-submarine warfare (ASW) capability, and frigate construction. Patrol boats were designed and produced locally. Coproduction agreements allowed the assembly in-country of F-5E fighters, helicopters, and rifles. Other agreements and technology exchanges were consummated with friendly nations such as Israel and South Africa.

The net result was that by late 1978, the Nationalist armed forces had taken solid strides in the quest for improved defense capability. With technological improvements of a high order made in every service, Taipei had the strong possibility of creating and maintaining one of the more sophisticated military establishments in the region. Just as noteworthy were the strides Taiwan had taken to move ahead of the PRC in the crucial technology development process.

China was certainly aware of its relative military position in relation to Taiwan – as well as to other potential foes – and responded. Its purchasing effort focused on technology development. While Taiwan, with its far smaller armed forces (470,000 regulars in the late 1970s) and the more limited scope of their possible employment, could realistically purchase both technology *and* a fair number of weapons systems to achieve an immediate upgrading of capabilities, China was barred from a similar course by the awesome size of the task confronting it. Indeed, it was estimated by various analysts that to reequip properly the Chinese armed forces (4.3 million strong in the late 1970s) would have taken more weapons and equipment than the

United States had in its entire inventory, both active and reserve. The cost would have been staggering. Consequently, while Peking could bow to necessity and make some large purchases of selected items critically necessary for an immediate upgrading of its force structure – helicopters and anti-tank guided missiles (ATGM), for instance – the desired result was a boost in self-sufficiency rather than dependence.[13]

By early 1977 a major effort was underway to push military modernization forward. A linchpin of this campaign was the return to power in July 1977 of Deng Xiao-ping. Deng shared the views of his mentor, the late Chou En-lai, that the 'liberation' of Taiwan was a sacred duty of sorts and publicly vowed as much. Simultaneously, just months after his official return to the upper levels of government, it became clear that he was the architect of far-reaching military reforms designed to pull the People's Liberation Army (PLA) into the technological world of the 1970s. Chinese 'shopping delegations' soon descended upon Europe in a virtual imitation of earlier Nationalist sprees. Naturally procurement could not proceed in a vacuum. A new emphasis upon proficiency was reflected in a spate of specialized warfare exercises, including a joint services maneuver in August 1977 opposite Taiwan. During the exercise attack aircraft were reported bombing and strafing in support of parachute and amphibious operations, with the entire force protected by interceptors. Although the exercise was elementary by Western or Soviet standards, it did show increased sophistication in the use of tactical airpower, as well as improvements in the techniques which would be needed for any invasion of Taiwan. Nevertheless, such an assault was unlikely if judged solely in military terms.[14]

Behind the scenes, however, it was not in the military field that China was preparing its trump card; the heart of its strategy was political. As the *Far Eastern Economic Review* was to put it, 'Taiwan will remember 1979 as the year that its most dreaded political nightmare – US recognition of Peking – finally came true'.[15] For on 15 December 1978 it was announced by the US administration of President Jimmy Carter that Washington was severing relations with Taipei in favor of its rival. There followed what was arguably the most difficult period in the Republic's post-civil war history.

The KMT leadership had not been unaware of diplomatic developments. The loss of Taiwan's UN seat in 1971 had been the writing on the wall and had triggered the reorientation of defense policy. Still, the event, when it finally came, was devastating. Neither did it occur in a vacuum. As early as 1970, Taipei had become concerned with the violent splinter of the Taiwan Independence Movement, the World United Formosans for Independence (WUFI). On 25 April, Chiang Ching-kuo, on a ten-day visit to the US, narrowly escaped assassination at the hands of Peter Huang, 32, a Taiwanese student in industrial engineering at Cornell. A member of WUFI, headed by Dr Trong R. Chai, Huang was detained with his accomplice, Cheng Tzu-tai, WUFI Executive Secretary.[16] WUFI itself was inspired by the contemporary liberation ideologies and direct action ethos, particularly in the US. It saw itself as a resistance movement and labelled its direct action units 'Commando Squads'. These were sent worldwide to engage in actions against the KMT 'oppressors'. A 1970 bombing of the United States Information Service (USIS) in Tainan and a February 1971 bombing of the Bank of America in Taipei, which caused several casualties, were typical actions. Security measures were consequently tightened, leading to further denunciations of 'repression' by the exile community and opposition figures in Taiwan. WUFI's next significant action was to use explosives in January 1976 to cause a power blackout over a wide area of southern Taiwan. Later in the year, a WUFI operative, Wang Hsing-nan, while visiting Taiwan, sent letter bombs to Hsieh Tung-min, governor of Taiwan; Huang Chieh, a former governor of Taiwan; and Li Huan, by that time director of the KMT's Department of Organizational Affairs (he would hold this position 1972–78). Wang Sheng was also apparently meant to be a target.[17] Only the first of the recipients actually opened his package, suffering serious injuries, to include the loss of his left arm and an eye. This 'punitive action' against Hsieh Tung-min, 'the number one traitor of Taiwan and puppet of the Chiang family', WUFI said in an announcement, was taken because the government had failed to show 'sincerity' following the power sabotage.[18]

Of more concern, though, were undoubtedly WUFI's published plans to foment domestic unrest for seizing state power.[19] The connections, real and purported, between WUFI, the Taiwan Independence Movement (TIM), and Taiwanese opposition figures within the island thus became a subject of increasing official attention. This attention seemed warranted when the opposition became involved in the November 1977 'Chungli riot, Taiwan's first violent mob scene in more than 20 years'.[20] Sparked by allegations of voter fraud, the riot led to an intensified security crackdown which had begun following the letter bomb attacks the previous year. It was in such a context that the US derecognition occurred in December 1978. Emboldened, the opposition, using as an organizational front a new periodical, *Formosa*, maneuvered for advantage. Through intent or misjudgment, their activities reached a peak in a substantial riot on 10 December 1979 in Kaohsiung,[21] 'the largest display of political violence since the February 1947 incident in which thousands died'.[22] The government response was swift and comprehensive, as those deemed responsible for the episode were arrested, tried in open court, and convicted under martial law provisions.

Often overlooked is that the Kaohsiung incident occurred amid another round of WUFI bombing attacks, this time in the US but again directed against KMT targets.[23] The perpetrator of the 1976 bombings had been apprehended,[24] but the American authorities were unable to apprehend those responsible for the attacks on their soil. Thus the Taiwan authorities were undoubtedly in a sensitive state when the opposition violated what had been seen as a bargain struck as to the terms under which protests would be allowed so as not to be subject to the sedition and treason sections of the martial law. As further arrests followed the Kaohsiung trial and a highly publicized incident wherein three family members of one of the accused were murdered while he was under detention,[25] 11 more attacks of various sorts, against 'KMT targets' in the US, occurred between 19 December 1979 and 29 July 1980.[26] The two principal targets were those deemed responsible for suppression of the Kaohsiung riots and the subsequent moves against the opposition, Wang Sheng and Kaohsiung Mayor Wang Yu-yueng (no relation). Unable to get at their targets, however, WUFI struck at their families. Bombs planted at the Los Angeles home of Wang Sheng's second son, Wang Pu-tien on 17 February 1980, and at the home (in the same city) of Wang Yu-yueng's son on 29 July 1980, caused substantial damage and resulted in one death, Mayor Wang's brother-in-law, Lee Chian-lin.[27] In between the two bombings, in Taiwan itself, a sensational death occurred when visiting American Chen Wen-chen, a 31-year-old professor of statistics at Carnegie-Mellon University, Pennsylvania, was found dead on 3 July at the National Taiwan University campus after having spent the day being questioned at Taiwan General Garrison

Command concerning his alleged links with the Taiwan Independence Movement. No perpetrator was apprehended, and the case quickly became a source of major irritation in US–ROC relations.[28] Congressional hearings on the murder rapidly expanded to include the activities of Taiwan's representatives on US university campuses and the oversight mechanisms used by the ROC.[29]

What the ROC now saw at stake in all of this was nothing less than its survival – and the survival of the KMT revolution. The attacks on family members were the final straw. WUFI, of course, would argue that it was simply fighting fire with fire, that the KMT's own actions against innocents far exceeded anything the militant exiles had even planned much less executed. The KMT response would have been that everything it had done had been in accordance with the law. Whether one agreed with the law was quite another matter. There were ways to change it, but as long as a state of conflict existed, normalcy could not reign. WUFI would respond that this was a canard and did not, in any case, excuse abuses such as torture and imprisonment for political crimes. The KMT would claim that abuses were inherent to any system and were in Taiwan punished when found out. Of course, no such debate between these mutually exclusive positions actually occurred, and bombs were the result. Some on Taiwan, however, were unwilling to wait for the enemy to come to them. Relates Wang Sheng's second son Wang Pu-tien:

> After this [the bombing in which Lee Chian-lin died], I learned that there were people who [went and] hired some gang types in the US, Mafia types – paid them a lot of money – to kill all the important Taiwan Independence Movement members in the US. They had been connected with the police before, so they knew a lot about 'black society' people. But they themselves [those doing the hiring] were liberals. Underworld representatives came to Taiwan and thought my father should agree. The individuals concerned came to see my father and explained [their intentions]. Father told them he represented the ROC and never should do this. The individuals concerned tried to bring these people to see my father, but he would not [see them]. He said he cannot. So the individuals concerned gave up. If father had not intervened, the case would have been much bigger than that of Henry

Liu; because there were at least seven to ten Taiwan Independence Movement leaders who were targeted. They are all in Taiwan now![30]

The Realities of Power

Pu-tien's is a telling point and serves to highlight the role Wang Sheng actually played during these difficult years. It is a point which needs to be made, because even as highly regarded a source as the *Far Eastern Economic Review* of Hong Kong was at this time replete with references to Chiang Ching-kuo, 'ruthless czar of the Kuomintang (KMT) secret police',[31] and to Wang Sheng, 'one of Chiang Ching-kuo's most powerful aides'.[32] And it was Wang Sheng who was seen to be in competition for position in the KMT hierarchy, as well as to be the shadowy figure behind the government's efforts to maintain control of internal security. When his long-time associate Li Huan was removed as head of the KMT Department of Organizational Affairs in 1978 and appointed head of National Sun Yat-sen University, for instance, Li having been held responsible for the party's less-than-anticipated showing in the November elections which had culminated in the Chungli riot,[33] the *Review* set forth a typical passage:

> According to some reports, Wang Sheng had shrewdly taken advantage of the electoral battles between the KMT and the opposition in order to eliminate rival Li from the political scene. Subsequent shuffles in crucial government posts reflected a consolidation of Wang's retinue and a strengthening of military influence in general. Although President Chiang was unquestionably the nucleus of government clout – with no apparent plans to relinquish the political spotlight – Wang Sheng's muscle was perceived behind many of the year's methodical actions intended to counter the nascent opposition movement.[34]

Little in such a passage jibed with reality. Neither Li Huan nor Wang Sheng, for all their important contributions to the KMT, had yet achieved the status necessary to be on the Standing Committee, though Admiral Soong Chang-chih, Chief of General Staff and Wang Sheng's superior, was a member (and on the National

Constantly visiting units to assess their readiness and morale, Wang Sheng (center) talks with marines on Christmas 1978.

Chiang Ching-kuo (center) and Wang Sheng (left) view exercises in 1979. (Note seating arrangements, with no preference shown to Wang Sheng upon the basis of past friendship with Chiang Ching-kuo).

Security Council, of which Wang Sheng was a member). Thus for commentators to have Wang Sheng and Li Huan, or any other combination, battling for position was to ignore all of those who already had superior positions – in the party, the government, the armed forces, and the alleged affections of superiors such as Chiang Ching-kuo. Neither, as has been demonstrated previously, was there a Wang Sheng 'retinue', because for such to have meaning would be to grant to Political Warfare operational power which it simply did not have. Indeed, in a further point, it has been detailed that Wang Sheng had no operational authority over the Taiwan General Garrison Command, the organization actually carrying out the campaign to safeguard internal security. (Whether it was, in fact, an 'instrument of repression' remains quite another matter altogether, though certainly Wang Sheng has argued that it was not.) The reality of the chain of command was visible in May 1978, even as Li Huan was shifted, when Lieutenant-General Wang Ching-hsu, chief of the Intelligence Bureau, was made commander of Taiwan General Garrison Command (and promoted to general).[35] Like all of the Command's previous commanders, he was a line officer, engineer branch by commission, and had no connections with GPWD. He was to hold his position until the end of 1981, at which time he assumed command of the National Security Bureau.[36] The head of the so-called 'secret police', in other words, so that the point cannot be missed, was the direct subordinate of Admiral Soong, himself a Standing Committee member together with the 'ruthless czar of the secret police' himself, Chiang Ching-kuo. Wang Sheng was not in his chain of command.

Highlighted for us in the *Review* passage, therefore, are not the realities of the KMT power equation at the time but rather the analytical confusion which prevailed, then as now, as to the precise roles personalities actually played in the important events under discussion. For all its awkward timing for the Republic, caught as it was amidst a rapidly changing strategic situation, the April 1975 death of Chiang Kai-shek does allow us a window through which we may once again peer at Wang Sheng's actual position within the hierarchy.

Though he had withdrawn from public affairs in the years immediately prior to his death, leaving effective control of the country to Chiang Ching-kuo, Chiang Kai-shek had until that time been the final arbiter in national decisionmaking. It was he, for instance, as noted previously, who decided that Wang Sheng should finally be made the Director of GPWD; and apparently the signed order to do so was his last official act in the month of his death. Though much in the KMT's decisonmaking had become more rational with Chiang Ching-kuo managing day to day affairs, it remained the elder Chiang's methodology to gather information by summoning individuals, irrespective of position or duties, and having them report on their work. Wang Sheng, who had only met Chiang Kai-shek twice before coming to Taiwan, had been so summoned by him a dozen or so times. He notes:

> When Chiang Kai-shek was in power, I never saw him upon my initiative. He would always call me. His conversation was always very brief and organized. He would ask me how morale was, how was the situation in Vietnam, how was training? He wanted my opinion. My rank was low, but he knew I had great responsibility. When I was the Deputy Director of GPWD, there were, in turn, four generals over me as my superiors; but Chiang Kai-shek knew they were not the person holding certain responsibilities – I was the one. It was he, for example, who sent me to Vietnam, so of course he wanted me to report on the situation there. Besides my official positions, I was also a member [after 19 May 1959] of the Central Committee, of which he was the *Tsung-ts'ai*, so he was also speaking to me in this capacity [when he summoned me]. He wanted information on everything; he was a very cautious decisionmaker.[37]

Hence Chiang Kai-shek, throughout his life, remained the KMT's strategic compass. To have him depart amidst threatening international events was a serious blow. 'The Kuomintang lost its center of gravity with Chiang's death', observes Ch'en Li-fu. 'It needed reorganization, with Chiang Ching-kuo as the party's leader'.[38] This was done, with the KMT 'wise men's council', the Central Committee for Deliberation and Consultation, playing an important role.[39] Chiang Ching-kuo became head of the KMT; he was already premier. The vice-president, Yen Chia-kan, became president and remained as such until completion of his term. Chiang Ching-kuo became president in 1978 at the age of 68 and would serve a decade until his own death. From 1975 until 1983, Wang Sheng was the Director of GPWD.

Almost 60 in mid-1975, Wang Sheng would seem to have 'arrived'. As noted earlier, certain commentators, foreign and domestic, reached this conclusion. Wang Sheng's powerful 'mentor', went the line of reasoning, was himself at the center of Taiwan's power structure – and would become the undisputed leader after 1978 – and Wang Sheng himself controlled 'the political commissar system'. Reality, of course, was quite different. The heady days of intense pressure to reform the party and its organizations, to build anew; of providing for the national defense, when thousands of shells were crashing down upon Quemoy, and hurried, dangerous visits to 'the front lines' were made to inspire the troops; of wondering, at times, if their revolution had a future; these days were gone. In their place had come routinization. Both men, never intimate in the sense of secrets and friends shared, had thrown themselves into the mundane ritual which came with nation-building. Wang Sheng himself observes:

> Before Chiang Ching-kuo became premier [in 1969 he became vice-premier, in 1972 premier], I would talk to him quite often, especially when he was Defense Minister [1965–69]. We would talk about all sorts of personal and professional issues. After he became premier, we did not talk that often, only once in a while, because he had so many issues to address. After he became president, he was even busier, so I really didn't see him much, as I had when he was defense minister. I had my superiors, we had a hierarchy, so I couldn't just go see him. He always asked me to come to see him more than I could go to see him [on my own initiative]. Most of the time when we met, we were visiting military bases or the front line [the offshore islands]. As we drove, I'd be sitting in the back behind him, and we would talk. Whenever he called me to his office, we would never talk more than half an hour. His manner of speaking was very succinct, and he controlled time very well. In his later years, when his health wasn't very good, I tried to avoid burdening him with the problems I was encountering. I just wanted him to get better.[40]

Wang Sheng's own schedule grew all the more intense when his life was shattered by the death of Hu Hsiang-li and the estrangement of his children. Chiang Ching-kuo had already been that route once, only to take it again with Chiang Kai-shek's passing. Already, the sheer burdens and loneliness of power had separated him from Wang Sheng. In his numerous, almost weekly visits to the countryside to mingle with the people, Chiang Ching-kuo was most often accompanied by the man who would be his KMT Secretary-General for six years, Chiang Yen-shih ('Y.S. Chiang', as he is frequently termed).[41] He was to analyze Chiang Ching-kuo thus:

> Many even now do not understand his ideas or what he was really like. He really liked people, to make contact with the people. He especially liked poor people. I would go with him all the time into the countryside. We would sit out in the evening wherever we were staying, with a bowl of fruit, and all the small children would come up, and he would play with them. He really liked that. He was very mild mannered and liked to tell them stories.[42]

It is impossible to imagine such a story ever being told of Wang Sheng. He, in contrast, spent every spare moment visiting troop units. Recalls Wang Li-tien ('Mao Ti'), Wang Sheng's youngest child:

> What I remember most about him was that he was always busy. We could hardly have dinner with him once a week, especially after 1975 when he became Director of Political Warfare. The first three years he had no holidays, no weekends. He would just come home to sleep. When we'd wake up, he'd be gone. In our home we don't take Chinese holidays that seriously, like New Year's and so forth. We don't go through a lot of ceremony. So that wasn't a problem. He would always be out with the troops. Sometimes, I would go out with him. The troops really appreciated his presence, I could tell. On weekends, when he went out [to visit units], he never informed the troops in advance. He would just tell the driver where to go. When he went in, he didn't go to the main office. He would go right to the troops. Once we went to a compound at Tao Yuan. After we had finished everything, the commander came in. He was in tears. But my father liked to see the reality of things, not just the words.[43]

Such was not a methodology designed to endear him to those upon whom he descended, even though Wang Sheng is not known to have used his myriad visits as grounds for taking direct action against individual officers (there are no recorded incidents, for instance, of summary reliefs). Yet his approach violated certain accepted ways of doing things, almost as if Wang Sheng, culturally the quintessential Chinese gentleman, was quite unable to stay in character politically where *revolutionary* matters were concerned. His visits, to use the case at hand, were to obtain an honest picture of the situation. *Truth*, therefore, was the issue, not niceties; and all should understand that there was only one way to gain it. He seems to have been singularly incapable of putting his mind to rest so long as the revolution had needs, which it always did. Daughter Wang Tsiao-li puts this into perspective:

> There are things I have noticed about my father. He is different from his colleagues. People tell me he was so powerful – people will think anything – they think they can get things done if only they can talk to Wang Sheng. Maybe it is because he has this intense personality. One time he took me to dinner. There were all sorts of important people there. He's not very cautious. One person was in charge of justice work, another in charge of something else – all had their areas of responsibility – my father was talking about police problems – we should see about this, maybe we should do that. I could see that these people were trying to avoid talking about these things. They really didn't want to hear about them – you're telling *me* how to run a police force. There is a realistic side to his stories. He really does try to do everything better. That's how he gets this kind of reputation. He has this kind of personality.[44]

Even Chiang Ching-kuo was not immune to Wang Sheng's constant drive for perfection. 'If Chiang Ching-kuo did something wrong', recalls Wang Pu-tien, 'my father always tried to correct him. Whenever Chiang Ching-kuo had a problem, like the Kaoshiung riots, he would come ask my father to find a solution. But he wasn't that close to my father, not like he was to Li Huan or others'.[45] Chiang Ching-kuo, however, particularly as he advanced in years, was not the only one who could not go at the pace Wang Sheng demanded of himself. His *sincerity* had become all-consuming.

Wang Sheng thus had become incapable of resting for more

than a moment, so great were the tasks at hand. His life revolved about his duty to the revolution. He was given to innumerable acts of kindness, was always decent to those around him, and was mild mannered in approach and speech. Yet these were pauses along a highway filled with onrushing traffic. He regularly checked on Chiang Ching-kuo's twins, born of Chang Ya-juo, for instance, and did the same with his own children, wherever they were living – it was not that he did not love them – but he served a higher calling.[46] Given the makeup of the man, it is unlikely that he ever, in his own mind, thought of the passing of the years in terms of being *called*. For he was the product of a unique era in which momentous events and the roles they demanded were as hand to glove. Even *destiny*, ironically, was possibly never to be spoken of, except perhaps by the likes of Chiang Kai-shek or Chiang Ching-kuo. Certainly destiny could not be considered by a man such as Wang Sheng, he would claim, because to do so was to abandon humility, an essential characteristic of a pupil and scholar.

This is judged ironic, because one of the adjectives commonly associated with Wang Sheng was 'ambitious'.[47] Yet he was consistent in turning down appointment to high office, choosing instead to patiently labor in the niche he had chosen for himself. The most common retort is that he was building his own faction, but this logic collapses before the evidence. What was central for Wang Sheng was the revolution, cast by the mold of fate as the counterrevolution. Says Wang Li-tien, 'My father's favorite words go: No matter where you go, no matter what you want to do, no matter what you want to be, I only ask two things – love the country and be against communism'.[48]

It is an accurate statement of what motivated Wang Sheng. How strange, then, must have seemed – to those who knew him, knew his frugal and simple habits – the constant references, through rumor and yellow journalism, to his alleged 'power and wealth'. In pushing this line, as well as numerous others, a key figure was Henry Liu, writing under the pen name 'Chiang Nan'. Prior to his murder in 1984, Liu was tireless in penning criticism of Wang Sheng (and Chiang Ching-kuo) for the US and foreign (e.g. Hong Kong) Chinese-language press, its bile matched only by its inaccuracy.[49] His subject's own tangled finances and puzzling motives have been insufficiently covered by David E. Kaplan,[50] but what is relevant here is the extent to which inaccuracies, when penned in the Chinese language and coming from those ostensibly

informed by inside sources, gained acceptance in circles generally
given to a more careful weighing of evidence. Surely a criticism
such as that which claimed Wang Sheng was allegedly
accumulating wealth by virtue of his position – a point which was
demonstrably false – should have set off alarm bells concerning
other points of analysis. It seems not to have done so.

His daughter, Wang Hsiao-li, was to observe, 'I think coming
from a poor family is quite important to his [Wang Sheng]
character. So when I read in these magazines all those bad things
about him and wealth, I am so embarrassed. I know how
inaccurate they are'.[51] Inaccurate, too, were the attempts to accuse
him of squiring a young woman about Taipei,[52] since the only
young woman with whom he was ever to appear alone, at
functions private or public, was none other than Wang Hsiao-li, his
daughter. As for the charges of using his influence to help his
friends, a favorite theme with Henry Liu, few knew as well as
Wang Hsiao-tien, Wang Sheng's third son, how completely his
father was devoted to the principle of merit:

> When I was in the army [under universal service], I asked for
> no special favors. I was in the army engineers. That was the
> time of the Vietnam War, when we repaired a lot of vehicles.
> I received no special favors because I was General Wang's son.
> And he did not try to gain any for me. To the contrary, when
> we graduated [from university] we all had to take an exam to
> become officers. I didn't prepare very well for it, because I
> didn't care. Of our 23 classmates, only three of us didn't pass.
> I was one of them, so I became a private. All my other
> classmates, those twenty, were second lieutenants. Actually, I
> stayed up the entire night before the exam playing *mah jong*!
> My father did not try to influence the process. They even used
> it as an example: even General Wang's son didn't pass, so
> don't think it's so easy![53]

Despite all the evidence to the contrary, for any who took the
time to find it, the drumroll of criticism would continue
throughout Wang Sheng's career. Chiang Yen-shih, who today is
the Secretary-General of the President's Office in Taiwan,
comments knowledgeably upon the price of being at the center of
momentous affairs, 'You can't expect all people to like you. Some
of those who didn't like him [Wang Sheng] are the ones who are

really totally ambitious and dangerous'.[54] As it was, the most
predictable element of Wang Sheng's response to gossip was that
he ignored it. As he was to note in an interview, 'It's not up to me
to say I'm not setting up a power or not thinking only of myself.
Those who would weaken our society spread such rumors to create
factions'.[55]

What we see, therefore, is a Wang Sheng who was vitally
important to Taiwan and the KMT revolution, a man who had in
many ways singlehandedly created a critical structure and ethos –
Political Warfare – which had given tensile strength to both the
military and society. Yet until his December 1979 appointment,
aged 64, to the Standing Committee, he was a man who had
become increasingly marginalized from the locus of power, both
by choice and circumstance. He was content to labor in the
shadow, secure in the knowledge that *service* was its own reward;
sincerity will out. This was to change dramatically as Peking's
political approach to its 'Taiwan problem' kicked into high gear
with American derecognition of Taipei. Wang Sheng was asked to
lead a new campaign against the enemy, a Political Warfare
campaign. Little did he suspect that it would be his last as head of
GPWD.

Liu Shao Kang – Strategic Counterrevolution

For Taiwan, 'the seventies of the Republic of China (1981–90)', as
Premier Sun Yun-suan ('Y. S. Sun') observed, promised to be 'a
crucial decade'.[56] US derecognition in December 1978 had been
followed by actual establishment of relations with China on 1
January 1979. In April of the same year, passage of the US Taiwan
Relations Act had clarified American commitments to Taiwan.
Henceforth, Taiwan's affairs were to be conducted by a
Coordination Council for North American Affairs (CCNAA). The
US maintained its commitment to provide those weapons
necessary for Taiwan's national defense. Yet the subsequent
manner in which this guarantee was actually implemented was
unacceptable to Taipei, because it left decisions of strategic posture
and military hardware in the hands of Washington. Relations
between the two erstwhile allies were strained for years.
Simultaneously, to press its advantage, China worked
systematically to replace Taiwan in all international forums,

ranging from the World Bank and International Monetary Fund (IMF) to the International Olympic Committee (IOC). With Taiwan's only major supporter having cut it adrift, this CCP campaign was quite successful. Taiwan was only able to maintain its position in certain organizations, most commonly those associated with sports, by accepting designation as a part of China – the renamed 'Chinese Taipei Olympic Committee', for instance, regaining membership in the IOC after its earlier expulsion in favor of the 'Chinese Olympic Committee' which represented Peking.[57]

Such efforts by China had been of long standing, yet it was US derecognition which served to inaugurate a new phase in the offensive. The American announcement of derecognition coincided to the month with the third plenum of the Eleventh Central Committee (CC) of the CCP. There, Deng Xiao-ping, who had been rehabilitated for the second time little more than a year before, not only consolidated his leadership of the party but also made a strong appeal for 'the great cause of reunification'. When formal relations were announced between Peking and Washington, the Chinese National People's Congress (NPC), in an 'open letter to the people of Taiwan', called for establishment of postal, trade, and transportation links. This offer was made again in a 30 September 1981 address to the CCP Standing Committee by Ye Jian-ying, its chairman. 'His nine-point policy clearly stated that after the reunification, Taiwan would be a special administrative region (SAR) of China which would maintain its present capitalist economic, political, and social systems and would be able to maintain its own army and its economic, cultural, and other ties with foreign countries'.[58] As soon as possible, it was further proposed, 'three links and four exchanges' should be established. 'The 'three links' referred to the earliest possible start in direct trade, transportation, and postal services between the Mainland and Taiwan; the 'four exchanges' referred to the establishment of exchanges between relatives and tourists, academic groups, cultural groups, and sports representatives'.[59]

The 'three links and four exchanges' were the most tangible element in these pronouncements and sought to tap latent fraternal impulses in the Taiwan polity. Officially, they did not, as would be expressed in direct terms by the KMT leadership, especially Chiang Ching-kuo, in the days – and years – which followed.[60] Yet unofficially the walls between Taiwan and China had begun to crumble. Exchanges were occurring, particularly investment by businessmen from Taiwan in mainland enterprises (where, among other things, labor was priced lower than in Taiwan itself). Chiang Ching-kuo, therefore, sought a coordinated response to the CCP's political offensive. Since Political Warfare seemed the issue at hand, and Wang Sheng had recently been brought into the KMT Standing Committee, he seemed the man for what Chiang Ching-kuo had in mind, an 'office' tasked with 'countering the CCP united front offensive'.

As Wang Sheng recalls the way the office actually unfolded,[61] one day in early 1980, after a meeting of the KMT Standing Committee, Chiang Ching-kuo asked him to come to his office. 'At this time the situation was very ominous, very serious', he recalls, 'because of the political developments'. Chiang Ching-kuo said that in order to cope with 'this united front strategy of the communists', Taiwan needed to strengthen its defenses. 'Before, we had only had a defensive posture. Now, we were also going to have an offense'. His words, as Wang Sheng recalls them, were to the effect: 'The job of countering the united front, conducted by the original 'Solidify the Country Group' *(Gu guo hsiao tsu)*, was not creative and aggressive enough. Now we want to start an all-out struggle against the enemy. I want you to take the responsibility'. It was not what Wang Sheng had expected to hear. 'In shock, I responded, "I absolutely cannot shoulder such a huge task. It is beyond my capability". In my career, I could never turn down the orders of my teacher, Chiang Ching-kuo; but this time I was concerned and answered immediately that this was very important work and that I was not qualified. I asked him if he would reconsider'. Chiang Ching-kuo was adamant, 'I've already done all the considering. You're the person. You're on the Standing Committee, so you can take this job'.

What swirled before Wang Sheng was the enormous nature of the undertaking, for what Chiang Ching-kuo had in mind was nothing less than coordinating the strategic and operational response of Taiwan to China's multifaceted offensive. Where could such a charge lead? 'As long as the communists were still around, the campaign would go on', he analyzed. 'There would be no deadline, so I was afraid that such a responsibility would be very broad and open-ended'. Wang Sheng asked that the task go to someone 'in a higher position with a higher reputation, and that I would be his [that person's] assistant'. Chiang Ching-kuo denied his request and continued, 'You don't need anyone higher than you'. He was very serious, direct, and firm, speaking a sentence at a time with a little impatience. Still looking for a way out, Wang Sheng, sitting in a chair in front of his former instructor's desk, changed his form of address, 'Teacher, you know me. Once I take a job, I throw myself into it and get it done. You know I won't be able to finish this job. It will be very controversial and will make lots of enemies. Eventually, this problem will extend not just to me but even to you. I don't care about myself, but it is not best for you'. Chiang Ching-kuo only repeated, 'I have already done my considering'.

Wang Sheng continues:

> The reason I thought the job was so dangerous was because of its tremendous scope. As soon as he mentioned it, my mind was racing over the whole scope of the problems. For instance, I would be the Number One enemy of the communists, because I would be attacking their strategy. Second, inside the country [Taiwan], I would be everyone's Number One enemy, because I would have to get many offices to coordinate, involve myself in everything they did. I could see all the dangers in this. Under the circumstances, I started to bargain with him. At the time, Chiang Yen-shih [Y.S. Chiang] was the Secretary-General of the Kuomintang. I suggested that he set up an office to take care of this, with my having a small office under him. I would do the work, but the office would be the one exercising the authority. Although I had accepted the order, I was still trying to relieve some of the pressure. Chiang Ching-kuo grew a bit impatient. He said he didn't care how I managed it, it was still my responsibility. What I wanted was to avoid being the main target. I wanted to be under the Secretary-General, so that he could take the lead. That was in 1980. That's the way the *Liu Shao Kang* Office came into being.[62]

Liu Shao Kang, as it was simply termed, the meaning taken from the name of an emperor in the Han dynasty linked with the Chinese character for 'rejuvenate', was actually a product of more than a Chiang Ching-kuo whim. It had initially been without label, but it had originated in detailed discussions between the president and KMT Secretary-General Y. S. Chiang[63] concerning the possibilities of a political strategic counteroffensive against the communists. 'We thought we must have a small group of people who were sincere who could study certain projects', Y. S. Chiang recalls: 'I didn't know General Wang very well, but I knew he had a keen mind and was devoted to the country. He was very competent, so we got him to head the office'.[64] What Wang Sheng was first specifically charged with was 'to make a thorough study of the mainland situation and how Taiwan could cope with it'.[65] He was then to produce policy recommendations. These would be passed on to the president.

The mechanism for this was specific. *Liu Shao Kang* itself had no command authority. It was to be an *ad hoc* KMT organization under the office of the Secretary-General, drawing its personnel from other offices on a part-time, loan basis. All of its recommendations were to be agreed upon by the two key individuals involved, Secretary-General Y. S. Chiang, representing the KMT, and Premier Y. S. Sun, representing the government. In actual fact, this process was fairly informal, because the three individuals passing judgement on *Liu Shao Kang*'s recommendations – Chiang Ching-kuo, Y. S. Chiang, and Y. S. Sun – knew each other well.[66] Wang Sheng, though he had hitherto not been a member of the inner circle, of course knew Chiang Ching-kuo. He soon developed a close working relationship with Y. S. Chiang and Y. S. Sun. Wang Sheng would meet with the two men two or three times a week to discuss possible strategic moves. Either Y. S. Chiang or Y. S. Sun would pass on recommendations to Chiang Ching-kuo in meetings scheduled for every third week.[67] As time went on, and *Liu Shao Kang* proved valuable, the procedure became even more informal. Recalls Y. S. Chiang:

> There were very few issues upon which the three of us disagreed. I would say that 99 per cent of what General Wang came up with, we would approve. These were the matters we recommended to Chiang Ching-kuo. The other one per cent we never formally recommended. We only submitted those things upon which we could agree. The premier, especially, had to give his agreement, because his office and his subordinate agencies would be the ones to carry out our recommendations. As time passed, the procedure became whichever of us three saw the president first would pass on to him our recommendations and inform the others.[68]

What happened rapidly, then, was that *Liu Shao Kang*, as might have been expected, given that Wang Sheng was involved, became far more than its original terms of reference suggested. It did not deal simply with the communist threat, but became instead a policy advisory body, a think tank, serving Chiang Ching-kuo and the upper leadership. As such, it tapped some of the brightest minds in Taiwan to provide advice on virtually *any* policy question, advice framed from within the particular perspective of Political Warfare – that is, strategic counterrevolution. To conceptualize this, one need only harken back to the early period of exile on Taiwan, when the overriding question was, 'What went wrong?' Now, in the 'crucial decade', the question was repeated, with the same solution: reform. *Liu Shao Kang* identified the targets and proposed solutions. Its concentration, however, was upon policy formulation as opposed to structural change. How, in other words, to make the pieces fit together better so as to turn around a strategic situation which showed signs of becoming another Civil War-like rout?

To answer this question, Wang Sheng formed three committees which matched the three committees of the KMT's own structure: domestic affairs, overseas affairs, and mainland affairs. Each had fewer than 20 members, all individuals with other, permanent positions who met for two meetings a month, usually in the third and fourth weeks of the month. Y. S. Chiang and Y. S. Sun would alternate as meeting chairmen, the former taking the third week, the latter the fourth. The participants with whom they met were a logical product of Political Warfare's emphasis upon service, for Wang Sheng, in a throwback to his own formative years, sought out the most vigorous talent in Taiwan. In practice, this meant those tapped were often relatively junior in rank and quite young. They would discuss issues, on a nonattribution basis, free from considerations of rank; Wang Sheng would package the product for Y. S. Chiang and Y. S. Sun.

Remembers Liu Kuo-chih, now senior vice-president for Taiwan Aerospace, then a recent PhD from MIT working for the Institute of Technology:

> I was very concerned with the political situation, so I was called to work at *Liu Shao Kang*. It was one of those 'your country needs you'. I was all in favor of working with them. How to cope with this new situation in which we found

ourselves? That's what the office was for. I became the part-time secretary of Overseas Affairs. I was very junior and not thinking about high-ranking things. I just liked to talk to Wang Sheng. We were just like a think-tank which pulled people out from all over the government, the best and the brightest. We drew our people from regular offices on a part-time basis. The Deputy Head of North American Affairs, for example, was a perfect match. And the Deputy Director of the KMT Overseas Department was also in *Liu Shao Kang*. He was one of many key players, just as was the Deputy Director of the International Trade Bureau. We were not in an operational role. We would just *meet*. As soon as a meeting was over, everyone would go back to their assignments. I myself, though, was a special case. I was very eager and was working in the *Liu Shao Kang* office four or five days per week. I also had a part-time teaching job. I was very young, so I had lots of new ideas I presented to Wang Sheng. I was very eager. If he agreed with my ideas, he took immediate action; so I thought he was a good boss, and I worked very hard. There were no set hours. I would go every day from about seven to eleven in the morning to our office in the *Li Ming* Book Company Building.[69]

The passage of the years has not dulled the excitement which those such as Liu Kuo-chih obviously felt at being able to break loose from hierarchy and participate directly, in a meaningful way, in the governance of the country. As for Wang Sheng's methodology, the influence of Jiangxi and the Youth Corps are plainly visible, above all in the effort to fulfill his obligation to Chiang Ching-kuo and the revolution in the most effective manner possible. His recommendations were far-ranging and a consistent voice of moderation. In 1980, for example, when internal debate raged over whether to allow citizens of Taiwan to go as tourists to the mainland, Wang Sheng was in favor not only of allowing the visits but of setting up a center to brief those departing. His argument was that the crisis of confidence many in Taiwan were experiencing could best be addressed by letting the people compare their own lot with that of the mainland population. Likewise, he pushed education as the best weapon both in the battle to remain strong internally and to comprehend the external world. More than a decade before, he had been the driving force behind a policy change which allowed military officers to complete advanced degrees abroad in the social sciences, rather than only in the sciences as had previously been the case. In *Liu Shao Kang* he sought to find means to encourage this same broadening of the mind. One such project was to encourage formation of professional groups and the holding of conferences where information could be exchanged. *Liu Shao Kang* would seek out the means to sponsor them. In another project, to strengthen the banking structure, *Liu Shao Kang*, in a recommendation written by Wang Sheng, urged establishment of numerous overseas branches of Taiwan banks.[70] Significantly, states Y. S. Chiang, 'He [Wang Sheng] never made his recommendations directly. Everything went out of the office in my name, not his name'.[71]

One of the best illustrations of a policy issue handled by *Liu Shao Kang* was the dilemma which arose when Taiwan sought to host the fifth World Women's Softball Championship in July 1982. Having fought repeated battles to prevent ostracization in the world of sports, the bid was important to Taipei but would only be gained if it was agreed that China could compete. In the intra-governmental debate which ensued prior to Taiwan's acceptance of the condition (in February 1982), it was *Liu Shao Kang* which supported sponsorship; it was the Ministry of Foreign Affairs, adhering to its policy of 'no contact' with the mainland, which was opposed. Wang Sheng's advice was that it would be best 'to let those girls come', to show them what Taiwan had to offer. This, then, was the position Y. S. Chiang presented at an early morning meeting called by Chiang Ching-kuo the day the decision had to be made. A dozen individuals attended and were informed of the *Liu Shao Kang* analysis: Peking had already offered itself as an alternative site and wanted to put Taiwan in the position of having to refuse to participate; yet another public relations disaster loomed if the hardline was allowed to prevail; to take the offensive, accept the bid and invite the mainland – it seemed clear that Peking would not actually let its women compete; and even if it did, Taiwan would still come out ahead – 'We should show them the island, take them everywhere. They will go back and tell what they have seen'.

When the Ministry of Foreign Affairs continued to resist, Chiang Ching-kuo, who was quite ill, signalled the meeting to an inconclusive end. On his own authority, therefore, acting upon the *Liu Shao Kang* recommendation, KMT Secretary-General Y. S.

Chiang called the appropriate officials and gave permission for the tournament. 'You should have seen the positive response!' he relates. 'Headlines, cables from all over abroad; and China didn't let their girls come anyway. Later, Chiang Ching-kuo told me, "Your decision was right"'.[72] Premier Y. S. Sun built upon this success with a 10 June 1982 speech concerning Taiwan's attitude towards China's political offensive. Addressing a group of American experts on Chinese affairs, he impressed them with his frank, sophisticated analysis of the issues at hand. The result was further diplomatic kudos.[73] *Liu Shao Kang* seemed well on its way to making a signal contribution to the effectiveness of KMT policymaking.

Its very success, however, aroused resentment. There can be no doubt that *Liu Shao Kang* was effective and that it performed in precisely the manner dictated by its creators, Chiang Ching-kuo and Y. S. Chiang. Indeed, Y. S. Chiang has stated as much. Yet in the very descriptions of success above are visible the seeds of disaster should a misstep occur. First, the selection of youthful, vigorous talent to staff the office, even though part-time, aroused the same resistance from the hierarchies of both the party and the government which had been such a feature of the Youth Corps versus KMT struggle decades previously. In fact, the tensions could be judged as heightened, since bureaucracy had become far more entrenched and routinized than ever it was in the Republican decade on the mainland. That policy was being made by 'them' rather than by its rightful owners became a recurring theme in whispered conversations.[74] Second, in order for any number of *Liu Shao Kang*'s proposals to work, coordination, even action, was necessary; and this, increasingly, was done by the personnel of *Liu Shao Kang* itself. There was, after all, no one else. This not only fuelled the resentment just noted but also, undoubtedly, provided grounds for individual abuse, minimally a certain flaunting of one's access to the levers of power. It would seem unrealistic to expect that even the most highly motivated, patriotic group would be less than human in this regard. Finally, to all of this must be added the personality of Wang Sheng. Already a lightning rod of sorts for discontent, the energy with which he made *Liu Shao Kang* a success convinced some that he was dangerously ambitious. Civilians, in particular, appear to have resented 'military' influence upon their authority. That Wang Sheng performed in accordance with the protocol set forth by his superiors could not be known to detractors. Neither could it be known that he was merely formulating the recommendations which went to Y. S. Chiang and Y. S. Sun, thence to Chiang Ching-kuo, that he carried out no actions of his own. Even within the KMT Central Standing Committee, therefore, there was complaint of a 'Standing Committee of the Central Standing Committee'. Reflects Y. S. Sun, '*Liu Shao Kang* was very effective in taking coordination and action. It was a good agency. It made good recommendations, but it was too strong for the party. Many people felt it was above even the Secretary-General of the party'.[75]

Such a criticism could have made sense had *Liu Shao Kang* been actually bypassing the Secretary-General himself, Y. S. Chiang. Yet it was reporting to him. He observes, 'Very often we met for breakfast, at least once a week. For very important issues, we would meet in the premier's office, Y. S. Sun, to coordinate. Then the recommendations would be submitted to the president'.[76]

Since *Liu Shao Kang* was performing as instructed, criticism might have remained meaningless had it not been for a critical intervening factor, the health of Chiang Ching-kuo. Afflicted with severe diabetes, which led to complications ranging from open sores on his feet to difficulties with his eyes,[77] the president's health took a precipitous turn for the worse shortly after *Liu Shao Kang* was inaugurated.[78] In late 1981 and early 1982, he underwent surgery, and there was open speculation as to the order of succession.[79] More importantly, Chiang Ching-kuo's health problems affected his stamina, powers of concentration, and judgement. These effects, common enough in severe diabetes, were magnified by the intense pressure of the time, with Taiwan, as judged by many, fighting for its life. Numerous sources speak of a 'transition team' or a 'five-man "crisis-management team"' having been formed, but the ultimate source of this information would appear to have been uninformed press speculation.[80] Though such cannot be ruled out, it would seem more likely that it was *Liu Shao Kang* being discussed.

Faced with Chiang Ching-kuo's illness, the office assumed an even higher profile, because the two senior individuals involved, Y. S. Sun and Y. S. Chiang, were, in fact, the logical crisis managers. To this duo was added a third individual, Ma Chi-chuang, Secretary-General to the President (the position now held by Y. S. Chiang). 'We were known as the Iron Triangle', says Y. S. Sun. 'Our three offices coordinated very well. We would meet at least once a

week. We worked on all the problems of the country, because
Chiang Ching-kuo was sick. Wang Sheng was not a part of the
triangle'.[81] What he was, however, was the man to whom the 'Iron
Triangle' turned to provide the position papers for its
decisionmaking. Even Wang Sheng's prodigious energies were
strained to the breaking point as he ran both GPWD and *Liu Shao
Kang*. The demands became still more intense as Chiang Ching-
kuo's health deteriorated further. Y. S. Sun adds:

> Chiang Ching-kuo was very sick. We tried to keep him from
> having to make difficult decisions. We met daily and only
> presented very difficult issues to him. The person who talked
> to him depended upon the issue. For example, on government
> matters, I would talk to him. We would see him almost every
> day. His judgement was not very good. We made very critical
> decisions in those years. Whenever we made decisions, he
> agreed. He never overruled us. We gave him alternative
> courses [of action] with our recommendation. We worked
> [together] very well.[82]

Again, it was Wang Sheng and *Liu Shao Kang* who provided the
data upon which 'alternative courses' could be worked out. That
they did so stemmed principally from the need for two qualities
which they could provide: timeliness and effectiveness. In time of
crisis, established modes of operation and normal bureaucratic
structure rarely suffice; the early 1980s in Taiwan were no
exception. Observes Wang Sheng:

> We continued for three years like this, during which time we
> did lots of work. I reported to my superiors and asked for
> nothing in return, no money or power. I went to all sorts of
> organizations to get the job done, trying to persuade them to
> get the job done. I never reported the obstacles, because
> Chiang Ching-kuo's health had begun to decline, and I didn't
> want to burden him. I never criticized any person, unit, or
> organization. I just kept patiently, with dedication, trying to
> do the job.[83]

As Wang Sheng 'tried to do the job', the rumors multiplied.
'Some said I was trying to take Chiang Ching-kuo's place, to be his
successor'. Wang Sheng continues. 'Another rumor said that while
the Standing Committee had originally been the highest office in

the country, the *Liu Shao Kang* Office was now actually controlling the Standing Committee. People said I had unlimited authority on Taiwan'.[84] These rumors found their way to Chiang Ching-kuo's ear. A life built upon a struggle against destructive factionalism in the KMT made the president wary of any recurrence. His altered judgement magnified the threat. Where before he had been quite capable of sorting rumor from fact, he now found himself seeing unbridled ambition. The harder Wang Sheng worked, the more he appeared to be ambitious. Wang Sheng's own driven personality, together with his deference for Chiang Ching-kuo, made matters worse, as Wang Sheng has since realized:

> My strong desire to sacrifice for my country led me to become too subjective and to neglect some of the objective elements of the environment. I didn't care if I had to suffer a great deal – it was for Chiang Ching-kuo and the party. It was during the years of *Liu Shao Kang* that Chiang Ching-kuo's health was at its worst. I thought I was being considerate by not going in for too many visits. Further, the president's dignity required that I make my own decisions. I shouldn't be asking him about every little thing. So for three years I rarely went in. Had I done so, he would have asked how things were going. I never lied, so he would then have had worries. I wanted to take the burden from him. I felt guilty about making things worse for him, so I tried not to add to his burdens – Chiang Ching-kuo had such an enormous burden on him already. But because of my approach, he lacked knowledge of what was really going on in the office. Simultaneously, there were some people who intentionally wanted to foster trouble between Chiang Ching-kuo and me. I take responsibility for the way things worked out; but, in fact, another reason I seldom went in was because I wanted to avoid criticism that Chiang Ching-kuo only favored his former students. I should have gone in often as per normal circumstances to keep him informed. Instead, I asked the Secretary-General of the Kuomintang, Y.S. Chiang, to go in for me, to deliver all of the messages for me.[85]

Y.S. Chiang himself put Wang Sheng's behavior in cultural context:

> General Wang was a student of Chiang Ching-kuo from the Gannan period. I was not. They had worked together. Wang

Sheng considered Chiang Ching-kuo as his teacher and paid
his respects accordingly. We [Chiang Ching-kuo and I],
though, were like friends. I didn't know him before. I knew
Chiang Kai-shek; it was he who introduced me to Chiang
Ching-kuo. Then we got acquainted. Thus our relationship
was different. General Wang always paid his respects. He
called Chiang Ching-kuo 'teacher'. That's the Chinese way.
Even I still respect the teachers I have had in the past, even the
ones when I was young. It's a lifelong view. General Wang
respected Chiang Ching-kuo as his teacher, not as a friend. So
the recommendations of the *Liu Shau Kang* Office always
went out in my name, never directly to Chiang Ching-kuo
[from Wang Sheng], unless he called General Wang and asked
for them. Elsewise, they always went out in my name.[86]

Wang Sheng's attempting to stay in the background so as not to
burden Chiang Ching-kuo; his deference which gave the
impression of being devious when filtered through a seriously ill
mind; even his blunt manner of speaking to the president when
they were alone – as they always had spoken – all served to
convince Chiang Ching-kuo that perhaps the rumors he heard
about 'ambitious' Wang Sheng were true, that perhaps something
was afoot. This impression was reinforced by the actions of some
individuals around Wang Sheng who took advantage of his name.
Thomas B. Lee of Tamkhang University observes, 'Wang Sheng's
problem was that he was surrounded by people who were
minimally qualified to be his lieutenants. He had too much faith in
humanity'.[87] It was this faith, too, which made Wang Sheng loath
to discipline those around him, only to take note of their
imperfection and use a different individual for a task the next time
such was required. Unfortunately, as had happened with Chiang
Kai-shek, this left the problem in place. Ironically, then, as with the
elder Chiang, Wang Sheng, far from being 'ruthless', was not
ruthless enough. Lee's observation about his faith in humanity
rings true.

There were no outrageous breaches, abuses of power, by Wang
Sheng's subordinates, at least none which could have been so
serious as to attract the attention of Chiang Ching-kuo. Rather the
normal abuse of a superior's name which is inherent to situations
of power – and perceived power – played differently in the altered
theater of Taiwan bureaucratic politics now that Chiang Ching-kuo

was no longer capable of sorting out rumor from fact, abuse from human weakness, overworked loyalty from deviousness. This played together with what Chiang Ching-kuo thought he heard as a growing refrain of factionalism to produce a discordant cacophony. Ill, his overwhelming desire was not to work through the buzz but for it to stop altogether. Wang Sheng's not being at hand to put an end to rumors as they arose was a capital error. The carping of detractors behind the scenes went unanswered; scenting an opening, enemies apparently pushed home their advantage. In such a context, the actual episode – or individuals – which brought about a rupture between the two men becomes unimportant. It was a crisis whose time had come.

As events developed, the continued pressure from the mainland served as the catalyst. In March 1983, giving in to repeated requests from personnel of the American Institute in Taiwan (AIT), the unofficial US Embassy following derecognition, Wang Sheng agreed to visit the United States. Ironically, some sources have suggested that Wang Sheng had 'a poor image in the US, Taiwan's most important benefactor'.[88] A poor image he had, perhaps, among those opposed to the KMT, but certainly not amongst most American officials. To the contrary, during his second visit to the US in April–May 1968, Wang Sheng had so impressed Professor Robert Scalapino at Berkeley with his analysis of Chinese affairs that he had arranged through the State Department to have Wang Sheng meet with scholars at leading American universities.[89] In a double irony, Scalapino was at the time *persona non grata* in Taiwan for his perceived hostility towards the KMT. Subsequently, Wang Sheng intervened directly with Chiang Ching-kuo to have the ban lifted and introduced the two men. Scalapino became a regular visitor and would meet with Chiang Ching-kuo, who would note his suggestions, some of which appeared in policy changes.[90] Similarly, during the same period, Wang Sheng, though not yet head of GPWD, had been meeting weekly with the Political Officer of the American Embassy, David Dean, to discuss the situation on the mainland. Dean had been impressed and had commented often to Y. S. Chiang on the depth of Wang Sheng's knowledge and the value of the meetings.[91] Wang Sheng was, in other words, anything but 'unpopular' with the Americans; instead, he was regarded in much the same fashion as he was by his own superiors – as a dedicated, knowledgeable official. His analysis of the situation was considered useful; and it was for this reason that James Lilly, the AIT head (and an active-duty CIA official seconded to the Department of State), requested that Wang Sheng visit the US for discussions with appropriate officials.[92]

Chiang Ching-kuo gave his approval and suggested that Wang Sheng take his wife – the funding was provided by the US. He was accompanied by a single ROC Army escort officer, Colonel Omar Ted Mah (now a retired major-general). There was no US escort officer, because the March visit involved but slightly more than a week of meetings in San Francisco and Washington, DC. If the timing of the trip was prompted by American concern at a possible succession struggle, this was not evident in the meetings, which dwelt upon the overall continued difficult strategic situation. A. Doak Barnett did inquire at one point concerning the possible successor to Chiang Ching-kuo; but Wang Sheng replied that a transfer of power would take place in accordance with the constitution, which stipulated that the vice-president would become president. It was but one question among a far more substantive conversation and created no stir at the time. In any case, notes of all meetings were kept by Colonel Mah, and regular reports were sent back to Taipei. Though not seen by Wang Sheng, the reports were filed by the ROC 'ambassador', Fred Chien, who had headed the Overseas Affairs Committee for *Liu Shao Kang* before moving to Washington, DC.[93] Thus it is unlikely there was anything untoward in them. Certainly nothing out of the ordinary occurred on the trip.

Upon his return, Wang Sheng briefly informed Chiang Ching-kuo as to what had occurred. 'His mannerisms were slightly different', Wang Sheng recalls. 'I could sense it. He was a little bit cold. But I made my report orally and thought nothing more of it. Life went on, and we had no meetings'.[94] Then, on 22 April 1983, Wang Sheng was summoned by Chiang Ching-kuo. Angry, he demanded to know why *Liu Shao Kang* had continued to push for the 'Academic Seminar' program despite his explicit orders to the contrary. Wang Sheng was stunned, for not only had no such instructions been given, the program in question had been advanced in a memorandum through Y. S. Chiang, which had been approved by Y. S. Sun, as head of the government, as well as Chiang Ching-kuo himself. Chiang Ching-kuo continued, 'How many times have I told you not to do those academic talk programs? Yet you're still pushing for them! Now everyone is upset with us! The Executive Yuan is upset!' Wang Sheng could only state that he must have misunderstood the instructions. The program in question, 'Academic Seminar', had arisen from the continuing quest for unity. Wang Sheng had suggested that the same concept used in the military – where entire days were set aside solely for Political Warfare training, especially in citizenship – be extended to the government in a much revised form. Each Monday morning a 30-minute broadcast discussion would be put out on a topic of current national importance; anyone who wanted could listen, of course, but doing so would be mandatory for government employees. Wang Sheng relates what transpired:

> My intent was that you give the whole nation a chance to continue its education. Anything could be the subject, from taxes to the budget. We could get experts to talk, giving the pros and cons of an issue. It would have been good for everyone, giving all an educational chance. If they had carried through with it, this would be a much better country. By presenting both sides of all manner of issues, we could have benefited all. When we started to push for this academic talks program, the Ministry of Education was to be in charge. At the end of the first year, it still had not started. But whenever I have a job, I see it through, I check on it. So I asked the Ministry of Education in a meeting [what the problem was]. They said it was a very difficult job and could be better performed by the Government Information Office. GIO, though, said that the program should go under the Bureau of Personnel Administration of the Executive Yuan. Ultimately, the fact was that no one was willing to take responsibility. What seems to have happened is that there simply was no will to carry out the program. Actually, it was never carried out. It was only intended to be an extension of the classroom. But the Premier reported to Chiang Ching-kuo that no one wanted to do the job. This got thrown together in Chiang Ching-kuo's mind with what he had heard about dissatisfaction about the program itself. At this time, he didn't like everyone always coming to him with bad news. And at this point I could have declared myself, told him the program had been approved by him, briefed the Premier (who was very supportive), and so forth. But I didn't want to be seen as arguing. I would rather just take the blame.[95]

Counterrevolution in China

He did not, and Chiang Ching-kuo went on: 'And why is it necessary for all universities to have flag-raising ceremonies?' Yet there was no such mandatory program. He said that two other Standing Committee members had also complained to him that *Liu Shao Kang* was involved in too much other people's business. 'I didn't even answer', says Wang Sheng. 'So he said to end the *Liu Shao Kang* Office. I was very happy about that. He was a bit angry when he said this, but I had a very happy face'.[96]

Thus ended *Liu Shao Kang*, a brief experiment which had begun as strategic counterrevolution, a means to attack the communists even as they seemed to have momentarily gained the upper hand. It had ended as an overextended body for policy formulation which had run its course. KMT Secretary-General Y. S. Chiang was pungent in his own analysis as to why *Liu Shao Kang* ended, 'The *Liu Shao Kang* Office, to be frank, was closed because someone close to the president recommended that this be done, someone who was jealous'.[97] Many pointed the finger at Premier Y. S. Sun himself, since much of the criticism seemed to come from government offices, which ultimately reported to him; but he responds, 'I never told Chiang Ching-kuo that *Liu Shao Kang* had completed its effectiveness. I knew the end was coming, but I was not consulted. It was a party matter, because of intra-party squabbling. This combined with personal jealousy to get them out'.[98] Perhaps the most telling analysis, though, was provided by Liu Kuo-chih, 'Maybe *Liu Shao Kang* needed an image builder'.[99]

Image-building was precisely what Wang Sheng was incapable of doing. Indeed, while his own insight into why *Liu Shao Kang* had been disbanded was remarkably shrewd and echoed the factors noted above,[100] what concerned him more were the personal implications of the situation: 'I thought it was a virtue to take the blame, but not telling the truth to my superior was the failure. The fact is that Chiang Ching-kuo's health was not good, which impaired his judgement. But perhaps if I had revealed all the facts to him, he would have made better decisions'.[101]

On Into Exile

It was this intense faith by Wang Sheng, that *sincerity* would always prevail, which he brought to bear on the situation. About the loss of *Liu Shao Kang*, he was stoical: 'I had always thought Chiang

Ching-kuo would be the one to save our country, so I chose to follow him. I didn't expect him to reward me with positions. I just asked, 'Did I do my best to serve Chiang?' Ambition is not an admirable quality'.[102] For Wang Sheng, disappointment was mixed with relief at having his workload cut considerably. He returned full-time to his role as Director of GPWD. Just two and a half weeks later, however, on 10 May 1983, Chiang Ching-kuo called him in again. At first he made small talk: He had observed, he said, that when Wang Sheng had been ordered to end *Liu Shao Kang*, he had been very happy. Wang Sheng replied that, yes, a great weight had been lifted from his shoulders. It was a peculiar conversation, though, observed Wang Sheng: 'Chiang Ching-kuo's memory was declining at this time. As his health declined, both his physical and mental faculties went down'.[103] Then the bombshell was dropped – Wang Sheng was to be removed from GPWD and transferred to a position as director of the Joint Operations and Training Department – 'a very insignificant position'.

The removal sent shock waves throughout Taiwan. To supporters, Wang Sheng had been 'Mr Political Warfare' for as long as anyone could remember, a sheet anchor which had held the *San Min Chu-i* revolution firm. In the eyes of the system's detractors, he was the linchpin of the mechanisms of repression. Helen Liu, for instance, was later to claim that Wang Sheng had threatened her husband, Henry Liu, before he was murdered, a charge picked up by David E. Kaplan in *Fires of the Dragon*.[104] Tien Hung-mao, in the same Congressional testimony mentioned above, was to claim, 'Had the President not recovered in time and the general [Wang Sheng] succeeded in filling the leadership vacuum, political consequences of such a military *coup de grace* would have been profound, insofar as the nature and developmental direction of Taiwan's political system were concerned'.[105] Speaking after Tien, Martin L. Lasatar, a former Congressional staffer, claimed: 'While the cause may be open to speculation, the effect of General Wang's removal from the center of power has been critical to political liberalization on the island. Since Wang was the chief spokesman for hardline security forces, his removal has had the effect of diminishing conservative objections to such liberal policies as making Taiwan a free trade zone and loosening the restraints on the Dang Xai [Wai] and other non-KMT political activists'.[106]

The inaccuracy of such assertions is substantial. To take but several assertions by Lasatar: Wang Sheng and *Liu Shao Kang* had been strong advocates of 'liberal policies' such as the free trade zone; and it was Wang Sheng who had recommended, in 1956 at the KMT's Eighth Party Congress, 'bipartisan politics'. The KMT Deputy Secretary-General had visited him afterwards and told him the time was not yet right, but it was a position he had maintained – even while doing his utmost to insure national unity through socialization and all the mechanisms in his hands. Even if one accepts the Lasatar analysis on its merits, the departure of Wang Sheng could only have strengthened conservative forces. That political liberalization did eventually proceed, within the context of continued strong economic transformation and expansion, is true. That this was connected to the departure of Wang Sheng is incorrect.

Regardless, the change was momentous. Yet Wang Sheng again took it as placidly as he had the demise of *Liu Shao Kang*. His youngest son, 'Mao Ti', recalls being elated, 'I was especially happy. Eventually, we all felt happy. He could spend more time at home!'[107] Daughter Wang Hsiao-li, far more analytical in her observations concerning the sea-change, comments:

> I was here [Taiwan] when he lost his job. We wondered what happened. I still don't really know. I was watching him. I didn't know how to talk to him, how to ask him what had happened. He wasn't sad, though. Stepmother would talk to people. For us children, there was not really that much change in our lives; for me, the whole family, that was the good part. [For] none of us were taking advantage of my father's position. We had all made our own way. Number One [Wang Kung-tien] went out very early. Number Two [Wang Pu-tien] was always in fights with everyone. He was strong and opinionated and didn't make friends easily. Number Three [Wang Hsiao-tien] was wild, into music, playing guitars. All of us, after college or the army, went to the States. We never worked here. We never got a job because of him [Wang Sheng]. So we weren't, 'Uh-oh', like that.[108]

For many, of course, it was 'Uh-oh, like that'. A constant stream of visitors found their way to his new office – leading to new whispers that a Wang Sheng 'faction' was forming. Finally, on 16 August 1983, Chiang Ching-kuo sent Premier Y. S. Sun to inform

Wang Sheng that it had been decided he should go as ambassador to Paraguay, one of the few staunch allies Taiwan had left anywhere in the world. Furthermore, Sun pointed out, Peking was making an all-out push to marginalize Taipei completely in Latin America, so his services would be of service to the revolution. Wang Sheng replied, 'At this moment, I am still a military man. I have no diplomatic expertise and may jeopardize our standing, but I obey orders. If you tell me to go, if those are the president's orders, I will obey'. He observes, 'I heard later that Chiang Ching-kuo was very pleased to hear that I would go if ordered'.[109] Yet again, Wang Sheng took his continued ostracization by his former mentor in his stride. Relates 'Mao Ti': 'I remember clearly, vividly, how one day he [Wang Sheng] came back with a smile, talked to my mom in the living room. She told me there might be a new assignment. There was a precedent, so I guessed, "Ambassador?" He said, "Yes"'.[110]

On 6 November Chiang Ching-kuo called Wang Sheng to the president's office to bid him farewell formally. He was relaxed but spoke of his fears of faction. It was not a comfortable conversation. Wang Sheng departed. Ten days later, on the 16th, he left for Paraguay with his wife. Summarizes daughter Wang Hsiao-li:

> I was watching him when he stepped down. The only sign of weakness was his asking me to go to Paraguay with him. I thought about it. Though I knew it would be a hard time for him, I knew myself. I wouldn't be happy, so I wouldn't be able to make him happy. After he went, I was asked about him 'as a man'. Look at what he did in Paraguay – that's his personality! Wherever he sees something which can be done better, he does it.[111]

'Look at what he did in Paraguay...' None could imagine then that Wang Sheng, sent into exile, at the age of 68 – for there were few who doubted that such was what Chiang Ching-kuo had in mind – would turn personal defeat into victory. For he knew but one life, to serve the revolution. And in a forgotten backwater, he continued to do just that. Throughout, he kept in his heart lines he himself had written about Chiang Ching-kuo, his teacher: 'Many of his old subordinates, his students or his fellow-students who have a comparatively good understanding of him know that he does not really ignore his personal relationships with others, but that he holds the existence of our country to be much more important'.[112] Wang Sheng would have seven long years to ponder his foresight; and in the end, it would be he who would deliver the lesson.

NOTES

1. Some material in this chapter has been used previously in my 'The Future of Taiwan', *South-East Asian Spectrum* [Bangkok], 4/3 (April–June 1976), pp. 7–17; and 'Two Chinese Roads to Military Modernization – and a US Dilemma', *Strategic Survey* [Washington, DC], VIII/3 (Summer 1980), pp. 18–28.
2. A vote to that effect was defeated in 1972 amidst heavy lobbying on both sides. Ultimately, in 1974 – just as both South Vietnam and Cambodia slid into evermore dire straits – the Resolution was, in fact, repealed.
3. Cf. my 'Two Chinese Roads to Military Modernization' (note 1).
4. For a hostile view of this effort cf. Kaplan, *passim*. An embroidered account of ROC efforts to obtain the US Mark-37 torpedo may be found at pp. 184–91.
5. Israel and Taiwan had no exchanges involving Political Warfare. No Israeli students have attended the Institute of Political Warfare.
6. For an analysis of some of the technological implications, though not addressed specifically to Taiwan, see Gerald J. Keller, 'Israeli-South African Trade: An Analysis of Recent Developments', *Naval War College Review* (Spring 1978), pp. 74–80.
7. Interview with Soong Chang-chih, 13 July 1993 in Taipei..
8. Ibid.
9. Ibid.
10. Cf. Steve Weismann and Herbert Krosney, *The Islamic Bomb* (New York: *New York Times* Book Co., 1986), esp. pp. 74–5, 152–3.
11. Cf. my 'Two Chinese Roads to Military Modernization – and a US Dilemma'. The systems sought fell into two main categories: (1) Air defense, for which Taipei desired *Mirage* F-1 aircraft and a variety of advanced technology anti-aircraft guns; and (2) Ground defense, the desired tank models being the German *Leopard* A-3 or A-4, together with overhauled US M-48A5s with standard M-60 equipment.
12. Ibid. The *Kfir* sale caused additional friction with the US, because it required Washington's approval; the plane incorporated an American-manufactured engine. An earlier sale to Ecuador had been blocked, as was this one to Taiwan.
13. For a more detailed discussion, to include strategic context, cf. Monte R. Bullard, 'The US-China Defense Relationship', *Parameters*, XIII/1 (March 1993), pp. 43–50.
14. Ibid. The PRC's airborne/air-transportable forces at the time consisted of three airborne divisions of some 9,000 men each. These units, though they might have been used in conjunction with amphibious operations, had no tanks and only limited artillery, anti-tank, and anti-aircraft weapons. Chinese airborne-lift capability was only sufficient to support regiment-size operations against objectives within a 500 nautical-mile radius of base. A lightly armed force of this size (approx. 2,500 men) would have been decimated in any attack on a strong position such as Taiwan. China's amphibious capabilities were likewise limited. The PRC conducted its first joint forces amphibious operation in 1955 against I Chiang Shan Island about 17 miles off the East China coast. Subsequently, amphibious training had an important place in the schedule of units stationed in or near the PRC's coastal areas. Large-scale amphibious maneuvers were held off the coast of Fukien Province in the summer of 1976. Yet China's total amphibious operation troop-lift capability extended to a force of some three infantry divisions. This over-the-beach capability could have been augmented by merchant ships and several thousand coastal junks, but the success of an invasion

mounted through a combination of all the assets discussed here was doubtful.

15. See p. 285 of 'Taiwan', *Asia 1980 Yearbook* (Hong Kong: *Far Eastern Economic Review* [hereafter *FEER*], 1980), pp. 285–9.
16. Further details may be found in *Martial Law on Taiwan and United States Foreign Policy Interests* (Ch. 4, note 109), pp. 124–5.
17. Interview with Wang Sheng, 24 July 1993 in Taipei.
18. Cf. 'Announcement of Taiwan Headquarters, World United Formosans for Independence (WUFI), dated Nov. 1976, contained as 'Exhibit' to App. 4 ('Material Submitted by A. James Gregor') in *Martial Law on Taiwan and United States Foreign Policy Interests*, pp. 201–4.
19. Ibid. The material Gregor provides, he notes, was extracted from the WUFI publication *Tai-tu (Independent Taiwan)*, 57, 28 Nov. 1976.
20. See pp. 315–16 of 'Taiwan', *Asia 1978 Yearbook* (Hong Kong: *FEER*, 1979), pp. 313–20.
21. Cf. John Kaplan (Ch. 4, note 112).
22. See p. 250 of 'Taiwan', *Asia 1982 Yearbook* (Hong Kong: *FEER*, 1982), pp. 250–4.
23. On 9 Aug. 1979 a bomb hidden in the ceiling destroyed the communications facilities of the Coordination Council for North American Affairs (CCNAA) office in New York City; on 20 Aug. a bomb exploded at the CCNAA Info. Section in NYC, 14 blocks from the CCNAA office; and on 23 Aug. a bomb was defused before it could explode at the CCNAA office near Washington, DC. For a complete list see *Taiwan Agents in America and the Death of Prof. Wen-Chen Chen: Hearings before the Subcommittees on Asian and Pacific Affairs and on Human Rights and International Organizations of the Committee on Foreign Affairs*, House of Representatives (97th Congress, 1st Session), 30 July and 6 Oct. 1981 (Washington, DC: US GPO, p. 82.
24. Details are contained in *Human Rights in Taiwan*, pp. 97–101. Apparently Wang Hsing-nan was traced through his fingerprints on the parcels. He was arrested in Jan. 1977 while on a flight which made a stopover in Taipei which he had not realized would occur (according to his confession). Though relatives attempted to claim he had been kidnapped from Hong Kong, sources claim he was actually maneuvered out of the transit lounge after his ill-timed stop. Wang Sheng adds, 'He mentioned training in Cuba'. (Interview, 24 July 1993 in Taipei.)
25. Cf. John Kaplan (Ch. 4, note 112), pp. 25–7; also *Taiwan Agents in America, passim.*
26. Refer again to the list in *Taiwan Agents in America*, p. 82.
27. Wang Pu-tien survived due to a stroke of luck: 'I worked one year at the Kennedy Space Center as an electrical engineer. In 1977 I moved to Los Angeles to work for Hughes Aircraft as a design engineer. I was at my own house in Los Angeles, but I had gone to stay for several nights at a friend's house. Sunday, we usually play basketball, so I went to UC-Irvine [before returning home]. Afterwards, I drove home. It was raining, so I parked in front of the garage. Since I had no remote control, I ran to my gate. I was very tired and wanted to eat some ice cream. I was falling asleep, so I went into the kitchen from the living room. I was in the kitchen when the explosion went off. The whole front end of the house was gone. The FBI and everyone came; the Commerce Department has a division which deals with these things. They came and collected the pieces and so forth. They said it wasn't a time bomb but rather a pressure bomb. They [the bombers] waited until I came home, then put it against my door; but the rain short-circuited it. The FBI said I was very lucky, because it rarely rains at that time of the year'. The other target was less lucky, though Mayor Wang's son himself was not the unfortunate victim. Wang Pu-tien continues: 'A few months later, they [WUFI] put a bomb in the mayor's son's house. He was in Taiwan on vacation. The mayor's wife's younger brother, from San Francisco, was just married and was there in Los Angeles for his honeymoon. He parked his car in the driveway, leaving his bride in the car. When the husband went to open the door, he saw a paper bag. He picked it up and was killed'. (Interview, 24 July 1993 in Taipei.)

28. Cf. *Taiwan Agents in America* (note 23), as well as *The Reminiscences of Mr Wang Ching-Hsu*, Oral History Series No. 1 (Taipei: Academica Historica, 1993). Wang Ching-Hsu was the commander of TGGC at the time of Chen Wen-chen's death. The case remains unsolved at this writing, though carried officially as an apparent suicide or accident. Understandably, it has over the years provoked considerable comment, not all of it particularly well informed. See e.g. 'Taiwan', *Asia 1982 Yearbook* (Hong Kong: FEER, 1983), pp. 248–9: 'An American forensic pathologist who came to Taiwan in September [1981] to investigate the case concluded that Chen had been murdered. The pathologist cut open the corpse and performed what he later described in the US as an extensive autopsy. The Taiwan Government maintained, however, that it was not a true autopsy because according to local law one must have the permission of the prosecutor and judge in a case to perform an autopsy. The government stripped an Associated Press reporter of her press credentials for writing that an autopsy had been performed and for refusing to retract the statement. Some observers saw the action as a warning to the local press not to be too zealous in reporting the Chen case'. Leaving aside the indelicate wording, the bruised feelings of the press, and the weak analysis (use of the phrase, 'some observers..'., having become at this time in *Review* coverage of Taiwan virtually a tacit admission of ignorance as to what had actually occurred), the accusation of murder, as allegedly made by the pathologist, was a serious one which should have warranted investigation. It had been raised by Chen's widow, Chen Su-jen, in her Congressional testimony on 6 Oct. 1981: 'On July 2, 1981, my husband was interrogated by the Taiwan Garrison Command for more than 12 hours. The next morning his body was found on the grounds of the National Taiwan University. ... My husband's death was not a suicide or an accident. It was murder. ... Three weeks ago [in Sept.], my husband's former colleague, Professor DeGroot, and a forensic pathologist, Dr Wecht [sic], had the privilege to go to Taiwan and re-examined the case of my husband's death. In the press conference upon their return on September 24 they reaffirmed my original judgement and conviction that he was murdered. I believe my husband had been badly tortured before he died. There were too many external wounds which could not be explained by a fall. In the Taiwan official autopsy report these wounds were either mentioned briefly without any explanation of how they might have occurred, or they were not mentioned at all [continues]' (*Taiwan Agents in America*, note 23, p. 71). The difficulty is that the autopsy report, as recorded by Dr. Cyril Hecht during the procedure, is enclosed (pp. 77–80) and, as it reads, does not support Mrs. Chen's assertions – or those of the *Review*. The report also contains a description of the actions of Taiwan authorities in facilitating the autopsy which is completely at variance with the impression created in the *Review*. Finally, the statement made by Morris DeGroot and pathologist Hecht upon their return, as reported by the Associated Press, is also enclosed (p. 83) and also directly contradicts the testimony of Mrs. Chen and the *Review*: 'Dr Hecht said he found nothing to contradict Taiwan's findings about bodily injuries, but he could not support the government's conclusions about how Chen died...Hecht said he found no evidence that Chen was tortured...Despite Taiwan's earlier refusal to allow an independent autopsy, there were no impediments, no limitations, Hecht said. Nobody withheld anything from us in the scientific end of the case'. From the evidence presented, we are thus left with a mystery, but one certainly befitting more careful prose than has hitherto often been the case.

29. Cf. ibid.; also *Martial Law on Taiwan and United States Foreign Policy Interests*.

30. Interview with Wang Pu-tien, 24 July 1993 in Taipei.

31. Ibid., 313.

32. See pp. 301 of 'Taiwan', *Asia 1979 Yearbook* (Hong Kong: FEER, 1980), pp. 299–306.

33. Cf. ibid., esp. pp. 314–16. The FEER observes (p. 315): 'Balloting on November 19 polled unexpected victories for almost every prominent non-KMT candidate,

including Hsu Hsin-liang in Taoyuan County, where an election-day riot erupted after citizens reportedly found proof of ballot-tampering. Four independents were elected in the 20 mayoral and magistrate slots, recognized as the most important elected provincial posts, which the KMT had monopolised during the previous term. Of 77 Provincial Assembly seats, 21 went to non-KMT candidates and another eight independents numbered among the 51 new Taipei municipal councillors. Numerous independents also appeared in the local posts of county and city councillors and town and village mayors. Although local newspapers lauded a "landslide Kuomintang victory" after the ruling party captured a hefty 85 per cent of 1,318 provincial seats, the proportion of elected independents was unprecedented in Taiwan, where the KMT party machine and martial law leave little margin for political free-lancing. Moreover, the public elected several well-known ex-KMT politicians who had either withdrawn or been expelled from the ruling party and who therefore represented even more explicitly an attempt to buck the one-party system'.

34. Ibid., p. 302.
35. He took over from Gen. Cheng Wei-yuan, who had begun his own tenure in 1975. Cheng went on to become the head of the Vocational Commission for Retired Servicemen (VACARS), what would hardly seem a 'career move'. Yet in 1987 he was elevated to Minister of National Defense; he would remain as such until 1989.
36. Interestingly, a much better case for a Wang Sheng 'retinue' could be made with Wang Ching-hsu's successor at TGGC, Gen. Chen Shou-san, than with the individuals in place when the *Review* wrote its analysis cited above. Chen, a native Taiwanese and Whampoa Military Academy graduate, was a former commandant of *Fu Hsing Kang*, as well as a former deputy executive director of GPWD. Thus he would have been Wang Sheng's subordinate for some years. He was also a line officer, commissioned in the infantry, and thus outside Wang Sheng's chain of command. Regardless, as will become clear in the text, such an effort at analytical empire building falls apart under the weight of actual events. Chen, in any case, was to continue as TGGC head until 1989.
37. Interview with Wang Sheng, 4 Aug. 1994 in Carmel, California.
38. Ch'en Li-fu, p. 239.
39. See ibid., p. 241. Elsewhere (p. 233), Ch'en records: 'Chiang [Kai-shek] passed away after midnight on 5 April 1975. Early the next day I learned the sad news. I rushed to the Veterans Hospital to offer my condolence. Ching-kuo kneeled down in front of me and sobbed: "I've lost my father. You are my only elder brother. I beg you to do what you can to help me!" I helped him up to his feet and expressed my sympathy: 'Of course I will help you. Please restrain your grief and take care of yourself to prepare to shoulder your huge responsibility'.
40. Interview with Wang Sheng, 4 Aug. 1994 in Carmel, California.
41. Chiang Yen-shih has noted: 'We [Chiang Ching-kuo and he] used to be together daily [Chiang Yen-shih was KMT Secretary-General] and even weekends in the field. On weekends, he would always go out into the countryside and spend the night there. I would always go with him. So we had a relationship where we talked freely and frankly, about what was good for the country and for the people. We would also talk about specific personalities'. (Interview, 20 July 1993 in Taipei.)
42. Ibid.
43. Interview with Wang Li-tien, 23 July 1993 in Taipei.
44. Interview with Wang Tsiao-li, 25 July 1993 in Taipei.
45. Interview with Wang Pu-tien, 24 July 1993 in Taipei.
46. A rumor which was to circulate throughout Wang Sheng's entire career was that he 'raised' Chiang Ching-kuo's twins. This was not so. Wang Pu-tien says, 'Father was very solicitous of Chiang Ching-kuo's children [the twins], but they didn't live with us. He didn't raise them for Chiang Ching-kuo, either, here or in China. They lived forty miles south of Taipei with an uncle on the mother's side. He did not raise them

but rather visited them periodically. Their mother was fond of my father'. (Interview, 24 July 1993 in Taipei.) Adds Wang Tsiao-li, 'I met two of his [Chiang Ching-kuo] sons from Gannan when I was very, very little. We went swimming. I didn't know who they were. They didn't live at our house. Father would go to visit them. He told them their father was 'on the mainland', I think'. (Interview, 25 July 1993 in Taipei.) Wang Li-tien also observes, 'It is purely a rumor that father raised Chiang Ching-kuo's illegitimate kids. Chiang Ching-kuo really does have two children by a woman, but they just came to visit once a year or so. People say they saw two young men playing with my brothers at *Fu Hsing Kang*, where I was born, but those two were the sons of a Chinese-Filipino family who were at my house quite often'. (Interview, 23 July 1993 in Taipei.)

47. See e.g. p. 307 in Thomas B. Gold, 'The Status Quo is not Static: Mainland-Taiwan Relations', *Asian Survey*, XXVII/3 (March 1987), pp. 300–15. From this and comments in his other works, about Wang Sheng as well as other leading KMT figures such as Chiang Ching-kuo, it seems clear that Gold has derived his knowledge secondhand. They cannot be judged particularly accurate.

48. Interview with Wang Li-tien, 23 July 1993 in Taipei.

49. David E. Kaplan, (Ch. 1, note 24), p. 537, cites several anthologies of Henry Liu's work. Kaplan has relied heavily upon this work in his own book, apparently taking much of it at face value. Helen Liu, in her Congressional testimony on 7 Feb. 1985, stated, 'Many people have compared Henry's work to that of William Shirer, Theodore White and Louis Fischer. Henry's work was widely published and read all throughout Asia, in China, Japan, Hongkong, and in Taiwan, despite repeated Government efforts to suppress it'. (See *The Murder of Henry Liu*, p. 51.) Though understandable in its sentiments, given that she was speaking of her late husband, the actual facts are otherwise. The best that can be said of Liu's peculiar body of writing is that, while it does stylistically reflect the power of a driven personality, it is quite inaccurate in content. It can certainly not be compared with any of the authors mentioned. See e.g. the Henry Liu work cited previously, 'Wang Sheng the Man'. One of the more curious lines Liu pursues in this work is his contention that 'Wang [Sheng] was not popular with Chiang Kai-shek'. More typical of the Liu style and tone, taken from the same piece, is the following passage: 'Wang Sheng always had a couple of "educated" people around to help him. For example, when he went to Vietnam to assist Nguyen Khanh in establishing a political cadre system, he wrote a little book entitled *Political Warfare*, evidently with the aim of achieving lasting fame through literature. It was translated into English by Wen Ha-hsiung for presentation to American and Vietnamese friends. The book opens: "What is politics? According to Sun Yat-sen, politics is the management of the people's affairs. What is warfare?..". Perhaps an illiterate soldier or a plebe at a cadre school could find anything in this shallow, immature writing. Supposedly, Wang presented a copy to an American journalist, who after reading half a page threw it in the garbage can. The author asked a former secretary of Wang's why Wang didn't get someone really competent to write his book. He answered in a shy but humerous way that generals have their own taste and that Wang likes to be the boss'. Unfortunately, Liu's work appears to have been relied upon, in the absence of other sources, by at least several scholars; he is cited e.g. in Maria Hsia Chang, 'Political Succession in the Republic of China' (Ch. 4, note 108).

50. David E. Kaplan (Ch. 1, note 24). Kaplan does not seriously explore what would seem to be the most obvious explanation for Liu's behavior; namely, that he had a very large ax to grind. He had failed to graduate from *Fu Hsing Kang* under circumstances which have yet to be adequately explained; apparently he was dissatisfied with his announced posting to follow graduation. (Kaplan, pp. 62–9, deals with this episode in such a manner that it fits neatly into his own overall attack on the KMT.) That Wang Sheng and Chiang Ching-kuo came to represent whatever demons Liu carried

with him, however, is plain from a reading of his work and the eagerness with which he grasps any rumor or bit of gossip to attack his subjects (an approach, one might add, repeated by Kaplan).

51. Interview with Wang Hsiao-li, 25 July 1993 in Taipei. Wang Li-tien ('Mao Ti') adds: 'When I left Taiwan in 1983, there was a rumor that I had two personal guards with lots of money. The first three years in the US I didn't even have my own bed! I slept on a mattress on the floor (my first year was in Oklahoma City, then two years in Philadelphia). I had a one-bedroom apartment with two or three of us living there [students]. I bought a car for $400. It was my first car, a Chevy Impala. When it got hit, I received $500 from the insurance company, so I was able to get rid of the car at a modest profit!' (Interview, 23 July 1993 in Taipei.)

52. This was yet another theme pursued by Henry Liu. See esp. his 'Wang Sheng's Mysterious Misstep' (translated), *Ch'i-shih Nien-tai Yueh Kan (The Seventies Monthly)*(June 1983), pp. 55–7. This article may be profitably read with 'Wang Sheng the Man' as a typical example of Henry Liu's questionable work.

53. Interview with Wang Hsiao-tien, 13 July 1993 in Taipei.

54. Interview with Chiang Yen-shih, 20 July 1993 in Taipei.

55. Interview with Wang Sheng, 29 July 1993 in Taipei.

56. Cf. Liu K'ang-sheng, 'China's Crucial Decade', *Free China Review* (April 1981), pp. 14–20.

57. Cf. Gerald Chan, 'The 'Two Chinas' Problem and the Olympic Formula', *Pacific Affairs*, 58/3 (Fall 1985), pp. 473–90.

58. See p. 469 of C.L. Chiou, 'Dilemmas in China's Reunification Policy toward Taiwan', *Asian Survey*, XXVI/4 (April 1986), pp. 467–82.

59. See p. 1097 of John Quan-sheng Zhao, 'An Analysis of Unification: The PRC Perspective', *Asian Survey*, XXIII/10 (Oct. 1983), pp. 1095–1114. Zhao gives the date of Ye Jian-ying's speech as 30 Sept. 1981, which I have used; it is reported as such in *Asia 1983 Yearbook* (p. 260). There is confusion, however: Chiou (note 39), gives the date as Sept. 1979; Bullard, 'The US–China Defense Relationship', uses 1 Oct. 1980. Regardless, Wang Sheng has stated that the 'three links and four exchanges' were well known in 1980 and a factor in the formation of *Liu Shao Kang*. (Interview, 16 July 1993 in Taipei.)

60. For a representative sampling see: Ts'ai Ch'ing-yuan, 'Unification the Free Chinese Way', *Free China Review* (Nov. 1981), pp. 16–19 (includes text of Chiang Ching-kuo's response to Ye Jian-ying); Liu K'ang-sheng, 'No Unification the Communist Way', ibid. (Nov. 1981), pp. 20–5 (includes text of response to Ye Jian-ying by ROC government spokesman James Soong); Liu K'ang-sheng, 'Red China's Biggest Lie', ibid. (Dec. 1981), pp. 23–8; K.T. Li, 'Communist China's "Peace Offer"', ibid. (June 1982), pp. 2-3; James C.Y. Soong, 'Nation: That Perpetual Peking Peace Plan', ibid. (March 1984), pp. 20–3 (includes a summary of each of Peking's nine points for reunification); and 'Documents: China's Reunification and World Peace', ibid. (May 1986), pp. 60–3 (includes Chiang Ching-kuo's address to the third plenum of the KMT Twelfth Central Committee).

61. The information and quotations which follow are from Interview with Wang Sheng, 16 July 1993 in Taipei.

62. Ibid.

63. The Chiang of Y.S. Chiang is frequently spelled Jiang so as to differentiate it from the Chiang of Chiang Kai-shek or Chiang Ching-kuo. In Chinese characters, however, their family names are the same. In my interview notes, I have Y.S. Chiang as rendering his name as I have done.

64. Interview with Chiang Yen-Shih, 20 July 1993 in Taipei.

65. Ibid.

66. When the US severed relations with Taiwan, the then-Minister of Foreign Affairs, Shen Chang-huan, took responsibility and resigned. Premier Y.S. Sun also submitted

his resignation, but it was not accepted. He subsequently was appointed concurrent Minister of Foreign Affairs. That, however, lasted but four days, because the pressure of both jobs was overwhelming. Thus Y.S. Chiang, who at the time was Minister of Education, a position he had held for five years (for part of which Y.S. Sun had been Minister of Commerce and Economic Activity), was given the position. He was to hold it for just one year, after which he switched to Sec.-Gen. of the KMT. Y.S. Sun was to remain Premier until early 1984, when he suffered a stroke on 24 Feb. He was formally replaced by Yu Kuo-hwa on 25 May. Y.S. Chiang, as stated in earlier notes, remains active in government and party affairs.

67. Interview with Chiang Yen-shih, 20 July 1993 in Taipei.
68. Ibid.
69. Interview with Liu Kuo-chih, 27 July 1993 in Taipei.
70. Ibid. and Interview with Chiang Yen-shih, 20 July 1993 in Taipei.
71. Interview with Chiang Yen-shih, 20 July 1993 in Taipei.
72. Ibid.
73. Cf. Parris Chang, 'Taiwan in 1982: Diplomatic Setback Abroad and Demands for Reforms at Home', *Asian Survey*, XXIII/1 (Jan. 1983), pp. 38–46.
74. A useful source for background to this reality is Jurgen Domes, 'Political Differentiation in Taiwan: Group Formation within the Ruling Party and the Opposition Circles 1979–1980', *Asian Survey*, XXI/10 (Oct. 1981), pp. 1011–28.
75. Interview with Sun Yun-Suan, 29 July 1993 in Taipei. Obviously, this interview took place nine years after Premier Sun suffered his debilitating stroke. The effects have impaired his faculties to a considerable degree, and he is confined to a wheelchair. Nevertheless, his mind is quite clear on numerous subjects, particularly their broad outlines. I have found the information he provided to be accurate in all respects, though at times events tend to be compressed temporally.
76. Interview with Chiang Yen-shih, 20 July 1993 in Taipei.
77. For what is one of the more compelling accounts of Chiang Ching-kuo's illnesses – certainly the most comprehensive that I know in the open literature – cf. Ch'en Li-fu, pp. 242–3.
78. Chiang Ching-kuo's change in appearance is marked, even in news photos. See e.g. the picture in *Free China Review* (April 1981), p. 7.
79. See e.g. Parris Chang, 'Taiwan in 1982: Diplomatic Setbacks Abroad and Demands for Reforms at Home', esp. 42–4. The later work by Maria Hsia Chang, 'Political Succession in the Republic of China', despite containing inaccuracies (in Ch. 4, note 119), is the most comprehensive attempt to discuss the topic in a dispassionate manner. A subsequent, post-*Liu Shao Kang* effort to examine the succession within the framework of the larger political changes occurring in Taiwan is Yangsun Chou and Andrew J. Nathan, 'Democratizing Transition in Taiwan', *Asian Survey*, XXVII/3 (March 1987), pp. 277–99.
80. See e.g. Maria Hsia Chang, 'Political Succession in the Republic of China', p. 425 (text and notes).
81. Interview with Sun Yun-Husan, 29 July 1993 in Taipei. This version contradicts that by Tien Hung-mao in Congressional testimony on 31 May 1984, wherein he stated: 'Chiang Ching-kuo... became inactive in decision-making. An *ad hoc* group consisting of approximately half-a-dozen leaders filled in to exercise *de facto* collective leadership. Within this group, General Wang Sheng gradually emerged as the pivotal figure...Operational base of the group reportedly centered on the so-called 'Liu Shao-Kang Office' (a pseudo name [sic])...From 1981 to the spring of 1983, this informal group superseded high-level policy-making on matters of political and security concerns. With a staff consisting of mostly General Wang's intimates, the office became the ultimate operational locus of political power. In light of this, there were speculations that General Wang was positioning himself for possible succession to President Chiang in the event that the latter became incapacitated'. Cf. *Political*

Developments in Taiwan: Hearing and Markup before the Subcommittee on Asian and Pacific Affairs of the Committee on Foreign Affairs, House of Representatives (98th Congress, 2nd Session), 31 May 1984 on House Congressional Resolution 129 (Washington, DC: US GPO, 1985), p. 9. As discussed in my own Ch. 6 and its notes, this version of events is inaccurate both in substance and thrust.

82. Ibid.
83. Interview with Wang Sheng, 16 July 1993 in Taipei.
84. Ibid.
85. Interview with Wang Sheng, 24 July 1993 in Taipei.
86. Interview with Chiang Yen-shih, 20 July 1993 in Taipei.
87. Interview with Dr Thomas B. Lee, Chairman of American Studies, Tamkhang University, 29 July 1993 in Taipei.
88. See e.g. p. 269 of 'Taiwan', *Asia 1984 Yearbook* (Hong Kong: FEER, 1985), pp. 268–73.
89. For a detailed discussion of this trip cf. Wang Sheng, *Notes on American Trip* (Taipei: China Daily Newspaper Agency, 1969). Schools at which discussions took place included: Stanford, Berkeley, Columbia, MIT, Cornell, Michigan, Georgetown, Harvard, NYU, and American University. Henry Liu, 'Wang Sheng the Man', claims these academic seminars were conducted under the auspices of the CIA, which is not accurate. Wang Sheng was accompanied throughout his trip by a lone US Army escort officer, a major.
90. Interview with Wang Sheng, 9 July 1993 in Carmel, California.
91. Interview with Chiang Yen-shih, 20 July 1993 in Taipei.
92. Interview with Wang Sheng, 16 July 1993 in Taipei.
93. Trip details come from Interview with Omar Ted Mah, 28 July 1993 in Taipei; Fred Chien's position in *Liu Shao Kang* is from Interview with Liu Kuo-chih, 27 July 1993 in Taipei.
94. Interview with Wang Sheng, 16 July 1993 in Taipei.
95. Ibid.
96. Ibid.
97. Interview with Chiang Yen-shih, 20 July 1993 in Taipei.
98. Interview with Sun Yun-suan, 29 July 1993 in Taipei.
99. Interview with Liu Kuo-chih, 27 July 1993 in Taipei.
100. Interview with Wang Sheng, 24 July 1993 in Taipei: 'Chiang Ching-kuo saw the *Liu Shao Kang* job as enormously complicated and a great responsibility. It was not a special privilege or power. All that was required was to silently dedicate your efforts to the party and the country. That's all that was necessary. It was not necessary to report to the Central Standing Committee of the party. Simultaneously, I thought this was a very tremendous responsibility, a heavy burden. I kept reminding myself that I had to pick up the burden and go on. I was willing to do this, to shoulder the heavy burden. I neglected to suggest to Chiang Ching-kuo that I should report to the Central Standing Committee. So over time, some of the members felt left out and uninformed. This was combined with the situation that some people deliberately instigated vicious disharmony. Some claimed we had a dual chain of command. They even said that the *Liu Shao Kang* Office was the Central Standing Committee above the Central Standing Committee. In my three years of office, I did not have the power to regulate, command, grade, reward, or punish. Our only way to get things done was through coordination and request. All the other units in the government could not do an effective job, but *Liu Shao Kang* would constantly request that they do extra work. So those people were very vexed at not living up to the standards of the request. They were worried that Wang Sheng would go in and tell Chiang Ching-kuo. The fact was, the *Liu Shao Kang* Office went through so many difficulties and met so many obstacles that we never dared report anything without true evidence. We were concerned that any report going in would add to Chiang Ching-kuo's worries and create instability

involving personnel. But, in turn, some of the other units went in and reported to the president for pre-emptive reasons. Before I could even go in, they went in. They said *Liu Shao Kang* should not have so many requests. These sort of reports gave Chiang Ching-kuo the impression that perhaps the areas of responsibility of *Liu Shao Kang* were too many and too broad – and it went against his original intention that *Liu Shao Kang* should be a unit concerned with far-reaching, broad concepts not mired in minor matters'.

101. Ibid.
102. Ibid.
103. Ibid.
104. Helen Liu's charge, contained in *The Murder of Henry Liu*, says in full (p. 48): 'Henry began writing articles about the Chiang family in the early 1970s as part of his graduate study work, and he arranged for publication of some of this work in several Hongkong magazines. Around that time he received a letter from General Wang Sheng, the powerful head of Taiwanese Security Bureau, who told Henry to 'take heed' of three things before he published his biography of Chiang Ching-kuo. He was told to consult with as many people as possible before publishing, to think of what was good for Taiwan, and should "move cautiously, and think twice", before publishing such a book. As reported in a recently published letter Henry wrote to a friend in Hongkong, [*] Henry wrote General Wang back bluntly telling him: "I'm living in America and I am independent. No one could tell me what I should write about!" This correspondence with General Wang Sheng was in 1973'. David E. Kaplan, pp. 175–6, uses this testimony virtually verbatim for his own description of the incident. The point in Helen Liu's testimony which I have marked [*] is significant, because the original text, lined out but still visible in the Congressional publication, reads: 'which we have translated and attached to this statement'. Obviously, Mrs Liu, either on her own or with counsel, decided that a translation of hearsay thrice removed was not appropriate (i.e. I say a Hongkong journalist says that Henry said what Wang Sheng said), though this is one of the few times in the testimony when such sensibilities prevail. As noted previously, such personal distress is understandable; less so is the use which has been made of such unsubstantiated material. David E. Kaplan, for example, refers to the same threatening letter at least three additional times in his text (pp. 196–7, 259, 328–9). Yet there is no assurance that the episode was not concocted by Henry Liu. Wang Sheng, for instance, has no recollection of having sent such a letter (Interview, 13 July 1993 in Taipei); neither does his aide of some two decades, Wang Yao-hwa: 'I managed all of Wang Sheng's correspondence and affairs. There was, according to my memory, no such letter. Henry Liu never communicated with him. Neither I nor the general drafted any such reply'. (Interview, 13 Aug. 1993 in Asuncion, Paraguay.) No such letter has emerged from the papers Henry Liu left behind.
105. *Political Developments in Taiwan*, p. 9. I have noted previously (Ch. 6, note 81) my exception taken to Tien Hung-mao's analysis. His understanding of *Liu Shao Kang*, as amplified in *The Great Transition* (esp. pp. 80–1), is flawed. He misconstrues the body as 'an *ad hoc* leadership group consisting of General Wang Sheng, KMT Secretary-General Tsiang Yen-si, Premier Sun Yun-hsuen, Secretary-General of the Presidential Office, Ma Chi-chuang, and Defense Minister Kao Kuei-yuan', which was disbanded when Chiang Ching-kuo became alarmed by Wang Sheng's 'political ambition'. Some elements in this description are factual; taken as a whole the passage is flawed. Most importantly, that an ill Chiang Ching-kuo may have given credence to talk that Wang Sheng was running amok is not questioned; but Tien turns the specter into his analytical point. As concerns the Congressional testimony at hand, it proceeds from a flawed model of civil-military relations. That a Wang Sheng rise to power would somehow have represented a military takeover of the government is fanciful. That this might not have been the best thing for the country, which is surely Tien's point, is an

altogether different matter which he does not pursue – but which the speaker [Martin L. Lasatar] who followed him in the hearings did, as discussed in my text which follows.

106. Ibid.
107. Interview with Wang Li-Tien ('Mao Ti'), 23 July 1993 in Taipei.
108. Interview with Wang Hsiao-li, 25 July 1993 in Taipei.
109. Interview with Wang Sheng, 16 July 1993 in Taipei.
110. Interview with Wang Li-tien ('Mao Ti'), 23 July 1993 in Taipei. The precedent to which 'Mao Ti' refers was that of Gen. Lo You-lun, the GPWD Director before Wang Sheng, who had gone on to become ambassador to El Salvador.
111. Interview with Wang Tsiao-li, 25 July 1993 in Taipei.
112. Wang Sheng, *What I Know about President Chiang Ching-kuo* (Ch. 2, note 82), p. 25.

7   Paraguay: Back to Jiangxi

Statue of Chiang Kai-shek in Asunción, Paraguay, visited by then Vice-President
(now President) Lee Teng-hui in March 1985. Wang Sheng is at right.

STEPPING down from the plane in Asunción, capital of Paraguay, on 18 November 1983, Wang Sheng could have been forgiven had he felt he had been exiled to the ends of the earth. A California-sized piece of flat, essentially featureless real estate, home to but three and a half million people, Paraguay existed as a political entity only because the Spanish, attracted by its central location and embrace of three major rivers, had once thought to make it the capital of their South American empire – a notion they quickly abandoned when the manifest disadvantages of the climate and setting became plain.[1] Development, such as it was, had subsequently been left to the famed Jesuit missions until the black robes themselves were expelled in 1767.[2] It could not be said that much had changed economically since those days; underdeveloped farming and ranching remained the essence of the productive sector. Politically, too, underdevelopment was the order of the day. The best that could be said of Paraguay's political history up to 1983 was that it had produced an impressive string of dictators, the latest of whom, the then 71-year-old General Alfredo Stroessner, had assumed power in 1954.[3] In short, the country was a backwater in every way.

That Taiwan was involved at all in such a remote nation stemmed almost wholly from its need to avoid diplomatic isolation. Stroessner saw in Chiang Kai-shek and the *Kuomintang* a model of sorts for his version of anti-communism and thus had long been a staunch supporter of Taipei. He maintained this posture even as his neighbors began to switch their formal recognition to Peking. Though China itself had for some decades shown little interest in as remote an area as Latin America in general, or Paraguay in particular, its campaign to marginalize the ROC had resulted, especially as the decade of the 1980s began, in a far more vigorous effort to effect state-to-state relations with the countries of the region. By 1988, in fact, less than five years after Wang Sheng's arrival, a majority of the local states would have recognized Peking, a roll call which included major players such as Argentina, Brazil, and Peru. It was just this sort of communist offensive, it will be recalled, that had been one of the rationales behind formation of the *Liu Shao Kang*. But, of course, that organization's fate had been integrally linked to Wang Sheng's own; hence the unfavorable outcome. The result was that only in spots such as Asunción had Taipei been able to hang on.

Paraguay's ruler, Stroessner, had gone so far as to erect a statue

of Chiang Kai-shek and to name a street after him. During a visit
to Taiwan, he had met Wang Sheng, among numerous other
generals, and thus was not unaware of his stature. He could not
have been unaware, either, that Wang Sheng's appointment as
ambassador, though a welcome sign of respect from Taipei, came
as a result of unusual circumstances. Nonetheless, the latter's
presence was a personal triumph of sorts for Stroessner, and he
met regularly with Wang Sheng. Significantly, a constant theme to
which Wang Sheng returned in these meetings was the need to
'open up' Paraguayan life by allowing more freedom and by
encouraging people to organize.[4]

On the face of it, this would hardly seem the sort of advice to
offer a dictator. Yet, given what we have explored in the previous
chapters, particularly in Chapter 5, there was no contradiction. As
a KMT stalwart such as Wang Sheng interpreted the world, an
interpretation explicitly laid out in *San Min Chu-i*, the two
qualities of freedom and organization were not opposites but
linked in symbiotic relationship. And far from licking his wounds,
Wang Sheng had hit the ground running. No sooner had he arrived
in Paraguay then he had taken the measure of the place and
discerned that he had, in a sense, returned to Jiangxi. The same
problems of political, economic, and social underdevelopment
loomed, with the same enemy, the communists, lurking behind the
next strategic hill. Thus, in his mind, he might have been sent as
the ROC's representative to what many regarded as a God-
forsaken Timbuktu, but *sincerity* would serve as his compass, as it
had throughout his life. He threw himself into his work.

Recalls Tseng Cheng-te, Commercial Attaché with the ROC
Embassy:

> He was so aggressive. He would work very late into the
> evening. One day at 11 o'clock at night, he had just come back
> from a social function and said he wanted to talk to me about
> a way to strengthen relations through commercial means. He
> called me on the phone, so I went over. The point is that he
> worked so hard that even at that late hour, he was still doing
> things. And while he talked to me, he kept doing other things!
> He took his work very seriously. He was very dedicated.[5]

Lee Shi-lin, the ROC Military Attaché at the time, has a similar
recollection:

During the eight years that Wang Sheng was there, I was ready to assist him on a moment's notice. He was very enthusiastic and dedicated to his job. There was a weekend when he called me in to talk about something and asked me to call the appropriate Paraguayan person immediately. I pointed out that it was Sunday. 'Oh!' was his reaction. He didn't even know what day it was! All he wanted to do was finish the job.[6]

It would be tempting to see Wang Sheng as throwing himself into his work 'to forget', but such an interpretation does not stand up when considered in light of the man's life. He was simply performing in the manner he always had. For the sleepy posting that had hitherto been Asunción, it was an exhilarating change. 'He was a *real* general', observes Chou Chen-ta, a retired commando now a businessman in Paraguay.[7]

For the 'real general', Paraguay was a political warfare challenge. His mission, as he analyzed it, had three facets: first, to secure Taiwan's diplomatic position in what ultimately was to become the only South American state with which Taipei was to have relations; second, as an integral part of this first aspect, to assist Paraguay in developing so that it could not fall victim to communist subversion; and, third, to work with the small Chinese community within Paraguay itself.

A Community in Search of Itself

It was naturally to this third facet that Wang Sheng initially turned his attention. Small though it was – Wang Sheng was unable even to get an accurate count of its numbers, though it seemed to consist of about 7,000 – the Chinese community was important economically in a country which had few entrepreneurs of any sort. Stroessner's seizure of power in 1954[8] had come after a post-World War II period of considerable political instability and economic stagnation (the economic growth rate between 1947 and 1954 had been 0.8 per cent per annum[9]). The world war itself had followed the 1932–35 Chaco War with Bolivia, a boundary dispute which had escalated to a conflict fought over the 60 per cent of Paraguay that was the non-arable marshland of 'the Chaco'. Successful though it was, the Chaco War was extremely costly in money and lives. Combined with the post-World War II stagnation

Wang Sheng (right) presides at the 1985 opening of the Chinese Cultural School in Asunción.

and Paraguay's lack of traditional natural resources (it *does* have enormous hydroelectric potential), the result was a situation where any economic steps at all should have been salutary. These Stroessner had provided, improving agriculture, foreign trade, and infrastructure. Hence the 29 years of his regime prior to the arrival of Wang Sheng had been marked by steady economic development.

The progress was fragile, though, and built largely upon revenues realized through joint development, with Paraguay's neighbors, of hydroelectric projects. When these were completed, just as the 1980s began, a serious recession set in. Wang Sheng had arrived just as it hit full force. This storm had begun to hurt the Chinese not only for the expected economic reasons but also because their economic prowess made them a target for many in positions of power who needed to find new sources of income now that the boom was over. In short, the normal problems of criminal activity and corruption, which were always of concern to colonies of 'pariah entrepreneurs' – outsiders performing commercial functions in societies not given, for reasons of culture or structure, to such activity – had reached a new level of concern.

What Wang Sheng discerned early on was that it was not just its wealth and 'foreign' characteristics which made the Chinese community such an inviting target. Most of the Chinese, after all, by any objective standards, even within Paraguay, should have been considered small potatoes as targets for extortion, especially when compared to the Paraguayan elite. Rather, it was their lack of organization which made the Chinese a target. 'Why not?' must have been the logic of those who victimized them.

A typical situation is related by George Wang, a young interpreter working in Asunción:

> My family provides an example of what goes on here: In 1980 we were accused of breaking and entering and threatening a neighbor. The accuser got other people to sign accusations, and we, my father and I, were taken to jail. There, the police laid out the deal. The accuser had a nephew who needed an operation, so they needed to 'borrow' US $3,000. 'If you'll loan it, we'll let you out'. The Chinese Embassy got involved in trying to help, which is normal. Ultimately, the Military Attaché was able to get us out, because he talked to an army colonel, now a general, who was a *Fu Hsing Kang* graduate. Of course, the military and the police are distinct, but the colonel was putting the police through a special training program next door to the jail, so after eight days he was able to get us transferred to his place. But we spent 44 days there. There are so many corrupt groups that they are often at cross purposes. The judge in our case received a bribe from someone *not* to let us go, so he didn't want to let us go. You can see how our embassy finds itself accused both of doing too much and too little. The motives of the parties involved get all scrambled. Before [Wang Sheng came], we just looked at a thing such as this as bad luck.[10]

With Wang Sheng as ambassador, the situation improved substantially. He recognized that the existing 'associations' of Chinese were precisely that, flaccid groups which needed to become muscular organizations that could represent their members. Comments Kao Lung-sheng, a businessman who was to play an important role in Wang Sheng's plans, 'Before, all were just individuals. They cared nothing for other people. General Wang brought them together into groups'.[11] During Wang Sheng's tenure, in fact, 24 geographic organizations, patterned on the traditional Chinese mutual aid societies, were formed, linked to the existing but largely inactive Chinese Association. All of the officers were elected. Analyzes Wang Yao-hwa, longtime aide to Wang Sheng who accompanied him to Paraguay in the same capacity:

> These organizations had nothing to do with the line of work people were in. People who lived in the same area now worked to help each other. For example, when a man needed a blood transfusion, the organizations would seek to find someone with the same type. At special holidays, we called together all these groups to have special events, such as picnics. What General Wang did was according to the principles of Pol War [Political Warfare]. It was organizational, to get people organized. Everyone supported the idea, because they saw when people have more organization, police and others leave you alone. They don't come asking for 'squeeze'. Because of the way General Wang proposed these ideas, [Chinese] people here felt more calm. There were no longer disturbances.[12]

Formation of the 24 'friendship groups', as they were termed, was just part of Wang Sheng's plan to ensure that the Chinese community did not again fragment. The atomization which was at the root of its problems grew, he judged, from the community's lack of belonging, its lack of cohesion. This stemmed directly from its having been separated from its cultural roots. It was useless, at such a stage, to speak of *San Min Chu-i* when the individuals concerned were 'Chinese' in name only (and had not become 'Paraguayan', either). The splits within the Chinese community were those which were normal to any society undergoing change – young versus old, traditional versus modern, and so on. To these were added the normal human shortcomings occasioned by position, ambition, and personality clashes. There were even two rival Chinese-language newspapers. Faction, then, built upon individual isolation, to the advantage of those who would exploit the whole. It had been the same in Jiangxi.

The obvious solution, judged Wang Sheng, was education. The

Chinese community in Paraguay had to be taught to appreciate its own culture, to draw strength from it, starting with the young. Using as his two main contact points Kao Lung-sheng and Chao Ju-pi, the latter a specialist in aircraft maintenance who was working in Paraguay as a businessman, Wang Sheng worked to make a 'Chinese Cultural School' a reality. True, the Chinese community had been holding a few classes using rented rooms, but there was no systematic *campaign* as such, no plan to accomplish a specific end as envisaged by the man who had used *Fu Hsing Kang* to accomplish the same end. An energetic fund raising effort built upon the growing solidarity within the Chinese community and the increased pride its members felt in its strengths. The US $250,000 it raised were matched by an equal grant Wang Sheng obtained from Taiwan, so that by 1985 the cultural center was a reality. At its center was a school, accredited by both the ROC government and the Paraguayan authorities and open to non-Chinese, as well, which added a Chinese component to the regular curriculum.[13] A special scholarship fund was set up to send top Paraguayan students to Taiwan for university training.[14] A professional staff delivered normal academic instruction; Chinese, for the most part volunteers who received only an honorarium, taught Chinese subjects.

Getting individuals, such as the volunteers at the school, to understand that they could thus help themselves and others became a central theme of Wang Sheng's tenure. 'An ambassador has his job as a diplomat', observes Kao Lung-sheng, now the school director. 'It was not necessary for him to do these things, but he saw that our children were just drifting, that there was nothing for them. His specialty was organization, so he helped us to get organized. Before that, everyone was an island unto himself'.[15] To further link those islands, Wang Sheng and his officials moved constantly throughout the Chinese community. Where previously the embassy officials had kept mainly to themselves, their ambassador now had them systematically visiting 'their' community. 'Most of the people who had come to Paraguay recently could not handle the language', says Chao Ju-pi, 'so General Wang got embassy officials to go visit them, to ask about their needs, to provide assistance. Through his leadership, our Chinese officials and businessmen, who previously rarely functioned outside their areas, interacted and mixed more together. Our lives became intertwined'.[16]

Remarkably, so, too, did the lives of Wang Sheng and wife, Hsiung Hwei-ying, become intertwined to an extent which had never been possible amidst the pressures of Taiwan. As her husband worked to develop 'community' amongst the Chinese in Paraguay, Hwei-ying – who was accompanied by 'Mao Ti', her own son who would shortly depart for university in the United States – performed a similar function using a religious approach. Her own school in Taipei had been left under the control of its board of directors, so it was natural that her considerable energies should find an outlet through her religion. In Paraguay she found the Chinese evangelical Christian community, a minority amongst a minority, drifting and holding services in a rented apartment. In a fashion which mirrored that of her husband, Hwei-ying provided a dynamism which resulted in a leap in membership and a move, ultimately, to an actual church. She even had a preacher sent out from her original congregation in Taiwan. As the number of converts grew, to include more than 500 Paraguayans, some ten branch chapels were opened in rented quarters. Separate Chinese- and Spanish-language services were held, but each month the congregations came together for a dual-language service.

Perhaps Hwei-ying's greatest achievement, however, at least in her own eyes, was the conversion of Wang Sheng himself.[17] Again, it would be tempting to find a Wang Sheng, beaten to his knees, grasping a proffered limb in a desperate effort to rise. And again, such an interpretation would fall short. Instead, what seems to have happened was that, in his usual fashion, Wang Sheng – having control over his schedule that he had never possessed in Taiwan – took the time to examine more carefully Christianity, the Bible in particular. Hitherto, his attitude had been as succinctly summarized by 'Mao Ti', 'He [once] said to one of the [church] elders that if God would help him overthrow the communists and go back to China, he would embrace Him!'[18] Yet as he explored the religion which his wife had long pressed upon him, he found, as had Sun Yat-sen and Chiang Kai-shek, who had both converted to Christianity, that it offered a philosophy which seemed to encompass all that he believed in, philosophically and morally. It was, in other words, like everything in his life, a decision based upon careful consideration and study. Adds 'Mao Ti', 'He wasn't looking for inner peace'.[19]

Indeed, there was no visible change in Wang Sheng. His whirlwind existence continued apace. His reputation as a *leader* reached a peak when, on the night of 2 February 1989, intense fighting broke out in the center of Asunción. A coup, mounted by Stroessner intimate and heir apparent General Andres Rodriguez, involved a battle between the presidential guard regiment and coup units that included the street in front of the ambassador's residence, which itself was half a block down from the embassy. As embassy personnel frantically tried to get him to escape, Wang Sheng stood his ground. Recalls the Ambassador's aide Wang Yao-hwa, 'I told the guards to prepare to leave [with him], but he said, 'If I die here, at least I died on the job'. After that, no one dared to think of leaving. The next day we went all over picking up shell fragments. They weighed more than three kilos!'[20] Adds Kao Lung-sheng of the 'Chinese Cultural School':

> We heard shots. I called General Wang [on the telephone]. He said, 'Tell all Chinese not to go out of their houses; it's not safe'. His first reflex was to think not of himself but of the Chinese people here. Yet the battlefield was right in front of his residence! At about two or three o'clock in the morning, I called again and said he should leave his residence. He said, 'I'm where I should be. This is the ambassador's residence, so I shall stay'. Afterwards, some of the officials of the embassy tried to get him out, but he refused to abandon his post. Fortunately, the whole thing ended in time. Had the fight continued, the air force was going to bomb the area. It was a close call, a matter of 5–10 minutes. Our Foreign Ministry had even ordered him to leave, but he refused.[21]

So in character, Wang Sheng's actions were able to serve as more than an example of personal bravery. Summarizes Wang Yao-hwa:

> Even amidst such circumstances, General Wang never left his post. Because of his attitude and actions, embassy people realized that even the ambassador was exceeding his limits. He had been trying to get people at the embassy to extend themselves for the people. In one instant he got them to redouble their efforts. He stayed at his post and set an example, while other self-appointed leaders were fleeing to Brazil. There were other groups amongst the Chinese people, but their leaders wavered, while General Wang stood his ground. Due to this episode, he was treated with even more respect by the people.[22]

The reference to 'self-appointed leaders', of course, alludes to a reaction, hardly surprising, which surfaced in some circles of the Chinese community against what they viewed as the overly aggressive, unwanted approach to his duties adopted by Wang Sheng. Though most welcomed the structure and purpose the ambassador's efforts brought to their lives, there were naturally enough of those who wanted to be left alone – and those who were resentful because their stake in the status quo was affected. Among these were elements engaged in illicit or criminal activities.[23]

Paraguay in Search of 'Development'

Ironically, it was just such terms which many might have applied to the regime of Stroessner itself. It has been mentioned early on in this chapter (and discussed explicitly in Chapter 5) that for critics, Taiwan's association with a state such as Paraguay was more than a marriage of convenience, rather a case of water seeking its own level (though 'slime' might be the more appropriate term when rendered from a position of hostility). On the surface, the two countries certainly appeared to share much in common. In particular, Stroessner had built up as the linchpin of his power a dominant *Asociación Nacional Republicana*, or Colorado Party, founded in 1887, which operated behind a facade of democratic process to co-opt all segments and sectors of Paraguayan society. As political scientist Carlos R. Miranda has observed, 'The ideological manipulation, extreme control of opposition groups, and co-optation through economic benefits created a foundation that seemed destined to last'.[24] Indeed, it had become 'one of the most stable authoritarian political systems ever to have held power in Latin America'.[25] Nevertheless, on 2 February 1989, it came crashing down.

Though unexpected, the coup was predictable. Judging by the advance warnings issued to American personnel in Asunción , as well as the enhanced guard force deployed, it seems clear that the US Embassy knew what was afoot. Viewed from a more analytical perspective, it should also have been clear that it was the very failure of Colorado rule to model itself after the KMT (not that this was ever consciously done except in Stroessner's mind) which left it vulnerable to dislocation when economic growth fizzled. Despite Wang Sheng's urgings, there really was no organization in

Wang Sheng (right) and ROC Military Attaché, Lee Shi-lin, talk with now-deposed ruler of Paraguay, Alfredo Stroessner.

Wang Sheng (right) at the opening of a Chinese-sponsored agricultural center in November 1986.

Paraguay beyond the Colorado Party, certainly no robust civil
society as there was in Taiwan. Corruption was rampant, feedback
mechanisms at a minimum. Neither had institutionalization
replaced personalism at an operative level. Consequently, the
forces unleashed, first, by prosperity, then, by recession, had no
outlets save within the very narrowly defined political world that
was the Colorado Party. In a crisis, in other words, the party, as
represented by Stroessner, was the only target available for attack.

Ironically, Paraguayan personnel had long been sent to Taiwan
for training, to include at *Fu Hsing Kang*'s Institute of Political
Warfare, precisely for the purpose of creating a cadre to staff newly
formed organizations, such as unions. These individuals included
representatives of both the military and civilian sectors. Military
officers, in fact, were required to join the Colorado Party.
Regardless of affiliation, however, the attraction of Taiwan to
Paraguayans was manifest. 'Taiwan is of such interest', observes
Colonel Victor A. Segovia, former Paraguayan Military Attaché in
Washington, DC, 'because it has been able to combine all factors –
especially domestic stability and economic progress with liberal
democracy – to become a world power. Political Warfare played a
key role in this'.[26] This much Stroessner could grasp; it was the
substance, the heart of the matter, which eluded him. He simply
did not grasp that Taiwan's stability had been built upon a
multifaceted commitment to developing all aspects of society.
'Apparently, someone like Stroessner only saw the anti-communist
aspects of the course [Institute of Political Warfare]', analyzes
Bernardo Antonio Aponte Carballo (mentioned previously in
Chapter 5). 'He didn't really understand that much of the course
is about democratic method. It's a course which teaches about
politics'.[27] And it was a failure to develop Paraguay politically, to
use political tools to facilitate the growth of a human and
organizational foundation, which resulted in Stroessner's downfall
after almost 35 years. He had moved in precisely the opposite
direction as had the KMT – or as had Wang Sheng within the
Paraguayan Chinese community.

Regardless, the overthrow initially posed difficulties for Wang
Sheng and the ROC position. Stroessner's regime had not been
particularly violent by Latin American standards – most of its
intimidation had taken the form of shuffling people in and out of
jail – but neither had it been gentle with those perceived as its foes.
It had ruled with an iron fist and kept files on all it suspected of

disloyalty.[28] As one of Stroessner's perceived supporters, Taiwan found itself accosted. Recalls Kao Lung-sheng of the 'Chinese Cultural School':

> After the coup, some Paraguayan people were against the Chinese. Taiwan had been friendly to Stroessner. They would say, 'Now we're in a new era, so we don't want you here any more'. I was even turned away when I went to give a blood transfusion. A nurse asked me if I was Japanese or Chinese. Upon learning that I was Chinese, she told me to go away: 'You all supported Stroessner, so we don't want you here anymore'. I told General Wang what was going on. 'Should we try to explain our position in the press?' He said, 'What we are doing here is for the benefit of Paraguayan society. People can see for themselves. I don't need to restate my position in the press. People will believe their own eyes'.[29]

Of course, Wang Sheng was not naive. Within two days of the coup, reports he received said, Peking's ambassador to Brazil, Shen Yuen-au, had made contact with the Rodriguez camp offering to establish relations and to provide substantial economic aid. In a private meeting with General Rodriguez, Wang Sheng laid out his case. Not only did Peking have a history, worldwide, of promising much but delivering little to states in exchange for ostracizing Taipei, but Taiwan was already doing far more to aid Paraguay than could ever conceivably be gained from China. Bilateral trade alone, for instance, stood at $60 million; 80 per cent of Paraguay's total exports of cotton and soyabeans, went to Taiwan. Tiny by Taiwan's standards, the relationship was hence of great importance to Paraguay – and was a product of extensive effort by the Taiwan embassy which China was highly unlikely to duplicate. 'I tried constantly to figure out what we could buy from them', Commercial Attaché Tseng Cheng-te was to explain later. 'It was very difficult, because they have nothing to offer'. It was equally unlikely that Peking would or could duplicate the training for Paraguayans provided by Taipei. And, finally, China was in no position to provide to Paraguay the development assistance which Taiwan *already had in place*.[30]

This last point was the trump card. For even while working assiduously to build a community of the Chinese population, Wang Sheng had not ignored his mission of securing Taiwan's position through development assistance to Paraguay. Though the political aspects of the ROC approach may have escaped Stroessner, the economics had not. Wang Sheng had endeavored to sketch out for him the parallels he saw between the Paraguayan situation and that which, as a much younger man, Wang had encountered in Jiangxi, more specifically in Gannan. The rural welfare schemes (e.g. cooperatives and rural credit banks) which had worked well there seemed ideal, given the low level of development in the Paraguayan countryside. Especially appropriate, Wang Sheng reasoned, would be the Rural Welfare Centers project (discussed in Chapter 2), with its bringing together of expertise under one roof to make technical information and education available to villagers. Significantly, Paraguayan development personnel, many schooled in the American concept of extension services, were also keen to try such a concept.[31] Hence, the first center had been set up in 1985, soon to be followed by two more.

Two aspects of these centers were most significant, particularly as detailed to Rodriguez after the 1989 coup. First, they were funded with US $200,000 each by the government of Taiwan, exclusive of the Chinese technicians who manned them together with Paraguayan personnel; and, second, they were the initial efforts of a far more extensive, comprehensive scheme for rural development which already existed on paper.[32] What Wang Sheng envisaged was nothing less than using the centers as *foci* for the political and economic advancement of the hinterland. In a variant of the *baojia* system (as described in the Gannan section of Chapter 2), each center was to serve some 100 families. Of the initial US $200,000 allocated to a center, half was given over to start-up and operating costs; the other half was used as an endowment to generate interest (at approximately 6.0 per cent per annum) which, in turn, was used to create rural credit.[33] Chinese development personnel – contract individuals with the Chinese Agro-technology Mission – worked with Paraguayan counterparts (employees of Asunción's own Ministry of Agriculture), not only to administer the funding aspects but, more importantly, to advance new concepts such as work teams, cooperative marketing, and handicraft production, all self-supervising. The desired result was to improve, in the short term, productivity and income, in the long-term, self-sufficiency through proactive rather than reactive planning. The social component of the outreach effort, therefore, was as salient as the technical, economic dimension. Necessarily, such grassroots socio-economic organizing would serve as a basis for the growth of political activity.[34]

This was just what Wang Sheng had in mind. The three centers in operation at the time of the Rodriguez coup were experimental, the prototypes for the larger program. The Gannan experience had given it its particular slant, which was to achieve the most with the least – and to work oneself out of a job. Relates Lee Shi-lin:

> To minimize the use of people, each year we were to set up five villages. For each there were to be two people. Thus each year only five would be established. At the end of five years, we would have 25 villages with only 50 people needed. At the sixth year, we would take people from the first year's villages and use them, turning the first villages over to the Paraguayan Ministry of Agriculture. By using such a five year cycle, we would minimize the number of personnel required. Our minimum goal was within five years to train enough people to keep on preparing farmers with knowledge of techniques. Wang Sheng designed the idea. He wanted it to work as a yeast which proliferates. He wanted it to keep growing from 100 to 1,000, so that eventually the whole country would receive help – and that this help would be seen as coming from the Taiwan government. People would benefit but would understand that the help came from Taiwan. This would improve our relationship with Paraguay.[35]

In a sense, the sky was the limit, because as Wang Sheng envisaged the plan, the specifics were but a means to an end, 'development'. *Anything* which contributed to that end, be it social, economic, or political, could legitimately be folded under a Rural Welfare Center's purview. One plan which originated with Wang Sheng, for example, was a scheme whereby each household would be encouraged to plant 100 trees of economic value, so that the mature wood could not only be sold but could be used to rebuild the family quarters themselves. No idea was off-limits. The crucial point was that solutions be self-sustaining and self-administered by the *campesinos* (peasants). Beyond the centers, too, Wang Sheng worked to establish a chain of service. Paraguay's poor soil required fertilizer, yet this was too expensive for the average peasant farmer. The unavailability of the raw materials and the need to order customized mixes abroad was responsible for a good bit of this problem. Hence, plans were implemented to lower costs by building a plant which could import the raw materials (they were brought in from Florida) and mix them for specific sites. To raise capital for the first purchases, which, regardless of price, would be beyond the reach of a normal *campesino*, the mechanism of an endowment fund to generate loan cash was used. To ensure that such help was applied neither haphazardly nor overwhelmingly, the extension services at the centers were supported by enhanced basic research at appropriate university facilities in Asunción. If specific taskings proved beyond the capability of local resources, direct Chinese inputs were utilized.

As a Stroessner confidant, Rodriguez had not been unaware of these activities and plans. Yet the scope of what Wang Sheng had in mind, and its relevance to local conditions and resources, had hitherto not been within his responsibilities. He was impressed. Relations with Taiwan were maintained. Subsequently, Rodriguez led a group of government officials and business people on an official visit to Taiwan, where details for the more vigorous pursuit of Wang Sheng's plans were completed.[36] 'Wang Sheng had the idea, created the thinking behind all this to improve the Paraguayan people's way of life', observes Huang Wen-jung, a technician at the Ita center in Paraguay's Central Department. 'Yet under Stroessner, before the coup, our plan for centers had been experimental. After the coup it became a full-fledged program. Rodriguez was responsible for this. He went to see for himself and liked what he saw. The local people really liked the concept, too'.[37]

It was, in fact, far easier for Wang Sheng and his cohorts to work in the new, more open political environment than it had been previously, particularly after Rodriguez was legally chosen president on 1 May 1989 in what was regarded as the most free election in Paraguayan history. For with democracy, however imperfect, came the ethos of service, an ethos which had long been, in China and Taiwan, at the foundation of *San Min Chu-i* and the KMT. This allowed Wang Sheng's development ideas to have a resonance that had been impossible previously. Stroessner had been able to appreciate the benefits individual projects might have for economic development and thus political stability; he saw the central role these two facets played in anti-communism. Yet he had been incapable of grasping an overall scheme of things, of seeing how such projects had to be allowed to take on a life of their own, with all the attendant political implications. Rodriguez played his cards more shrewdly, either through inclination or external pressure – there were many who claimed that his alleged past involvement with narcotics trafficking had allowed Washington to make it clear that either a new order would appear or he, like Stroessner, would be made to disappear – and ultimately gave way peacefully to a new president in 1993.

During the Rodriguez presidency, then, Wang Sheng's plans enjoyed their greatest success. The number of development centers expanded to 21 (see Map 8 for locations), with another nine planned to complete the first phase (these were in the process of being implemented in 1993). The fertilizer mixing plant was opened; the credit scheme implemented. An Economic Cooperation Commission began to function, with meetings alternating between Taiwan and Paraguay. A project was carried out which made the Paraguayan Army self-sufficient in rice and, simultaneously, opened up the potential for a major new crop.[38] Military cooperation continued, with technical and training missions arriving from Taiwan. Likewise, steady numbers of Paraguayans, both military and civilian, were sent to Taiwan itself for training, especially to *Fu Hsing Kang*.[39]

The manner in which the Paraguayans viewed this latter program, which had, at the time of the coup, been widely regarded in some circles as a linchpin of support for the old-regime, is articulated by Lieutenant-General Lino Oviedo, who, as the commander of the Army's 1st Corps, was to emerge as a key figure in Rodriguez's power base:

> We send people to *Fu Hsing Kang* because Taiwan has had the most experience in defending itself against communism. Even though mainland China is more powerful and has a greater population, the people who withdrew to Taiwan, thanks to their political strategy of anti-communism, have built a respected nation. We would like all our qualified officers and civilians to go there for training. We want them to learn to defend themselves against communism. In fact, if you look at Taiwan's present prosperity, you will see that it is built upon the manner in which they combine the political and the economic. This kind of system has allowed their country to develop, to the point where we may judge that it is one of the most successful cases of development under difficult circumstances. Economically, they have become a power, hence a model for us.[40]

MAP 8
ROC DEVELOPMENT CENTERS IN PARAGUAY

It was a telling point. Certainly, considered from any number of angles, Taiwan and Paraguay would have to be considered an odd couple. Their relationship was not without problems. In the field, there were the expected dissimilarities of culture and behavior. Assesses Hung Wen-jung, fluent in Spanish because he was raised in the Dominican Republic:

> At a center we look at everything to improve the people's lives. I give marketing ideas and plans, how to do it right. The Paraguayan coordinators carry out the operational part. A lot of how a center actually works depends upon the interaction of individuals, especially their language abilities. There are, of course, more fundamental problems which affect our relationship. Paraguayans tend to look to the present, not the future. One of our jobs [therefore] is to look into the future, to look at how the market will develop. For example, a typical Paraguayan farmer grows one crop which takes six months to a year to ripen. If we can get them to diversify, we can get ahead of the market rhythm. Our products can be ready when demand peaks, so we can get the best prices. My being here teaching technology is only one thing. Most important is to teach the technique of modifying your way of production to increase your income. You have to be flexible and think ahead. This has not been the Paraguayan way. It must never be forgotten that it took Taiwan 40 years to get to where it is. Here, the soil is of poor quality, and the local people don't want to work more than four hours per day. These qualities will in time give them lots of trouble.[41]

At a more basic level, there was the echo of the charge levelled against Taiwan itself by critics: how could a purported democracy justify its association with a dictatorship such as that of Stroessner? This regime which, in addition to all of its other aforementioned shortcomings,[42] had also become known as a refuge of sorts for renegade Nazi war criminals. We have explored this topic previously in Chapter 5, but it is useful to highlight how Taiwan saw the problem, as aptly summarized by Wang Sheng's long-serving aide Wang Yao-hwa:

> All governments have their own ways of ordering their affairs. Back then, we could not classify people and countries as simply as we do now. Paraguay had its way of doing things,

the intimate details of which we knew little. We had no way to find out for sure; neither did we have the right to interfere in their affairs. They were a country with which we had relations which asked for training. Taiwan itself was in a very difficult situation. The communists were trying to cut us off. When we trained these people [Paraguayans], we expected it to strengthen their country [which was anti-communist]. Of course, we expected to benefit, as well. We must try to maintain our diplomatic relations. If we can make their country better, [our expectation is that] they'll show their gratitude. *Fu Hsing Kang* trains people. They are selected by the [Paraguayan] government, not us. We give them classes on how to organize their lives in many different fields. Those [Paraguayans] who went back [to Taiwan] were from all fields, not just the military. Each works in his own field. We would like these people to use what they have learned to change their lives. They have much experience already when they come to us. *Fu Hsing Kang* takes what is best and gives lessons to make it better. It has nothing to do with torture and all the things the opposition is talking about. For example, this waiter here went back to *Fu Hsing Kang*. From the opposition standpoint, he should be a torturer. Yet he's still a waiter.[43]

Thus the small Taiwan mission, which totalled some 15 individuals, excluding the contract personnel brought in to work at the development centers, went about the business of accomplishing the mission as Wang Sheng conceived it. Wang Sheng himself obviously did not dwell upon what he saw as philosophical fine points, but took the world as he found it and endeavored to make it a better place. He had experienced success throughout his life by utilizing the same philosophy, in circumstances far more forbidding than those he found in Paraguay. Indeed, though there were periodic security scares – such as when individuals known to be connected with the Taiwan Independence Movement appeared at Wang Sheng's church with a pistol in their possession (he was not present) – there was little that happened in Asunción which would suggest that the ambassador from Taiwan had once been, at least by reputation, one of the most powerful men in the Chinese-speaking world. Indeed, the only concession to his position was that the embassy guard force was augmented by physically impressive newcomers throughout Wang

Sheng's tenure (steps, though, which had never been necessary in Taiwan itself).

Wang family life, too, achieved a harmony it had not known in Taiwan. Hsiung Hwei-ying, in fact, was ultimately to become chairman of the group maintained by the ambassadors' wives, a unique position given that most of the nations so-represented did not even have relations with Taiwan. As was to be expected, she quickly put a degree of vigor into the sedate organization which left a considerable mark. As Wang Sheng grew older, she – ten years his junior – served another function as well. Recalls Tseng Cheng-te, the Commercial Attaché:

> He [Wang Sheng] always saw the best in people. If anything, he was too soft-hearted. Not everyone worked with one heart. Sometimes people in the embassy would take advantage of his kindness. His softness was counterbalanced by the personality of his wife. She could distinguish very well between good and bad. If she thought someone deserved punishment, she would see that he got it.[44]

Two strong-willed individuals, the Wangs had become a team of sorts at last. In Paraguay, it was certainly an effective team. For whatever flaws either might have, what they shared was a deep faith in the perfectibility of man. Where they had differed was in personality and emphasis. What is fascinating about Wang Sheng himself is the degree to which his subordinates and associates in Paraguay recognized that they were in the company of someone extraordinary – and were touched by him. Wang Yao-hwa, who had spent a lifetime in Wang Sheng's company as his aide, observes:

> When he came to Paraguay, General Wang realized that people were atomized, they had no cohesion. So he put together a political warfare strategy. He saw clearly the need to get people together, to increase their incomes – this is the basis of a stable society. In his approach, General Wang is in effect pointing out to people that if he invites you to dinner to eat fish, it will under normal circumstances soon be gone. What he does is not simply to invite you to eat; he tells you how to obtain the fish and provides you with a fishing pole. He wants to make sure you always have enough fish. This is his way of doing things; in a phrase, independent living, be

self-sufficient. As the saying goes (we also have this in Chinese): 'If you want God to help you, you must help yourself'. So instead of just giving the Paraguayans money, we show them what they *can* have and how to get it. This was Wang Sheng's main purpose in creating the agricultural centers.[45]

Likewise, Tseng Cheng-te, the Commercial Attaché, put his finger on the essence of the man when he recalled:

Sometimes he [Wang Sheng] would repeat a saying by Confucius, 'Rotten wood cannot be used for sculpture'. He disagreed on this point, even though he was a follower of Confucius. 'I don't believe the whole wood is rotten', he would say. 'There must be some part which is good – and we can use that part for our sculpture'.[46]

Such a man would have been difficult to replace in even the most desirable of postings. In Paraguay, it would prove impossible. When the turn of events dictated in 1991 that it was time to return home, a private reception was hosted by President Rodriguez, who pointed out the obvious: Wang Sheng's contributions to Paraguay had been immeasurable. Wang Sheng, who had studied throughout his stay, gave his own farewell speech in Spanish.

Return to Taiwan

During the entire time Wang Sheng had been posted to Paraguay, he had not returned home to Taiwan. So much had changed that it was almost safe to say that he came back to a different country than the one he had left. Most particularly, the momentum which had been building up just as he left had transformed the island. It had become an economic powerhouse and a functioning, multi-party democracy. Wang Sheng's mentor, Chiang Ching-kuo, had guided the state until his death on 13 January 1988. He and Wang Sheng were not to see each other after their strained parting over four years before.

Yet Chiang Ching-kuo had not forgotten the man with whom he had been so closely associated. Chiang Yen-shih, the KMT Secretary-General when Wang Sheng left for Paraguay and now Secretary-General of the President's Office, recounts:

About four months before he passed away, Chiang Ching-kuo called me. I had not seen him for several years, because I had resigned from the KMT about the same time as the *Liu Shao Kang* office closed. I had gone to the Science and Technology Center as its Chairman of the Board (my formal training was as a geneticist). For all those years [prior to my departure], Chiang Ching-kuo and I had been together daily, even on weekends in the countryside. We had talked freely and frankly. Now, suddenly, after more than three years without seeing each other, he called me. We talked for an hour, sitting in chairs just like now, he on the right, I on the left, very close. 'I've been thinking of you', he said. 'I have been missing you. So now I must talk to you. All the misunderstandings are clear'. We talked like that. I understood that he now knew the past criticisms and rumors about the *Liu Shao Kang* office were not true. In those years, Chiang Ching-kuo had been sick [so he had believed the rumors], but he was telling me that he had come to know the truth. I can tell you the fact. As we talked that day, General Wang was in Paraguay. Chiang Ching-kuo said, 'Wang Sheng is a good man. We should use him'.[47]

It was as fitting a tribute as Wang Sheng's modesty would have allowed.[48] That his absolution came when he was already an old man would not have bothered him in the slightest – Chiang Yen-shih, in fact, never passed on the information contained in the quotation above. Wang Sheng had made plain decades before that it was the *revolution* which he served, not individuals. He had followed Chiang Ching-kuo, because they shared a common dedication to an ideal of service to the Chinese people. That he had been cast down from the peak of power to the furthest reaches of civilization worried him not in the slightest, as was proved by his actions. As his daughter Wang Hsiao-li noted earlier, his only sign of wavering was in asking her to accompany him to Paraguay, which she had declined to do. In the country itself, he did not miss a step. Seemingly cast aside, he performed, during his eight years of exile, in precisely the same manner he had throughout his life. Judging by the accolades heaped upon his tenure, his guiding star – his *sincerity* – had not deserted him.

Astonishingly, David E. Kaplan was to write of him as 'an ineffectual ambassador'.[49] To the contrary, the KMT's temporary loss had worked to Paraguay's permanent gain. Thus had Taiwan gained as well.

NOTES

1. For details, one of the most useful, definitive works is Andrew Nickson, *Historical Dictionary of Paraguay* (NY: Scarecrow Press, 1992). Certainly the most delightful source on the country in general, a book which uses a journey to Paraguay as a vehicle for a larger philosophical exploration, is Ben MacIntyre, *Forgotten Fatherland: The Search for Elisabeth Nietzsche* (NY: Farrar Straus Giroux, 1992).
2. Cf. R.B. Cunninghame Graham, *A Vanished Arcadia* (NY: Haskell House, 1968). The expulsion itself has achieved a certain public recognition as a result of the critical success of the major motion picture, *The Mission*.
3. For complete details see Carlos R. Miranda, *The Stroessner Era: Authoritarian Rule in Paraguay* (Boulder, CO: Westview Press, 1990). Among Stroessner's notable nineteenth-century predecessors were José Gaspar Rodriguez de Francia (1814–40); Carlos Antonio López (1840–62); his son Francisco Solano López (1862–70). The latter led Paraguay into the disastrous Triple Alliance War (1864–70), in which the country was devastated. Also useful for the early part of the Stroessner regime is Andre Nickson, *Paraguay: Power Game* (London: Latin America Bureau, 1982).
4. Interview with Wang Yao-hwa, 13 Aug. 1993 in Asunción, Paraguay.
5. Interview with Tseng Cheng-te ('Timothy'), 19 July 1993 in Taipei.
6. Interview with Lee Shi-lin, 22 July 1993 in Taipei.
7. Interview with Chou Chen-ta, 10 Aug. 1993 in Asunción, Paraguay.
8. Stroessner, it must be added, though the guiding hand in the May 1954 coup, did not seize power directly. Instead, he stage-managed events from behind the scene and was legally elected president on 14 June 1954. Miranda (note 3), p. 46.
9. Miranda (note 3), p. 103.
10. Interview with George Wang, 13 Aug. 1993 in Asunción, Paraguay.
11. Interview with Kao Lung-sheng, 19 Aug. 1993 in Asunción, Paraguay
12. Interview with Wang Yao-hwa, 10 Aug. 1993 in Asunción, Paraguay. In an interview conducted over several days , on 13 Aug., Wang Yao-hwa was to add, 'Of course, this whole business [of being exploited by others] goes to why General Wang wanted to get the Chinese [in Paraguay] organized. They're not like the Koreans, who automatically get organized. General Wang came to Paraguay on 18 November 1983. I can't give you an exact date when he outlined his plans, though I remember he did so. You could see them in his actions. When he first arrived here, though, I recall one day that we took a walk to meet the people. We saw some Chinese getting picked on by some Paraguayans. He said, "Hey, we're not organized". Thus this became his first goal. Simultaneously, he started helping people to improve their lives'.
13. The school, which runs from the lower grades through the secondary level, uses the weekdays to provide the same subject matter as would a traditional Paraguayan equivalent. After regular hours and on weekends, however, Chinese students normally attend additional instruction, particularly in Chinese language skills. Payment of tuition by students, as at other private schools, makes the institution self-supporting.
14. At the time I visited the school, in Aug. 1993, this program was in abeyance pending the sorting out of 'problems' which appeared to center about ensuring that the program was used by its Paraguayan beneficiaries, as intended, to further their education. As Wang Yao-hwa noted ruefully at one point, 'In fact, one of the Paraguayans who went back to Taiwan to study in a university even ended up engaging in business instead!' (Interview, 10 Aug. 1993 in Asunción, Paraguay.)

15. Interview with Kao Lung-sheng, 10 Aug. 1993 in Asunción, Paraguay.
16. Interview with Chao Ju-pi, ibid.
17. I base this judgement upon numerous interviews with Hsiung Hwei-ying, to include an entire day of discussions held 30 July 1993 in Taipei.
18. Interview with Wang Li-tien, 23 July 1993 in Taipei.
19. Ibid.
20. Interview with Wang Yao-hwa, 10 Aug. 1993 in Asunción, Paraguay.
21. Interview with Kao Lung-sheng, ibid.
22. Interview with Wang Yao-hwa, ibid.
23. Interview with Wu Wei-shai, 10 Aug. 1993 in Asunción, Paraguay. Engaged in business and a volunteer teacher at the Chinese Cultural Center, Ms Wu was well-informed on the subject. As she put the matter succinctly, 'In one word, we're talking about people with personal interests'.
24. Miranda (note 3), p. 124.
25. Ibid.
26. Interview with Victor A. Segovia, 17 Aug. 1993 in Asunción, Paraguay.
27. Interview with Bernardo Antonio Aponte Carballo, 20 Aug. 1993 in Asunción, Paraguay.
28. Interview with Andrew Nickson, 15 Aug. 1993 in Asunción, Paraguay.
29. Interview with Kao Lung-sheng, 10 Aug. 1993 in Asunción, Paraguay.
30. Source for this paragraph in general is Interview with Wang Yao-hwa, 10 Aug. 1993 in Asunción, Paraguay. Specifics of trade were related during Interview with Tseng Cheng-te, 19 July 1993 in Taipei.
31. Interview with Juan Ignacio Torales, Vice Director of Paraguayan Ministry of Agriculture, 17 Aug. 1993 in Asunción, Paraguay.
32. Wang Sheng, as he had done in the implementation of *Fu Hsing Kang*, would employ 52-month timelines to map out his future plans. In the case of the centers, he had already completed such documents, showing the roles of all key individuals, organizations, and functions. Goals and projected costs were included, together with anticipated needs for external resources and the actions required for obtaining them.
33. Of the $100,000 used to make a center a going concern, $50,000 was required for plant construction, $30,000 for the purchase of machinery, $10,000 for the operating costs of demonstration plots and so forth, and $10,000 for local personnel expenses (e.g. per diem). Cf. *Ministerio de Agricultura y Ganadería, 'Centros de Capacitación y Servicios (CCS), SE AG – Misión Técnica China'*, undtd 1993 mimeo (Asunción, Paraguay), 5 pp.
34. Interview with Ricardo Pedretti (Coordinator) and Guillermo Cespedes (Assistant Coordinator), Council of Rural Development (*Conselo de Desarrollo Rural – CDR*), 17 Aug. 1993 in Asunción, Paraguay.
35. Interview with Lee Shi-lin, 22 July 1993 in Taipei.
36. Interview with Hu Chih-min, former Chancellor at the Taiwan Embassy in Asunción, 19 July 1993 in Taipei.
37. Interview with Huang Wen-jung, 18 Aug. in Asunción, Paraguay.
38. This was a particularly interesting operation which highlights the manner in which the Chinese mission functioned under Wang Sheng. As related by Lee Shi-lin: 'The Paraguayan president made a request to Wang Sheng asking if Taiwan could provide specialty people to assess the feasibility of rice production on a 45,000 hectare military farm located 180 miles outside Asunción, in the Chaco region. We did research on the soil, the weather, and so forth. After assessment, we did some trials which proved that rice could actually be grown there. Then we provided the machinery. The timetable we came up with was that the first year we would plant 200 hectares of rice; the second year, 250 hectares. Eventually, we wanted to have 1,000 hectares. Now they are growing rice. Production each year is enough to meet the military's needs, with some left over to sell on the market. The reason why the president made his request for this specific area was that it was in the Chaco, thus very poor and not very populated. Our

project is significant, because the Chaco region (essentially the left side of the River Paraguay), though it makes up three-fifths of Paraguay, is little used due to its poor qualities'. (Interview, 22 July 1993 in Taipei.)

39. The numbers, while important to Paraguay, should not be overestimated. Apparently, up to the present, approx. 120 Paraguayans have received *Fu Hsing Kang* courses of four or more weeks. Such political training, of course, is quite separate from the agricultural, economic, or technical instruction which has been offered under the auspices of appropriate Taiwan government agencies.

40. Interview with Lt.-Gen. Lino Oviedo, 17 Aug. 1993 in Asunción, Paraguay.

41. Interview with Huang Wen-jung, 18 Aug. 1993 in Asunción, Paraguay. At the time I visited the Ita Center, Huang was in Asunción attending a meeting at the Ministry of Agriculture. We subsequently met in the capital. One of his more humorous observations concerning cultural differences was related at that time: 'I have been cutting the poles necessary to put up electric lines. The electricity was only connected the day after you left the center. It has taken us two years to get it [Paraguay has a substantial power surplus]. That's illustrative of the speed at which things work around here'. Significantly, lest Huang be considered overly blunt in his assessment, the same analysis (though expressed somewhat differently) came in an interview with Leoncio Quintana, Coordinator of the Agricultural Extension Div. (*Dirección de Extensión Agraria – DEA*) of the Ministry of Agriculture, 18 Aug. 1993 in Asunción, Paraguay.

42. Cf. John Vinocur, 'A Republic of Fear', *The New York Times Magazine*, 23 Sept. 1984.

43. Interview with Wang Yao-hwa, 13 Aug. 1993 in Asunción, Paraguay. Though I was unable to interview the waiter in question, in conversation he did confirm that he had attended *Fu Hsing Kang*.

44. Interview with Tseng Cheng-te, 19 July 1993 in Taipei.

45. Interview with Wang Yao-hwa, 18 Aug. 1993 in Asunción, Paraguay.

46. Interview with Tseng Cheng-te, 19 July 1993 in Taipei.

47. Interview with Chiang Yen-shih, 20 July 1993 in Taipei.

48. In the same interview, Chiang Yen-shih added his own words of praise: 'And he [Chiang Ching-kuo] told me, "You're several years younger than I. You should be up to work for the government and the party!" He called me Y.S., using the initials of my name. A few years ago [from July 1993] we had a party congress. At that time, we had trouble [within the KMT], so I jumped back in – because I didn't like to see this. General Wang is a very good man. *Liu Shao Kang* was a good office'.

49. David E. Kaplan (Ch. 1, note 24), p. 329.

8 A New Era?

Wang Sheng addresses law students in 1969.

BACK IN Taiwan in 1991, Wang Sheng assiduously steered clear of politics, though many urged him to return to the fray. For not all were pleased with the changes which had swept Taiwan. Under the leadership of Lee Teng-hui, who had been chosen personally to assume the mantel of leadership by Chiang Ching-kuo, the civil war had been declared officially over (1 May 1991) and the state of emergency had been lifted; the Taiwan General Garrison Command abolished (August 1992); full elections for the National Assembly had been held (December 1991), as well as elections for the Legislative Yuan (December 1992) and for local government (November 1993). Constitutional changes had been implemented in an effort to make positions more accountable to the popular will (May 1992). Relations with China had begun to approach normalization using quasi-official agencies, Taiwan's Straits Exchange Foundation (SEF) and China's Association for Relations Across the Taiwan Strait (ARATS). Taken together, particularly amidst continued economic buoyancy, these developments opened up the social and political spheres.

What rushed in to fill the space was not altogether pleasing. A rising crime rate coupled with a decline in traditionally accepted modes of conduct created a sense of unease among large sections of the populace. Meanwhile a growing problem of official corruption and factionalism tarnished the KMT image and hindered its ability to respond effectively to the growing challenge of the opposition Democratic Progressive Party (DPP, *Min-chu chin-pu tang)*. For its part, the DPP, which had captured 50 of 161 seats in the Legislative Yuan elections (as opposed to the KMT's 103 seats[1]), downplayed publicly its commitment to 'Taiwan independence' yet took every other opportunity to assert that it was essential to its party platform. China loomed ominously in the background, threatening to take 'appropriate action' should independence be formally declared.

It was against such a background that the KMT held its Fourteenth Party Congress, 16–22 August 1993. Wang Sheng, who had not been returned to the Central Standing Committee in the election which had followed his departure for Paraguay, was still a member of the Central Committee itself. Strong support surfaced for his renewed candidacy, but he declined to stand for election. In deference to his service and continued influence, he was named to the KMT 'wise men's body', the Central Committee for Deliberation and Consultation. This was the extent to which Wang

Sheng desired to be involved in official matters. 'His idea is that because his age is very high, he should not hold a government job', observes Hsiung Hwei-ying of her husband. 'What the country needs now are good young people, strong in terms of learning and character. He will just offer advice, because his mind is still young. He should do this to accomplish his goals'.[2]

To give substance to this desire, Wang Sheng had founded, in 1992, a private, non-profit organization, the Foundation for the Promotion of Chinese Modernization (also translated as the Foundation for the Promotion of the Modernization of China). Most members of its Board of Directors were university presidents. Its principal activity was to hold an annual conference, alternating between Taiwan and China, to discuss Chinese modernization in six areas: (1) citizen; (2) family; (3) society; (4) education; (5) economics; and (6) politics. The first such conference was held in Taipei in conjunction with the Fourteenth Party Congress. Twenty-eight scholars from China's Institute of Social Sciences in Peking, a government agency, attended, though they declined to discuss modernization of the citizen or politics. The second conference, the next year, was held in Peking in August 1994. The Chinese agreed to discuss the 'citizen' category but replaced 'politics' with 'management'.[3] Though the mainlanders were keen to have Wang Sheng lead Taiwan's delegation, an emergency appendectomy and a consequent convalescence in the United States kept him away.

Wang Sheng took advantage of his presence there to meet privately with the staff of the San Francisco chapter of the Whampoa Alumni Association. He had begun a two-year term as the chairman of the national association in 1993, so when the opportunity presented itself to communicate directly with a constituent unit, he took advantage of it. At the one-and-a-half hour meeting was echoed the unease many at home felt over the turn their country had taken. The discussion was frank, with the old soldiers eager to hear Wang Sheng's views on the situation at home and the issues which had surfaced. He offered his opinions but refused to be drawn into a discussion of personalities, noting at one point, 'I don't belong to any stream, mainstream or anti-stream. I belong to the *San Min Chu-i* stream'. Yet it was clear he was concerned, particularly about the course the opposition was taking:

We have to trust Lee Teng-hui. He is the chairman of the party and the president. Still, now we have the Taiwan Independence people saying that they will not follow the 1946 Constitution. But now the Constitution has been amended [1992; the DPP walked out prior to the official votes], so the DPP must follow it. If the DPP will not follow, Lee Teng-hui will have to take some action. He has tolerated them in the past, but now all parties concerned, through the amendment process, have legally agreed on the ground rules.[3]

In this analysis we find raised the single most prominent issue threatening the future of Taiwan, that of 'Taiwan independence' as advocated by the DPP. It threatens, because China has plainly stated that such a declaration would be 'unacceptable'. The implementation of that word, 'unacceptable', would in all probability mean military action. Such a conflict would rapidly escalate as other major concerned states were drawn in, particularly the US and Japan.

Yet such concerns do not seem to enter into the DPP's calculus of decisionmaking. Perhaps the greatest irony of Wang Sheng's life is that, having been a key part of the Chinese Revolution for so many years, having seen it reach its most developed form while in exile, he should see his very success spawning separatism. Why go home, asks the exiled population, when we are already there? In an age of resurgent nationalism, it is certainly understandable that the DPP, a party born of repressed tribal sentiment ('Taiwan for the Taiwanese'), its legitimacy rooted in mythohistory (a 'Taiwanese Taiwan' which never was), should continue to push its narrow agenda. It also sought to conceal it from public scrutiny lest its perilous implications prompt the same sort of debate it has for years demanded on the KMT agenda. Less understandable is the unwillingness of its members, regardless of their years of opposition, to see the peripheral importance of ideological zealotry amidst an historical transformation which has created a new Taiwan. It is as if, with the society of *San Min Chu-i* at hand, the opposition is intent upon seeing if it can withstand a punishing blow from afar.

Of the DPP's poor timing, there can be no doubt. China itself, as is well known, is undergoing its own historical transformation. But whereas the issue in Taiwan is the demand by a political group that society deliberately tempt fate, in China fate is being determined by structural forces beyond purposive control. It is the efforts of the CCP to ride the whirlwind, to maintain, at all costs, the illusion of control, that create such a dangerous juncture for Taiwan. As linchpins of the Kuomintang faction of the Chinese Revolution, men such as Wang Sheng, enter their twilight years, they may experience the pain of not having brought the benefits of *San Min Chu-i* to China itself. Yet they can take solace and pride in having built in one province, Taiwan, a model of what the revolution, in their vision, was to be. In contrast, the communist fossils in Peking, heirs to a faction of the revolution which has cost since 1949, by some accounts, as many as 80 million Chinese their lives, can only cling to power. Their way, we now know incontrovertibly, produced little save corpses. Having built no structure capable of harnessing the forces of socio-economic-political development they have now unleashed, their only outlet is irredentism, the demand that alienated territories (Hong Kong, Macau, and Taiwan) return to the motherland – a perverse mirror image of the DPP's position.

If the strategic danger is clear enough, less so is the route to safety. There are few in Taiwan, Wang Sheng among them, who advocate a physical return to the mainland. Yet there are many – and in this camp I would place Wang Sheng – who feel an obligation, as *Chinese*, to work for the betterment of China as an entity – as missionaries of sorts, if the situation will allow the resurfacing of the religious imagery which I have earlier attached to *Fu Hsing Kang* and its graduates. This is hardly a frivolous undertaking. Considered coldly in light of historical circumstance and geostrategic position, it is actually the most viable course of action open to Taiwan. Only China's development into a version of Taiwan will ultimately safeguard the latter. That one need not share the philosophical underpinnings of 'the quest', as it is judged to be in many minds, only further recommends the course of action. Differing motives do not detract from the choice of rational alternative, and other options, such as declared independence, wither when examined.

An argument for the status quo? Wang Sheng would hardly call it such, for the very reasons embodied in the criteria which are the basis for the work of his foundation: 'development' is ongoing, particularly when the medium for change is humanity. The effort to perfect man, that his organizations and their actions will be correct, is never ending. It is the effort to which Wang Sheng has devoted his life. His more recent embrace of religion has been but a logical next step. He has not changed his approach one whit, but he has situated it within a more all-encompassing philosophical framework. When he returned to Taiwan in 1991, before he was interviewed at the airport, he stated to those around him, 'If you don't have God in your heart – or don't believe in God – you will respect nobody'.[4] He has, in other words, come to understand as God the very humanity, *sincerity*, and service which motivates any believer in the Chinese Revolution as articulated in *San Min Chu-i*. The one is impossible without the other. The form is unimportant, but the essence is constant.

It is here that Wang Sheng grows most disturbed when he views the actions of the DPP, or of so many others in Taiwan. Observes Kao Lung-sheng in Paraguay, 'I went back to Taiwan and met General Wang. He said our society was in turmoil. He said our people in their hearts were lost to God, so He was estranged from them'.[5] It is only too easy to hear Percival imparting to King Arthur 'the secret of the Holy Grail' in the film *Excalibur*: 'We have lost our way, Arthur. The king and the land are one. Drink from the chalice and you will be reborn and the land with you'.

Fu Hsing Kang was intended to teach 'the way'; its graduates were to be its champions. By insuring the purity of the key institutions of society, especially the military, which was at all costs to be kept free from corruption and the other ills which had destroyed it on the mainland, political warfare would secure the survival of the revolution. Having successfully carried out his mission, Wang Sheng now sees the very fruits of his labors, a prosperous and democratic society, causing citizens in increasing numbers to 'lose their way'. It is this imperfection which leads to all others, whether geostrategic miscue or simply criminal activity.

Ominously, Political Warfare itself, ill understood and much maligned, remains a prominent target of the opposition. They see it as a crucial element in the KMT structure of control. In such an analysis they have missed the forest for the trees. Certainly they have not even begun to consider the issues reflected in Wang Sheng's thinking above. Such will have to be done if Taiwan, on the verge of a success story with few parallels in history, is not to be undone from within – the very fate which befell the revolution on the Chinese mainland. If such happens, undoubtedly Wang Sheng will judge that a lack of *sincerity* produced the result.

NOTES

1. Only 96 seats were captured by party-sanctioned candidates; the additional KMT seats were captured by those KMT members who contested without the backing of the party.
2. Interview with Hsiung Hwei-ying, 9 Aug. 1994 in Carmel, California.
3. Interview with Wang Sheng, 9 Aug. 1994 in Carmel, California.
4. Interview with Wang Li-tien, 23 July 1993 in Taipei.
5. Interview with Kao Lung-sheng, 10 Aug. 1993 in Asunción, Paraguay.

Bibliography

BOOKS/PAMPHLETS/MONOGRAPHS:

Barnett, A. Doak (ed.). *Chinese Communist Politics in Action* (Seattle: University of Washington Press, 1969).

Be an Iron Man! (Chou-yige Gang-tei Hao-han) (Taipei: Li Ming Cultural Enterprises, 1978).

Bedeski, Robert E. *State Building in Modern China: The Kuomintang in the Prewar Period*, China Research Monograph No. 18 (Berkeley: Center for Chinese Studies, 1981).

Bullard, Monte R. *The Soldier and the Citizen: Taiwan's Military and Allegiance Warfare – 1950–1970* (draft manuscript).

Chang, Chi-yun. *The Rebirth of the Kuomintang (The Seventh National Congress)*, trans. Nee Yuan-ching; rev. and ed. Tsao Wen-yen (Taipei: China Cultural Service, nd/offprint).

Chang, Maria Hsia. *The Chinese Blue Shirt Society: Fascism and Developmental Nationalism*, Chinese Research Monograph No. 30 (Berkeley, CA: Center for Chinese Studies, Institute of East Asian Studies, 1985).

Chang, Sidney H. and Ramon H. Meyers (eds.). *The Storm Clouds Clear Over China: The Memoir of Ch'en Li-fu 1900–1993* (Stanford: Hoover Institution Press, 1994).

Chang, Wen-lung. *A Study of Political Coercion in Urban Taiwan* (Ann Arbor: University Microfilms, Northwestern University Ph.D. dissertation, 1972).

Ch'i, Hsi-sheng. *Nationalist China at War* (Ann Arbor: The University of Michigan Press, 1982).

Chiang, Kai-shek. *Soviet Russia in China: A Summing-Up at Seventy* (New York: Farrar, Straus and Cudahy, 1957).

Chiang Nan [Henry Liu]. *Chiang Ching-kuo Zhuan* (*A Biography of Chiang Ching-kuo*) (Montebello, CA: *Mei-guo Lun-tan Bao* [*The American Tribune*], 1984).

Chiang, Siang-tseh. *The Nien Rebellion* (Seattle, WA: University of Washington Press, 1954).

Chou, Yu-kou. *Chiang Ching-kuo yu Chang Ya-juo* [*Chiang Ching-kuo and Chang Ya-juo*] (Taipei: Lien Ching, 1990).

Cline, Ray S. *Chiang Ching-kuo Remembered: The Man and His Political Legacy* (Washington, DC: United States Global Strategy Council, 1989).

Collection of Speeches and Writings of President Chiang Ching-kuo (Chiang Ching-kuo Shensheng Yen-lun Chu-shu Hui-bien), vol. 1 [of 26] (Taipei: Li Ming Cultural Enterprises, 1981).

Crozier, Brian. *The Man Who Lost China: The First Full Biography of Chiang Kai-shek* (New York: Charles Scribner's Sons, 1976).

Cumings, Bruce. *The Origins of the Korean War: Vol. II The Roaring of the Cataract, 1947–50* (Princeton, NJ: Princeton University Press, 1990).

Deacon, Richard. *The Chinese Secret Service* (London: Grafton Books, 1989).

Dupuy, Trevor N. *The Chinese Civil War* (New York: Franklin Watts, 1969).

Eastman Lloyd E. *The Abortive Revolution: China Under Nationalist Rule, 1927–1937* (Cambridge: Harvard University Press, 1974).

—— *Seeds of Destruction: Nationalist China in War and Revolution, 1937–1949* (Stanford: Stanford University Press, 1984).

Fairbank, John King. *The United States and China*, 4th ed. (Cambridge, MA: Harvard University Press, 1983).

Fei, John C.H. 'A Historical Perspective on Economic Modernization in the ROC,' in Ramon H. Myers (ed.), *Two Societies in Opposition: The Republic of China and the People's Republic of China After Forty Years* (Stanford: Hoover Institution Press, 1991).

Fifty Years of Student Military Training (Shuei-sheng Juen-hsiung Wu-shr Nien) (Taipei: Military Training Department of the ROC Ministry of Education, 1978).

Finkelstein, David M. 'Acheson in Opposition: United States Policy Towards Formosa, 1949–1950' (dated 27 April 1983) and 'Crisis and Confusion: United States Policy Towards Formosa, June–November 1950' (dated March 1984) (unpublished manuscripts).

Galenson, Walter (ed.). *Economic Growth and Structural Change in Taiwan: The Postwar Experience in the Republic of China* (Ithaca, NY: Cornell University Press, 1979).

Gellner, Ernest. *Conditions of Liberty: Civil Society and its Rivals* (New York: Allen Lane/The Penguin Press, 1994).

General Political Warfare Department (GPWD), *General Briefing on Political Warfare System in the Chinese Armed Forces* (Taipei: Ministry of National Defense, npd [c.1960]).

Gold, Thomas B. *State and Society in the Taiwan Miracle* (Armonk, NY: M.E. Sharpe, 1986).

Goldstone, Jack A. (ed.) *Revolutions: Theoretical, Comparative, and Historical Studies* (Chicago: Harcourt Brace Jovanovich, 1985).

Graham, R.B. Cunninghame. *A Vanished Arcadia* (NY: Haskell House, 1968).

Grasso, M. *Truman's Two China Policy* (Armonk, NY: M.E. Sharpe, 1987).

Griffith, Samuel B. (ed. and trans.) *Sun Tzu: The Art of War* (London: Oxford University Press, 1963).

Haggard, Stephen. *Pathways From the Periphery: The Politics of Growth in the Newly Industrializing Countries* (Ithaca, NY: Cornell University Press, 1990).

Harrison, James Pinckney. *The Long March to Power: A History of the Chinese Communist Party, 1921–1972* (New York: Praeger, 1972).

Hart, John N. *The Making of an Army 'Old China Hand': A Memoir of Colonel David D. Barrett*, Chinese Research Monograph No. 27 (Berkeley: Center for Chinese Studies, 1985).

Hartford, Kathleen J. and Steven M. Goldstein (eds.). *Single Sparks: China's Rural Revolutions* (Armonk, N.Y.: M.E. Sharpe, 1989).

Heinlein, Joseph J. *Political Warfare: The Chinese Nationalist Model* (Washington, DC: American University Ph.D. dissertation, 1974).

Ho, Samuel P. S. *Economic Development of Taiwan, 1860–1970* (New Haven, CT: Yale University Press, 1978).

Hooton, E.R. *The Greatest Tumult: The Chinese Civil War 1936–49* (New York: Brasseys [UK], 1991).

House Congressional Hearing, 20 May 1982. *Martial Law on Taiwan and United States Foreign Policy Interests: Hearing Before the Subcommittee on Asian and Pacific Affairs of the Committee on Foreign Affairs, House of Representatives (97th Congress, 2nd Session)*(Washington, DC: US Government Printing Office, 1982).

House Congressional Hearing. *Human Rights in Taiwan: Hearing Before the Subcommittee on International Organizations of the Committee on International Relations, House of Representatives (95th Congress, 1st Session)*(Washington, DC: US Government Printing Office, 1977).

House Congressional Hearing. *Taiwan Agents in America and the Death of Prof. Wen-Chen Chen: Hearings Before the Subcommittees on Asian and Pacific Affairs and on Human Rights and International Organizations of the Committee on Foreign Affairs*, House of Representatives (97th Congress, 1st Session), 30 July and 6 October 1981 (Washington, DC: US Government Printing Office).

House Congressional Resolution 129, 31 May 1984. *Political Developments in Taiwan: Hearings and Markup Before the Subcommittee on Asian and Pacific Affairs of the Committee on Foreign Affairs, House of Representatives (98th Congress, 2nd Session)*(Washington, DC: US Government Printing Office, 1984).

House Congressional Resolutions 49 and 110, 7 February 1985. *The*

Murder of Henry Liu: Hearings and Markup Before the Committee on Foreign Affairs and its Subcommittee on Asian and Pacific Affairs, House of Representatives (99th Congress, 1st Session)(Washington, DC: US Government Printing Office, 1985).

Hsiung, James C. *Contemporary Republic of China: The Taiwan Experience, 1950–1980* (New York, Praeger Publisher, 1981).

Hsu, En-tseng. *The Invisible Conflict: The Behind-the-Scenes Battle in Pre-'49 China* (Hong Kong: The Green Pagoda Press, 1962).

Hu, Kuo-tai. 'The Struggle Between the Kuomintang and the Chinese Communist Party on Campus During the War of Resistance, 1937–45,' *The China Quarterly*, 118 (June 1989), pp. 300–323.

Hu, Shin. *Jiang Jing-guo yu Zhang Ya-ruo Chih Lien* [*The Affair of Chiang Ching-kuo and Chang Ya-juo*](Changchun, Manchuria: 'Literature of the Times' Publishers, 1993).

Huang, J.H. (ed. and trans.) *Sun Tzu: The New Translation* (New York: William Morrow and Company, 1993).

Huang, Philip C.C., Lynda Schaefer Bell, and Kathy Lemons Walker. *Chinese Communists and Rural Society, 1927–1934*, Chinese Research Monograph No. 13 (Berkeley: Center for Chinese Studies, 1978).

Huntington, Samuel P. *The Soldier and the State: The Theory and Politics of Civil-Military Relations* (Cambridge, MA: Harvard University Press, 1964).

Jacobs, Dan N. *Borodin: Stalin's Man in China* (Cambridge, MA: Harvard University Press, 1981).

Jin, Kai-shin (ed.). *Twenty Years of CTS* (Taipei: China Television Service, 1991).

Johnson, Chalmers. *Peasant Nationalism and Communist Power in China* (Berkeley: University of California Press, 1962).

Kaplan, David E. *Fires of the Dragon* (New York: Atheneum Press, 1992).

Kaplan, John. *The Court-Martial of the Kaohsiung Defendants*, Research Papers and Policy Studies Number 2 (Berkeley: Institute of East Asian Studies, University of California, 1981).

Kerr, George. *Formosa Betrayed* (Boston: Houghton, Mifflin Company, 1965).

—— *Formosa: Licensed Revolution and the Home Rule Movement, 1895–1945* (Honolulu: University Press of Hawaii, 1974).

Kwan, Ha Yim (ed.). *China and the U.S. 1955–63* (New York: Facts on File, 1973).

Lai, Tse-han, Ramon H. Myers, and Wei Wou, *A Tragic Beginning: The Taiwan Uprising of February 28, 1947* (Stanford: Stanford University Press, 1991).

Lerman, Arthur J. *Taiwan's Politics: The Provincial Assemblyman's World* (Washington, DC: University Press of America, 1978).

Levine, Steven. *Anvil of Victory: The Communist Revolution in*

Manchuria, 1945–1948 (New York: Columbia University Press, 1987).

Lin, Ching-yuan. *Industrialization in Taiwan, 1946–72: Trade and Import-Substitution Policies for Developing Countries* (New York: Praeger Publishers, 1973).

Linebarger, Paul M.A. *The China of Chiang Kai-shek: A Political Study* (Boston: World Peace Foundation, 1941).

Lintner, Bertil. *Burma in Revolt: Opium and Insurgency Since 1948* (Boulder, CO: Westview Press and Bangkok: White Lotus, 1994).

Liu, F. F. *A Military History of Modern China 1924–1949* (Princeton, NJ: Princeton University Press, 1956).

Liu, Jing-shing. *Wo Sheng You Shing – Liu Jing-shing Chi- Shih Sheng-chen-chi (I Was Fortunate in my Life – Recollecting the Past on my Seventieth Birthday)* (Taipei: private imprint, Quan Qing Color Printing Company, 11 November 1989).

Lo, Hsuan. *The Saga of Chiang Ching-kuo in Jiangsi* (Canton: South China Press, 1988).

Loh, Pichon P. Y. *The Early Chiang Kai-shek: A Study of his Personality and Politics, 1887–1924* (New York: Columbia University Press, 1971).

—— (ed.). *The Kuomintang Debacle of 1949: Conquest or Collapse* (Boston: D.C. Heath and Company, 1965).

Macintyre, Ben. *Forgotten Fatherland: The Search for Elisabeth Nietzsche* (NY: Farrar Straus Giroux, 1992).

Marks, Thomas A. *Making Revolution: The Insurgency of the Communist Party of Thailand in Structural Perspective* (Bangkok: White Lotus Press, 1995).

—— *Maoist Insurgency Since Vietnam* (London: Frank Cass Publishers, 1996).

Mao, Tse-tung. *Report From Xunwu*, released in a new edition, Roger Thompson (ed. and trans.) (Stanford: Stanford University Press, 1990).

Mendel, Douglas. *The Politics of Formosan Nationalism* (Berkeley: University of California Press, 1970).

Miranda, Carlos R. *The Stroessner Era: Authoritarian Rule in Paraguay* (Boulder, CO: Westview Press, 1990).

Myers, Ramon H. (ed.) *Two Societies in Opposition: The Republic of China and the People's Republic of China After Forty Years* (Stanford: Hoover Institution Press, 1991).

—— and Mark R. Peattie (eds.). *The Japanese Colonial Empire, 1895–1945* (Princeton: Princeton University Press, 1984).

Nickson, Andrew. *Historical Dictionary of Paraguay* (NY: Scarecrow Press, 1992).

—— *Paraguay: Power Game* (London: Latin America Bureau, 1982).

Obeyesekere, Gananath. *The Apotheosis of Captain Cook: European Mythmaking in the Pacific* (Princeton, NJ: Princeton University Press, 1992).

Paribatra, Sukhumbhand. *The Taiwan Straits Crisis of 1958: A Study of the Use of Naval Power*, Asian Studies Monographs No. 030 (Bangkok: Institute of Asian Studies, Chulalongkorn University, 1981).

Payne, Robert. *Chiang Kai-shek* (New York: Weybright and Talley, 1969).

Pepper, Suzanne. *Civil War in China* (Berkeley: University of California Press, 1978).

Perry, Elizabeth J. *Chinese Perspectives on the Nien Rebellion* (Armonk, NY: M. E. Sharpe, 1981).

The Political Establishment in the Chinese Armed Forces (Taipei: Political Department, Ministry of National Defense, February 1960).

Price, Frank W. *The Three Principles of the People* (Taipei: China Publishing Company, 1981).

Price, Jane Lois. *The Training of Revolutionary Leadership in the Chinese Communist Party, 1920–1945* (New York: Columbia University Ph.D. dissertation, 1974).

Pye, Lucien W. *The Mandarin and the Cadre: China's Political Cultures* (Ann Arbor, MI: Center for Chinese Studies, University of Michigan, 1988).

— *The Spirit of Chinese Politics* (Cambridge, MA: MIT Press, 1968).

Republic of China Yearbook 1958 (Taipei: ROC Yearbook Society, 1958).

Republic of China Yearbook 1989 (Taipei: Kwang Hwa Publishing Company, 1989).

Republic of China Yearbook 1993 (Taipei: Kwang Hwa Publishing Company, 1993).

Robinson, Thomas W. (ed.) *Democracy and Development in East Asia: Taiwan, South Korea, and the Philippines* (Washington, DC: The American Enterprise Institute Press, 1991).

Romanus, Charles F. and Riley Sutherland. *The History of the China-Burma-India Theater*, 3 vols. (Washington, DC: Department of the Army, 1959).

Rummel, R.J. *China's Bloody Century: Genocide and Mass Murder Since 1900* (New Brunswick, NJ: Transaction Press, 1991).

— *Death by Government: Genocide and Mass Murder Since 1900* (New Brunswick, NJ: Transaction Press, 1994).

Sahlins, Marshall. *How Natives Think: About Captain Cook, For Example* (Chicago, IL: The University of Chicago Press, 1995).

Sawyer, Ralph D. (ed. and trans.) *The Seven Military Classics of Ancient China* (Boulder, CO: Westview Press, 1993).

Seagrave, Sterling. *The Soong Dynasty* (New York: Harper & Row Publishers, 1985).

Selden, Mark. *The Yenan Way in Revolutionary China* (Cambridge: Harvard University Press, 1971).

Seligman, Adam. *The Idea of Civil Society* (New York: The Free Press, 1992).

Shaw, Yu-ming. *Beyond the Economic Miracle: Reflections: Reflections on the Republic of China on Taiwan, Mainland China, and Sino-American Relations*, 2nd ed. (Taipei: personal imprint; Kwang Hwa Publishing Company, 1990).

Shen, T.H. *The Sino-American Joint Commission on Rural Reconstruction* (Ithaca, NY: Cornell University Press, 1970).

Short, Anthony. *The Origins of the Vietnam War* (London: Longman Group, 1989).

Skocpol, Theda. *States and Social Revolutions* (New York: Cambridge University Press, 1979).

Spence, Jonathan D. *The Search for Modern China* (New York: W. W. Norton & Company, 1990).

Takekoshi, Yosaburo. *Japanese Rule in Formosa* (New York: Longmans, Green & Co., 1907).

Tang, Tsou. *The Embroilment Over Quemoy: Mao, Xhang, and Dulles*, International Study Paper No. 2 (Ogdan, UT: Institute of International Studies, University of Utah, 1959).

Teng, Ssu-yu. *The Nien Army and Their Guerrilla Warfare, 1851–1868* (Paris: Mouton & Co. La Haye, 1961).

Thomson, James C. Jr. *While China Faced West: American Reformers in Nationalist China, 1928–1937* (Cambridge, MA: Harvard University Press, 1969).

Tien, Hung-mao. *Government and Politics in Kuomintang China 1927–1937* (Stanford, CA: Stanford University Press, 1972).

— *The Great Transition: Political and Social Change in the Republic of China* (Stanford, CA: Hoover Institution Press, 1989).

Tilly, Charles. *From Mobilization to Revolution* (Reading, MA: Addison-Wesley, 1978).

Tong, Hollington K. *Chiang Kai-shek* (Taipei: China Publishing Company, 1953).

— *China Handbook 1937–1943: A Comprehensive Survey of Major Developments in China in Six Years of War* (New York: The Macmillan Company, 1943).

Tuan, Chia-feng. 'A Comparison of the Land Reform Programs in the Republic of China on Taiwan and Communist China', *Issues & Studies*, XVIII/12 (December 1982), pp. 62–83.

Tuchman, Barbara W. *Stilwell and the American Experience in China, 1911–45* (New York: Macmillan Press, 1971).

Van Slyke, Lyman P. (ed.) *The Chinese Communist Movement: A Report of the United States War Department, July 1945* (Stanford, CA: Stanford University Press, 1968).

Wade, Robert. *Governing the Market: Economic Theory and the Role of Government in East Asian Industrialization* (Princeton, NJ: Princeton University Press, 1990).

Wang, Sheng. *The Theory and Practice of Political Warfare*, (Taipei: *Fu Hsing Kang* College, 1959)
—— *The Thought of Dr. Sun Yat-sen* (Taipei: Li Ming Cultural Enterprise Co., 1981).
—— *What I Know About President Chiang Ching-kuo* (Taipei: Li Ming Cultural Enterprise Co., 1980).
Wei, William. *Counterrevolution in China: The Nationalists in Jiangxi During the Soviet Period* (Ann Arbor: The University of Michigan Press, 1985).
Weismann, Steve and Herbert Krosney. *The Islamic Bomb* (New York: *The New York Times* Book Company, 1986).
Whitson, William W. with Huang Chen-hsia. *The Chinese High Command: A History of Communist Military Politics, 1927–71* (New York: Praeger Publishers, 1973).
Wilbur, C. Martin. *Sun Yat-sen: Frustrated Patriot* (New York: Columbia University Press, 1976).
Wilson, Richard W. *Learning to be Chinese: The Political Socialization of Children in Taiwan* (Cambridge, MA: The MIT Press, 1970).
Wright, Mary C. *The Last Stand of Chinese Conservatism: The T'ung-chih Restoration, 1862–1874* (Stanford, CA: Stanford University Press, 1957).
Yager, Joseph A. *Transforming Agriculture in Taiwan: The Experience of the Joint Commission on Rural Reconstruction* (Ithaca, NY: Cornell University Press, 1988).
Yang, Tsun. *Chiang Ching-kuo Wai Chuan: Tsung Chiko dau Gannan* [*Chiang Ching-kuo's Untold Story: From Chiko to Gannan*] (Taipei: New Tide Cultural Enterprises, 1993).
Young, Arthur N. *China's Nation-Building Effort, 1927–1937* (Stanford: Hoover Institution Press, 1971).
—— *China's Wartime Finance and Inflation, 1937–1945* (Cambridge, MA: Harvard University Press, 1965).

ARTICLES:

Appleton, Sheldon. 'Taiwanese and Mainlanders on Taiwan: A Survey of Student Attitudes', *The China Quarterly*, 44 (October–December 1970), 38–65.
Arrigo, Linda Gail. 'Land Concentration in China: The Buck Survey Revisited,' *Modern China*, 12/3 (July 1986), 259–360.
Averill, Stephen C. 'Local Elites and Communist Revolution in the Jiangxi Hill Country,' Chapter 11 in Joseph W. Esherick and Mary Backus Rankin (eds.), *Chinese Local Elites and Patterns of Dominance*

(Berkeley: University of California Press, 1990), 282–304.

—— 'Party, Society, and Local Elite in the Jiangxi Communist Movement,' *The Journal of Asian Studies*, 46/2 (May 1987), 279–303,

—— 'The Shed People and the Opening of the Yangzi Highlands,' *Modern China*, 9/1 (January 1983), 84–126.

Bedeski, Robert E. 'Pre-Communist State-Building in Modern China: The Political Thought of Chiang Kai-shek,' *Asian Perspective* [Seoul], 4/2 (Fall-Winter 1980), 149–70.

Billingsley, Phil. 'Bandits, Bosses, and Bare Sticks: Beneath the Surface of Local Control in Early Republican China,' *Modern China*, 7/3 (July 1981), 235–88.

Brick, Andrew B. 'The East Asian Development Miracle: Taiwan as a Model,' *Issues & Studies*, 28/8 (August 1992), 1–13.

Bullard, Monte R. 'Political Warfare in Vietnam,' *Military Review*, XLIX/10 (October 1969), 54–59.

—— 'The US-China Defense Relationship,' *Parameters*, XIII/1 (March 1993), 43–50.

Buss, Claude A. Book Review of *Two China Policy* in *The Journal of Asian Studies*, 47/2 (May 1988), 346–47.

'Challenge: Students Flock to Vacation "Battle Camp",' *Free China Review* (April 1983), 36–43.

Chan, Gerald. 'The "Two Chinas" Problem and the Olympic Formula,' *Pacific Affairs*, 58/3 (Fall 1985), 473–90.

Chang, David Wen-wei. 'Political Development in Taiwan: The Sun Yat-sen Model for National Reconstruction,' *Issues & Studies*, 25/5 (May 1989), 11–32.

Chang, Kia-ngau. 'War and Inflation' in Pinchon P. Y. Loh (ed.) *The Kuomintang Debacle of 1949: Conquest or Collapse* (Boston: D.C. Heath and Company, 1965).

Chang, Maria Hsia. 'Political Succession in the Republic of China on Taiwan,' *Asian Survey*, XXIV/4 (April 1984), 423–46.

Chang, Parris. 'Taiwan in 1982: Diplomatic Setback Abroad and Demands for Reforms at Home,' *Asian Survey*, XXIII/1 (January 1983), 38–46.

Chang, Su. 'Chiang Ching-kuo and Chang Ya-juo,' in 'Chiang Ching-kuo in Southern Jiangxi (Gannan)' section of *Jiangxi Historical Records Selections* [Nanchang], No. 35 (August 1989), 349–65.

Chen, David. 'What Was Truman's China Policy?', *Free China Review* (July 1988), 24–25.

Chen, Jian. 'China and the First Indo-China War,' *The China Quarterly*, 133 (March 1933), 85–110.

Cheng, Peter P.C. 'Taiwan Under Chiang Kai-shek's Era: 1945–1976,' *Asian Profile*, 16/4 (August 1988), 299–315.

Chern, Kenneth S. 'The Ideology of American China Policy, 1945–1960,'

Journal of Oriental Studies [Hong Kong], XX/2 (1982), 155–72.

Chiang, Ching-kuo. 'My Days in Soviet Russia,' reprinted in Ray S. Cline, *Chiang Ching-kuo Remembered: The Man and His Political Legacy* (Washington, DC: United States Global Strategy Council, 1989).

Chiang, Kai-shek. '*Chung-yang kan-hsiao ch'eng-li tian-li chi yen-chiu-pu ti-yich'i k'ai-hsueh tian-li hsun-tz'u*' ('Address at the Ceremony Establishing the Central Cadre Academy and First Research Class') in *Chung-yang kan-pu hsueh-hsiao yen-chiu-pu ti-yi ch'i pi-yeh shih-chou-nien chi-nien t'e-k'an* (*Special Issue Commemorating the Fortieth Anniversary of the Graduation of the First Research Division of the Central Cadre Academy*), 11–14.

Chiang Nan [Henry Liu]. ' ['Wang Sheng the Man'] '*Wang Sheng hsien-sheng che-ko-jen*', *Ch'i-shih Nien-tai Yueh Kan* [*The Seventies Monthly*], No. 103 (August 1978), 52–54.

—— 'Wang Sheng's Mysterious Misstep' [translated], *Ch'i-shih Nien-tai Yueh Kan* (*The Seventies Monthly*) (June 1983), 55–57.

Chiou, C.L. Book Review of *A Tragic Beginning: The Taiwan Uprising of February 28, 1947* in *The Australian Journal of Chinese Affairs*, 28 (July 1992), 206–9.

—— 'Dilemmas in China's Reunification Policy Toward Taiwan,' *Asian Survey*, XXVI/4 (April 1986), 467–82.

Chiu, Hung-dah. 'Law and Justice,' in James C. Hsiung (ed.), *Contemporary Republic of China: The Taiwan Experience 1950–1980* (New York: Praeger Publishers, 1981).

Chou, Yangsun and Andrew J. Nathan. 'Democratizing Transition in Taiwan,' *Asian Survey*, XXVII/3 (March 1987), 277–99.

Copper, James Franklin. 'Taiwan in 1981: In a Holding Pattern,' *Asian Survey*, XXII/1 (January 1982), 47–55.

Diamond, Norma. 'Women Under Kuomintang Rule: Variations on the Feminine Mystique,' *Modern China*, 1/1 (January 1975), 3–45.

Dickson, Bruce J. 'The Lessons of Defeat: The Reorganization of the Kuomintang on Taiwan, 1950-52,' *The China Quarterly*, 133 (March 1993), 56–84.

Domes, Jurgen. 'Political Differentiation in Taiwan: Group Formation Within the Ruling Party and the Opposition Circles 1979–1980,' *Asian Survey*, XXI/10 (October 1981), 1011–28.

Dorris Carl E. 'Peasant Mobilization in North China and the Origins of Yenan Communism,' *The China Quarterly*, 68 (December 1976), 697–719.

Eastman, Lloyd E. 'Fascism in Kuomintang China: The Blue Shirts,' *The China Quarterly*, 49 (January-March 1972), 1–31.

—— 'Research Note: Who Lost China? Chiang Kai-shek Testifies,' *The China Quarterly*, 87 (September 1981), 658–68.

—— 'The Rise and Fall of the "Blue Shirts": A Review Article,' *Republican*

China, XIII/1 (November 1987), 25–48.

Eberstadt, Nicholas. 'Who Wanted Mr. Liu Dead?' *New York Times Book Review*, 25 October 1992, 32.

Elkins, W.F. 'Fascism in China: The Blue Shirts Society, 1932–1937,' *Science and Society*, 33/4 (1969), 426–33.

Esherick, Joseph W. 'Number Games: A Note on Land Distribution in Prerevolutionary China,' *Modern China*, 7/4 (October 1981), 387–41.

Eto, Shinkichi. 'Hai-lu-feng – The First Chinese Soviet Government,' Parts I & II, *The China Quarterly*, 8 (October–December 1961), I: 161–83; 9 (January-March 1962), II: 149–81.

Fang, Ch'ing-yen. 'Wang Sheng During the Pre-Taiwan Period,' in 'Chiang Ching-kuo in Southern Jiangxi (Gannan)' section of *Jiangxi Historical Records Selections* [Manchang], No. 35 (August 1989), 369–74.

Faure, David. 'The Plight of the Farmers: A Study of the Rural Economy of Jiangnan and the Pearl River Delta, 1870–1937,' *Modern China*, 11/1 (January 1985), 3–37.

'Foreign Affairs: Premier Asks Free World Backing for El Salvador,' *Free China Review* (April 1982), 3.

Garver, John W. 'The Chinese Threat in the Vietnam War,' *Parameters*, XXII/1 (Spring 1992), 73–85.

Gillin, Donald G. 'Review Article: 'Peasant Nationalism' in the History of Chinese Communism,' *The Journal of Asian Studies*, XXIII/2 (February 1964), 269–87.

Gold, Thomas B. 'The Status Quo is not Static: Mainland-Taiwan Relations,' *Asian Survey*, XXVII/3 (March 1987), 300–15.

Goldfrank, Walter L. 'Theories of Revolution and Revolution Without Theory: The Case of Mexico,' *Theory & Society*, 7 (1979), 135–65.

Goldstone, Jack A. 'Theories of Revolution: The Third Generation,' *World Politics*, XXXII/3 (April 1980), 425–53.

Gole, Henry G. 'Shadow Wars and Secret Wars: Phoenix and MACV-SOG,' *Parameters*, XXI/4 (Winter 1991–92), 95–105.

Grove, Linda. 'Creating a Northern Soviet,' *Modern China*, 1/3 (July 1975), 243–70.

Gurtov, Melvin. 'The Taiwan Strait Crisis Revisited: Politics and Foreign Policy in Chinese Motives,' *Modern China*, 2/1 (January 1976), 49–103.

Halloran, Richard. 'China Road Force in Laos at 20,000,' *New York Times*, 16 October 1969, 1.

Ho, Samuel P. S. 'South Korea and Taiwan: Development Prospects and Problems in the 1980s,' *Asian Survey*, XXI/12 (December 1981), 1175–96.

Hofheinz, Roy Jr. 'The Ecology of Chinese Communist Success: Rural Influence Patterns, 1923–45,' in A. Doak Barnett (ed.), *Chinese*

Communist Politics in Action (Seattle: University of Washington Press, 1969), 3–77.

Hsiao, Hsin-Huang Michael. 'The Changing State-Society Relation in the ROC: Economic Change, the Transformation of the Class Structure, and the Rise of Social Movements,' Chapter 6 in Ramon Myers (ed.), *Two Societies in Opposition: The Republic of China and the People's Republic of China After Forty Years* (Stanford: Hoover Institution Press, 1991), 127–40.

—— 'Emerging Social Movements and the Rise of a Demanding Civil Society in Taiwan,' *The Australian Journal of Chinese Affairs*, 24 (July 1990), 163–79.

Hsiung, James C. 'Taiwan in 1984: Festivity, New Hope, and Caution,' *Asian Survey*, XXV/1 (January 1985), 90–96.

Hsu Cho-yun. 'Historical Setting for the Rise of Chiang Ching-kuo,' in Leng Shao-chuan (ed.), *Chiang Ching-kuo's Leadership in the Development of the Republic of China on Taiwan*, Vol. III (New York: University Press of America, 1993), 1–29.

Hsu Hao-jan as told to Wu Shih-ts'ang. 'Wang Sheng in Gannan,' in 'Chiang Ching-kuo in Southern Jiangxi (Gannan)' section of *Jiangxi Historical Records Selections* [Nanchang], No. 35 (August 1989), 366–67.

Hu, Chi-hsi. 'The Sexual Revolution in the Kiangsi Soviet,' *The China Quarterly*, 59 (September 1974), 477–90.

Huang, Philip C.C. 'The Jiangxi Period: an Introduction,' in Huang, Lynda Schaefer Bell, Kathy Lemons Walker, *Chinese Communists and Rural Society, 1927–1934*, Chinese Research Monograph No. 13 (Berkeley, CA: Center for Chinese Studies, 1978), 1–4.

—— '"Public Sphere/Civil Society" in China? The Third Realm Between State and Society,' *Modern China*, 19/2 (April 1993), 107–239.

Huebner, Jon W. 'The Abortive Liberation of Taiwan,' *The China Quarterly*, 110 (June 1987), 256–75.

—— 'The Americanization of the Taiwan Straits,' *Asian Profile*, 13/3 (June 1985), 187–99.

Johnson, Chalmers. 'Peasant Nationalism Revisited: The Biography of a Book,' *The China Quarterly*, 72 (December 1977), 766–85.

Keller, Gerald J. 'Israeli-South African Trade: An Analysis of Recent Developments,' *Naval War College Review* (Spring 1978), 74–80.

Krauss, Clifford. 'U.S., Aware of Killings, Worked With Salvador's Rightists, Papers Suggest,' *The New York Times*, 9 November 1993, A1.

Lamley, Harry J. Book Review of *A Tragic Beginning: The Taiwan Uprising of February 28, 1947* in *The Journal of Asian Studies*, 51/3 (August 1992), 652–54.

Lan, Ke-jeng and Jiann-chyuan Wang. 'The Taiwan Experience in

Economic Development,' *Issues & Studies*, 27/10 (October 1991), 135–57.

Lancashire, Edel. 'The Lock of the Heart Controversy in Taiwan, 1962–63: A Question of Artistic Freedom and a Writer's Social Responsibility,' *The China Quarterly*, 103 (September 1985), 462–88.

—— 'Popeye and the Case of Guo Yidong, Alias Bo Yang,' *The China Quarterly*, 92 (December 1982), 663–86.

Lee, Huan, 'Chiang Kai-shek and Chinese Youth' (p. 684) in *Proceedings of Conference on Chiang Kai-shek and Modern China*, Vol. III: *Chiang Kai-shek and China's Modernization* (Taipei: China Cultural Service, 1987).

Lee, Kuo-wei. 'The Road to Democracy: Taiwan Experience,' *Asian Profile* [Hong Kong], 19/6 (December 1991), 489–504.

Li, K.T. 'Communist China's 'Peace Offer',' *Free China Review* (June 1982), 2–3.

Li, Yun-han. 'Chiang Ching-kuo's Struggles During the War of Resistance Against Japan,' *Chin-tai Chung-kuo*, No. 76 (30 April 1990).

Lintner, Bertil. 'The CIA's First Secret War: Americans Helped Stage Raids Into China From Burma,' *Far Eastern Economic Review*, 16 September 1993, 56–58.

Liu, K'ang-sheng. 'China's Crucial Decade,' *Free China Review* (April 1981), 14–20.

—— 'No Unification the Communist Way,' *Free China Review* (November 1981), 20–25.

—— 'Red China's Biggest Lie,' *Free China Review* (December 1981), 23–28.

Mann, Jim. 'Taiwan Thriving Four Decades After CIA Predicted its Fall,' *Los Angeles Times*, 6 November 1993, A3.

Marks, Thomas A. 'The Future of Taiwan,' *South-East Asian Spectrum* [Bangkok], 4/3 (April–June 1976), 7–17.

—— 'Insurgency by the Numbers II: The Search for a Quantitative Relationship Between Agrarian Revolution and Land Tenure in South and Southeast Asia,' *Small Wars and Insurgencies* [London], 5/2 (Autumn 1994), 218–91.

—— 'Korea's Search for Identity Tests U.S.,' *The Asian Wall Street Journal*, 6–7 July 1990, 10; reprinted as 'U.S. Must Understand a Changing Korea,' *The Asian Wall Street Journal Weekly*, 27 August 1990, 14.

—- 'Making Revolution: *Sendero Luminoso* in Peru,' *Small Wars and Insurgencies* [London], 3/1 (Spring 1992), 22–46.

—— 'This Taiwan Exposé Sheds More Heat Than Light,' *The Asian Wall Street Journal*, 26–27 November 1993, 8.

—— 'Two Chinese Roads to Military Modernization – and a U.S. Dilemma,' *Strategic Survey* [Washington, DC], VIII/3 (Summer 1980), 18–28.

Martin, Roberta. 'The Socialization of Children in China and on Taiwan: An Analysis of Elementary School Textbooks,' *The China Quarterly*, 62 (June 1975), 242–61.

Meisner, Maurice. 'The Development of Formosan Nationalism,' *The China Quarterly*, 15 (July–September 1963), 91–114.

Metzger, Thomas A. 'Did Sun Yat-sen Understand the Idea of Democracy? The Conceptualization of Democracy in the Three Principles of the People and in John Stuart Mill's "On Liberty",' *The American Asian Review*, X/1 (Spring 1992), 1–41.

Meyer, Jeffrey E. 'Teaching Morality in Taiwan Schools: The Message of the Textbooks,' *The China Quarterly*, 114 (June 1988), 267–84.

Michael, Franz. 'The Role of Law in Traditional, Nationalist and Communist China,' *The China Quarterly*, 9 (January–March 1962), 124–48.

Myers, Ramon H. 'The Economic Transformation of the Republic of China on Taiwan,' *The China Quarterly*, 99 (September 1984), 500–28.

—- 'Taiwan as an Imperial Colony of Japan: 1895–1945,' *Journal of the Institute of Chinese Studies of the Chinese University of Hong Kong*, 6/2 (1973), 425–53.

Omicinski, John. 'Earth's Deadliest Century,' *The Honolulu Advertiser*, 11 December 1994, B1.

Peng, Ming-min. 'Political Offences in Taiwan: Laws and Problems,' *The China Quarterly*, 47 (July/September 1971), 471–93.

Peng, Thomas Ching-peng. 'President Lee's Rise to Power and His Reform Program,' *Issues & Studies*, 28/6 (June 1992), 59–69.

Penrose, Sandra. Book Review of *Two China Policy*, *The Australian Journal of Chinese Studies*, 22 (July 1989), 197–99.

Polachek, James M. 'The Moral Economy of the Kiangsi Soviet (1928–1934),' *Journal of Asian Studies*, XLII/4 (August 1983), 805–29.

Porch, Douglas. 'Bugeaud, Gallieni, Lyautey: The Development of French Colonial Warfare,' in Peter Paret (ed.), *Makers of Modern Strategy from Machiavelli to the Nuclear Age* (Princeton: Princeton University Press, 1986), 376–407.

Pye, Lucien W. 'The State and the Individual: An Overview Interpretation, *The China Quarterly*, 127 (September 1991), 443–66.

Selden, Mark. 'The Guerrilla Movement in Northwest China: The Origins of the Shensi-Kansu-Ninghsia Border Region,' Parts I & II, *The China Quarterly*, 28 (October–December 1966), I: 63–81; 29 (January–March 1967), II: 61–81.

—— 'People's War and the Transformation of Peasant Society: China and Vietnam,' in Mark Selden and Edward Freedman (eds.), *America's Asia*, offprint (nfd).

She, Colleen S. 'Toward Ideology: Views of the May Fourth Intelligentsia on Love, Marriage, and Divorce,' *Issues & Studies* [Taipei], 27/2 (February 1991), 104–32.

Shewmaker, Kenneth E. 'The "Agrarian Reformer" Myth,' *The China Quarterly*, 34 (April–June 1968), 66–81.

Soong, James C.Y. 'Documents: China's Reunification and World Peace,' *Free China Review* (May 1986), 60–63.

—— 'Nation: That Perpetual Peking Peace Plan,' *Free China Review* (March 1984).

Stross, Randy. 'Number Games Rejected: The Misleading Allure of Tenancy Estimates,' *Republican China*, X/3 (Special June 1985 Issue), 1–17.

'Taiwan,' *Asia 1978 Yearbook* (Hong Kong: *Far Eastern Economic Review*, 1979), 313–20.

'Taiwan,' *Asia 1979 Yearbook* (Hong Kong: *Far Eastern Economic Review*, 1980), 299–306.

'Taiwan,' *Asia 1980 Yearbook* (Hong Kong: *Far Eastern Economic Review*, 1980), 285–89.

'Taiwan,' *Asia 1981 Yearbook* (Hong Kong: *Far Eastern Economic Review*, 1982), 250–54.

'Taiwan,' *Asia 1982 Yearbook* (Hong Kong: *Far Eastern Economic Review*, 1983), 248–49.

'Taiwan,' *Asia 1984 Yearbook* (Hong Kong: *Far Eastern Economic Review*, 1985), 268–73.

Tien, Hung-mao. 'Taiwan in Transition: Prospects for Socio-Political Change,' *The China Quarterly*, 64 (December 1975), 615–44.

Tozer, W. 'Taiwan's "Cultural Renaissance": A Preliminary View,' *The China Quarterly*, 43 (July–September 1970), 81–99.

Tsai, Ch'ing-yuan. 'Unification the Free Chinese Way,' *Free China Review* (November 1981), 16–19.

Tsai, Wen-hui. 'Protest Movements in Taiwan in the 1980s,' *The American Asian Review*, VIII/4 (Winter 1990), 116–34.

Vinocur, John. 'A Republic of Fear,' *The New York Times Magazine* (23 September 1984), nfd.

Wang, Betty. 'Foreign Affairs: A Policy of Intensive Cooperation – ROC's Technical Missions Abroad,' *Free China Review* (December 1985), 39–49.

—— 'Technical Exchanges: Forging Ahead in the Dominican Republic – International Cooperation Builds Progress, Friendship,' *Free China Review* (March 1986), 46–53.

—— 'Technical Exchanges: Panama,' *Free China Review* (January 1986), 47–53.

Wang, Chien-hui. 'Anniversary: Bombardment of Quemoy,' *Free China Review* (August 1988), 32–41.

Wang, Yu San. 'The Republic of China's Technical Cooperation Programs With the Third World,' *Issues & Studies*, XIX/5 (May 1983), 64–79.

Watt, John. 'Book Review of *A Tragic Beginning: The Taiwan Uprising of February 28, 1947* in *The American Asian Review*, X/2 (Summer 1992), 152–59.

Wei, William. 'Five Encirclement and Suppression Campaigns (1930–1934),' in Edwin Pak-wah Leung (ed.), *Historical Dictionary of Revolutionary China, 1839–1976* (New York: Greenwood Press, 1992), 121–23.

—— 'The Guomindang's Three Parts Military and Seven Parts Politics Policy,' *Asian Profile* [Hong Kong], 10/2 (April 1982), 111–27.

—— 'Insurgency by the Numbers I: A Reconsideration of the Ecology of Communist Success in Jiangxi Province, China,' *Small Wars and Insurgencies* [London], 5/2 (Autumn 1994), 201–17.

—— 'Law and Order: The Role of Guomindang Security Forces in the Suppression of the Communist Bases During the Soviet Period,' Chapter 2 in Hartford and Goldstein, 34–61 (notes on 182–88).

—— 'The Role of the German Advisors in the Suppression of the Central Soviet: Myth and Reality,' in Bernd Martin, ed., *The German Advisory Group in China: Military, Economic, and Political Issues in Sino-German Relations, 1927–1938* [or *Die deutsche Beraterschaft in China 1927–1938* (Dusseldorf: Droste, 1981).

—— 'Warlordism and Factionalism in the Guomindang's Encirclement Campaigns in Jiangxi,' in *Illinois Papers in Asian Studies 1983, Pt. II: Kuomintang Development Efforts During the Nanking Decade* (Urbana: Center for Asian Studies, University of Illinois, 1983), 87–120.

Whiting, Allen S. 'Mystery Man of Formosa,' *Saturday Evening Post* (12 March 1955).

—— 'New Light on Mao – 3. Quemoy 1958: Mao's Miscalculations,' *The China Quarterly*, 62 (June 1975), 263–70.

Winckler, Edwin A. 'Institutionalization and Participation on Taiwan: From Hard to Soft Authoritarianism?', *The China Quarterly*, 99 (September 1984), 481–99.

Wright, Mary C. 'From Revolution to Restoration: The Transformation of Kuomintang Ideology,' *The Far Eastern Quarterly*, XIV/4 (August 1955), 515–32.

Wu, Jau-shieh Joseph. 'Analysis of Individual Level Transformation in Taiwan: A Note on Development Theory and the Implications for Third World Communism,' *Issues & Studies*, 26/11 (November 1990), 116–33.

Yang, Ming-che. 'Kuomintang on the Move for the 1980s,' *Free China Review* (January 1980), 13–22.

Yang, Yung-shan. 'Foreign Affairs: Growing With Panama – ROC Mission

Specializes in Agricultural Diplomacy,' *Free China Review* (October 1982), 8–16.

Yeh, K.C. *The Chinese Communist Revolutionary Strategy and the Land Reform Problem, 1921–1927*, Memorandum RM-6077-ARPA (Santa Monica, CA: The Rand Corporation, April 1970).

Zhao, John Quansheng. 'An Analysis of Unification: The PRC Perspective,' *Asian Survey*, XXIII/10 (October 1983), 1095–1114.

Index